Contemporary Plays by Women

Susan Smith Blackburn

Contemporary PLAYS BY WOMEN

Outstanding Winners and Runners-Up for The Susan Smith Blackburn Prize (1978–1990)

Edited by

Emilie S. Kilgore

PRENTICE HALL PRESS

New York   London   Toronto   Sydney   Tokyo   Singapore

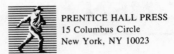

PRENTICE HALL PRESS
15 Columbus Circle
New York, NY 10023

PRENTICE HALL PRESS and colophons are registered trademarks of Simon & Schuster, Inc.

Library of Congress Cataloging in Publication Data
Contemporary plays by women: outstanding winners and runners-up for The Susan Smith Blackburn Prize,
1978–1990 / edited by Emilie S. Kilgore.
   p. cm.
   Summary: Introduction / Wendy Wasserstein—Getting out / Marsha Norman—My sister in this house / Wendy
Kesselman—Coyote ugly / Lynn Siefert—Painting Churches / Tina Howe—Ourselves alone / Anne Devlin—
Serious money / Caryl Churchill—Keeping Tom nice / Lucy Gannon.
   ISBN 0-13-183690-0
   ISBN 0-13-183708-7 (pbk.)
   1. American drama—Women authors. 2. American drama—20th century. 3. Women—Drama. I. Kilgore,
Emilie S.
PS628.W6C66 1991
812′.540809287—dc20
       90-7963
       CIP

Designed by Richard Oriolo

Manufactured in the United States of America

10 9 8 7 6 5 4 3 2 1

First Edition

Quality printing and binding by:
  Arcata Graphics/Fairfield
  100 North Miller Street
  Fairfield, Pa. 17320
  U.S.A.

To Susan

Acknowledgments

I am grateful to Gail Winston of Prentice Hall Press for asking me to do this book. It is something I had had in the back of my mind for several years. Her guidance, resourceful support, and cheerful readiness to help at every turn made the task of producing this book much easier than it might otherwise have been.

Of course I would not have been asked to do the book at all had it not been for the existence of The Susan Smith Blackburn Prize. In this light, I would like to thank my brother-in-law, William V. Blackburn; my father, C. Cabanné Smith; and all those who were involved in making the Prize a reality.

I am most appreciative to Michael Attenborough and to Leslie Samuels for their help in numerous negotiations. I am very grateful to Bertrand Davezac, Charles Perlitz, Ronny Wells, and Edwin Wilson for their friendly and generous assistance. Vi Morton helped me a great deal with the correspondence.

I want to thank Wendy Wasserstein for her introduction to the book and for being helpful in many other ways.

Each of the seven playwrights represented in the book was asked to write a brief personal statement to accompany her play. I want to thank them for their thoughtful contributions. I hope the reader will enjoy them as much as I did.

Contents

Preface
Emilie S. Kilgore

xiii

Introduction
Wendy Wasserstein

xvii

Getting Out
Marsha Norman

I

My Sister in This House
Wendy Kesselman

67

Coyote Ugly
Lynn Siefert

119

Painting Churches
Tina Howe

165

Ourselves Alone
Anne Devlin

229

Serious Money
Caryl Churchill

309

Keeping Tom Nice
Lucy Gannon

439

Appendix A
*Chronological Listing of The
Susan Smith Blackburn Prize
Finalists, Plays, Judges, and
Presenters (1978–1990)*

491

Appendix B
*Members of the
Board of Directors of
The Susan Smith Blackburn Prize*

504

Preface

The Susan Smith Blackburn Prize was established in 1978 as a memorial to my sister. It is awarded annually to a woman who deserves recognition for having written a work of outstanding quality for the English-speaking theater. Susan believed that society urgently needed more influence from talented women, and she encouraged many to excel. The aim of the Prize is to extend the creative influence of women in the theater, to encourage them to write for the theater, and to recognize excellence in the works of those who do.

Those who knew her felt this Prize was a fitting tribute to Susan. She had a gift for writing and a lifelong love of the theater. As a child she wrote plays that we children performed for visiting guests and relatives. Later she acted in plays at the Alley Theatre and the Little Theater in Houston, where we grew up, and at Smith College. After graduating with honors, Susan studied acting with Uta Hagan in New York and played several leading roles in productions on and off Broadway. In 1960 she married William Blackburn, and two years later they moved to London where Susan would spend the last 15 years of her life. Their two children, Adam and Lucy, live in London today. Susan gave drama classes to school children while working as a journalist, and she had many interests in addition to the theater. She was a delegate to the Democratic National Convention in 1972, cochairing the McGovern campaign in Europe. Her sense of justice led her to organize a large and successful benefit in London for the American Indians. She was a strong supporter of the Women's Liberation Movement and an enthusiastic worker for the English National Opera. She wrote a superb guidebook to London, which she revised and updated in the last year of her life. To all of her activities and her many friendships she brought energy and passion and intelligence. These qualities were ex-

hibited in the last months of her life, which were devoted to a search for
a way to conquer her illness, cancer.

After her much too early death, it was impossible not to do something;
among her family and friends there was a spontaneous stirring to perpetuate
the reaching out that was in her life. The result was the Susan Smith Blackburn Prize.

We got in touch with Lillian Hellman and asked her to join us as a director. She thought it was a wonderful idea. At that time, in 1978, only 7
percent of the plays presented across the United States were written by
women. A similar situation existed in the United Kingdom. Today, 12 years
later, that figure has approximately tripled.

We realized from the beginning that if the Prize was to be a prestigious
one, the judges must be persons whose views are taken seriously and whose
award therefore carries the weight we intended the prize to carry. In the
intervening years, many highly distinguished men and women on both sides
of the Atlantic have served on the panels, which consist of six judges each
year, three from the United States and three from the United Kingdom.
(Names of judges who have served to date appears in Appendix A.)

In September of each year, prominent professionals in the theater throughout the English-speaking world are asked to submit full-length plays for
consideration. The plays need not have been produced; if, however, a play
has been produced, the first production must have taken place within the
preceding 12 months. Each script is read by at least three members of a
reading committee in order to select 10 to 12 finalists. All final nominations
are read by all six judges. Finalists are notified in December, and the Prize
is awarded in February at a ceremony, in New York or London, which
honors all finalists. Willem de Kooning, a friend and admirer of Susan's,
made and signed a limited edition of prints especially for the Prize. These
prints are given to winners, judges, directors of the Prize, and major con-
tributors.

In the first 12 years there have been 138 finalist plays by 99 playwrights,
62 of whom are American and 37 British or Irish (a listing of finalists,
both alphabetically by author and grouped by year, is in Appendix A). The
award has not only motivated women to write for the theater but in many
cases has anticipated later recognition. It has also fostered the interchange of plays between America and England. In addition, there have
been many instances of benefits to playwrights as a direct result of having
been nominated, including productions, grants, and public recognition.
The lists of finalists have become an important resource for theaters interested in new plays. In Houston, where I live, 30 Blackburn finalists
have been produced.

I am especially pleased that Gail Winston of Prentice Hall Press asked
me to edit a volume of contemporary plays by women, chosen from the

finalists of The Susan Smith Blackburn Prize. I would hope that this is the first volume in an ongoing series.

In making the selection of plays to be included, I was mindful of wanting a balance. My field is the visual arts, and I did not proceed differently from selecting and hanging an exhibition of paintings. A primary concern is how things relate together. I chose a representative group of plays, some American, some British or Irish, covering a span of 12 years and showing the range and diversity in both subject and style. At the same time, I chose plays to which I had a strong personal response, and which I particularly admired. I asked Wendy Wasserstein to write an introduction to the book, as I felt that the ideas and views of a playwright would be pertinent and interesting.

The playwrights in this book, as well as the other finalists, have the scope and the imagination that Susan had. The Prize reaches out in a way that Susan might have in her own work had she lived. The Prize, therefore, is not only a tribute to her. It is the fulfillment of a promise.

Emilie S. Kilgore
June 1990

Introduction

When I was a playwrighting student at the Yale Drama School in 1976, my thesis play was a piece I wrote for eight women which was called *Uncommon Women and Others*. I wrote the play partly because I'd spent my graduate years reading a great deal of Jacobean Drama in which, to put it simply, men kissed the poisoned lips of women and promptly dropped dead. My honest reaction to these works was that although I found the drama compelling, this particular experience was not familiar to me nor to any of my friends.

Uncommon Women and Others, a play about a women's college reunion, was performed for the first time in the basement of the Yale Drama School. As in all good graduate schools there was an after-play discussion and evaluation. I will never forget the moment when one rather literate and informed theatergoer raised his hand and said, "I can't get into this. It's about women."

"Well," I whispered to a friend, "I've spent my life getting into Hamlet and Lawrence of Arabia. Why doesn't he just try it?"

Two years later *Uncommon Women and Others* was a finalist for the first Susan Smith Blackburn Prize. When Mimi Kilgore, the late Susan Blackburn's sister, called me from Houston to inform me of the honor, I had no idea who Susan Blackburn was or that a prize had been established in her name for plays by women; much less that the prize honored both British and American women. However, as Mimi informed me about the details of the prize, my immediate response was, "I can get into this. It's about women!"

As Mimi mentioned the names of the ten other finalists to me, I began to feel, for the first time, part of a community of emerging women writers. Some of the finalists' work, like Marsha Norman's *Getting Out* and Leigh Curran's *The Lunch Girls,* I had already seen and admired; others, like plays by the British writers Pam Gems and Mary O'Malley. I had only read. Some of the finalists were completely unfamiliar to me as I'm very sure I was to them. But the point was that we shared a commonality as women playwrights in a world that didn't directly discourage plays by women, but didn't exactly encourage their voices either.

The establishment of The Susan Smith Blackburn Prize said to each of us women playwrights that someone knew we were out there, someone knew we were working, and someone thought that our work was worthy of recognition. This is not to say that that at the time of the first Blackburn Prize in 1978 that the better known drama awards, Broadway's Antoinette Perry "Tony" Awards, or England's *Evening Standard* Outstanding Play Prize were specifically designated as recognition to male playwrights. But somehow it always seemed to come out that way.

In the past decade three of the Blackburn finalists—Marsha Norman, Beth Henley, and myself—have been awarded the Pulitzer Prize for Drama, and as recently as 1989 Timberlake Wertenbaker's *Our Country's Good*, a Blackburn finalist, was awarded the *Evening Standard* Prize. Women playwrights have obviously come a long way from the days of Hrotsvitha of Gandersheim, the first woman playwright on record. Hrotsvitha, an eighth-century canoness, was a closet dramatist; in other words, her plays were never performed. The recognition offered by The Susan Smith Blackburn Prize will hopefully signal to this and future generations of women playwrights that they will never have to settle again for anonymity.

Recently my niece, a senior at a traditional New Hampshire high school, proudly informed me that her school was making a real effort to include more women writers on its reading lists. An academic dictum had been passed down demanding that every literature class include one female writer per semester. The good intentions of this measure seemed to highlight for me the current dilemma faced by women playwrights—we are still considered a specialty act, a once-a-semester tangent.

Happily, The Susan Smith Blackburn Prize refuses to accept this subset status. The plays included in this volume are not competing with one another for that single well-intentioned "women's slot." In fact, their range proves how really preposterous the notion is that one woman writer can be representative of all.

This volume of plays illustrates the overwhelming diversity of a woman's perspective. To ignore it is limiting, and to categorize it equally so. One can certainly make a case for some thematic similarities in plays by women. All of the writers included in this collection have spent both their artistic and personal lives as women. How much and in what way this affects the characters, language, and subject matter of each play will vary from author to author.

In Marsha Norman's riveting *Getting Out* there are two main characters. Arlene, a woman who has just served an eight-year prison term in Kentucky, and Arlie, her younger and more volatile self. There is nothing dainty or timid about Ms. Norman's language. She is not afraid to be raw or even ugly, but she always remains true to her heroine's point of view.

At the end of Act One, Arlene is almost raped by a prison guard who boorishly asks her, "That what you think this is rape?" Pulling no punches, Arlene answers him, "I oughta know." Both the playwright's words and craft here are immaculate. The transition from Arlie to Arlene is seamless. *Getting Out* is compellingly theatrical, even on the printed page. Perhaps this is because Marsha Norman has created without sentimentality a vital woman who in a less enlightened playwright's hand could be demeaned and certainly has been traditionally ignored.

The difficult balance of merging craft with an individual voice is of course one of the theatrical pursuits of every playwright—male or female. And the legacies of those who accomplished these stage-worthy feats are also the rightful inheritance of every playwright—male or female. But perhaps it is the woman playwright who feels the keener urgency to reexamine theatrical traditions and thereby revitalize them.

Caryl Churchill also creates her individual dramaturgy from an extremely well-versed knowledge of theatrical traditions. Her play *Serious Money* begins with a scene from Thomas Shadwell's *The Stockjobbers,* written in 1692. The master (or is it mistress) playwright then proceeds to write her modern comedy in rhyming couplets with the confident authority of Shadwell, Shakespeare, and the women playwrights of the Restoration—Aphra Behn and Katherine Philips—firmly behind her.

Serious Money is an indictment of the fast money and easy greed of the 1980s. Moreover, the satiric lances are not gender specific. In other words, this is not a play in which the men make money and the little ladies stay home and spend it. Scilla Todd, a trader in the City of London, learns to be as greedy as any man. In the denouement of the play she confronts Mary Lou Barnes, an American arbitrageur, as to why her brother, a paper dealer, disappeared shortly before he was to speak to government investigators. Scilla is not appalled by the hints of illegal insider trading, but rather she resents that "They left me out because I'm a girl and it's terribly unfair. . . . I'm greedy and completely amoral."

Caryl Churchill breaks both form and traditional roles. Ultimately Scilla Todd moves to New York and is named by *Business Week* as "Wall Street's Rising Star." Mary Lou, on the other hand, runs for President in 1996. Ms. Churchill is not degrading her women, but she's not afraid to acknowledge their power either. The result is a play of great energy by a writer who is both acute and fearless.

Looking for traces of similarities in these plays one notices not so much the predominance of but the equal opportunity given to female characters. Wendy Kesselman's play, *My Sister in This House* tells the story of sisters,

maids, who work in a French home in Le Mans, France, 1933. The sisters'
employers, Madame Danzard and her daughter Isabelle, live in a suffocating
bourgeois world of faded linens and endless card games. When the sisters first
arrive Madame is ecstatic. "Sisters!" she exclaims. "What could be better?
And almost two for the price of one. We'll save on everything."

Ms. Kesselman is able to unravel from the smallest domestic detail an
almost Grimm's Fairy tale of the darkest proportions. She moves her story
delicately from the most innocuous incident to a harrowing finale. Through
it all Ms. Kesselman remains both a knowing and accepting eye. She is
never judgmental. The writer's hand here is both gentle and firm. What
could have been merely sensational becomes a very moving portrait of sup-
pression and class conflict.

Anne Devlin's *Ourselves Alone* is another play in which specifically women
and their relationships, accomplishments, and disappointments are the thrust
of the drama. Through the eyes and needs of Freida, Josie, and Donna we
come to understand the complicated politics of Northern Ireland and the fact
that we can no longer separate the war at the front from the one at home.

As the play begins, Frieda, a nightclub singer, refuses to sing a song that
calls for every man to stand beside the men behind the wire. "I'm fed up
with songs where the women are doormats," she says. Devlin's women are
hardly doormats; they are full, passionate, and committed to their cause.
Furthermore, if because of a romance they exhibit doormat behavior, they
are complicated enough to acknowledge it.

I can't say if a man could write about the Belfast struggle from a woman's
point of view as clearly as Devlin has. Chances are, however, he wouldn't
and some would say he couldn't. Moreover it would be small-minded and
ignorant to say that men don't write fine women characters and tell their
stories with conviction. But given a similar collection by male playwrights,
which by the way would be called "British and American Plays" without
any gender reference, I'm certain that the proportion of leading female figures would be considerably less.

Consider, for instance, Tina Howe's play, *Painting Churches*. It is the
portrait of a family and a marriage as seen through the eyes of a daughter,
who happens to be an artist. In Ms. Howe's play, Margaret, "Mags", Church
comes home to Boston to paint a portrait of her aging parents—Gardner
Church, the eminent New England poet, and Fanny Church, his equally
well-born and eccentric wife. Church's parents are packing up their life in
Boston and reducing it all down to a Cape Cod cottage. Like Mags, the
artist, Ms. Howe is able to capture all the light and texture of the Churches.
Her portrait is vivid, lyrical, and deeply moving.

Mags, very much needs her parents to realize that she has abilities, "very
strong abilities." And Ms. Howe, the excellent playwright, is able to show
us that Mags's often insufferable mother, who organizes her books not by

subject or author but by their jacket colors, also had abilities. Sadly, however she has no creative outlet except for buying mad hats from thrift stores. Fanny Church is trapped by her own imagination and inevitable aging.

Ms. Howe not only understands her milieu, but she, like the best of artists, is willing to look at it deeply. She brings the texture of painting and the lyricism of poetry to her writing for the theater. The world of *Painting Churches* is that of a daughter looking honestly and lovingly at her parents. As I read it I thought how lucky we are that Ms. Howe and other daughters are now finally beginning to be fairly represented on our stages.

Clearly what all these plays have most in common is the strength of their writing. When Scarlet Pewsy, the twelve-year-old "survivor" in Lynn Siefert's *Coyote Ugly,* goes after her brother with "a fish head in one hand and a scaling knife in the other," the author's not looking to be pleasing or cute. Ms. Siefert's American landscape is spare. As opposed to Wendy Kesselman's play which is dotted with the semi-precious and useless objects of bourgeois life, *Coyote Ugly* is external and direct.

Lynn Siefert's language in this play is staccato. The scenes are short, the antagonisms are both violent and economical. It is as if this author has completely eradicated the traditional woman's place as the light composer of comedy of manners, and by doing so has allowed herself and all the women writers to follow her new tones, new angles, and interestingly, new manners.

Keeping Tom Nice by Lucy Gannon also takes the staccato approach of Siefert but is set in an entirely different culture. Tom, a retarded twenty-four-year-old man who has "razor bones on paper skin" is the central focus of a working class British family. Every day they place his wheel chair on the same patch of carpet facing the same strip of wallpaper. Tom and the family's futile attempts at "keeping him nice" become symbols of the family's dashed hopes, frustrations, and the uselessness of their entire lives.

Lucy Gannon manages to tell this story of domestic abuse in the most poetic fashion. Almost musically, the beauty of the language underscores the desperation of Tom's life. Finally, a social worker engages Tom's father in a duet of good and evil. Ms. Gannon's triumph is that she understands the complexity and even the sanctimony of evil. Through this knowledge she expands the range and power of domestic drama.

I'm sure there are as many personal motivations and hindrances to writing a play for the seven authors selected for this book as there are for any other playwrights. Some of the writers would say they write plays about women because they are untold stories and therefore theatrical. Others would resent the limitation of subject. And still others would argue that there is indeed a female perspective, and it hasn't been fairly represented on the American or British stage because of a traditional lack of female producers, directors, and dramaturges. Moreover, I'm sure a few would never venture to say why they write. The point is, however, to quote Governor Arthur Philip in *Our Country's Good,* another Blackburn finalist, ''The Theatre is an expression of civilisation.'' And civilization consists of both men and women, and men and women playwrights.

The connection the Blackburn Prize makes between American and British women playwrights is a very pertinent one. Appropriately in *Ourselves Alone* a character asks her Irish friend why she is going to England and the friend responds simply, ''Why not? It's my language.'' Most of these plays were developed in nonprofit theaters devoted to new playwrights. Two of the British plays were first presented by Max Stafford Clark at London's Royal Court Theatre. British and American women writers share not only a common language but a common theatrical tradition. Our voices, our characters, our forms have an urgency and a vitality that comes only after centuries of silence.

For me there is still no artistic experience as exciting be it Broadway, off-Broadway, Louisville, The West End, or Sloane Square as being inside a theater at the moment when the lights go down and the drama begins. And what makes this volume of plays, and the more than 100 Susan Smith Blackburn finalists' plays, so especially crucial to me and to our theater is that when the curtain goes up, the world of the play has been infinitely expanded for the audience by the art and eye of these women authors. For that I am beyond grateful to The Susan Smith Blackburn Prize and to every woman playwright who has ever been considered for it. I am very proud to be counted among them.

WENDY WASSERSTEIN
1990

GETTING
OUT

Marsha Norman

Getting Out received its world premiere at Actors Theatre of Louisville, Kentucky. The West Coast premiere was produced by the Center Theatre Group of Los Angeles, Mark Taper Forum. Original production in New York by the Phoenix Theatre. Produced Off-Broadway in New York City by Lester Osterman, Lucille Lortel, and Marc Howard.

In one of my early conversations about writing plays, before I had ever written one, that is, Jon Jory, of Actors Theatre of Louisville, told me, "Go back at least ten years and write about some time when you were really scared."

Getting Out, my first play, was the result of that advice. The scary time was the two years I spent teaching in the children's unit of a state mental hospital. I was indeed injured there, we all were, but the most frightening thing was the realization that once a violent child got into the system, there was almost no way out for her. The children were also aware of this, and consequently ran away as often as they could. Which, if the truth be told, we didn't really mind, as it gave us a chance to rest until the police brought them back.

But later, when I sat down to write, I wondered what would happen if one of our girls ever found herself some place she couldn't get out of. Like solitary confinement in federal prison.

I know now, all these years and plays later, that I always write about solitary confinement. But *Getting Out* was my first crack at it. And the best comment I ever had about the play was a question asked of me by a prisoner from Terminal Island, who wanted to know where I had done my time.

My other plays include *'Night, Mother,* which won both The Susan Smith Blackburn Prize and the Pulitzer Prize; *Third and Oak: The Laundromat; The Pool Hall; The Holdup; Traveler in the Dark;* and *Sarah and Abraham.*

I have received grants from the National Endowment for the Arts and the Rockefeller Foundation, the American Academy, and Institute of Arts and Letters, and have been playwright-in-residence at the Actors Theatre of Louisville and the Mark Taper Forum. I serve on the Board of the Young Playwrights Festival and am the Treasurer of the Council of the Dramatists Guild.

MARSHA NORMAN
1990

3

Characters

ARLENE, a thin, drawn woman in her late 20's, who has just served an 8-year prison term for murder.

ARLIE, Arlene at various times earlier in her life.

BENNIE, an Alabama prison guard in his 50's.

EVANS, a prison guard.

DOCTOR, a psychiatrist in a juvenile institution.

CALDWELL, a prison guard.

MOTHER, Arlene's mother.

SCHOOL PRINCIPAL

RONNIE, a teenager in a juvenile institution.

CARL, Arlene's former pimp and partner in various crimes, in his late 20's.

WARDEN, Superintendent of Pine Ridge Correctional Institute for Women.

RUBY, Arlene's upstairs neighbor, a cook in a diner, also an ex-con, in her late 30's.

Both acts are set in a dingy one-room apartment in a rundown section of downtown Louisville, Kentucky. There is a twin bed and one chair. There is a sink, an apartment-size combination stove and refrigerator, and a counter with cabinets above. Dirty curtains conceal the bars on the outside of the single window. There is one closet and a door to the bathroom. The door to the apartment opens into a hall.

A catwalk stretches above the apartment and a prison cell, Stage Right, connects to it by stairways. An apron Downstage and Stage Left completes the enclosure of the apartment in playing areas for the past. The apartment must seem imprisoned.

The time is the present.

4

Notes

Arlie is the violent kid Arlene was until her last stretch in prison. She may walk through the apartment quite freely, but no one there will acknowledge her presence. Most of her scenes take place in the prison areas.

Arlie, in a sense, is Arlene's memory of herself, called up by fears, needs and even simple word cues. The memory haunts, attacks, and warns. But mainly, the memory will not go away.

Arlie's life should be as vivid as Arlene's, if not as continuous. There must be hints in both physical type and gesture that Arlie and Arlene are the same person, though seen at different times in her life. They both speak with a country twang, but Arlene is suspicious and guarded, withdrawal is always a possibility. Arlie is unpredictable and incorrigible. The change seen in Arlie during the second act represents a movement toward the adult Arlene, but the transition should never be complete. Only in the final scene are they enjoyably aware of each other.

The life in the prison "surround" needs to convince without distracting. The guards do not belong to any specific institution, but rather, to all the places where Arlene has done time.

Over Loudspeaker—Before Act One Curtain

These announcements will be broadcast beginning 5 minutes before the house lights come down for Act One. A woman's voice is preferred, a droning loudspeaker tone is essential.

Kitchen workers, all kitchen workers report immediately to the kitchen. Kitchen workers to the kitchen. The library will not be open today. Those scheduled for book check-out should remain in morning work assignments. Kitchen workers to the kitchen. No library hours today. Library hours resume tomorrow as usual. All kitchen workers to the kitchen.

Frances Mills, you have a visitor at the front gate. All residents and staff, all residents and staff . . . Do not, repeat, Do not, walk on the front lawn today or use the picnic tables on the front lawn during your break after lunch or dinner.

Your attention please. The exercise class for Dorm A residents has been cancelled. Mrs. Fischer should be back at work in another month. She thanks you for your cards and wants all her girls to know she had an 8 pound baby girl.

Doris Creech, see Mrs. Adams at the library before lunch. Frances Mills, you have a visitor at the front gate. The Women's Associates' picnic for the beauty school class has been postponed until Friday. As picnic lunches have already been prepared, any beauty school member who so wishes, may pick up a picnic lunch and eat it at her assigned lunch table during the regular lunch period.

Frances Mills, you have a visitor at the front gate. Doris Creech to see Mrs. Adams at the library before lunch. I'm sorry, that's Frankie Hill, you have a visitor at the front gate. Repeat, Frankie Hill, not Frances Mills, you have a visitor at the front gate.

6

ACT ONE

The warden's voice on tape is heard in the blackout.

WARDEN'S VOICE: The Alabama State Parole Board hereby grants parole to Holsclaw, Arlene, subject having served eight years at Pine Ridge Correctional Institute for the second degree murder of a cab driver in conjunction with a filling station robbery involving attempted kidnapping of attendant. Crime occurred during escape from Lakewood State Prison where subject Holsclaw was serving three years for forgery and prostitution. Extensive juvenile records from the state of Kentucky appended hereto. (*As* WARDEN *continues, light comes up on* ARLENE, *walking around the cell, waiting to be picked up for the ride home.* ARLIE *is visible, but just barely, D.C. Warden's voice, continuing.*) Subject now considered completely rehabilitated is returned to Kentucky under inter-state parole agreement in consideration of family residence and appropriate support personnel in the area. Subject will remain under the supervision of Kentucky parole officers for a period of five years. Prospects for successful integration into community rated good. Psychological evaluation, institutional history and health records attached in Appendix C, this document.

BENNIE'S VOICE: Arlie! (ARLENE *leaves the cell, light comes up on* ARLIE, *seated D.C. She tells this story rather simply. She enjoys it, but its horror is not lost on her. She may be doing some semi-absorbing activity such as painting her toenails.*)

ARLIE: So, there was this little kid, see, this creepy little fucker next door. Had glasses an somethin wrong with his foot. I don't know, seven, maybe. Anyhow, ever time his daddy went fishin, he'd bring this kid back some frogs. They built this little fence around em in the back yard like they was pets or somethin. An we'd try to go over an see em but he'd start screamin to his mother to come out an git rid of us. Real snotty like. So we got sick of him bein such a goody-goody an one night me an June snuck over there an put all his dumb ol frogs in this sack. You never heard such a fuss. (*Makes croaking sounds.*) Slimy bastards, frogs. We was plannin to let em go all over the place, but when they started jumpin an all, we just figured they was askin for it. So, we taken em out front to the porch an we throwed em, one at a time, into the street. (*Laughs.*) Some of em hit cars goin by but most of em jus got squashed, you know, runned over? It was great, seein how far we could throw em, over back of our backs an under our legs an God, it was really fun watchin em fly through the air then SPLAT (*Claps*

7

hands.) all over somebody's car window or somethin. Then the next day, we was waitin and this little kid comes out in his back yard lookin for his stupid frogs and he don't seen any an he gets so crazy, cryin and everything. So me an June goes over an tells him we seen this big mess out in the street, an he goes out an sees all them frogs legs and bodies an shit all over the everwhere, an, man, it was so funny. We bout killed ourselves laughin. Then his mother come out and she wouldn't let him go out an pick up all the pieces, so he jus had to stand there watchin all the cars go by smush his little babies right into the street. I's gonna run out an git him a frog's head, but June yellin at me "Arlie git over here for some car slips on them frog guts an crashes into you." (*Pause.*) I never had so much fun in one day in my whole life. (ARLIE *will remain seated as* ARLENE *enters the apartment. It is late evening. Two sets of footsteps are heard coming up the stairs.* ARLENE *opens the door and walks into the room. She stands still, surveying the littered apartment.* BENNIE *is heard dragging a heavy trunk up the stairs.* BENNIE *is wearing his guard uniform. He is a heavy man, but obviously used to physical work.*)

BENNIE: (*From outside.*) Arlie?

ARLENE: Arlene.

BENNIE: Arlene? (*Bringing the trunk just inside the door.*)

ARLENE: Leave it. I'll git it later.

BENNIE: Oh, now, let me bring it in for you. You ain't as strong as you was.

ARLENE: I ain't as mean as I was. I'm strong as ever. You go on now. (*Beginning to walk around the room.*)

ARLIE: (*Irritated, as though someone is calling her.*) Lay off! (*Gets up and walks past* BENNIE.)

BENNIE: (*Scoots the trunk into the room a little further.*) Go on where, Arlie?

ARLENE: I don't know where. How'd I know where you'd be goin?

BENNIE: I can't go til I know you're gonna do all right.

ARLENE: Look, I'm gonna do all right. I done all right before Pine Ridge, an I done all right at Pine Ridge. An I'm gonna do all right here.

BENNIE: But you don't know nobody. I mean, nobody nice.

ARLENE: Lay off.

BENNIE: Nobody to take care of you.

ARLENE: (*Picking up old newspapers and other trash from the floor.*) I kin take care of myself. I been doin it long enough.

BENNIE: Sure you have, an you landed yourself in prison doin it, Arlie girl.

ARLENE: (*Wheels around, won't this guy ever shut up?*) Arlie girl landed herself in prison. Arlene is out, O.K.?

BENNIE: Hey, now, I know we said we wasn't gonna say nuthin about that, but I been lookin after you for a long time. I been watchin you eat your dinner for 8 years now. I got used to it, you know?

ARLENE: Well, you kin jus' git unused to it.

BENNIE: Then why'd you ask me to drive you all the way up here?

ARLENE: I didn't, now. That was all your big ideal.

BENNIE: And what were you gonna do? Ride the bus, pick up some soldier, git yourself in another mess of trouble?

ARLIE: (*Struts back into the apartment from the closet door, going over as if to a soldier sitting at a bar.*) O.K., who's gonna buy me a beer?

ARLENE: You oughta go by Fort Knox on your way home.

ARLIE: Fuckin soldiers, don't care where they get theirself drunk. (*Stops.*)

ARLENE: You'd like it.

ARLIE: Well, Arlie girl, take your pick.

ARLENE: They got tanks right out on the grass to look at.

ARLIE: (*Now appears to lean on a bar rail.*) You git that haircut today, honey?

BENNIE: I just didn't want you given your 20 dollars the warden gave you to the first pusher you come across. (ARLIE *laughs.*)

ARLENE: That's what you think I been waiting for? (*A guard appears and motions for* ARLIE *to follow him.*)

ARLIE: Yeah! I heard ya. (*The guard "escorts"* ARLIE *to the cell and slams the door.*)

BENNIE: But God Almighty, I hate to think what you'd done to the first ol bugger tried to make you in that bus station. You got grit, Arlie girl. I gotta credit you for that.

ARLIE: (*From the cell, as she dumps a plate of food on the floor.*) Officer!

BENNIE: The screamin you'd do. Wake the dead.

ARLENE: Uh-huh.

BENNIE: An there ain't nobody can beat you for throwin plates. (*Proudly.*)

ARLIE: Are you gonna clean up this shit or do I have to sit here and look at it til I vomit? (*As the guard comes in to clean it up.*)

BENNIE: Listen, ever prison in Alabama's usin' plastic forks now on account of what you done.

ARLENE: You can quit talkin' just any time now.

ARLIE: Some life you got, fatso. Bringin me my dinner then wipin it off the walls. (*Laughs.*)

BENNIE: Some of them officers was pretty leery of you. Even the chaplain.

ARLENE: No he wasn't either.

BENNIE: Not me, though. You was just wild, that's all.

ARLENE: Animals is wild, not people. That's what he said.

ARLIE: (*Mocking.*) Good behavior, good behavior. Shit.

BENNIE: Now what could that four-eyes chaplain know about wild? (ARLENE *looks up sharply.*) O.K. Not wild, then . . .

ARLIE: I kin git outta here anytime I want. (*Leaves the cell.*)

BENNIE: But you got grit, Arlie.

ARLENE: I have said for you to call me Arlene.

BENNIE: O.K. O.K.

ARLENE: Huh?

BENNIE: Don't git riled. You want me to call you Arlene, then Arlene it is. Yes Ma'am. Now, (*Slapping the trunk.*) where do you want this? (*No response.*) Arlene, I said, where do you want this trunk?

ARLENE: I don't care. (BENNIE *starts to put it at the foot of the bed.* ARLENE sees him.) No! (*Then calmer.*) I seen it there too long. (BENNIE *is understandably irritated.*) Maybe over here. (*Points to a spot near the window.*) I could put a cloth on it and sit an look out the . . . (*She pulls the curtains apart, sees the bars on the window.*) What's these bars doin here?

BENNIE: (*Stops moving the trunk.*) I think they're to keep out burglars, you know. (*Sits on the trunk.*)

ARLENE: Yeah, I know.

ARLIE: (*Appearing on the catwalk as if stopped during a break in.*) We ain't breakin in, cop, we're just admirin this beautiful window.

ARLENE: I don't want them there. Pull them out.

BENNIE: You can't go tearin up the place, Arlene. Landlord wouldn't like it.

ARLIE: (*To the unseen policeman.*) Maybe I got a brick in my hand and maybe I don't.

BENNIE: Not one bit.

ARLIE: An I'm standin on this garbage can because I like to, all right?

ARLENE: I ain't gonna let no landlord tell me what to do. (*Fairly strong, walking back toward him.*)

BENNIE: The landlord owns the building. You gotta do what he says or he'll throw you out right on your pretty little behind. (*Gives her a familiar pat.*)

ARLENE: (*Slaps his hand away.*) You watch your mouth. I won't have no dirty talk.

ARLIE: Just shut the fuck up, cop! Go bust a wino or something. (*Returns to the cell.*)

ARLENE: Here, put the trunk over here. (*Points D.R.*)

BENNIE: What you got in here, anyhow? Rocks? Rocks from the rock pile? (*Carrying the trunk over to the spot she has picked.*)

ARLENE: That ain't funny.

BENNIE: Oh sweetie, I didn't mean nuthin by that.

ARLENE: And I ain't your sweetie.

BENNIE: We really did have us a rock pile, you know, at the old Men's Prison, yes we did. And those boys, time they did nine or ten years carryin' rocks around, they was pret-ty mean, I'm here to tell you. And strong? God.

ARLENE: Well, what did you expect? (*Beginning to unpack the trunk.*)

BENNIE: You're tellin' me. It was dumb, I kept tellin the warden that. They coulda killed us all, easy, any time, that outfit. Except, we did have the guns.

ARLENE: Uh-huh.

BENNIE: One old bastard sailed a throwin-rock at me one day, would took my eye out if I hadn't turned around just then. Still got the scar, see? (*Reaches up to the back of his head.*)

ARLENE: You shoot him?

BENNIE: Nope. Somebody else did. I forget who. Hey! (*Walking over to the window.*) These bars won't be so bad. Maybe you could get you some plants so's you don't even see them. Yeah, plants'd do it up just fine. Just fine.

ARLENE: (*Pulls a cheaply framed picture of Jesus out of the trunk.*) Chaplain give me this.

BENNIE: He got it for free, I bet.

ARLENE: Now, look here. That chaplain was good to me, so you can shut up about him.

BENNIE: Fine. Fine. (*Backing down.*)

ARLENE: Here. (*Handing him the picture.*) You might as well be useful 'fore you go.

BENNIE: Where you want it?

ARLENE: Don't matter.

BENNIE: Course it matters. Wouldn't want me puttin it inside the closet, would you? You gotta make decisions now, Arlene. Gotta decide things.

ARLENE: I don't care.

BENNIE: (*Insisting.*) Arlene.

ARLENE: There. (*Pointing to a prominent position on the apartment wall, C.*)

BENNIE: Yeah. Good place. See it first thing when you get up. (ARLENE *lights a cigarette, as* ARLIE *retrieves a hidden lighter from the toilet in the cell.*)

ARLIE: There's ways . . . gettin outta bars . . . (*Appears to light a fire in the cell, catching her blouse on fire too.*)

BENNIE: (*As* ARLIE *is lighting the fire.*) This ol nail's pretty loose. I'll find something better to hang it with . . . somewhere or other . . .

ARLIE: (*Screams and the* DOCTOR *runs toward her, getting the attention of* EVANS, *a guard who has been goofing off on the catwalk.*) Let me outta here! There's a fuckin fire in here! (DOCTOR *arrives at the cell, pats his pockets as if looking for the keys.*) Officer!

DOCTOR: Guard! (GUARD *begins his run to the cell.*)

ARLIE: It's burnin me!

DOCTOR: Hurry!

GUARD-EVANS: I'm comin! I'm comin!

DOCTOR: What the hell were you . . .

GUARD-EVANS: Come on, come on. (*Fumbling for the right key.*)

DOCTOR: For Chrissake! (*Urgent.* GUARD *gets the door open, they rush in.* DOCTOR, *wrestling* ARLIE *to the ground, opens his bag.*) Lay still, dammit. (ARLIE *collapses.* DOCTOR *may appear to given an injection.*) Ow! (*Grabbing his hand.*)

GUARD-EVANS: (*Lifting* ARLIE *up to the bed.*) Get bit, Doc?

DOCTOR: You going to let her burn this place down before you start payin attention up there?

GUARD-EVANS: (*Walks to the toilet, feels under the rim.*) Uh-huh.

BENNIE: There, that what you had in mind?

ARLENE: Yeah, thanks.

GUARD-EVANS: She musta had them matches hid right here.

BENNIE: (*Who has hung the picture and is now staring at it.*) How you think he kept his beard trimmed all nice?

ARLENE: (*Preoccupied with unloading the trunk.*) Who?

BENNIE: (*Pointing to the picture.*) Jesus.

DOCTOR: (*Quite stern.*) I'll have to report you for this.

ARLENE: I don't know.

DOCTOR: That injection should hold her. I'll check back later. (*Leaves.*)

GUARD-EVANS: (*Walking over to the bed.*) Report me, my ass. We got cells don't have potties, Holsclaw. (*Begins to search her and the bed, handling her very roughly.*) So where is it now? Got it up your pookie, I bet. Oh, that'd be good. Doc comin back an me with my fingers up your . . . roll over . . . don't weigh hardly nuthin, do you, dollie?

BENNIE: Never seen him without a moustache either.

ARLENE: Huh?

BENNIE: The picture.

GUARD-EVANS: Aw now . . . (*Finding the lighter under the mattress.*) That wasn't hard at all. Don't you know bout hide an seek, Arlie girl? Gonna hide somethin, hide it where it's fun to find it. (*Standing up, going to the door.*) Crazy fuckin someday-we-ain't-gonna-come-save-you bitch!

BENNIE: Well, Arlie girl, (GUARD *slams cell door and leaves.*) That ol trunk's bout as empty as my belly.

ARLENE: You have been talkin bout your belly ever since we left this mornin.

BENNIE: You hungry? Them hotdogs we had give out around Nashville.

ARLENE: No. Not really.

BENNIE: You gotta eat, Arlene.

ARLENE: Says who?

BENNIE: (*Laughs, this is a familiar response.*) How bout I pick us up some chicken, give you time to clean yourself up. We'll have a nice little dinner, just the two of us.

ARLENE: I git sick if I eat this late. Besides, I'm tired.

BENNIE: You'll feel better soon's you git somethin on your stomach. Like I always said, "Can't plow less'n you feed the mule."

ARLENE: I ain't never heard you say that.

BENNIE: There's lots you don't know about me, Arlene. You been seein me ever day, but you ain't been payin attention. You'll get to like me now we're out.

. ARLENE: You . . . was always out.

BENNIE: Yes sir, I'm gonna like bein retired. I kin tell already. An I can take care of you, like I been, only now . . .

ARLENE: (*Interrupting.*) You tol me you was jus takin a vacation.

BENNIE: I was gonna tell you.

ARLENE: You had some time off an nothin to do . . .

BENNIE: Figured you knew already.

ARLENE: You said you ain't never seen Kentucky like you always wanted to. Now you tell me you done quit at the prison? (*Increasingly angry.*)

BENNIE: They wouldn't let me drive you up here if I was still on the payroll, you know. Rules, against the rules. Coulda got me in big trouble doin that.

ARLENE: You ain't goin back to Pine Ridge?

BENNIE: Nope.

ARLENE: An you drove me all the way up here plannin to stay here?

BENNIE: I was thinkin on it.

ARLENE: Well what are you gonna do?

BENNIE: (*Not positive, just a possibility.*) Hardware.

ARLENE: Sell guns?

BENNIE: (*Laughs and shakes his head ''no.''*) Nails. Always wanted to. Some little store with bins and barrels full of nails and screws. Count em out. Put em in little sacks.

ARLENE: I don't need nobody hangin around remindin me where I been.

BENNIE: We had us a good time drivin up here, didn't we? You throwin that tomato outta the car . . . hit that No Litterin sign square in the middle. (*Grabs her arm as if to feel the muscle.*) Good arm you got.

ARLENE: (*Pulling away sharply.*) Don't you go grabbin me.

BENNIE: Listen, you take off them clothes and have yourself a nice hot bath. (*Heading for the bathroom.*) See, I'll start the water. And me, I'll go get us some chicken. (*Coming out of the bathroom.*) You like slaw or potato salad?

ARLENE: Don't matter.

BENNIE: (*Asking her to decide.*) Arlene . . .

ARLENE: Slaw.

BENNIE: One big bucket of slaw comin right up. An extra rolls. You have a nice bath, now, you hear? I'll take my time so's you don't have to hurry fixin yourself up.

ARLENE: I ain't gonna do no fixin.

BENNIE: (*A knowing smile.*) I know how you gals are when you get in the tub. You got any bubbles?

ARLENE: What?

BENNIE: Bubbles. You know, stuff to make bubbles with . . . bubble bath.

ARLENE: I thought you was goin.

BENNIE: Right. Right. Goin right now. (BENNIE *leaves, locking the door behind him. He has left his hat on the bed.* ARLENE *checks the stove and refrigerator, then goes into the bathroom when noted.*)

GUARD-CALDWELL: (*Opening the cell door, carrying a plastic dinner carton.*) Got your grub, girlie.

ARLIE: Get out!

GUARD-CALDWELL: Can't. Doc says you gotta take the sun today.

ARLIE: You take it! I ain't hungry. (GUARD *and* ARLIE *begin walk to the D. table area.*)

GUARD-CALDWELL: You gotta eat, Arlie.

ARLIE: Says who?

GUARD-CALDWELL: Says me. Says the Warden. Says the Department of Corrections. Brung you two rolls.

ARLIE: And you know what you can do with your . . .

GUARD-CALDWELL: Stuff em in your bra, why don't you?

ARLIE: Ain't you got somebody to go beat up somewhere?

GUARD-CALDWELL: Gotta see you get fattened up.

ARLIE: What do you care? (ARLENE *goes into the bathroom.*)

GUARD-CALDWELL: Oh, we care all right. (*Setting the food down on the table.*) Got us a two-way mirror in the shower room. (*She looks up, hostile.*) And you don't know which one it is, do you? (*He forces her onto the seat.*) Yes Ma'am. Eat. (*Pointing to the food.*) We sure do care if you go gittin too skinny. (*Walks away, folding his arms and standing watching her, her anger building, despite her hunger.*) Yes Mam. We care a hog lickin lot.

ARLIE: Sons-a-bitches! (*Throws the whole carton at him. Mother's knock is heard on the apartment door.*)

MOTHER: Arlie? Arlie girl you in there? (ARLENE *walks out of the bathroom, stands still, looking at the door.* ARLIE *hears the knock at the same time and slips into the apartment and over to the bed, putting the pillow between her legs and holding the yellow teddy bear* ARLENE *has unpacked. Knocking louder.*) Arlie?

ARLIE: (*Pulling herself up weakly on one elbow, speaking with the voice of a very young child.*) Mama? Mama? (ARLENE *walks slowly toward the door.*)

MOTHER: (*Now pulling the doorknob from the outside, angry that the door is locked.*) Arlie? I know you're in there.

ARLIE: I can't git up, Mama. (*Hands between her legs.*) My legs is hurt.

MOTHER: What's takin you so long?

ARLENE: (*Smoothing out her dress.*) Yeah, I'm comin. (*Puts* BENNIE'S *hat out of sight under the bed.*) Hold on.

MOTHER: I brung you some stuff but I ain't gonna stand here all night. (ARLENE *opens the door and stands back.* MOTHER *looks strong but badly worn. She is wearing her cab driver's uniform and is carrying a plastic laundry basket stuffed with cleaning fluids, towels, bug spray, etc.*)

ARLENE: I didn't know if you'd come.

MOTHER: Ain't I always?

ARLENE: How are you? (*Moves as if to hug her.* MOTHER *stands still,* ARLENE *backs off.*)

MOTHER: Bout the same. (*Walking into the room.*)

ARLENE: I'm glad to see you.

MOTHER: (*Not looking at* ARLENE.) You look tired.

ARLENE: It was a long drive.

MOTHER: (*Putting the laundry basket on the trunk.*) Didn't fatten you up none, I see. (*Walks around the room looking the place over.*) You always was too skinny (ARLENE *straightens her clothes again.*) Shoulda beat you like your daddy said. Make you eat.

ARLIE: Nobody done this to me, Mama. (*Protesting, in pain*) No! No!

MOTHER: He weren't a mean man, though, your daddy.

ARLIE: Was . . . (*Quickly.*) my bike. My bike hurt me. The seat bumped me.

MOTHER: You remember that black chewing gum he got you when you was sick?

ARLENE: I remember he beat up on you.

MOTHER: Yeah, (*Proudly.*) and he was real sorry a coupla times. (*Looking in the closet.*) Filthy dirty. Hey! (*Slamming the closet door,* ARLENE *jumps at the noise.*) I brung you all kinda stuff. Just like Candy not leavin you nuthin. (*Walking back to the basket.*) Some kids I got.

ARLIE: (*Curling up into a ball.*) No, Mama, don't touch it. It'll git well. It git well before.

ARLENE: Where is Candy?

MOTHER: You got her place so what do you care? I got her outta my house so whatta I care? This'll be a good place for you.

ARLENE: (*Going to the window.*) Wish there was a yard, here.

MOTHER: (*Beginning to empty the basket.*) Nice things, see? Bet you ain't had no colored towels where you been.

ARLENE: No.

MOTHER: (*Putting some things away in cabinets.*) No place like home. Got that up on the kitchen wall now.

ARLIE: I don't want no tea, Mama.

ARLENE: Yeah?

MOTHER: (*Repeating* ARLENE'S *answers.*) No . . . yeah? . . . You forgit how to talk? I ain't gonna be here all that long. Least you can talk to me while I'm here.

ARLENE: You ever git that swing you wanted?

MOTHER: Dish towels, an see here? June sent along this teapot. You drink tea, Arlie?

ARLENE: No.

MOTHER: June's havin another baby. Don't know when to quit, that girl. Course, I ain't one to talk. (*Starting to pick up trash on the floors, etc.*)

ARLENE: Have you seen Joey?

ARLIE: I'm tellin you the truth.

MOTHER: An Ray . . .

ARLIE: (*Pleading.*) Daddy didn't do nuthin to me.

MOTHER: Ray ain't had a day of luck in his life.

ARLIE: Ask him. He saw me fall on my bike.

MOTHER: Least bein locked up now, he'll keep off June til the baby gits here.

ARLENE: Have you seen Joey?

MOTHER: Your daddy ain't doin' too good right now. Man's been dyin for ten years, to hear him tell it. You'd think he'd git tired of it an just go ahead . . . pass on.

ARLENE: Mother . . . (*Wanting an answer.*)

MOTHER: Yeah, I seen 'im. Bout two years ago. Got your stringy hair.

ARLENE: You got a picture?

MOTHER: You was right to give him up. Foster homes is good for some kids.

ARLIE: Where's my Joey-bear? Yellow Joey-bear? Mama?

ARLENE: How'd you see him?

MOTHER: I was down at Detention Center pickin up Pete. (*Beginning her serious cleaning now.*)

ARLENE: How is he? (*Less than interested.*)

MOTHER: I could be workin at the Detention Center I been there so much. All I gotta do's have somethin big goin on an I git a call to come after one of you. Can't jus have kids, no, gotta be pickin em up all over town.

ARLENE: You was just tellin me . . .

MOTHER: Pete is taller, that's all.

ARLENE: You was just tellin me how you saw Joey.

MOTHER: I'm comin back in the cab an I seen him waitin for the bus.

ARLENE: What'd he say?

MOTHER: Oh, I didn't stop. (ARLENE *looks up quickly, hurt and angry.*) If the kid don't even know you, Arlie, he sure ain't gonna know who I am.

ARLENE: How come he couldn't stay at Shirley's?

MOTHER: Cause Shirley never was crazy about washin more diapers. She's the only smart kid I got. Anyway, social worker only put him there til she could find him a foster home.

ARLENE: But I coulda seen him.

MOTHER: Thatta been trouble, him bein in the family. Kid wouldn't have known who to listen to, Shirley or you.

ARLENE: But I'm his mother.

MOTHER: (*Interrupting.*) See, now you don't have to be worryin about him. No kids, no worryin.

ARLENE: He just had his birthday, you know.

ARLIE: Don't let daddy come in here, Mama. Just you an me. Mama?

ARLENE: When I git workin, I'll git a nice rug for this place. He could come live here with me.

MOTHER: Fat chance.

ARLENE: I done my time.

MOTHER: You never really got attached to him anyway.

ARLENE: How do you know that? (*Furious.*)

MOTHER: Now don't you go gettin het up. I'm tellin you . . .

ARLENE: But . . .

MOTHER: Kids need rules to go by an he'll get em over there.

ARLIE: No Daddy! I didn't tell her nuthin. I didn't! I didn't! (*Screaming, gets up from the bed, terrified.*)

MOTHER: Here, help me with these sheets. (*Hands* ARLENE *the sheets from the laundry basket.*) Even got you a spread. Kinda goes with them curtains. (ARLENE *is silent.*) You ain't thanked me, Arlie girl.

ARLENE: (*Going to the other side of the bed.*) They don't call me Arlie no more. It's Arlene now. (ARLENE *and* MOTHER *make up the bed.* ARLIE *jumps up, looks around and goes over to* MOTHER'S *purse. She looks through it hurriedly and pulls out the wallet. She takes some money and runs D.L. where she is caught by a* SCHOOL PRINCIPAL.)

PRINCIPAL: Arlie? You're in an awfully big hurry for such a little girl. (*Brushes at* ARLIE'S *hair.*) That is you under all that hair, isn't it? (ARLIE *resists this gesture.*) Now, you can watch where you're going.

ARLIE: Gotta git home.

PRINCIPAL: But school isn't over for another three hours. And there's peanut butter and chili today. (*As if this mattered.*)

ARLIE: Ain't hungry. (*Struggling free.*)

PRINCIPAL: (*Now sees* ARLIE'S *hands clenched behind her back.*) What do we have in our hands, Arlie? (*Sticky sweet over suspicion.*)

ARLIE: Nuthin.

PRINCIPAL: Let me see your hands, Arlie. Open up your hands. (*Expecting the worse.*)

ARLIE: (*Bringing hands around in front, opening them, showing crumpled dollars.*) It's my money. I earned it.

PRINCIPAL: (*Taking the money.*) And how did we earn this money?

ARLIE: Doin things.

PRINCIPAL: What kind of things?

ARLIE: For my daddy.

PRINCIPAL: Well, we'll see about that. You'll have to come with me.

ARLIE: No. (*Resisting as* PRINCIPAL *pulls her.*)

PRINCIPAL: Your mother was right after all. She said put you in a special school. (*Quickly.*) No, what she said was put you away somewhere and I said, No, she's too young, well I was wrong. I have four hundred other children to take care of here and what have I been doing? Breaking up your fights, talking to your truant officer and washing your writing off the bathroom wall. Well, I've had enough. You've made your choice. You *want* out of regular school and you're going to *get* out of regular school.

ARLIE: (*Becoming more violent.*) You can't make me go nowhere, bitch!

PRINCIPAL: (*Backing off in cold anger.*) I'm not making you go. You've earned it. You've worked hard for this, well, they're used to your type over there. They'll know exactly what to do with you. (PRINCIPAL *stalks off, leaving* ARLIE *alone.*)

MOTHER: (*Smoothing out the spread.*) Spread ain't new, but it don't look so bad. Think we got it right after we got you. No, I remember now. I was pregnant with you an been real sick the whole time. (ARLENE *lights a cigarette,* MOTHER *takes one,* ARLENE *retrieves the pack quickly.*) Your daddy brung me home this big bowl of chili an some jelly doughnuts. Some fare from the airport give him a big tip. Anyway, I'd been eatin peanut brittle all day, only thing that tasted any good. Then in he come with this chili an no sooner'n I got in bed I thrown up all over everwhere. Lucky I didn't throw you up, Arlie girl. Anyhow, that's how come us to get a new spread. This one here. (*Sits on the bed.*)

ARLENE: You drivin the cab any?

MOTHER: Any? Your daddy ain't drove it at all a long time now. 6 years, 7 maybe.

ARLENE: You meet anybody nice?

MOTHER: Not any more. Mostly drivin old ladies to get their shoes. Guess it got around the nursin homes I was reliable. (*Sounds funny to her.*) You remember that time I took you drivin with me that night after you been in a fight an that soldier bought us a beer? Shitty place, hole in the wall?

ARLENE: You made me wait in the car.

MOTHER: (*Standing up.*) Think I'd take a child of mine into a dump like that?

ARLENE: You went in.

MOTHER: Weren't no harm in it. (*Walking over for the bug spray.*) I didn't always look so bad, you know.

ARLENE: You was pretty.

MOTHER: (*Beginning to spray the floors.*) You could look better'n you do. Do somethin with your hair. I always thought if you'd looked better you wouldn't have got in so much trouble.

ARLENE: (*Pleased and curious.*) Joey got my hair?

MOTHER: And skinny.

ARLENE: I took some beauty school at Pine Ridge.

MOTHER: Yeah, a beautician?

ARLENE: I don't guess so.

MOTHER: Said you was gonna work.

ARLENE: They got a law here. Ex-cons can't get no license.

MOTHER: Shoulda stayed in Alabama, then. Worked there.

ARLENE: They got a law there, too.

MOTHER: Then why'd they give you the trainin?

ARLENE: I don't know.

MOTHER: Maybe they thought it'd straighten you out.

ARLENE: Yeah.

MOTHER: But you are gonna work, right? (*Doesn't want another burden.*)

ARLENE: Yeah. Cookin maybe. Something that pays good.

MOTHER: You? Cook? (*Laughs.*)

ARLENE: I could learn it.

MOTHER: Your daddy ain't never forgive you for that bologna sandwich. (ARLENE *laughs a little, finally enjoying a memory.*) Oh, I wish I'd seen you spreadin that Colgate on that bread. He'd have smelled that toothpaste if he hadn't been so sloshed. Little snotty-nosed kid tryin to kill her daddy with a bologna sandwich. An him bein so pleased when you brung it to him . . . (*Laughing.*)

ARLENE: (*No longer enjoying the memory.*) He beat me good.

MOTHER: Well, now, Arlie, you gotta admit you had it comin to you. (*Wiping tears from laughing.*)

ARLENE: I guess.

MOTHER: You got a broom?

ARLENE: No.

MOTHER: Well, I got one in the cab I brung just in case. I can't leave it here, but I'll sweep up fore I go. (*Walking toward the door.*) You jus rest til I git back. Won't find no work lookin the way you do. (MOTHER *leaves,* ARLENE *finds some lipstick and a mirror in her purse, she makes an attempt to look better while* MOTHER *is gone.*)

ARLIE: (*Jumps up, as if talking to another kid.*) She is not skinny!

ARLENE: (*Looking at herself in the mirror.*) I guess I could . . .

ARLIE: And she don't have to git them stinky permanents. Her hair just comes outta her head curly.

ARLENE: Some lipstick.

ARLIE: (*Serious.*) She drives the cab to buy us stuff, cause we don't take no charity from nobody, cause we got money cause she earned it.

ARLENE: (*Closing the mirror, dejected, afraid* MOTHER *might be right.*) But you're too skinny and you got stringy hair. (*Sitting on the floor.*)

ARLIE: (*More angry.*) She drives at night cause people needs rides at night. People goin to see their friends that are sick, or people's cars broken down an they gotta get to work at the . . . nobody calls my Mama a whore!

MOTHER: (*Coming back in with the broom.*) If I'd known you were gonna sweep up with your butt, I wouldn't have got this broom. Get up! (*Sweeps at* ARLENE *to get her to move.*)

ARLIE: You're gonna take that back or I'm gonna rip out all your ugly hair and stuff it down your ugly throat.

ARLENE: (*Tugging at her own hair.*) You still cut hair?

MOTHER: (*Noticing some spot on the floor.*) Gonna take a razor blade to get out this paint.

ARLENE: Nail polish.

ARLIE: Wanna know what I know about your Mama? She's dyin. Somethin's eatin up her insides piece by piece, only she don't want you to know it.

MOTHER: (*Continuing to sweep.*) So, you're callin' yourself Arlene, now?

ARLENE: Yes.

MOTHER: Don't want your girlie name no more?

ARLENE: Somethin like that.

MOTHER: They call you Arlene in prison?

ARLENE: Not at first when I was bein hateful. Just my number then.

MOTHER: You always been hateful.

ARLENE: There was this chaplain, he called me Arlene from the first day he come to talk to me. Here, let me help you. (ARLENE *reaches for the broom.*)

MOTHER: I'll do it.

ARLENE: You kin rest.

MOTHER: Since when? (ARLENE *backs off,* MOTHER *sweeping harder now.*) I ain't hateful, how come I got so many hateful kids? Poor dumb as hell Pat, stealin them wigs, Candy screwin since day one, Pete cuttin up ol Mac down at the grocery, June sellin dope like it was Girl Scout cookies, and you . . . thank God I can't remember it all.

ARLENE: (*A very serious request.*) Maybe I could come out on Sunday for . . . you still make that pot roast?

MOTHER: (*Now sweeping over by the picture of Jesus.*) That your picture?

ARLENE: That chaplain give it to me.

MOTHER: The one give you your "new name."

ARLENE: Yes.

MOTHER: It's crooked. (*Doesn't straighten it.*)

ARLENE: I liked those potatoes with no skins. An that ketchup squirter we had, jus like in a real restaurant.

MOTHER: People that run them institutions now, they jus don't know how to teach kids right. Let em run around an get in more trouble. They should get you up at the crack of dawn an set you to scrubbin the floor. That's what kids need. Trainin. Hard work.

ARLENE: (*A clear request.*) I'll probably git my Sundays off.

MOTHER: Sunday . . . is my day to clean house now. (ARLENE *gets the message, finally walks over to straighten the picture.* MOTHER *now feels a little bad about this rejection, stops sweeping for a moment.*) I woulda wrote you but I didn't have nuthin to say. An no money to send, so what's the use?

ARLENE: I made out.

MOTHER: They pay you for workin?

ARLENE: Bout three dollars a month.

MOTHER: How'd you make it on three dollars a month? (*Answers her own question.*) You do some favors?

ARLENE: (*Sitting down in the chair under the picture, a somewhat smug look.*) You jus can't make it by yourself.

MOTHER: (*Pauses, suspicious, then contemptuous.*) You play, Arlie?

ARLENE: You don't know nuthin about that.

MOTHER: I hear things. Girls callin each other "mommy" an bringin things back from the canteen for their "husbands." Makes me sick. You got family, Arlie, what you want with that playin? Don't want nobody like that in my house.

ARLENE: You don't know what you're talkin about.

MOTHER: I still got two kids at home. Don't want no bad example. (*Not finishing the sweeping. Has all the dirt in one place, but doesn't get it up off the floor yet.*)

ARLENE: I could tell them some things.

MOTHER: Like about that dab driver. (*Vicious.*)

ARLENE: Look, that was a long time ago. I wanna work, now, make somethin of myself. I learned to knit. People'll buy nice sweaters. Make some extra money.

MOTHER: We sure could use it.

ARLENE: An then if I have money, maybe they'd let me take Joey to the fair, buy him hotdogs an talk to him. Make sure he ain't foolin around.

MOTHER: What makes you think he'd listen to you? Alice, across the street? Her sister took care her kids while she was at Lexington. You think they pay any attention to her now? Ashamed, that's what. One of em told me his mother done died. Gone to see a friend and died there.

ARLENE: Be different with me and Joey.

MOTHER: He don't even know who you are, Arlie.

ARLENE: Arlene. (*She can't respond, this is all she can say.*)

MOTHER: You forget already what you was like as a kid. At Waverly, tellin them lies about that campin trip we took, sayin your Daddy make you watch while he an me . . . you know I'd have killed you then if them social workers hadn't been watchin.

ARLENE: Yeah.

MOTHER: Didn't want them thinkin I weren't fit. Well, what do they know? Each time you'd get out of one of them places, you'd be actin worse than ever. Go right back to that junkie, pimp, Carl, sellin the stuff he steals, savin his ass from the police. He follow you home this time, too?

ARLENE: He's got four more years at Bricktown.

MOTHER: Glad to hear it. Here . . . (*Handing her a bucket.*) Water. (ARLENE *fills up the bucket and* MOTHER *washes several dirty spots on the walls, floor and furniture.* ARLENE *knows better than to try to help. The* DOCTOR *walks* D. *to find* ARLIE *for their counseling session.*)

DOCTOR: So you refuse to go to camp?

ARLIE: Now why'd I want to go to your fuckin camp? Camp's for babies. You can go shit in the woods if you want to, but I ain't goin.

DOCTOR: Oh, you're goin.

ARLIE: Wanna bet?

MOTHER: Arlie, I'm waitin. (*For the water.*)

ARLIE: 'Sides, I'm waitin.

DOCTOR: Waiting for what?

ARLIE: For Carl to come git me.

DOCTOR: And who is Carl?

ARLIE: Jus some guy. We're goin to Alabama.

DOCTOR: You don't go till we say you can go.

ARLIE: Carl's got a car.

DOCTOR: Does he have a driver's license to go with it?

ARLIE: (*Enraged, impatient.*) I'm goin now. (*She stalks away, then backs up toward him again. He has information she wants.*)

DOCTOR: Hey!

ARLENE: June picked out a name for the baby?

MOTHER: Clara . . . or Clarence. Got it from this fancy shampoo she bought.

ARLIE: I don't feel good. I'm pregnant, you know.

DOCTOR: The test was negative.

ARLIE: Well, I should know, shouldn't I?

DOCTOR: No. You want to be pregnant, is that it?

ARLIE: I wouldn't mind. Kids need somebody to bring em up right.

DOCTOR: Raising children is a big responsibility, you know.

ARLIE: Yeah, I know it. I ain't dumb. Everybody always thinks I'm so dumb.

DOCTOR: You could learn if you wanted to. That's what the teachers are here for.

ARLIE: Shit.

DOCTOR: Or so they say.

ARLIE: All they teach us is about geography. Why'd I need to know about Africa. Jungles and shit.

DOCTOR: They want you to know about other parts of the world.

ARLIE: Well, I ain't goin there so whatta I care?

DOCTOR: What's this about Cindy?

ARLIE: (*Hostile.*) She told Mr. Dawson some lies about me.

DOCTOR: I bet.

ARLIE: She said I fuck my Daddy for money.

DOCTOR: And what did you do when she said that?

ARLIE: What do you think I did? I beat the shit out of her.

DOCTOR: And that's a good way to work out your problem?

ARLIE: She ain't done it since. (*Proud.*)

DOCTOR: She's been in traction, since.

ARLIE: So, whatta I care? She say it again, I'll do it again. Bitch!

ARLENE: (*Looking down at the dirt* MOTHER *is gathering on the floor.*) I ain't got a can. Just leave it.

MOTHER: And have you sweep it under the bed after I go? (*Wraps the dirt in a piece of newspaper and puts it in her laundry basket.*)

DOCTOR: (*Looking at his clipboard.*) You're on unit clean-up this week.

ARLIE: I done it last week!

DOCTOR: Then you should remember what to do. The session is over. (*Getting up, walking away.*) And stand up straight! And take off that hat! (DOCTOR *and* ARLIE *go offstage as* MOTHER *finds* BENNIE'S *hat.*)

MOTHER: This your hat?

ARLENE: No.

MOTHER: Guess Candy left it here.

ARLENE: Candy didn't leave nuthin. (*Then realizes this was a mistake.*)

MOTHER: Then whose is it? (ARLENE *doesn't answer.*) Do you know whose hat this is? (ARLENE *turns away.*) I'm askin you a question and I want an answer. (ARLENE *turns her back to* MOTHER.) Whose hat is this? You tell me right now, whose hat is this?

ARLENE: It's Bennie's.

MOTHER: And who's Bennie?

ARLENE: Guy drove me home from Pine Ridge. A guard.

MOTHER: (*Upset.*) I knew it. You been screwin a goddamn guard. (*Throws the hat on the bed.*)

ARLENE: He jus drove me up here, that's all.

MOTHER: Sure.

ARLENE: I git sick on the bus.

MOTHER: You expect me to believe that?

ARLENE: I'm tell you, he jus . . .

MOTHER: No man alive gonna drive a girl 500 miles for nuthin.

ARLENE: He ain't never seen Kentucky.

MOTHER: It ain't Kentucky he wants to see.

ARLENE: He ain't gettin nuthin from me.

MOTHER: That's what you think.

ARLENE: He done some nice things for me at Pine Ridge, funny stories.

MOTHER: He'd be tellin stories all right, tellin his buddies where to find you.

ARLENE: He's gettin us some dinner right now.

MOTHER: And how're you gonna pay him? Huh? Tell me that.

ARLENE: I ain't like that no more.

MOTHER: Oh you ain't. I'm your mother. I know what you'll do.

ARLENE: I tell you I ain't.

MOTHER: I knew it. Well, when you got another bastard in you, don't come cryin to me, cause I done told you.

ARLENE: Don't worry.

MOTHER: An I'm getting myself outta here fore your boyfriend comes back.

ARLENE: He ain't my boyfriend. (*Increasing anger.*)

MOTHER: I been a lotta things, but I ain't dumb, Arlene. (*"ARLENE" is mocking.*)

ARLENE: I didn't say you was. (*Beginning to know how this is going to turn out.*)

MOTHER: Oh no? You lied to me!

ARLENE: How?

MOTHER: You took my spread without even sayin thank you. (*Not an answer. Just going on with the fury.*) You're hintin at comin to my house for pot roast just like nuthin ever happened, an all the time you're hidin a goddamn guard under your bed. (*Furious.*) Uh-huh.

ARLENE: Mama? (*Quietly.*)

MOTHER: What? (*Cold, fierce.*)

ARLENE: What kind of meat makes a pot roast?

MOTHER: A roast makes a pot roast. Buy a roast. Shoulder, chuck . . .

ARLENE: Are you comin back?

MOTHER: You ain't got no need for me.

ARLENE: I gotta ask you to come see me?

MOTHER: I come tonight, didn't I, an nobody asked me?

ARLENE: Just forget it.

MOTHER: (*Getting her things together now, ready to go.*) An if I hadn't told them about this apartment, you wouldn't be out at all, how bout that!

ARLENE: Forget it! (*Stronger.*)

MOTHER: Don't you go talkin to me that way. You remember who I am. I'm the one took you back after all you done all them years. I brung you that teapot. I scrubbed your place. You remember that when you talk to me.

ARLENE: Sure.

MOTHER: Uh-huh. (*Now goes to the bed, rips off the spread and stuffs it in her basket.*) I knowed I shouldn't have come. You ain't changed a bit.

ARLENE: Same hateful brat, right? (*Back to* MOTHER.)

MOTHER: Same hateful brat. Right. (*Arms full, heading for the door.*)

ARLENE: (*Rushing toward her.*) Mama . . .

MOTHER: Don't you touch me. (MOTHER *leaves.* ARLENE *stares out the door, stunned and hurt, finally, she slams the door and turns back into the room.*)

ARLENE: No! Don't you touch Mama, Arlie.

RONNIE: (*A fellow juvenile offender, runs across the catwalk, waving a necklace and being chased by* ARLIE.) Arlie got a boyfriend, Arlie got a boyfriend. (*Throws the necklace D.*) Whoo!

ARLIE: (*Chasing him.*) Ronnie, you ugly mother, I'll smash your fuckin . . .

ARLENE: You might steal all . . . (*Getting more angry.*)

RONNIE: (*Running down the stairs.*) Arlie got a boyfriend . . .

ARLIE: Gimme that necklace or I'll . . .

ARLENE: . . . or eat all Mama's precious pot roast . . .

RONNIE: (*As they wrestle on the D. apron.*) You'll tell the Doctor on me? And get your private room back? (*Laughing.*)

ARLENE: (*Cold and hostile.*) No, don't touch Mama, Arlie. Cause you might slit Mama's throat. (*Goes into the bathroom.*)

ARLIE: You wanna swallow all them dirty teeth?

RONNIE: Tell me who give it to you.

ARLIE: No, you tell me where it's at.

RONNIE: (*Breaks away, pushing* ARLIE *in the opposite direction, runs for the necklace.*) It's right here. (*Drops it down his pants.*) Come an git it.

ARLIE: Oh now, that was really ignorant, you stupid pig.

RONNIE: (*Backing away, daring her.*) Jus reach right in. First come, first served.

ARLIE: Now, how you gonna pee after I throw your weenie over the fence?

RONNIE: You ain't gonna do that, girl. You gonna fall in love. (*She turns vicious, pins him down, attacking. This is no longer play. He screams.* DOCTOR *appears on the catwalk.*)

DOCTOR: Arlie! (*Heads down the stairs to stop this.*)

CARL: (*From outside the apartment door.*) Arlie!

DOCTOR: Arlie!

ARLIE: Stupid, ugly . . .

RONNIE: Help! (ARLIE *runs off, hides D.L.*)

DOCTOR: That's three more weeks of isolation, Arlie. (*Bending down to* RONNIE.) You all right? Can you walk?

RONNIE: (*Looking back to* ARLIE *as he gets up in great pain.*) She was tryin to kill me.

DOCTOR: Yeah. Easy now. You shouldn've known, Ronnie.

ARLIE: (*Yelling at* RONNIE.) You'll get yours, crybaby.

CARL: Arlie . . .

ARLIE: Yeah, I'm comin!

CARL: Bad-lookin dude says move your ass an open up this here door, girl. (ARLENE *does not come out of the bathroom.* CARL *twists the door knob violently, then kicks in the door and walks in.* CARL *is thin and cheaply dressed.* CARL'S *walk and manner are imitative of black pimps, but he can't quite carry if off.*) Where you at, Mama?

ARLENE: Carl?

CARL: Who else? You 'spectin' Leroy Brown?

ARLENE: I'm takin a bath!

CARL: (*Walking toward the bathroom.*) I like my ladies clean. Matter of professional pride.

ARLENE: Don't come in here.

CARL: (*Mocking her tone.*) Don't come in here. I seen it all before, girl.

ARLENE: I'm gittin out. Sit down or somethin.

CARL: (*Talking loud enough for her to hear him through the door.*) Ain't got the time. (*Opens her purse, then searches the trunk.*) Jus come by to tell you it's tomorrow. We be takin our feet to the New York street. (*As though she will be pleased.*) No more fuckin around with these jiveass southern turkeys. We're goin to the big city, baby. Get you some red shades an some red shorts an the john's be linin' up fore we hit town. Four tricks a night. How's that sound? No use wearin out that cute ass you got. Way I hear it, only way to git busted up there's be stupid, an I ain't lived this long bein stupid.

ARLENE: (*Coming out of the bathroom wearing a towel.*) That's exactly how you lived your whole life—bein stupid.

CARL: Arlie . . . (*Moving in on her.*) be sweet, sugar.

ARLENE: Still got your curls.

CARL: (*Trying to hug her.*) You're lookin O.K. yourself.

ARLENE: Oh, Carl. (*Noticing the damage to the door, breaking away from any closeness he might try to force.*)

CARL: (*Amused.*) Bent up your door, some.

ARLENE: How come you're out?

CARL: Sweetheart, you done broke out once, been nabbed and sent to Pine Ridge and got yourself paroled since I been in. I got a right to a little free time too, ain't that right?

ARLENE: You escape?

CARL: Am I standin here or am I standin here? They been fuckin with you, I can tell.

ARLENE: They gonna catch you.

CARL: (*Going to the window.*) Not where we're going. Not a chance.

ARLENE: Where you going they won't git you?

CARL: Remember that green hat you picked out for me down in Birmingham? Well, I ain't ever wore it yet, but I kin wear it in New York cause New York's where you wear whatever you feel like. One guy tol me he saw this dude wearin a whole ring of feathers roun his leg, right here (*Grabs his leg above the knee.*) an he weren't in no circus nor no Indian neither.

ARLENE: I ain't seen you since Birmingham. How come you think I wanna see you now?

ARLIE: (*Appearing suddenly, confronts* CARL.) Carl, I ain't goin with that dude, he's weird. (*Pointing as if there is a trick waiting.*)

CARL: Cause we gotta go collect the johns' money, that's "how come."

ARLIE: I don't need you pimpin for me.

ARLENE: (*Very strong.*) I'm gonna work.

CARL: Work?

ARLENE: Yeah.

CARL: What's this "work"?

ARLIE: You always sendin me to them ol' droolers . . .

CARL: You kin do two things, girl . . .

ARLIE: They slobberin all over me . . .

CARL: Breakin out an hookin.

ARLIE: They tyin me to the bed!

ARLENE: I mean real work.

ARLIE: (*Now screaming, gets further away from him.*) I could git killed working for you. Some sicko, some crazy drunk . . . (*Goes offstage, guard puts her in the cell sometime before* BENNIE'S *entrance.*)

CARL: You forget, we seen it all on TV in the dayroom, you bustin outta Lakewood like that. Fakin that palsy fit, then beatin that guard half to death with his own key ring. Whoo-ee! Then that spree you went on . . . stoppin at that fillin station for some cash, then kidnappin the old dude pumpin the gas.

ARLENE: Yeah.

CARL: Then that cab driver comes outta the bathroom an tries to mess with you and you shoots him with his own piece. (*Fires an imaginary pistol.*) That there's nice work, Mama. (*Going over to her, putting his arms around her.*)

ARLENE: That gun . . . it went off, Carl.

CARL: (*Getting more determined with his affection.*) That's what guns do, doll. They go off.

BENNIE'S VOICE: (*From outside.*) Arlene? Arlene?

CARL: Arlene? (*Jumping up.*) Well, la de da. (BENNIE *opens the door, car-*

rying the chicken dinners. He is confused seeing ARLENE *wearing a towel and talking to* CARL.)

ARLENE: Bennie, this here's Carl.

CARL: You're interruptin, Jack. Me an Arlie got business.

BENNIE: She's callin herself Arlene.

CARL: I call my ladies what I feel like, chicken man, an you call yourself "gone."

BENNIE: I don't take orders from you.

CARL: Well, you been takin orders from somebody, or did you git that outfit at the army surplus store?

ARLENE: Bennie brung me home from Pine Ridge.

CARL: (*Walking toward him.*) Oh, it's a guard now, is it? That chicken break out or what? (*Grabs the chicken.*)

BENNIE: I don't know what you're doin here, but . . .

CARL: What you gonna do about it, huh? Lock me up in the toilet? You an who else, Batman?

BENNIE: (*Taking the chicken back, walking calmly to the counter.*) Watch your mouth, punk. (*Condescending. Doesn't want a fight, for* ARLENE'S *sake, but doesn't want to appear threatened either.*)

CARL: (*Kicks a chair toward* BENNIE.) Punk!

ARLENE: (*Trying to stop this.*) I'm hungry.

BENNIE: You heard her, she's hungry.

CARL: (*Vicious.*) Shut up! (*Mocking.*) Ossifer.

BENNIE: Arlene, tell this guy if he knows what's good for him . . .

CARL: (*Walking to the counter where* BENNIE *has left the chicken.*) Why don't you write me a parkin ticket? (*Shoves the chicken on the floor.*) Don't fuck with me, Dad. It ain't healthy.

BENNIE: (*Pauses, a real standoff. Finally, bends down and picks up the chicken.*) You ain't worth dirtyin' my hands. (CARL *walks by him, laughing.*)

CARL: Hey, Arlie. I got some dude to see. (*For* BENNIE'S *benefit as he struts to the door.*) What I need with another beat up guard? All that blood, jus ugly up my threads. (*Very sarcastic.*) Bye y'all.

ARLENE: Bye, Carl.

CARL: (*Turns back quickly at the door, stopping* BENNIE *who was following him.*) You really oughta shine them shoes, man. (*Vindictive laugh, slams the door on* BENNIE's *face.*)

BENNIE: (*Relieved, trying to change the atmosphere*) Well, how bout if we eat? You'll catch your death dressed like that.

ARLENE: Turn around then. (ARLENE *gets a shabby housecoat from the closet. She puts it on over her towel, buttons it up, then pulls the towel out from under it. This has the look of a prison ritual.*)

BENNIE: (*As she is dressing.*) Your parole officer's gonna tell you to keep away from guys like that . . . for your own good, you know. Those types, just like the suckers on my tomatoes back home. Take everything right outta you. Gotta pull em off, Arlie, uh, Arlene.

ARLENE: Now, I'm decent now.

BENNIE: You hear what I said?

ARLENE: I told him that. That's exactly what I did tell him. (*Going to the bathroom for her hairbrush.*)

BENNIE: Who was that anyhow? (*Sits down on the bed, opens up the chicken.*)

ARLENE: (*From the bathroom.*) Long time ago, me an Carl took a trip to-gether.

BENNIE: When you was a kid, you mean?

ARLENE: I was at this place for kids.

BENNIE: And Carl was there?

ARLENE: No, he picked me up an we went to Alabama. There was this wreck an all. I ended up at Lakewood for forgery. It was him that done it. Got me pregnant too.

BENNIE: That was Joey's father?

ARLENE: Yeah, but he don't know that. (*Sits down.*)

BENNIE: Just as well. Guy like that, don't know what they'd do.

ARLENE: Mother was here while ago. Says she's seen Joey. (*Taking a napkin from* BENNIE.)

BENNIE: Wish I had a kid. Life ain't, well, complete, without no kids to play ball with an take fishin. Dorrie, though, she had them backaches an that neuralgia, day I married her to the day she died. Good woman though.

No drinkin, no card playin, real sweet voice . . . what was that song she used to sing? . . . Oh, yeah . . .

ARLENE: She says Joey's a real good-lookin kid.

BENNIE: Well, his Mom ain't bad.

ARLENE: At Lakewood, they tried to git me to have an abortion.

BENNIE: They was just thinkin of you, Arlene.

ARLENE: I told em I'd kill myself if they done that. I would have too. (*Matter-of-fact, no self-pity.*)

BENNIE: But they took him away after he was born.

ARLENE: Yeah. (BENNIE *waits, knowing she is about to say more.*) An I guess I went crazy after that. Thought if I could jus git out an find him . . .

BENNIE: I don't remember any of that on the TV.

ARLENE: No.

BENNIE: Just remember you smilin at the cameras, yellin how you tol that cab driver not to touch you.

ARLENE: I never seen his cab. (*Now forces herself to begin to eat.*)

ARLIE: (*In the cell, holding a pillow and singing.*) Rock-a-bye baby, on the tree top, when the wind blows, the cradle will . . . (*Not remembering.*) cradle will . . . (*Now talking.*) what you gonna be when you grow up, pretty boy baby? You gonna be a doctor? You gonna give people medicine an take out they . . . no, don't be no doctor . . . be . . . be a preacher . . . sayin Our Father who is in Heaven . . . Heaven, that's where people go when they dies, when doctors can't save em or somebody kills em fore they even git a chance to . . . no, don't be no preacher neither . . . be . . . go to school an learn good (*Tone begins to change.*) so you kin . . . make everbody else feel so stupid all the time. Best thing you to be is stay a baby cause nobody beats up on babies or puts them . . . (*Much more quiet.*) that ain't true, baby. People is mean to babies, so you stay right here with me so nobody kin git you an make you cry an they lay one finger on you (*Hostile.*) an I'll beat the screamin shit right out of em. They even blow on you an I'll kill em. (BENNIE *and* ARLENE *have finished their dinner. Bennie puts one carton of slaw in the refrigerator, then picks up all the paper, making a garbage bag out of one of the sacks.*)

BENNIE: Ain't got a can, I guess. Jus use this ol sack for now.

ARLENE: I ain't never emptyin another garbage can.

BENNIE: Yeah, I reckon you know how by now. (*Yawns*). You bout ready for bed?

ARLENE: (*Stands up.*) I spose.

BENNIE: (*Stretches.*) Little tired myself.

ARLENE: Thanks for the chicken. (*Dusting the crumbs off the bed.*)

BENNIE: You're right welcome. You look beat. How bout I rub your back. (*Grabs her shoulders.*)

ARLENE: (*Pulling away.*) No. (*Walking to the sink.*) You go on now.

BENNIE: Oh come on. (*Wiping his hands on his pants.*) I ain't all that tired.

ARLENE: I'm tired.

BENNIE: Well, see then, a back rub is just what the doctor ordered.

ARLENE: No. I don't . . . (*Pulling away.*)

BENNIE: (*Grabs her shoulders and turns her around, sits her down hard on the trunk, starts rubbing her back and neck.*) Muscles git real tight like, right in here.

ARLENE: You hurtin me.

BENNIE: Has to hurt a little or it won't do no good.

ARLENE: (*Jumps, he has hurt her.*) Oh, stop it! (*Slips away from him and out into the room. she is frightened.*)

BENNIE: (*Smiling, coming after her, toward the bed.*) Be lot nicer if you was layin down. Wouldn't hurt as much.

ARLENE: Now, I ain't gonna start yellin I'm jus tellin you to go.

BENNIE: (*Straightens up as though he's going to cooperate*) O.K. then. I'll jus git my hat. (*He reaches for the hat then turns quickly, grabs her and throws her down on the bed. He starts rubbing again.*) Now, you just relax. Don't you go bein scared of me.

ARLENE: You ain't gettin nuthin from me.

BENNIE: I don't want nuthin, honey. Jus trying to help you sleep.

ARLENE: (*Struggling.*) Don't you call me honey.

BENNIE: (*Stops rubbing, but keeps one hand on her back. Rubs her hair with his free hand.*) See? Don't that feel better?

ARLENE: Let me up.

BENNIE: Why, I ain't holdin you down. (*So innocent.*)

ARLENE: Then let me up.

BENNIE: (*Takes hands off.*) O.K. Git up.

ARLENE: (*Turns over slowly, begins to lift herself up on her elbows.* BEN-NIE *puts one hand on her leg.*) Move your hand.

BENNIE: (ARLENE *gets up, moves across the room.*) I'd be happy to stay here with you tonight. Make sure you'll be all right. You ain't spent a night by yourself for a long time.

ARLENE: I remember how.

BENNIE: Well how you gonna git up? You got a alarm?

ARLENE: It ain't all that hard.

BENNIE: (*Puts one hand in his pocket, leers a little.*) Oh yeah it is. (*Walks toward her again.*) Gimme a kiss. Then I'll go.

ARLENE: You stay away from me. (*Edging along the counter, seeing she's trapped.*)

BENNIE: (*Reaches for her, clamping her hands behind her, pressing up against her.*) Now what's it going to hurt you to give me a little ol kiss?

ARLENE: Git out! I said git out! (*Struggling.*)

BENNIE: You don't want me to go. You're just beginning to git interested. Your ol girlie temper's flarin up. I like that in a woman.

ARLENE: Yeah, you'd love it if I'd swat you one. (*Gettin away from him.*)

BENNIE: I been hit by you before. I kin take anything you got.

ARLENE: I could mess you up good.

BENNIE: Now, Arlie. You ain't had a man in a long time. And the ones you had been no count.

ARLENE: Git out! (*Slaps him. He returns the slap.*)

BENNIE: (*Moving in.*) Ain't natural goin without it too long. Young thing like you. Git all shriveled up.

ARLENE: (ARLIE *turning on, now.*) All right, you sunuvabitch, you asked for it! (*Goes into a violent rage, hitting and kicking him.*)

BENNIE: (*Overpowering her capably, prison guard style.*) Little outta practice, ain't you? (*Amused.*)

ARLENE: (*Screaming.*) I'll kill you, you creep!

BENNIE: (*Struggle continues,* BENNIE *pinning her arms under his legs as he kneels over her on the bed.* ARLENE *is terrified and in pain.*) You will? You'll kill ol Bennie . . . kill ol Bennie like you done that cab driver? (*A cruel reminder he employs to stun and mock her.* ARLENE *looks as though she has been bit.* BENNIE *is still fired up, he unzips his pants.*)

ARLENE: (*Passive, cold and bitter.*) This how you got your Dorrie, rapin?

BENNIE: (*Unbuttoning his shirt.*) That what you think this is, rape?

ARLENE: I oughta know.

BENNIE: Uh-huh.

ARLENE: First they unzip their pants. (BENNIE *pulls his shirt out.*) Sometimes they take off their shirt.

BENNIE: They do huh?

ARLENE: But mostly, they just pull it out and stick it in. (BENNIE *stops, one hand goes to his fly, finally hearing what she has been saying. He straightens up, obviously shocked. He puts his arms back in his shirt.*)

BENNIE: Don't you call me no rapist. (*Pause, then insistent.*) No, I ain't no rapist, Arlie. (*Gets up, begins to tuck his shirt back in and zip up his pants.*)

ARLENE: And I ain't Arlie.

BENNIE: (ARLENE *remains on the bed as he continues dressing.*) No, I guess you ain't.

ARLENE: (*Quietly and painfully.*) Arlie coulda killed you.

Over Loudspeaker—Before Act Two Curtain

These announcements will be heard during the last 5 minutes of the intermission.

Garden workers will, repeat, will, report for work this afternoon. Bring a hat and raincoat and wear boots. All raincoats will be checked at the front gate at the end of work period and returned to you after supper.

Your attention please. A checkerboard was not returned to the recreation area after dinner last night. Anyone with information regarding the black and red checkerboard missing from the recreation area will please contact Mrs. Duvall after lunch. No checkerboards or checkers will be distributed until this board is returned.

Betty Rickey and Mary Alice Wolf report to the laundry. Doris Creech and Arlie Holsclaw report immediately to the superintendent's office. The movie this evening with be "Dirty Harry" starring Clint Eastwood. Doris Creech and Arlie Holsclaw report to the superintendent's office immediately.

The bus from St. Mary's this Sunday will arrive at 1:00 P.M. as usual. Those residents expecting visitors on that bus will gather on the front steps promptly at 1:20 and proceed with the duty officer to the visiting area after it has been confirmed that you have a visitor on the bus.

Attention all residents. Attention all residents. (*Pause.*) Mrs. Helen Carson has taught needlework classes here at Pine Ridge for 30 years. She will be retiring at the end of this month and moving to Florida where her husband has bought a trailer park. The resident council and the Superintendent's staff has decided on a suitable retirement present. We want every resident to participate in this project—which is—a quilt, made from scraps of material collected from the residents and sewn together by residents and staff alike. The procedure will be as follows. A quilting room has been set up in an empty storage area just off the infirmary. Scraps of fabric will be collected as officers do evening count. Those residents who would enjoy cutting up old uniforms and bedding no longer in use should sign up for this detail with your dorm officer. If you would like to sign your name or send Mrs. Carson some special

message on your square of fabric, the officers will have tubes of embroidery paint for that purpose. The backing for the quilt has been
donated by the Women's Associates as well as the refreshments for the
retirement party to be held after lunch on the 30th. Thank you very
much for your attention and participation in this worthwhile tribute to
someone we are all very fond of here. You may resume work at this
time. Doris Creech and Arlie Holsclaw report to the superintendent's
office immediately.

ACT TWO

The next morning. ARLENE *is asleep on the bed.* ARLIE *is locked in a maximum security cell. We do not see the officer to whom she speaks.*

ARLIE: No, I don't have to shut up, neither. You already got me in seg-re-ga-tion, what else you gonna do? I got all day to sleep, while everybody else is out bustin ass in the laundry. *(Laughs.)* Hey! I know . . . you ain't gotta go do no dorm count, I'll just tell you an you jus sit. Huh? You preciate that? Ease them corns you been moanin about . . . yeah . . . O.K. Write this down. *(Pride, mixed with alternating contempt and amusement.)* Startin down by the john on the back side, we got Mary Alice. Sleeps with her pillow stuffed in her mouth. Says her Mom says it'd keep her from grindin down her teeth or somethin. She be suckin that pillow like she gettin paid for it. *(Laughs.)* Next, it's Betty the Frog. Got her legs all opened out like some fuckin . . . *(Makes croaking noises.)* Then it's Doris eatin pork rinds. Thinks somebody gonna grab em outta her mouth if she eats em during the day. Doris ain't dumb. She fat, but she ain't dumb. Hey! You notice how many girls is fat here? Then it be Rhonda, snorin, Marvene, wheezin and Suzanne, coughin. Then Clara an Ellie be still whisperin. Family shit, who's gettin outta line, which girls is gittin a new work 'signment, an who kin git extra desserts an for how much. Them's the two really run this place. My bed right next to Ellie, for sure it's got some of her shit hid in it by now. Crackers or some crap gonna leak out all over my sheets. Last time I found a fuckin grilled cheese in my pillow. Even had two of them little warty pickles. Christ! O.K. Linda and Lucille. They be real quiet, but they ain't sleepin. Prayin, that's them. Linda be sayin them Hell Mary's till you kin just about scream. An Lucille, she tol me once she didn't believe in no God, jus some stupid spirits whooshin aroun everwhere makin people do stuff. Weird. Now, I'm goin back down the other side, there's . . . *(Screams.)* I'd like to see you try it! I been listenin at you for the last three hours. Your husband's gettin laid off an your lettuce is gettin eat by rabbits. Crap City. *You* shut up! Whadda I care if I wake everybody up? I want the nurse . . . I'm gittin sick in here . . . an there's bugs in here! *(The light comes up in the apartment. Faint morning traffic sounds are heard.* ARLENE *does not wake up. The Warden walks across the catwalk. The* GUARD-EVANS *catches up with him near* ARLIE'S *cell.* BENNIE *is stationed at the far end of the walk.)*

LOUDSPEAKER: Dorm A may now eat lunch.

GUARD-EVANS: Warden, I thought 456 . . . *(Nodding in* ARLIE'S *direction.)* was leavin here.

WARDEN: Is there some problem?

GUARD-EVANS: Oh, we can take care of her all right. We're just tired of takin her shit, if you'll pardon the expression.

ARLIE: *(Interrupting.)* You ain't seen nuthin yet, you mother.

WARDEN: Washington will decide on her transfer. Til then, you do your job.

GUARD-EVANS: She don't belong here. Rest of. . . .

LOUDSPEAKER: *(Interrupts him.)* Betty Rickey and Mary Alice Wolf report to the laundry.

GUARD-EVANS: Most of these girls are mostly nice people, go along with things. She needs a cage.

ARLIE: *(Vicious.)* I need a knife.

WARDEN: Had it occurred to you that we could send the rest of them home and just keep her? *(Very curt. Walks away.)*

LOUDSPEAKER: Dorm A may now eat lunch. A Dorm to lunch.

GUARD-EVANS: *(Turning around, muttering to himself.)* Oh, that's a swell idea. Let everybody out except bitches like Holsclaw. *(She makes an obscene gesture at him, he turns back toward the catwalk.)* Smartass Warden, thinks he's runnin a hotel.

BENNIE: *(Having overheard this last interchange.)* Give you some trouble, did she?

GUARD-EVANS: I can wait.

BENNIE: For what?

GUARD-EVANS: For the day she tries gettin out an I'm here by myself. I'll show that screachin slut a thing or . . .

BENNIE: That ain't the way, Evans.

GUARD-EVANS: The hell it ain't. Beat the livin . . .

BENNIE: Outta a little thing like her? Gotta do her like all the rest. You got your shorts washed by givin Betty Rickey Milky Ways. You git your chairs fixed givin Frankie Hill extra time in the shower with Lucille Smith. An you git ol Arlie girl to behave herself with a stick of gum. Gotta have her brand, though.

GUARD-EVANS: You screwin that wildcat?

BENNIE: *(Starts walk to* ARLIE'S *cell.)* Watch. (ARLIE *is silent as he approaches, but is watching intently.)* Now, *(To nobody in particular.)* where was that piece of Juicy Fruit I had in this pocket. Gotta be here somewhere. *(Takes a piece of gum out of his pocket and drops it within* ARLIE'S *reach.)* Well, *(Feigning disappointment.)* I guess I already chewed it. (ARLIE *reaches for the gum and gets it.)* Oh, *(Looking down at her now.)* how's it goin, kid?

ARLIE: O.K. (ARLIE *says nothing, but unwraps the gum and chews it. Bennie leaves the cell area, motioning to the other guard as if to say, "See, that's how it's done." A loud siren goes by in the street below the apartment.* ARLENE *bolts up out of bed, then turns back to it quickly, making it up in a frenzied, ritual manner. As she tucks the spread up under the pillow, the siren stops and so does she. For the first time, now, she looks around the room, realizing where she is and the habit she has just played out. A jackhammer noise gets louder. She walks over to the window and looks out. There is a wolf-whistle from a worker below. She shuts the window in a fury, then grabs the bars. She starts to shake them, but then her hand goes limp. She looks around the room, as if trying to remember what she is doing there. She looks at her watch, now aware that it is late and that she has slept in her clothes.)*

ARLENE: People don't sleep in their clothes, Arlene. An people git up fore noon. (ARLENE *makes a still disoriented attempt to pull herself together, changing shoes, combing her hair, washing her face, etc., as guards and other prison life continue on the catwalk.)*

WARDEN: *(Walking up to* ARLIE, *remaining some distance from her, but talking directly to her, as he appears to check files or papers.)* Good afternoon, Arlie.

ARLIE: Fuck you. *(WARDEN walks away.)* Wait! I wanna talk to you.

WARDEN: I'm listening.

ARLIE: When am I gittin outta here?

WARDEN: That's up to you.

ARLIE: The hell it is.

WARDEN: When you can show that you can be with the other girls, you can get out.

ARLIE: How'm I supposed to prove that bein in here?

WARDEN: And then you can have mail again and visitors.

ARLIE: You're just fuckin with me. You ain't ever gonna let me out. I been in this ad-just-ment room four months, I think.

WARDEN: Arlie, you see the other girls on the dorm walking around, free to do whatever they want? If we felt the way you seem to think we do, every-one would be in lockup. When you get out of segregation, you can go to the records office and have your time explained to you.

ARLIE: It won't make no sense.

WARDEN: They'll go through it all very slowly . . . when you're eligible for parole, how many days of good time you have, how many industrial days you've earned, what constitutes meritorious good time . . . and how many days you're set back for your write-ups and all your time in segregation.

ARLIE: I don't even remember what I done to git this lockup.

WARDEN: Well, I do. And if you ever do it again, or anything like it again, you'll be right back in lockup where you will stay until you forget *how* to do it.

ARLIE: What was it?

WARDEN: You just remember what I said.

ARLENE: Now, then . . . *(Sounds as if she has something in mind to do. Looks as though she doesn't.)*

ARLIE: What was it?

WARDEN: Oh, and Arlie, the prison chaplain will be coming by to visit you today.

ARLIE: I don't want to see no chaplain!

WARDEN: Did I ask you if you wanted to see the chaplain? No, I did not. I said, the chaplain will be coming by to visit you today. Mrs. Roberts, why hasn't this light bulb been replaced? *(To an unseen guard. Walks away.)*

ARLIE: *(Screaming.)* Get out of my hall! (WARDEN *walks away.* ARLENE *walks to the refrigerator and opens it. She picks out a carton of slaw* BENNIE *put there last night. She walks away from the door, then turns around, remembering to close it. She looks at the slaw, as* GUARD *comes up to* ARLIE'S *cell with a plate.)*

ARLENE: I ain't never eatin no more scrambled eggs.

GUARD-CALDWELL: Chow time, cutie pie.

ARLIE: These eggs ain't scrambled, they's throwed up! And I want a fork! (ARLENE *realizes she has no fork, then fishes one out of the garbage sack from last night. She returns to the bed, takes a bite of slaw and gets her wallet out of her purse. She lays the bills out on the bed one at a time.)*

ARLENE: That's for coffee . . . and that's for milk and bread . . . an that's cookies . . . an cheese an crackers . . . an shampoo an soap . . . an bacon an livercheese. No, pickle loaf . . . an ketchup and some onions . . . an peanut butter an jelly . . . an shoe polish. Well, ain't no need gettin everything all at once. Coffee, milk, ketchup, cookies, cheese, onions, jelly. Coffee, milk . . . oh, shampoo . . .

RUBY: *(Off banging on the door, yelling.)* Candy, I gotta have my five dollars back.

ARLENE: *(Quickly stuffing her money back in her wallet.)* Candy ain't here!

RUBY: It's Ruby, upstairs. She's got five dollars I loaned her . . . Arlie? That Arlie? Candy told me her sister be . . . (ARLENE *opens the door hesitantly.)* It is Arlie, right?

ARLENE: It's Arlene. *(Does not extend her hand.)*

RUBY: See, I got these shoes in layaway . . . *(Puts her hand back in her pocket.)* she said you been . . . you just got . . . you seen my money?

ARLENE: No.

RUBY: I don't get em out today they go back on the shelf.

ARLENE: *(Doesn't understand.)* They sell your shoes?

RUBY: Yeah. Welcome back.

ARLENE: Thank you. *(Embarrassed, but relieved.)*

RUBY: She coulda put it in my mailbox. (RUBY *starts to leave,* ARLENE *is closing the door behind her, when* RUBY *turns around.)* Uh . . . listen . . . if you need a phone, I got one most of the time.

ARLENE: I do have to make this call.

RUBY: Ain't got a book though . . . well, I got one but it's holdin up my bed. *(Laughs.)*

ARLENE: I got the number.

RUBY: Well, then . . . *(Awkward.)*

ARLENE: Would you . . . wanna come in?

RUBY: You sure I'm not interruptin anything?

ARLENE: I'm sposed to call my parole officer.

RUBY: Good girl. Most of them can't talk but you call em anyway. *(ARLENE does not laugh.)* Candy go back to that creep?

ARLENE: I guess.

RUBY: I's afraid of that. *(Looking around.)* Maybe an envelope with my name on it? Really cleaned out the place, didn't she?

ARLENE: Yeah. Took everything. *(They laugh a little.)*

RUBY: Didn't have much. Didn't do nuthin here 'cept . . . sleep.

ARLENE: Least the rent's paid til the end of the month. I'll be workin by then.

RUBY: You ain't seen Candy in a while.

ARLENE: No. Think she was in the 7th grade when . . .

RUBY: She's growed up now, you know.

ARLENE: Yeah. I was thinkin she might come by.

RUBY: Honey, she won't be comin by. He keeps all his . . . *(Starting over.)* his place is pretty far from here. But . . . *(Stops, trying to decide what to say.)*

ARLENE: But what?

RUBY: But she had a lot of friends, you know. *They* might be comin by.

ARLENE: Men, you mean.

RUBY: Yeah. *(Quietly, waiting for Arlene's reaction.)*

ARLENE: *(Realizing the truth.)* Mother said he was her boyfriend.

RUBY: I shouldn't have said nuthin. I jus didn't want you to be surprised if some john showed up, his tongue hangin out an all. *(Sits down on the bed.)*

ARLENE: It's O.K. I shoulda known anyway. *(Now suddenly angry.)* No, it ain't O.K. Guys got their dirty fingernails all over her. Some pimp's out buyin green pants while she . . . Goddamn her.

RUBY: Hey now, that ain't your problem. *(Moves toward her, ARLENE backs away.)*

ARLIE: *(Pointing.)* You stick your hand in here again Doris an I'll bite it off.

RUBY: She'll figure it out soon enough.

ARLIE: *(Pointing to another person.)* An you, you ain't my Mama, so you can cut the Mama crap.

ARLENE: I wasn't gonna cuss no more.

RUBY: Nuthin in the parole rules says you can't git pissed. My first day outta Gilbertsville I done the damn craziest . . . (ARLENE *looks around, surprised to hear* RUBY *has done time.*) Oh yeah, a long time ago, but . . . hell, I heaved a whole gallon of milk right out the window my first day.

ARLENE: *(Somewhat cheered.)* It hit anybody?

RUBY: It bounced! Make me feel a helluva lot better. I said, "Ruby, if a gallon of milk can bounce back, so kin you."

ARLENE: That's really what you thought?

RUBY: Well, not exactly. I had to keep sayin it for bout a year fore I finally believed it. I's moppin this lady's floor once an she come in an heard me sayin "gallon-a'-milk, gallon-a'-milk," fired me. She did. Thought I was too crazy to mop her floors. *(Laughs, but is still bitter.* ARLENE *wasn't listening.* RUBY *wants to change the subject now.)* Hey! You have a good trip? Candy said you was in Arkansas.

ARLENE: Alabama. It was O.K. This guard, well he used to be a guard, he just quit. He ain't never seen Kentucky, so he drove me. *(Watching for* RUBY'S *response.)*

RUBY: Pine Ridge?

ARLENE: Yeah.

RUBY: It's co-ed now, ain't it?

ARLENE: Yeah. That's dumb, you know. They put you with men so's they can git you if you're seen with em.

RUBY: Sposed to be more natural, I guess.

ARLENE: I guess.

RUBY: Well, I say it sucks. Still a prison. No matter how many pictures they stick up on the walls or how many dirty movies they show, you still gotta be counted 5 times a day. *(Now beginning to worry about* ARLENE'S *silence.)* You don't seem like Candy said.

ARLENE: She tell you I was a killer?

RUBY: More like the meanest bitch that ever walked. I seen lots worse than you.

ARLENE: I been lots worse.

RUBY: Got to you, didn't it? *(ARLENE doesn't respond, but RUBY knows she's right.)* Well, you jus gotta git over it. Bein out, you gotta . . .

ARLENE: Don't you start in on me.

RUBY: *(Realizing her tone.)* Right, sorry.

ARLENE: It's O.K.

RUBY: Ex-cons is the worst. I'm sorry.

ARLENE: It's O.K.

RUBY: Done that about a year ago. New waitress we had. Gave my little goin straight speech, "No booze, no men, no buyin on credit," shit like that, she quit that very night. Stole my fuckin raincoat on her way out. Some speech, huh? *(Laughs, no longer resenting this theft.)*

ARLENE: You a waitress?

RUBY: I am the Queen of Grease. Make the finest french fries you ever did see.

ARLENE: You make a lot of money?

RUBY: I sure know how to. But I ain't about to go back inside for doin it. Cookin out's better'n eatin in, I say.

ARLENE: You think up all these things you say?

RUBY: Know what I hate? Makin salads—cuttin up all that stuff 'n floppin it in a bowl. Some day . . . some day . . . I'm gonna hear "tossed salad" an I'm gonna do jus that. Toss out a tomato, toss out a head a' lettuce, toss out a big ol carrot. *(Miming the throwing act and enjoying herself immensely.)*

ARLENE: *(Laughing.)* Be funny seein all that stuff flyin outta the kitchen.

RUBY: Hey Arlene! *(Gives her a friendly pat.)* You had your lunch yet?

ARLENE: *(Pulling away immediately.)* I ain't hungry.

RUBY: *(Carefully.)* I got raisin toast.

ARLENE: No. *(Goes over to the sink, twists knobs as if to stop a leak.)*

ARLIE: Whaddaya mean, what did she do to me? You got eyes or is they broke? You only seein what you feel like seein. I git ready to protect myself from a bunch of weirdos an then you look.

ARLENE: Sink's stopped up. *(Begins to work on it.)*

ARLIE: You ain't seein when they's leavin packs of cigarettes on my bed an then thinking I owe em or somethin.

RUBY: Stopped up, huh? *(Squashing a bug on the floor.)*

ARLIE: You ain't lookin when them kitchen workers lets up their mommies in line nights they know they only baked half enough brownies.

RUBY: Let me try.

ARLIE: You ain't seen all the letters comin in an goin out with visitors. I'll tell you somethin. One of them workmen buries dope for Betty Rickey in little plastic bottles under them sticker bushes at the water tower. You see that? No, you only seein me. Well, you don't see shit.

RUBY: *(A quiet attempt.)* Gotta git you some Drano if you're gonna stay here.

ARLIE: I'll tell you what she done. Doris brung me some rollers from the beauty school class. 3 fuckin pink rollers. Them plastic ones with the little holes. I didn't ask her. She jus done it.

RUBY: Let me give her a try.

ARLENE: I can fix my own sink.

ARLIE: I's stupid. I's thinkin maybe she were different from all them others. Then that night everbody disappears from the john and she's wantin to brush my hair. Sure, brush my hair. How'd I know she was gonna crack her head open on the sink? I jus barely even touched her.

RUBY: *(Walking to the bed now, digging through her purse.)* Want a Chiclet?

ARLIE: You ain't asked what she was gonna do to me. Huh? When you gonna ask that? You don't give a shit about that cause Doris such a good girl.

ARLENE: Don't work. *(Giving up.)*

RUBY: We got a dishwasher quittin this week if you're interested.

ARLENE: I need somethin that pays good.

RUBY: You type?

ARLENE: No.

RUBY: Do any clerk work?

ARLENE: No.

RUBY: Any key punch?

ARLENE: No.

RUBY: Well, then I hate to tell you, but all us old-timers already got all the good cookin and cleanin jobs. *(Smashes another bug, goes to the cabinet to look for the bug spray.)* She even took the can of Raid! Just as well, empty anyway. *(ARLENE doesn't respond.)* She hit the bugs with it. *(Still no response.)* Now, there's that phone call you was talkin about.

ARLENE: Yeah.

RUBY: *(Walking toward the door.)* An I'll git you that number for the dishwashin job, just in case. *(ARLENE backs off.)* How bout cards? You play any cards? Course you do. I get sick of beatin myself all the time at solitaire. Damn borin bein so good at it.
ARLENE: *(Goes for her purse.)* Maybe I'll jus walk to the corner an make my call from there.

RUBY: It's always broke.

ARLENE: What?

RUBY: The phone . . . at the corner. Only it ain't at the corner. It's inside the A & P.

ARLENE: Maybe it'll be fixed.

RUBY: Look, I ain't gonna force you to play cards with me. It's time for my programs anyway.

ARLENE: I gotta git some pickle loaf an . . . things.

RUBY: Suit yourself. I'll be there if you change your mind.

ARLENE: I have some things I gotta do here first.

RUBY: *(Trying to leave on a friendly basis.)* Look, I'll charge you a dime if it'll make you feel better.

ARLENE: *(Takes her seriously.)* O.K.

RUBY: *(Laughs, then realizes ARLENE is serious.)* Mine's the one with the little picture of Johnny Cash on the door. *(Walks to the door and leaves. BENNIE'S singing begins almost immediately, as ARLENE walks toward the closet. She is delaying going to the store, but is determined to go. She checks little things in the room, remembers to get a scarf, changes shoes, checks her wallet, finally, as she is walking out, she stops and looks at the picture of Jesus, then moves closer, having noticed a dirty spot. She goes back into the bathroom for a tissue, wets it in her mouth, then dabs at the offending spot. She puts the tissue in her purse then leaves the room when noted.)*

BENNIE: *(To the tune of "I'll Toe The Line," walks across the catwalk carrying a tray with cups and a pitcher of water.)* I keep my pants up with a piece of twine. I keep my eyes wide open all the time, Da da da da-da da da da da da *(Doesn't know this line.)* If you'll be mine, please pull the twine.

ARLIE: You can't sing for shit.

BENNIE: *(Starts down the stairs toward* ARLIE'S *cell.)* You know what elephants got between their toes?

ARLIE: I don't care.

BENNIE: Slow natives. *(Laughs.)*

ARLIE: That ain't funny.

GUARD-EVANS: *(As* BENNIE *opens* ARLIE'S *door.)* Hey, Davis.

BENNIE: Conversation is rehabilitatin, Evans. Want some water?

ARLIE: O.K.

BENNIE: How bout some Kool-Aid to go in it? *(Gives her a glass of water.)*

ARLIE: When does the chaplain come?

BENNIE: Want some gum?

ARLIE: Is it today?

BENNIE: Kool-Aid's gone up, you know. 15 cents and tax. You get out, you'll learn all about that.

ARLIE: Does the chaplain come today?

BENNIE: *(Going back up the catwalk.)* Income tax, sales tax, property tax, gas and electric, water, rent . . .

ARLIE: Hey!

BENNIE: Yeah, he's comin, so don't mess up.

ARLIE: I ain't.

BENNIE: What's he tell you anyway, get you so starry-eyed?

ARLIE: He jus talks to me.

BENNIE: I talk to you.

ARLIE: Where's Frankie Hill?

BENNIE: Gone.

ARLIE: Out?

BENNIE: Pretty soon.

ARLIE: When.

BENNIE: Miss her don't you? Ain't got nobody to bullshit with. Stories you gals tell . . . whoo-ee!

ARLIE: Get to cut that grass now, Frankie, honey.

BENNIE: Huh?

ARLIE: Stupidest thing she said. *(Gently.)* Said first thing she was gonna do when she got out . . . (ARLENE *leaves the apartment.)*

BENNIE: Get laid.

ARLIE: Shut up. First thing was gonna be going to the garage. Said it always smelled like car grease an turpur . . . somethin.

BENNIE: Turpentine.

ARLIE: Yeah, an gasoline, wet. An she'll bend down an squirt oil in the lawnmower, red can with a long pointy spout. Then cut the grass in the back yard, up an back, up an back. They got this grass catcher on it. Says she likes scoopin up that cut grass an spreadin it out under the trees. Says it makes her real hungry for some lunch. *(A quiet curiosity about all this.)*

BENNIE: I got a power mower, myself.

ARLIE: They done somethin to her. Took out her nerves or somethin. She . . .

BENNIE: She jus got better, that's all.

ARLIE: Hah. Know what else? They give her a fork to eat with last week. A fork. A fuckin fork. Now how long's it been since I had a fork to eat with?

BENNIE: *(Getting ready to leave the cell.)* Wish I could help you with that, honey.

ARLIE: *(Loud.)* Don't call me honey.

BENNIE: *(Locks the door behind him.)* That's my girl.

ARLIE: I ain't your girl.

BENNIE: *(On his way back up the stairs.)* Screechin wildcat.

ARLIE: What time is it? *(Very quiet.* ARLENE *walks back into the apartment. She is out of breath and has some trouble getting the door open. She is carrying a big sack of groceries. As she sets the bag on the counter, it breaks open, spilling cans and packages all over the floor. She just stands and looks at the mess. She takes off her scarf and sets down her purse, still looking at the spilled groceries. Finally, she bends down and picks up the package of pickle loaf. She starts to put it on the counter, then turns suddenly and throws it at the door. She stares at it as it falls.)*

ARLENE: Bounce? *(In disgust.)* Shit. (ARLENE *sinks to the floor. She tears open the package of pickle loaf and eats a piece of it, tearing off the bites in her mouth. She is still angry, but is completely unable to do anything about her anger.)*

ARLIE: Who's out there? Is anybody out there? *(Reading.)* Depart from evil and do good. *(Yelling.)* Now, you pay attention out there cause this is right out of the Lord's mouth. *(Reading.)* And dwell, that means live, dwell forever-more. *(Speaking.)* That's like for longer than I've been in here or longer than . . . this Bible the chaplain give me's got my name right in the front of it. Hey! Somebody's sposed to be out there watchin me. Wanna hear some more? *(Reading.)* For the Lord for . . . *(The word is forsaketh.)* I can't read in here, you turn on my light, you hear me? Or let me out and I'll go read it in the TV room. Please let me out. I won't scream or nuthin. I'll just go right to sleep, O.K.? Somebody! I'll go right to sleep. O.K.? You won't even know I'm there. Hey! Goddammit, somebody let me out of here, I can't stand it in here any more. Somebody! *(Her spirit finally broken.)*

ARLENE: *(She draws her knees up, wraps her arms around them and rests her head on her arms.)* Jus gotta git a job an make some money an everything will be all right. You hear me, Arlene? You git yourself up an go find a job. *(Continues to sit.)* An you kin start by cleanin up this mess you made cause food don't belong on the floor. *(Still sitting.* CARL *appears in the doorway of the apartment. When he sees* ARLENE *on the floor, he goes into a fit of vicious, sadistic laughter.)*

CARL: What's happenin, Mama? You havin lunch with the bugs?

ARLENE: *(Quietly).* Fuck off.

CARL: *(Threatening.)* What'd you say?

ARLENE: *(Reconsidering.)* Go away.

CARL: You watch your mouth or I'll close it up for you.

ARLENE: *(Stands up now.* CARL *goes to the window and looks out, as if checking for someone.)* They after you, ain't they? (CARL *sniffs, scratches at his arm.)*

CARL: *(Finding a plastic bag near the bed, stuffed with brightly colored knitted things. He pulls out baby sweaters, booties and caps.)* What the fuck is this?

ARLENE: You leave them be.

CARL: You got a baby hid here somewhere? I foun its little shoes. *(Laughs, dangling them in front of him.)*

ARLENE: Them's mine. *(Chasing him.)*

CARL: Aw sugar, I ain't botherin nuthin. Just lookin. *(Pulls more out of the sack, dropping one or two on the floor, kicking them away with his feet.)*

ARLENE: *(Picking up what he's dropped.)* I ain't tellin you again. Give me them.

CARL: *(Turns around quickly, walking away with a few of the sweaters.)* How much these go for?

ARLENE: I don't know yet.

CARL: I'll jus take care of em for you—a few coin for the trip. You *are* gonna have to pay your share, you know.

ARLENE: You give me them. I ain't goin with you. *(She walks toward him.)*

CARL: You ain't? *(Mocking,* ARLENE *walks up close to him now, taking the bag in her hands. He knocks her away and onto the bed.)* Straighten up, girlie. *(Now kneels over her.)* You done forgot how to behave yourself. *(Moves as if to threaten her, but kisses her on the forehead, then moves out into the room.)*

ARLENE: *(Sitting up.)* I worked hard on them things. They's nice, too, for babies and little kids.

CARL: I bet you fooled them officers good, doin this shit. *(Throws the bag in the sink.)*

ARLENE: I weren't . . .

CARL: *(Interrupting.)* I kin see that scene. They sayin . . . *(Puts on a high Southern voice.)* "I'd jus love one a' them nice yella sweaters."

ARLENE: They liked them.

CARL: Those turkeys, sure they did. Where else you gonna git your free sweaters an free washin an free step-right-up-git-your-convict-special-shoe-shine. No, don't give me no money, officer. I's jus doin this cause I likes you. *(Uncle Tom talk.)*

ARLENE: They give em for Christmas presents.

CARL: *(Checks the window again, then peers into the grocery sack.)* What you got sweet, Mama? *(Pulls out a box of cookies and begins to eat them.)*

ARLIE: I'm sweepin, Doris, cause it's like a pigpen in here. So you might like it, but I don't, so if you get some mops, I'll take one of them, too.

ARLENE: You caught another habit, didn't you?

CARL: You turned into a narc or what?

ARLENE: You scratchin an sniffin like crazy.

CARL: I see a man eatin cookies an that's what you see too.

ARLENE: An you was laughin at me sittin on the floor! You got cops lookin for you an you ain't scored yet this mornin. You better git yourself back to prison where you can git all you need.

CARL: Since when Carl couldn't find it if he really wanted it?

ARLENE: An I bought them cookies for me.

CARL: An I wouldn't come no closer if I's you.

ARLENE: *(Stops, then walks to the door.)* Then take the cookies an git out.

CARL: *(Imitating* BENNIE.*)* Oh, please, Miss Arlene, come go with Carl to the big city. We'll jus have us the best time.

ARLENE: I'm gonna stay here an git a job an save up money so's I kin git Joey. *(Opening the door.)* Now, I ain't sposed to see no ex-cons.

CARL: *(Big laugh.)* You don't know nobody else. Huh, Arlie? Who you know ain't a "con-vict"?

ARLENE: I'll meet em.

CARL: And what if they don't wanna meet you? You ain't exactly a nice girl, you know. An you gotta be jivin about that job shit. *(Throws the sack of cookies on the floor.)*

ARLENE: I kin work. *(Retrieving the cookies.)*

CARL: Doin what?

ARLENE: I don't know. Cookin, cleanin, somethin that pays good.

CARL: You got your choice, honey. You can do cookin an cleanin OR you can do somethin that pays good. You ain't gonna git rich working on your knees. You come with me an you'll have money. You stay here, you won't have shit.

ARLENE: Ruby works an she does O.K.

CARL: You got any Kool-Aid? *(Looking in the cabinets, moving* ARLENE *out of his way.)* Ruby who?

ARLENE: Upstairs. She cooks. Works nights an has all day to do jus what she wants.

CARL: And what, exactly, do she do? See flicks? Take rides in cabs to pick up see-through shoes?

ARLENE: She watches TV, plays cards, you know.

CARL: Yeah, I know. Sounds just like the dayroom in the fuckin joint.

ARLENE: She likes it.

CARL: *(Exasperated.)* All right. Say you stay here an *finally* find yourself some job. *(Grabs the picture of Jesus off the wall.)* This your boyfriend?

ARLENE: This chaplain give it to me.

CARL: Say it's dishwashin, O.K.? *(*ARLENE *doesn't answer.)* O.K.?

ARLENE: O.K. *(Takes the picture, hangs it back up.)*

CARL: An you git maybe 75 a week. 75 for standin over a sink full of greasy gray water, fishin out blobs of bread an lettuce. People puttin pieces of chewed up meat in their napkins and you gotta pick it out. 8 hours a day, 6 days a week, to make 75 lousy pictures of Big Daddy George. Now, how long it'll take you to make 75 workin for me?

ARLENE: A night. *(Sits on the bed,* CARL *pacing in front of her.)*

CARL: Less than a night. Two hours maybe. Now, it's the same fuckin 75 bills. You can either work all week for it or make it in 2 hours. You work two hours a night for me an how much you got in a week? *(*ARLENE *looks puzzled by the multiplication required.* CARL *sits down beside her, even more disgusted.)* Two 75's is 150. Three 150s is 450. You stay here you git 75 a week. You come with me an you git 450 a week. Now, 450, Arlie, is *more* than 75. You stay here you gotta work 8 hours a day and your hands git wrinkled and your feet swell up *(Suddenly distracted.)* There was this guy at Bricktown had webby toes like a duck. *(Back now.)* You come home with me you work 2 hours a night an you kin sleep all mornin an spend the day buyin eyelashes an tryin out perfume. Come home, have some guy openin the door for you sayin, "Good Evenin, Miss Holsclaw, nice night now ain't it? *(Puts his arm around her.)*

ARLENE: It's Joey I'm thinkin about.

CARL: If you was a kid, would you want your Mom to git so dragged out washin dishes she don't have no time for you an no money to spend on you? You come with me, you kin send him big orange bears an Sting-Ray bikes with his name wrote on the fenders. He'll like that. Holsclaw. *(Amused.)* Kinda sounds like coleslaw, don't it? Joey be tellin all his friends bout his Mom livin up in New York City an bein so rich an sendin him stuff all the time.

ARLENE: I want to be with him.

CARL: *(Now stretches out on the bed, his head in her lap.)* So, fly him up to see you. Take him on that boat they got goes roun the island. Take him up to the Empire State Building, let him play King Kong. *(Rubs her hair, unstudied tenderness.)* He be talkin bout that trip his whole life.

ARLENE: *(Smoothing his hair.)* I don't want to go back to prison, Carl.

CARL: *(Jumps up, moves toward the refrigerator.)* There any chocolate milk? *(Distracted again.)* You know they got this motel down in Mexico named after me? Carlsbad Cabins. *(Proudly.)* Who said anything about goin back to prison? *(Slams the refrigerator door, really hostile.)* What do you think I'm gonna be doin? Keepin you out, that's what!

ARLENE: *(Stands up.)* Like last time? Like you gettin drunk? Like you lookin for kid junkies to beat up?

CARL: God, ain't it hot in this dump. You gonna come or not? You wanna wash dishes, I could give a shit. *(Now yelling.)* But you comin with me, you say it right now, lady! *(Grabs her by the arm.)* Huh?

RUBY: *(Knocks on the door.)* Arlene?

CARL: She ain't here! *(Yelling.)*

RUBY: *(Alarmed.)* Arlene! You all right?

ARLENE: That's Ruby I was tellin you about.

CARL: *(Catches her arm again, very rough.)* We ain't through!

RUBY: *(Opening the door.)* Hey! *(Seeing the rough treatment.)* Goin to the store. *(Very firm.)* Thought maybe you forgot somethin.

CARL: *(Turns ARLENE loose.)* You this cook I been hearin about?

RUBY: I cook. So what?

CARL: Buys you nice shoes, don't it, cookin? Why don't you hock your watch an have somethin done to your hair? If you got a watch.

RUBY: Why don't you drop by the coffee shop. I'll spit in your eggs.

CARL: They let you bring home the half-eat chili dogs?

RUBY: You . . . you got half-eat chili dogs for brains. *(To* ARLENE.*)* I'll stop by later. *(Contemptuous look for* CARL.*)*

ARLENE: No. Stay. *(*CARL *gets the message.)*

CARL: *(Goes over to the sink to get a drink of water out of the faucet, then looks down at his watch.)* Piece a' shit. *(Thumps it with his finger.)* Shoulda took the dude's hat, jack. Guy preachin about the end of the world ain't gonna own a watch that works.

ARLENE: *(Walks over to the sink, bends over* CARL.*)* You don't need me. I'm gittin too old for it, anyway.

CARL: I don't discuss my business with strangers in the room. *(Heads for the door.)*

ARLENE: When you leavin?

CARL: Six. You wanna come, meet me at this bar. *(Gives her a brightly colored matchbook.)* I'm havin my wheels delivered. *(With faintly uncertain pride.)*

ARLENE: You stealin a car?

CARL: Take a cab. *(Gives her a dollar.)* You don't come . . . well, I already laid it out for you. I ain't never lied to you, have I girl?

ARLENE: No.

CARL: Then you be there. That's all the words I got. *(Makes an unconscious move toward her.)* I don't beg nobody. *(Backs off.)* Be there. *(Turns abruptly and leaves.* ARLENE *watches him go, folding up the money in the matchbook. The door remains open.)*

ARLIE: *(Reading, or trying to, from a small testament.)* For the Lord forsaketh not his Saints, but the seed of the wicked shall be cut off.

RUBY: *(Walks over to the counter, starts to pick up some of the groceries lying on the floor, then stops.)* I 'magine you'll want to be puttin these up yourself. *(*ARLENE *continues to stare out the door.)* He do this?

ARLENE: No.

RUBY: Can't trust these sacks. I seen bag boys punchin holes in em at the store.

ARLENE: Can't trust anybody. *(Finally turning around.)*

RUBY: Well, you don't want to trust him, that's for sure.

ARLENE: We spent a lot of time together, me an Carl.

RUBY: He live here?

ARLENE: No, he jus broke outta Bricktown near where I was. I got word there sayin he'd meet me. I didn't believe it then, but he don't lie, Carl don't.

RUBY: You thinkin of goin with him?

ARLENE: They'll catch him. I told him but he don't listen.

RUBY: Funny ain't it, the number a' men come without ears.

ARLENE: How much that dishwashin job pay?

RUBY: I don't know. Maybe 75.

ARLENE: That's what he said.

RUBY: He tell you you was gonna wear out your hands and knees grubbin for nuthin, git old an be broke an never have a nice dress to wear? (*Sitting down.*)

ARLENE: Yeah.

RUBY: He tell you nobody's gonna wanna be with you cause you done time?

ARLENE: Yeah.

RUBY: He tell you your kid gonna be ashamed of you an nobody's gonna believe you if you tell em you changed?

ARLENE: Yeah.

RUBY: Then he was right. (*Pauses.*) But when you make your two nickels, you can keep both of em.

ARLENE: (*Shattered by these words.*) Well, I can't do that.

RUBY: Can't do what?

ARLENE: Live like that. Be like bein dead.

RUBY: You kin always call in sick . . . stay home, send out for pizza an watch your Jonny Carson on TV . . . or git a bus way out Preston Street an go bowlin . . .

ARLENE: (*Anger building.*) What am I gonna do? I can't git no work that will pay good cause I can't do nuthin. It'll be years fore I have a nice rug for this place. I'll never even have some ol Ford to drive around, I'll never take Joey to no fair. I won't be invited home for pot roast and I'll have to wear this fuckin dress for the rest of my life. What kind of life is that?

RUBY: It's outside.

ARLENE: Outside? Honey I'll either be *inside* this apartment or *inside* some kitchen sweatin over the sink. Outside's where you get to do what you want, not where you gotta do some shit job jus so's you can eat worse than you did in prison. That ain't why I quit bein so hateful, so I could come back and rot in some slum.

RUBY: *(Word ''slum'' hits hard.)* Well, you can wash dishes to pay the rent on your ''slum,'' or you can spread your legs for any shit that's got the ten dollars. *(With obvious contempt.)*

ARLENE: *(Not hostile).* An I don't need you agitatin me.

RUBY: An I don't live in no slum.

ARLENE: *(Sensing* RUBY's *hurt.)* Well, I'm sorry . . . it's just . . . I thought . . . *(Increasingly upset.)*

RUBY: *(Finishing her sentence to her.)* . . . it was gonna be different. Well, it ain't. And the sooner you believe it, the better off you'll be. *(A guard enters* ARLIE's *cell.)*

ARLIE: Where's the chaplain? I got somethin to tell him.

ARLENE: They said I's . . .

GUARD-CALDWELL: He ain't comin.

ARLENE: . . . he tol me if . . . I thought once Arlie . . .

ARLIE: It's Tuesday. He comes to see me on Tuesday.

GUARD-CALDWELL: Chaplain's been transferred, dollie. Gone. Bye-bye. You know.

ARLENE: He said the meek, meek, them that's quiet and good . . . the meek . . . as soon as Arlie . . .

RUBY: What, Arlene? Who said what?

ARLIE: He's not comin back?

ARLENE: At Pine Ridge there was . . .

ARLIE: He woulda told me if he couldn't come back.

ARLENE: I was . . .

GUARD-CALDWELL: He left this for you.

ARLENE: I was . . .

GUARD-CALDWELL: Picture of Jesus, looks like.

ARLENE: . . . this chaplain . . .

RUBY: Arlene . . . *(Trying to call her back from this hysteria.)*

ARLIE: *(Hysterical.)* I need to talk to him.

ARLENE: This chaplain . . .

ARLIE: You tell him to come back and see me.

ARLENE: I was in lockup . . .

ARLIE: *(A final, anguished plea.)* I want the chaplain!

ARLENE: I don't know . . . years . . .

RUBY: And . . .

ARLENE: This chaplain said I had . . . said Arlie was my hateful self and she was hurtin me and God would find some way to take her away . . . and it was God's will so I could be the meek . . . the meek, them that's quiet and good an git whatever they want . . . I forgit that word . . . they git the Earth.

RUBY: Inherit.

ARLENE: Yeah. And that's why I done it.

RUBY: Done what?

ARLENE: What I done. Cause the chaplain he said . . . I'd sit up nights waitin for him to come talk to me.

RUBY: Arlene, what did you do? What are you talkin about?

ARLENE: They tol me . . . after I's out an it was all over . . . they said after the chaplain got transferred . . . I didn't know why he didn't come no more til after . . . they said it was three whole nights at first, me screamin to God to come git Arlie an kill her. They give me this medicine an thought I's better . . . then that night it happened, the officer was in the dorm doin count . . . an they didn't hear nuthin but they come back out where I was an I'm standin there tellin em to come see, real quiet I'm tellin em, but there's all this blood all over my shirt an I got this fork I'm holdin real tight in my hand . . . *(Clenches one hand now, the other hand fumbling with the buttons as if she's going to show RUBY.)* this fork, they said Doris stole it from the kitchen an give it to me so I'd kill myself an shut up botherin her . . . an there's all these holes all over me where I been stabbin myself an I'm sayin Arlie is dead for what she done to me, Arlie is dead an it's God's will . . . I didn't scream it, I was jus sayin it over and over . . . Arlie is dead, Arlie is dead . . . they couldn't git that fork outta my hand til . . . I woke up in the infirmary an they said I almost died. They said they's glad I didn't. *(Smiling.)* They said did I feel better now an they was real nice, bringing me chocolate puddin . . .

RUBY: I'm sorry, Arlene. *(Reaches out for her, but* ARLENE *pulls away sharply.)*

ARLENE: I'd be eatin or jus lookin at the ceiling an git a tear in my eye, but it'd jus dry up, you know, it didn't run out or nuthin. An then pretty soon, I's well, an officers was sayin they's seein such a change in me an givin me yarn to knit sweaters an how'd I like to have a new skirt to wear an sometimes lettin me chew gum. They said things ain't never been as clean as when I's doin the housekeepin at the dorm. *(So proud.)* An then I got in the honor cottage an nobody was foolin with me no more or nuthin. An I didn't git mad like before or nuthin. I jus done my work an knit . . . an I don't think about it what happened, cept . . . *(Now losing control.)* people here keep callin me Arlie an . . . *(Has trouble saying "*ARLIE.*")* I didn't mean to do it, what I done . . .

RUBY: Oh, honey . . . *(Trying to help.)*

ARLENE: I did . . . *(This is very difficult.)* I mean, Arlie was a pretty mean kid, but I did . . . *(Very quickly.)* I didn't know what I . . . *(Breaks down completely, screaming, crying, falling over into* RUBY'S *lap.)* Arlie! *(Grieving for this lost self.)*

RUBY: *(Rubs her back, her hair, waiting for the calms she knows will come. Finally, but very quietly.)* You can still . . . *(Now obviously referring to some personal loss of her own.)* . . . you can still love people that's gone. *(*RUBY *continues to hold her tenderly, rocking as with a baby. A terrible crash is heard on the steps outside the apartment.)*

BENNIE'S VOICE: Well, chicken pluckin, hog kickin shit!

RUBY: Don't you move now, it's just somebody out in the hall.

ARLENE: That's . . .

RUBY: It's O.K., Arlene. Everything's gonna be just fine. Nice and quiet now.

ARLENE: That's Bennie that guard I told you about.

RUBY: I'll get it. You stay still now. *(She walks to the door, and looks out into the hall, hands on hips.)* Why you dumpin them flowers on the stairs like that? Won't git no sun at all! *(Turns back to* ARLENE.*)* Arlene, there's a man plantin a garden out in the hall. You think we should call the police or get him a waterin' can?

BENNIE: *(Appearing in the doorway, carrying a box of dead looking plants.)* I didn't try to fall, you know.

RUBY: Well, when you git ready to try, I wanna watch! *(Blocking the door.)*

ARLENE: I thought you's gone.

RUBY: *(To BENNIE.)* You got a visitin pass?

BENNIE: *(Coming into the room.)* Arlie . . . *(Quickly.)* Arlene. I brung you some plants. You know, plants for your window. Like we talked about, so's you don't see them bars.

RUBY: *(Picking up one of the plants.)* They sure is scraggly lookin things. Next time, git plastic.

BENNIE: I'm sorry I dropped em, Arlene. We kin get em back together an they'll do real good. *(Setting them down on the trunk.)* These ones don't take the sun. I asked just to make sure. Arlene?

RUBY: You up for seein this petunia killer?

ARLENE: It's O.K. Bennie, this is Ruby, upstairs.

BENNIE: *(Bringing one flower over to show ARLENE, stuffing it back into its pot.)* See? It ain't dead.

RUBY: Poor little plant. It comes from a broken home.

BENNIE: *(Walks over to the window, getting the box and holding it up to the window.)* That's gonna look real pretty. Cheerful-like.

RUBY: Arlene ain't gettin the picture yet. *(Walking to the window and holding her plant up, too, posing.)* Now. (ARLENE *looks, but is not amused.)*

BENNIE: *(Putting the plants back down.)* I jus thought, after what I done last night . . . I jus wanted to do somethin nice.

ARLENE: *(Calmer now.)* They is nice. Thanks.

RUBY: Arlene says you're a guard.

BENNIE: I was. I quit. Retired.

ARLENE: Bennie's goin back to Alabama.

BENNIE: Well, I ain't leavin right away. There's this guy at the motel says the bass is hittin pretty good right now. Thought I might fish some first.

ARLENE: Then he's goin back.

BENNIE: *(To* RUBY *as he washes his hands.)* I'm real fond of this little girl. I ain't goin til I'm sure she's gonna do O.K. Thought I might help some.

RUBY: Arlene's had about all the help she can stand.

BENNIE: I got a car, Arlene. An money. An . . . *(Reaching into his pocket.)* I brung you some gum.

ARLENE: That's real nice, too. An I 'preciate what you done, bringin me here an all, but . . .

BENNIE: Well, look. Least you can take my number at the motel an give me a ring if you need somethin. *(Gives her a piece of paper.)* Here, I wrote it down for you. *(*ARLENE *takes the paper.)* Oh, an somethin else, these towel things . . . *(Reaching into his pocket, pulling out the packaged towelettes.)* they was in the chicken last night. I thought I might be needin em, but they give us new towels every day at that motel.

ARLENE: O.K. then. I got your number.

BENNIE: *(Backing up toward the door.)* Right. Right. Any ol thing, now. Jus any ol thing. You even run outta gum an you call.

RUBY: Careful goin down.

ARLENE: Bye Bennie.

BENNIE: Right. The number now. Don't lose it. You know, in case you need somethin.

ARLENE: No. *(*BENNIE *leaves,* ARLENE *gets up and picks up the matchbook* CARL *gave her and holds it with* BENNIE'S *piece of paper.)*

RUBY: *(Watches a moment, sees* ARLENE *trying to make this decision, knowing that what she says now is very important.)* We had this waitress put her phone number in matchbooks, give em to guys left her nice tips. Anyway, one night this little ol guy calls her and comes over and says he works at this museum an he don't have any money but he's got this hat belonged to Queen Victoria. An she felt sorry for him so she screwed him for this little ol lacy hat. Then she takes the hat back the next day to the museum thinkin she'll git a reward or somethin an you know what they done? *(Pause.)* Give her a free membership. Tellin her thanks so much an we're so grateful an wouldn't she like to see this mummy they got downstairs . . . an all the time jus stallin . . . waiting cause they called the police.

ARLENE: You do any time for that?

RUBY: *(Admitting the story was about her.)* County jail.

ARLENE: *(Quietly, looking at the matchbook.)* County jail. *(ARLENE tears up the matchbook and drops it in the sack of trash.)* You got any Old Maids?

RUBY: Huh?

ARLENE: You know.

RUBY: Cards? *(Surprised and pleased.)*

ARLENE: *(Laughs a little.)* It's the only one I know.

RUBY: Old Maid, huh? *(Not her favorite game.)*

ARLENE: I gotta put my food up first.

RUBY: Bout an hour?

ARLENE: I'll come up.

RUBY: Great. *(Stopping by the plants on her way to the door.)* These plants is real ugly. *(Fondly. Exits. ARLENE watches her, then turns back to the groceries still on the floor. Slowly, but with great determination, she picks up the items one at a time and puts them away in the cabinet above the counter. ARLIE appears on the catwalk, one light on each of them.)*

ARLIE: Hey! You member that time we was playin policeman an June locked me up in Mama's closet an then took off swimmin? An I stood around with them dresses itchin my ears an crashin into that door tryin to git outta there? It was dark in there. So, finally, *(Very proud.)* I went around an peed in all Mama's shoes. But then she come home an tried to git in the closet only June taken the key so she said, "Who's in there?" an I said, "It's me!" and she said, "What you doin in there?" an I started gigglin an she started pullin on the door an yellin, "Arlie, what you doin in there?" *(Big laugh.)*

ARLIE and ARLENE: *(ARLENE has begun to smile during the story, now they say together, both standing as MAMA did, one hand on her hip.)* Arlie, what you doin in there?

ARLENE: *(Still smiling and remembering, stage dark except for one light on her face.)* Aw shoot. *(Light dims on her fond smile as ARLIE laughs once more.)*

END

MY SISTER IN THIS HOUSE

Wendy Kesselman

My Sister in This House was first produced by Actors Theatre of Louisville, Kentucky. Original production in New York City by The Second Stage.

On a cold and bitter February afternoon, I was reading Janet Flanner's *Paris Was Yesterday* when I came across a short article called "The Murder in Le Mans." Reading the story of the sisters Christine and Lea Papin, maids who, one cold and bitter February afternoon in 1933, murdered the mistress and daughter of the house they worked in, I became completely obsessed. It was an obsession that led me all the way to the house in Le Mans, up the dark tunnel-like staircase where the crime was committed to the shabby broken-down maid's room, where the sisters waited in a single bed for the police to come. The same obsession took me through countless readings, rejections, and revisions until *My Sister in This House* won The Susan Smith Blackburn Prize and was produced at Actors Theatre of Louisville's New Play Festival and then at The Second Stage in New York. My other plays—all obsessions—include *I Love You, I Love You Not; The Juniper Tree: A Tragic Household Tale; Becca; Maggie Magalita; The Griffin and the Minor Canon* (book); and *Merry-Go-Round* and have been, with *My Sister in This House*, widely produced in this country and abroad. I have received Guggenheim, McKnight, and two National Endowment for the Arts Playwriting Fellowships, as well as the First Annual Playbill Award and four ASCAP Popular Awards in Musical Theatre. I have published nine children's books and a novel and am presently at work on an adaptation of Dickens's *A Tale of Two Cities*, which will be produced in the fall of 1991. Ubu Repertory Theater commissioned me to write a play set in the French Revolution, *Olympe and the Executioner*, for which I was delighted once again this year to be a finalist for The Susan Smith Blackburn Prize.

WENDY KESSELMAN
1990

Characters

CHRISTINE

LEA*, her sister

MADAME DANZARD

ISABELLE, her daughter

VOICE OF PHOTOGRAPHER

VOICE OF MEDICAL EXAMINER

VOICE OF JUDGE

The play takes place in Le Mans, France, during the early 1930s. It is based on an historical incident which occurred in Le Mans in 1933.

*Pronounced Léa

ACT ONE
Scene 1

CHRISTINE: *(Voice over.) (Sings.)*
Sleep my little sister, sleep
Sleep through darkness
Sleep so deep

Light comes up slowly on the faces of CHRISTINE *and* LEA *as if framed in a photograph.*

CHRISTINE: *(Continues.)*
All the rivers find the sea
My little sister
Sleep for me.

Dream my little sister, dream
Dream I'm here now
Dream your dreams
All the things you want to be
My little sister
Dream for me.*

*(*CHRISTINE *and* LEA, *stand side by side at the edge of the stage.* CHRISTINE *wears a faded dress with a white apron,* LEA, *a simple childlike dress.* CHRISTINE'S *hair is wound either in two buns, one on each side of her face, or in braids circling her head.* LEA'S *hair hangs in a long braid.*

CHRISTINE *is just twenty.* LEA, *still an adolescent.* LEA *gazes vaguely into the distance.* CHRISTINE *looks straight ahead. They move apart.* CHRISTINE *begins polishing a brass candlestick.* LEA *looks out.)*

LEA: Dear Christine. When Maman left me here on Friday, I thought I would die. They didn't want to take me at first, but Maman told Madame Crespelle I was fifteen. Christine, I wish you could see what they eat. You can't imagine the desserts. The cook told me Madame's favorite dish is duck with cherries and Monsieur's, chicken with champagne. I'm hungry all the time. But it isn't as bad as I expected. I even have my own room. Do you think you could ask Madame Roussel to change your day off to Wednesday, like mine? *(She pauses.)* Today Madame Crespelle smiled at me. She was pleased with how the silver looked. I had been polishing it all morning. It was worth every minute for Madame's smile. When she smiles she looks just like Sister Veronica. *(A bell rings.* LEA *moves closer to* CHRISTINE.*)* Three days ago Maman came and took me away. She said I could earn more money somewhere else. I was just getting used to the Crespelles, but I'm getting four more francs a month and Maman's promised to let me keep one of them. The Cottins have one daughter, Mademoiselle Sophie. Her birthday is next week. She's only two months older than me. She's so pretty. Her skin is like milk. And Christine, you should hear her play the piano. *(She pauses.)* Madame Cottin counts everything. Even the chocolates in the glass bowl. But I remember everything you taught me. And I think Madame will be pleased with me. *(She pauses.)* Every morning Madame Cottin examines my fingernails before I make the beds. Her things are so delicate. So many ruffles. So many buttons. You wouldn't believe how many buttons. It takes me two hours to iron one dress. And even then Madame isn't satisfied. *(She pauses.)* In this house I'm always afraid I'll do something wrong. Not like you, Christine. You never make mistakes *(She pauses. Longingly.)* Oh Christine, if only Maman would place us together. *(A bell rings, almost interrupting* LEA'S *last sentence.* LEA *goes down on her hands and knees and begins polishing the floor.* CHRISTINE *looks out.)*

CHRISTINE: *(Tender.)* Don't worry, Lea. You don't have to worry. It's only a matter of time. Just time before you get used to it. *(She pauses.)* Don't worry what they say to you. *(She pauses.)* I mean . . . don't take it to heart. I know that's hard in the beginning. But you'll learn. It's just time. *(She pauses.)* You'll see. Remember what Maman says—"When you've worked for them as long as I have—then you'll see." *(She pauses.)* Some are better than others, Lea. Believe me. You just never know. *(She pauses.)* Don't worry about writing every day. I know how tired you must be. But don't hide anything from me. And if—if they make you cry—I want you to let me know right away. *(A bell rings. Light comes up on the interior of the* DAN- ZARD *house in Le Mans, France. A combined dining room and sitting room is divided from the kitchen by a narrow staircase going up to a landing, and continuing to a maid's room. The house can also be created in a less realistic way. However, the staircase is an intrinsic element of the structure of the set.)*

CHRISTINE *and* LEA *pick up shabby suitcases. They smile at each other. They go upstairs to the maid's room. The room is shabby, small. There is a single bed, a night table, a sink and a mirror. There is a small skylight.* LEA *opens the door and rushes into the room.* CHRISTINE *follows her.*

LEA: *(Excited.)* I can't believe it. I just can't believe it. *(She puts her suitcase down on the floor.)* How did you do it? How did you get Maman to agree? Tell me.

CHRISTINE: Shhh. They'll hear you downstairs.

LEA: Tell me. You're always keeping something from me. (CHRISTINE *turns away.)* Tell me.

CHRISTINE: *(Turning back, smiling.)* I told her there'd be more money for her this way.

LEA: You're so clever, so smart.

CHRISTINE: I said that till you learned, you had to have someone to protect you.

LEA: And that was you. That was you. Am I right, Christine? *(She reaches to hug* CHRISTINE.*)*

CHRISTINE: *(Shivering.)* The room's cold. *(She lifts her suitcase onto the bed.)*

LEA: Remember what you used to call me? My feet still get cold at night. They get like ice. (CHRISTINE *opens her suitcase, starts putting her things away. She has few belongings.)*

CHRISTINE: *(Smiling.)* Come on. Put your suitcase up here with mine. I'll unpack it for you. *(She picks up* LEA'S *suitcase and puts it on the bed. She begins to unpack it for* LEA.*)*

LEA: Now they'll be warm. (CHRISTINE *takes a small crocheted blanket out of* LEA'S *suitcase.)*

CHRISTINE: What—you still have this old thing?

LEA: I had to take it. She was with me when I packed.

CHRISTINE: *(Turning away.)* Well, I don't care. It has nothing to do with me.

LEA: Don't you like it?

CHRISTINE: It's old and falling apart. I never liked Maman's sewing. It's vulgar. *(Silently, she continues unpacking their things.)*

LEA: *(Watching her.)* What's the matter? Aren't you glad that we're together?

CHRISTINE: Why didn't you take the other room? They offered it to you.

LEA: But I wanted to be with you.

CHRISTINE: The other room was nice. Nicer than this one.

LEA: Christine? (CHRISTINE *is silent.*) I don't understand. You worked the whole thing out and now you don't even want me with you.

CHRISTINE: Of course I want you with me.

LEA: What's wrong then?

CHRISTINE: Nothing's wrong. *(There is a pause.)*

LEA: I'll throw the blanket away if you want. I don't care about it. I just want you to be happy.

CHRISTINE: *(Finally turning around.)* But I am happy, little cold feet. *(She takes the blanket from* LEA.*)* We'll put the blanket right here. *(She lays the blanket at the foot of the bed.)* The main thing is that now we are together. *(Slowly the light on* CHRISTINE *and* LEA *dims. Light has begun to come up on* MADAME DANZARD *and* MADEMOISELLE ISABELLE DANZARD *downstairs in the sitting room.* MADAME DANZARD *is polishing* ISABELLE'S *nails.* MADAME DANZARD *is in her early fifties.* ISABELLE *in her early twenties, the same age as* CHRISTINE.*)*

MADAME DANZARD: This pink is lovely on you. So much better than the clear. Clear, clear, clear. It seems to be all everyone's wearing. This is such a bright color.

ISABELLE: You don't think it's too bright, do you, Maman? Do you think it's too bright?

MADAME DANZARD: Too bright? Nonsense. Bright colors are coming back. Hold still. This is delicate work, my dear. Highly delicate. This has to be perfect. *(She finishes the last nail of* ISABELLE'S *left hand.)* There! Now the other one. (ISABELLE *examines her hand.*) I'm waiting. (ISABELLE *holds out her other hand.*) So my dear, what do you think?

ISABELLE: About what, Maman?

MADAME DANZARD: What do you mean—about what, Maman? About them. About what else?

ISABELLE: Oh . . . they seem fine.

MADAME DANZARD: Fine? Is that all you can say? As a matter of fact, I think we may be in for a pleasant surprise.

ISABELLE: If you say so, Maman.

MADAME DANZARD: *(After a pause.)* Can't you at least express an opinion? You know how I value your opinion, Isabelle.

ISABELLE: Yes Maman. I know.

MADAME DANZARD: I wouldn't have taken the younger one. It's always a risk. But seeing that she's in the family. *(Putting the nail brush in the bottle and shaking it vigorously.)* Sisters! What could be better? And two almost for the price of one. We'll save on everything. They didn't even want two rooms. *(Carefully touching up one nail.)* Just this little corner. Apparently the older one sews extraordinarily well. She's your age, you know. "Such embroidery, such needlework," they said. I've never seen recommendations like that from Saint Mary of the Fields.

ISABELLE: Sewing. That's all they ever teach them.

MADAME DANZARD: Well, it's all to the good. If there're any alterations on your new dress she'll make them. We won't even have to go to the dress-maker's.

ISABELLE: What luck.

MADAME DANZARD: I remember our neighbor Monsieur Blanqui hiding one of those convent girls. I saw her once from my window. She must have been just my age. She looked a little like the older sister. She'd run away from the convent.

ISABELLE: Run away. Really?

MADAME DANZARD: Every now and then one got away. I never understood how she escaped. That wall! There was not one place you could see inside. I used to hear her at night begging them not to send her back. "Not there. Not to that place." In the end even Madame Blanqui didn't want to give her up. Can you imagine—in this town? And believe me they came looking for her.

ISABELLE: They did, Maman?

MADAME DANZARD: They used to comb each house for those girls. *(She lifts up ISABELLE's hands.)* Look, my dear. Aren't they beautiful? How do you like my handiwork? *(The light fades.)*

S c e n e   2

Early morning. CHRISTINE *and* LEA's *room is almost dark. They are asleep. The alarm clock rings.* CHRISTINE *turns it off. She reaches out to touch* LEA, *curled up beside her. Gently she touches her shoulder, strokes her hair.*

LEA: *(Turning toward* CHRISTINE.*)* Is it time?

CHRISTINE: Sleep, turtle. Go back in your shell.

LEA: But—

CHRISTINE: Sleep. There's time. I'll wake you. (LEA *turns over again. She is holding the small blanket their Mother has made.* CHRISTINE *covers* LEA'S *shoulder with the blanket. Shivering, she gets out of bed, stands on the cold floor. She puts on her shoes.)* Lea . . . it's almost six.

LEA: Mmmm. Another minute, Christine. Just one more.

CHRISTINE: Just one—all right. *(At the sink, she washes her face and hands. She shivers from the cold water, fixes her hair in the mirror. She removes her long white nightgown and puts on her maid's uniform. She goes over to the bed. Tickling* LEA'S *feet.)* Come on now. Come on. *(She pulls the blanket off* LEA.)

LEA: *(Sitting up.)* It's freezing here. Is it always like this?

CHRISTINE: *(Laying out* LEA'S *uniform on the bed.)* Always.

LEA: Everywhere you've been?

CHRISTINE: Everywhere.

LEA: *(Putting on her shoes.)* I polished the banister yesterday. Did you notice how it shines?

CHRISTINE: I noticed. *(To herself.)* I thought it would be easier with two of us.

LEA: You're disappointed, aren't you? You're unhappy with me here. Tell me.

CHRISTINE: Don't be silly.

LEA: I can't seem to do anything right. I can't seem to please you.

CHRISTINE: You please me, turtle. You please me more than anything.

LEA: You're so quick. You get things done in a minute.

CHRISTINE: You're fine the way you are.

LEA: *(Struggling with her nightgown.)* Maybe this was a mistake. I slow you down.

CHRISTINE: Stop it, Lea.

LEA: *(Still struggling.)* Sister Veronica always said I was too slow. She said I'd never be as quick as you.

CHRISTINE: What did she know?

LEA: You used to think she knew everything.

CHRISTINE: *(Helping* LEA *take off her nightgown.)* That was a long time ago. I've gotten over all that now.

LEA: You were famous at the convent. Your sewing! They still have that dress you made for the Virgin Mary. She's still wearing it.

CHRISTINE: And yet I remember, when I was at Saint Mary's, I could never go down the stairs like the others. One, two, one, two. I could never take a step with my left foot. It was always my right, my right, my right. I used to envy them running down the stairs when it took me forever.

LEA: Tell me a story, Christine. Just one—before we go down.

CHRISTINE: Which one?

LEA: When I was little.

CHRISTINE: You're still little.

LEA: No, I mean really little—you know—the story with the horse.

CHRISTINE: Again? Don't you ever get tired of it.

LEA: No—tell me.

CHRISTINE: *(Making the bed.)* When you were just a tiny thing, Maman sent me out one day to get bread. You came with me, the way you always did. And as we were walking, you let go of my hand and ran into the street to pick something up.

LEA: Tell it slower. You're telling it too fast.

CHRISTINE: It was a *long* narrow street—you remember—on a hill. At the top of the street a horse and carriage loaded with bottles was coming down and galloping right toward you. I ran into the street and pulled you across and pushed you down into the gutter with me. *(Falling down on the bed with* LEA.) What a noise when the horse galloped by! Everyone was screaming. Maman said the horse had gone mad. And when we stood up, we were both bleeding. But it was the same wound. It started on my arm and went down across your wrist. Look—*(She lines up her arm with* LEA'S.) We have it still.

LEA: And Maman—what did she say?

CHRISTINE: Oh Maman. Maman was terrified. You know how her face gets. She screamed at us.

LEA: And then—then what happened?

CHRISTINE: Then there was the gypsy—Mad Flower they used to call her.

LEA: And what did she say?

CHRISTINE: She said—oh you—you know it so well.

LEA: But tell me again, Christine. Tell me again.

CHRISTINE: They're bound for life, Mad Flower said. Bound in blood. *(A bell rings.)*

S c e n e   3

In this scene the dining room and kitchen are seen simultaneously. MADAME DANZARD *and* ISABELLE *are sitting at the dining room table, finishing the first course of lunch.* CHRISTINE *and* LEA *come into the kitchen. They are wearing their uniforms:* CHRISTINE, *the long severe cook's apron,* LEA, *the delicate serving apron.*

MADAME DANZARD: Don't toy with your food, Isabelle. It's so disagreeable. Always making those little piles.

ISABELLE: I'm not, Maman.

MADAME DANZARD: You mean to tell me I don't see what you're doing.

ISABELLE: I'm not toying, Maman.

MADAME DANZARD: *(Coldly.)* Very well, my dear, call it what you will. *(She rings a small round bell.* LEA *and* CHRISTINE *come into the dining room.* MADAME DANZARD *looks them over carefully.* LEA *is carrying a platter of veal on a tray. She presents the platter for* MADAME DANZARD'S *inspection, as* CHRISTINE *stands to the side.* MADAME DANZARD *smiles to herself.* LEA *puts the platter down and she and* CHRISTINE *go back into the kitchen.* MADAME DANZARD *and* ISABELLE *serve themselves and eat in silence for a few moments.)*

CHRISTINE: *(Following* LEA *into the kitchen.)* She liked it. Did you see? Did you see her face?

LEA: She likes everything you do.

CHRISTINE: She sees everything. *(She sits down at the kitchen table and begins to prepare string beans. Everything* CHRISTINE *does in the kitchen is neat, quick, impeccable. The bowls and plates seem to move like magic beneath her fingers.* LEA *is clearly a beginner. She sits down beside* CHRISTINE *and begins, clumsily, to help her with the beans.)*

MADAME DANZARD: *(Savouring the veal.)* This veal is delicious.

ISABELLE: Of course, you love veal. *(She looks at her mother.)*

MADAME DANZARD: Don't you?

ISABELLE: You know I don't. It's too heavy in the middle of the day.

MADAME DANZARD: Not the way she's prepared it. Light as a feather.

ISABELLE: I've heard it ruins the complexion.

MADAME DANZARD: Where did you hear that?

ISABELLE: I read it.

MADAME DANZARD: *(Scornfully.)* Really. Where?

ISABELLE: Somewhere. I don't remember.

MADAME DANZARD: Certain days of the month, my dear, you really are worse than others.

ISABELLE: That shouldn't surprise *you.*

MADAME DANZARD: Isabelle, if you continue in this vein you're going to ruin my meal. *(She eats with a certain relish.)* Wait till the Blanchards come to dinner. I'll have her make her rabbit paté. Won't that surprise them! The best cook we've had in years.

ISABELLE: Oh I don't know—Marie wasn't so bad.

MADAME DANZARD: Marie? Please. The way she cooked a pot au feu— ahhh—It still makes me shudder.

ISABELLE: You exaggerate, Maman.

MADAME DANZARD: Exaggerate? I'm being kind. Marie would have mur- dered a veal like this. *(Wiping her mouth with her napkin.)* Done to perfec- tion. I hope we never lose her. And she always buys the best.

ISABELLE: I don't know how she does it with the money you give her.

MADAME DANZARD: It's what I've always given them. You have no idea how lucky we are, Isabelle. The servants I've seen in my day. *(She watches* ISABELLE *stuff potatoes into her mouth.)* They eat like birds. *(Looking at* ISABELLE.) Always looking so neat, so perfect. You wouldn't think they were maids at all. Though I must admit the younger one gives me trouble— she's so young.

ISABELLE: I like the younger one.

MADAME DANZARD: Well she's quiet. I'll say that for her.

ISABELLE: *(Mercilessly chewing on the veal.)* Quiet? She never speaks. Neither of them do.

MADAME DANZARD: I suppose they must talk between themselves.

ISABELLE: I can't imagine about what.

MADAME DANZARD: *(Looking at* ISABELLE.) Well, maybe they pray. *(She laughs.)* That's how it is when you're brought up by the nuns. *(They both laugh. Abruptly stopping the laughter.)* Will you stop it, Isabelle. Look at that plate. *(She rings the small round bell.* LEA *comes into the dining room with a platter of cheese.* MADAME DANZARD *and* ISABELLE *are instantly silent.* LEA *clears away the empty platter of veal and goes back into the kitchen.)* They're so discreet. Not the slightest prying. You can't imagine what it's like to have a prying maid. To have someone going through your things.

ISABELLE: The younger one washes my things so perfectly. And you know, she's almost pretty.

MADAME DANZARD: *(Cleaning her teeth with her tongue.)* When your father and I were first married—she was something that one. But these two are different. Mark my words.

CHRISTINE: *(Rapidly snapping off the ends of the beans.)* How lucky we are, Lea. The other houses I've been—they come into the kitchen and interfere. Madame knows her place.

MADAME DANZARD: I never even have to tell them anything.

CHRISTINE: I know what she wants before she says a word.

MADAME DANZARD: They take such pride in the house. Not a speck of dust under the carpet.

CHRISTINE: Madame checks everything. I like that.

LEA: You do? It scares me—the way she checks.

MADAME DANZARD: Not a speck.

CHRISTINE: Oh no, I like it. It's better that way. Believe me. In the end it's better.

MADAME DANZARD: Not under the lamps. Not a ring.

ISABELLE: Really?

MADAME DANZARD: Not one. They're extraordinarily clean.

CHRISTINE: Madame is so precise, so careful. Her lists! Everything down to the last second.

LEA: She doesn't let us get away with a thing.

ISABELLE: Well Maman, let's face it—you don't let them get away with a thing.

MADAME DANZARD: Why should I? I pay them enough.

CHRISTINE: Why should she? She wants the house a certain way.

MADAME DANZARD: This is my house.

ISABELLE: It certainly is.

MADAME DANZARD: Well, it will be yours one day, Isabelle.

CHRISTINE: But she always sees the little things we do.

MADAME DANZARD: The younger one may be pretty, but it's the older one who fascinates me. I've never had anyone like her.

CHRISTINE: I've never had anyone like Madame before.

MADAME DANZARD: Totally trustworthy. I never have to count the change when she comes back from marketing. Not one sou is missing.

CHRISTINE: *(Holding out her bowl to* LEA.*)* Put them all in here, Lea.

ISABELLE: They don't seem to have any friends.

MADAME DANZARD: Thank heaven for that. (LEA *spills the beans on the floor. She gasps.)*

CHRISTINE: You're so clumsy. *(She begins picking up the beans. Upset,* LEA *helps her.)*

MADAME DANZARD: I've seen those people's friends, my dear. Believe me— it's bad enough with that mother of theirs.

ISABELLE: What a horror! It's a lucky thing they have each other.

CHRISTINE: I didn't mean it. You're so silly. What a baby you are.

MADAME DANZARD: And they do love us. They're so devoted to us. You'll see—the whole town will envy us. *(Laughing.)* We have pearls on our hands, Isabelle. Two pearls. *(They clink their wine glasses.* MADAME DANZARD *rings the small round bell.* ISABELLE *goes over to the sitting room area and takes an evening bag with tiny seed pearls out of a sewing basket.* LEA *and* CHRISTINE *come into the dining room and begin to clear away the dishes.* MADAME DANZARD *goes over to the sewing basket and takes out her needle-*

point.) Let me see, Isabelle. (ISABELLE *holds out the evening bag.)* I can't see it from here. (ISABELLE *leans closer and hands her the bag.* CHRISTINE *and* LEA *work silently together in the kitchen.)* Nice, Very nice. It's coming along. Bit by bit. *(She hands it back to* ISABELLE, *sits down on the couch and begins doing needlepoint.)* You can't rush these things, my dear. Believe me. A bag like that could take you . . . *(She looks at* ISABELLE *laboring with the seed pearls.)* two years. (ISABELLE *looks at her.)* Maybe more. But there's no hurry, is there? Nothing to hurry for. You have all the time in the world.

ISABELLE: Yes Maman.

MADAME DANZARD: All the time. When I was your age I made a bag just like that. Seed pearls too—but mine had a blue background. And when I held it up to the light, it . . .

ISABELLE: It what?

MADAME DANZARD: Shone . . . like little moons. Night after night I worked on that bag. But in the end it was worth it.

ISABELLE: Why, Maman?

MADAME DANZARD: I don't remember. An evening out. A dance.

ISABELLE: Oh what happened, Maman? Tell me.

MADAME DANZARD: I don't know. Maybe nothing. Maybe nothing *ever* happened. Listen to that rain. It's been raining like that for a week. A full week. Who knows when it will stop. Do you hear it, Isabelle?

ISABELLE: I hear it.

MADAME DANZARD: It could go on like this for a month. That's all we need. Are you listening to me, Isabelle?

ISABELLE: I'm listening, Maman.

MADAME DANZARD: Last year it went on for three months. Remember?

ISABELLE: That was the year before.

MADAME DANZARD: Was it? Was it really. Well, in Paris it's no better. After all, they're further north.

ISABELLE: Do you really think it rains more in Paris than here?

MADAME DANZARD: More, Isabelle. Much more. I'm sure of it. *(After a pause.)* Maybe we'll go up to Paris this year.

ISABELLE: Oh Maman, could we?

MADAME DANZARD: For a little shopping.

ISABELLE: Oh Maman. When?

MADAME DANZARD: Though I don't know. The things they wear in Paris. And you don't look well in those clothes, Isabelle. You know you don't. Even I don't look well in them. How could one? Hand me the scissors, would you. (ISABELLE *looks around.*) There. Right behind you. *(Impatient.)* On the table. (ISABELLE *stands up and drops everything.*) What's the matter with you? *(She rings the small round bell. Pulling* ISABELLE *up, as she bends to pick up the seed pearls.)* Really, Isabelle. (LEA *comes in from the kitchen.* MADAME DANZARD *points to the floor.* LEA *kneels and starts collecting the tiny seed pearls that have fallen.* MADAME DANZARD *eyes the floor, making sure every last seed pearl has been picked up.)* Besides, I don't like to leave the house.

ISABELLE: But why, Maman? What could happen to it?

MADAME DANZARD: A lot can happen to a house when you're not there. And then—going to Paris—such a trip.

ISABELLE: A trip!

MADAME DANZARD: And such an expense. Think of the money. Mmmm— Paris.

ISABELLE: Paris!

MADAME DANZARD: Yes, I think we'll just have to skip Paris this year. *(A bell rings.* MADAME DANZARD *and* ISABELLE *jump.* LEA *goes to the door.)*

ISABELLE: Who's that?

MADAME DANZARD: Shhh. Let *me* listen. Who could it be? In this weather. (ISABELLE *puts her evening bag back into the sewing basket. She and* MADAME DANZARD *hurriedly sit down on the couch and wait, smiling, rubbing their cheeks to redden them.* LEA *comes back with the mail. She puts one letter in her pocket quickly, enters the sitting room with another letter on a tray. She presents the tray to* MADAME DANZARD *with a letter opener.)* Oh! Mail. *(She takes the letter.* LEA *goes up the stairs.)*

ISABELLE: Anything for me, Maman?

MADAME DANZARD: Look at this. Would you look at this, Isabelle. No return address. And look at the handwriting. What do you think it could be? *(She waves the letter toward* ISABELLE.)

ISABELLE: *(Taking the letter.)* Well, it's not a marriage.

MADAME DANZARD: *(Snatching it back. Excitedly.)* Maybe a funeral. Whose I wonder?

ISABELLE: What is it, Maman? (LEA *comes into the upstairs room, sits down on the bed, opens the letter and eagerly begins reading it.)*

MADAME DANZARD: *(Eagerly opening the letter.)* Just a minute. Just a minute. *(Crushed.)* Another letter from the Little Shepherds of Le Mans. Will they never stop asking for money. Those children must be eating out of golden bowls. *(Reflecting suddenly.)* Hmm. I wonder how much the Blanchards are giving.

ISABELLE: *(Staring out at the rain.)* Do you really think it will rain straight through the winter?

MADAME DANZARD: You can never tell. But it looks it, doesn't it? *(Going to stand beside* ISABELLE.*)* It certainly looks it. Rain, rain, rain. Those clouds. I've never seen it so grey. Well, don't complain, Isabelle. At least we don't have to go out. *(She walks out of the room.* ISABELLE *follows her.* CHRISTINE *finishes putting everything away in the kitchen and goes upstairs into their room.* LEA, *hastily folding up the letter, looks at her guiltily.)*

CHRISTINE: *(Softly.)* What is it, Lea? Another letter from Maman? (LEA *looks away. Gently.)* Well, go on. Read it. There's no reason to stop just because I came into the room. *(She takes off her long apron and folds it neatly.)*

LEA: I'll read it later.

CHRISTINE: You won't have time later. You're exhausted by ten. Read it now. (LEA *looks at her. Smiling.)* Why don't you read it out loud?

LEA: *(Nervously.)* Do you really want me to?

CHRISTINE: I wouldn't say it otherwise, would I?

LEA: *(Unfolding the letter, begins to read.)* "Lea, my pet, my little dove. I know I'll see you Sunday as usual, but I miss you. Little Lea. You'll always be little."

CHRISTINE: Go on.

LEA: *(Continuing.)* "Don't forget to bring me the money. You forgot last week."

CHRISTINE: Poor Maman.

LEA: Christine—Maman just—

CHRISTINE: Maman just what? *(Changing. Gentle.)* Go ahead. Keep reading.

LEA: *(Going on with the letter.)* "You can't wear your hair that way anymore, Lea. Like a child. All that long hair." *(She stops.)*

CHRISTINE: Well? Don't leave anything out.

LEA: *(Going on.)* "Next Sunday, when you come, I'll fix it for you. It'll be better that way. Like Christine's. Won't fall in the soup." (LEA *looks up, laughing.* CHRISTINE *doesn't smile.)* *(Going back to the letter. Quickly.)* "Or get Christine to fix it for you. But—" *(She stops.)*

CHRISTINE: But what?

LEA: "Tell her to be gentle."

CHRISTINE: *(Snatching the letter from LEA.)* I'm never going back.

LEA: Christine.

CHRISTINE: *(Folding the letter up very small.)* You can go if you want to.

LEA: You know I wouldn't without you.

CHRISTINE: But you still care for her. She loves you.

LEA: But Christine, Christine. Maman loves you too. She's just . . .

CHRISTINE: What?

LEA: . . . scared of you.

CHRISTINE: Scared of me? *(Giving the tiny folded up letter back to LEA.)* You never stick up for me. But that's right. Defend her. Take her part. Like you always do. *(Moving away.)* Once she said that just to look at me made her sick. She couldn't even keep me after the first year. She hated when I cried.

LEA: Christine.

CHRISTINE: At Saint Mary of the Fields, I used to escape. Once a month. No one in this town would have brought me back—you know what they call it here. But your Maman—our Maman—she brought me back every time. In the end all I wanted was to be a nun. A nun! *(She smiles.)* That's all I wanted. But then of course she took me out. She hadn't expected that. That was against all her plans. I had to work. I had to make money. And she kept all of it. She placed me—and each time I got used to it, she took me out again. Sometimes I'd run away. I ran back to the Sisters. They wanted to keep me. It was Maman, our beloved precious Maman, who would come and drag me out again.

LEA: Don't be angry with me.

CHRISTINE: I'm not angry with you.

LEA: Your face. It looks so—

CHRISTINE: *(Cutting in.)* What? What's the matter with my face?

LEA: It just looked . . . Your face is beautiful. There's nothing wrong with your face.

CHRISTINE: No? *(She takes the hairbrush.)* I'll fix it for you. Just like she said. I'll fix it. *(Tenderly starting to brush* LEA's *hair. Longingly.)* If we didn't go back we could have all our Sundays together, just to ourselves. We could walk, we could go to the station and watch the trains come in. We could sit in the square, we could—But no—you wouldn't want that, would you? You want to go back. Don't you? *(Pleading.)* Don't you, Lea? *(*LEA *is silent.* CHRISTINE *changes, violently brushes* LEA's *hair.)* Of course you do. *(Roughly, she twists* LEA's *hair into two buns on either side of her face.)* There. Like this. That's what she meant. *(Pulling* LEA *over to the mirror above the sink. Raging.)* Look. How do you like it?

LEA: *(Tearing out her hair and sobbing.)* I hate it. *(She grabs the brush from* CHRISTINE *and tries to fix her own hair, putting it back the way it was. She does this clumsily, jerkily—too upset to get it right.* CHRISTINE *watches her in silence, suddenly overwhelmed at what she has done.)*

CHRISTINE: I am a monster—aren't I? Just like she says.

LEA: You're not a monster. *(She stops fixing her hair.)*

CHRISTINE: Here. Let me. *(Cautiously, she reaches for the brush.* LEA *hesitates, turns away.)* I'll do it for you. *(*LEA *still hesitates.)* Let me do it— please. *(*LEA *is silent.)* Please. *(Tentatively,* LEA *holds out the brush.* CHRISTINE *takes it from her gently. Softly, slowly, she starts brushing* LEA's *hair.)* What did you mean when you said my face was beautiful?

LEA: What I said.

CHRISTINE: What's beautiful about it? Tell me one thing.

LEA: *(Looking up at her.)* Your eyes.

S c e n e   4

The sound of a radio. In the sitting room MADAME DANZARD *is turning the dial of a radio. She stops at a station which is playing the overture of Offenbach's "La Vie Parisienne." She smiles. She stands beside the radio, listening, and starts humming along. She goes over to the dining room cabinet and takes out an old photograph album. She looks through the album, sighing to herself, gently tapping her foot. She puts the album down on the table in front of the couch and begins dancing to the music.* ISABELLE *comes down the stairs, slowly at first, then quicker, interrupting* MADAME DAN-ZARD'S *dance. Startled,* MADAME DANZARD *immediately switches to a station playing a Bach organ prelude.* She looks at* ISABELLE. ISABELLE *walks across the room and takes a chocolate out of a glass bowl, puts it into her mouth and looks at her mother.* MADAME DANZARD *snatches the bowl away and puts it in the dining room cabinet.* ISABELLE *sits down on the couch and starts looking through the photograph album.* MADAME DANZARD *takes a white glove from the cabinet and carefully puts it on. She rings the small round bell.* LEA *hurries in. She stands silently as* MADAME DANZARD, *wearing her white glove, slowly goes all around the room, testing the furniture and mouldings for dust.* LEA *smiles as* MADAME DANZARD *checks. On the radio, the Bach prelude continues.* MADAME DANZARD *walks up the staircase, smiling, checking the banister, kneeling down and touching the balustrades. Bending down in an awkward position on the staircase, she finds a spot of dust on the white glove, stands up, shows it to* LEA. MADAME DANZARD *removes the glove, puts it on the table on the landing and goes downstairs to the dining room.* LEA *rushes up the stairs to clean the place where the dust has been found.* CHRISTINE *comes into the dining room, carrying the pitcher of dried flowers.* MADAME DANZARD *checks the flowers, rearranges one or two.* CHRISTINE *takes the pewter pitcher upstairs to their table on the landing. She picks up the white glove, looks at* LEA *dusting the staircase. Their hands touch for an instant.* CHRISTINE *goes down the stairs and out the hallway carrying the white glove, as* LEA *continues up the stairs dusting between the railings of the banister.* MADAME DANZARD *goes over to the radio and turns it off.*

ISABELLE: Who's this, Maman?

MADAME DANZARD: *(Looking over* ISABELLE'S *shoulder.)* Ah. Your great aunt Dominique, whom you never knew. Lucky for you. *(Sitting down beside* ISABELLE *on the couch.)* She owned half the houses on the Rue Dutois. When your father and I were first married, she wouldn't take one franc off the rent. That's the mentality of the people on your father's side. *(Pointing.)* That dress! Always pretending to be poor as church mice. *(Turning the page.)* Ah. The Rue Dutois. A quiet street. Almost as quiet as this one.

ISABELLE: No street is as quiet as this one.

---

*Nun Komm der Heiden Heiland (BWV659) a 2 Clav. e Pedale J.S. Bach.

MADAME DANZARD: *(Turning the page.)* Oh. Look at you. Right here in the courtyard. Do you still have that little hat? Why don't you ever wear that little hat anymore, Isabelle?

ISABELLE: What hat? Oh. That hat. Of course not, Maman.

MADAME DANZARD: Too bad. You were delightful in that hat.

ISABELLE: Maman, do you know how old I was then?

MADAME DANZARD: *(Looking closely at the photograph.)* Oh yes. Yes. I suppose so, Isabelle. I suppose you were.

ISABELLE: Exactly. (MADAME DANZARD *turns the page.*)

MADAME DANZARD: Here you are again. Here we are. Oh look! *(Together they laugh over the photographs.* MADAME DANZARD, *still chuckling, continues to turn the pages of the photograph album. Suddenly* ISABELLE *smiles. She stifles a laugh.* MADAME DANZARD *looks up.* ISABELLE *begins laughing in earnest.* MADAME DANZARD *sees the photograph* ISABELLE *is looking at and stops laughing immediately. She slams the photograph album shut.* IS-ABELLE, *trying to stifle her laughter, leaves the room. After a few moments* MADAME DANZARD *goes up the stairs on tiptoe, silently opens the door to* CHRISTINE *and* LEA'S *room, one foot stepping in, and stares at the immaculate perfect order, as the light dims.*

Scene 5

LEA *and* CHRISTINE *come into their room, wearing their faded dresses and coats of the first scene.*

CHRISTINE: I don't want to force you.

LEA: You're not forcing me. We can never go back.

CHRISTINE: She didn't mean you when she told us to get out. She only meant me. *(She takes off her coat.)*

LEA: She meant both of us.

CHRISTINE: Not you, Lea. Not ever you. She'll never stop loving you.

LEA: She'll never forgive me for the money. Never, Christine. You know she won't.

CHRISTINE: But why shouldn't you keep your own money—instead of giving it to her. (LEA *sits on the bed, upset.)* She'll forgive you. You'll see. She'll forgive you. She always has. *(Looking at* LEA.) And Lea, Lea, you know what we'll do with that money? (LEA *is silent.*) We'll save it. We'll save all of it, from now on. We'll put it together—yours and mine—and save it. And someday, Lea, someday we'll—we'll—(LEA *looks at her.*)

LEA: Remember what you said—we could spend all our Sundays together.

CHRISTINE: I remember.

LEA: Promise?

CHRISTINE: Promise. (LEA *picks up the small blanket from their mother. She bites the wool with her teeth, loosening a strand. She pulls it, stops, pulls it again.*)

LEA: Here. Hold this. (*She hands* CHRISTINE *the blanket.*)

CHRISTINE: What are you doing? (LEA *keeps pulling.*) You've had that since you were four. (*As* LEA *pulls, the loosely crocheted blanket begins to unravel.*) Lea!

LEA: Just hold it. (*She pulls harder.*) Now pull from your end. (CHRISTINE *hesitates.*) Go ahead. Pull it!

CHRISTINE: But—

LEA: Go on. (CHRISTINE *cautiously begins to pull.*) That's it! That's right. Go ahead. Pull it. Pull it. Pull it harder. (CHRISTINE *looks at her.*) Harder. (CHRISTINE *really starts pulling in earnest.*) That's it. Harder. Oh harder. (*She pulls from her end.*) Harder. (*As the blanket unravels faster and faster, they run around the room. They are constricted by the confines of the narrow room. They wind the wool around the bed, the sink. They wind it around each other.* LEA, *laughing, falls on the bed.* CHRISTINE *falls beside her.*)

CHRISTINE: (*Laughing.*) No more, no more. (LEA *wraps* CHRISTINE *even closer to her with the wool.*) (*Breaking away suddenly.*) That's enough. I have to go downstairs.

LEA: It's not time yet. (*Playful.*) Don't you want to play anymore?

CHRISTINE: (*Putting on her apron. Abruptly.*) No.

S c e n e   6

MADAME DANZARD *comes down the hall, dressed to go out. She is holding two hats. In the maid's room,* CHRISTINE *is sitting on the bed, embroidering a white chemise with delicate lace and wide intricate shoulder straps.* LEA *sits beside her, hemming a long white nightgown.*

MADAME DANZARD: *(Calling.)* Isabelle! Isabelle. (ISABELLE *comes into the dining room.* MADAME DANZARD *holds out a particularly provincial hat.)* Charming, isn't it? (ISABELLE *is silent.)* Well, go ahead. There's no reason to be shy. *(She lunges toward* ISABELLE *with the hat.)*

ISABELLE: *(Drawing back.)* Oh. It's for me, Maman?

MADAME DANZARD: Of course it's for you. For whom else?

ISABELLE: And you want me to wear it now?

MADAME DANZARD: *(Very serious.)* I don't want you to wear anything else. You haven't forgotten how pretentious the Loupins looked last Sunday in their monstrosities.

ISABELLE: I remember.

MADAME DANZARD: Well, I can't wait to see their faces today. (ISABELLE *puts on the hat.)* Perfect. *(The bell rings.)*

ISABELLE: *(Anxious.)* It's them!

MADAME DANZARD: Early, as usual. Hoping to catch a glimpse of something. Well, they won't see anything today. They'll just have to wait. *(She stands still for a few moments, delightedly looking at her watch. She puts on another hat, if anything even more provincial than* ISABELLE'S. *Plunging in the stickpin of the hat.)* How do you like mine?

ISABELLE: *(After a pause.)* Adorable.

MADAME DANZARD: Well together—I must say—we make quite a pair. *(The bell rings again. They go out.)*

LEA: I'll never sew like you. Look at this hem. *(She holds up the nightgown and laughs.)* Even my hems are crooked. All those years with the Sisters and I never learned.

CHRISTINE: The Sisters didn't know how to teach you. Give it to me. I'll do it. (LEA *gives her the nightgown.)* Remember when I used to visit you at the convent? You waited for me at the gate. You were so little and so hungry all the time. *(She laughs.)* You're still hungry all the time.

LEA: Christine.

CHRISTINE: Hmm?

LEA: Can I . . .

CHRISTINE: *(Knowing what* LEA *wants.)* Can you what?

LEA: Can I look at them again?

CHRISTINE: Of course you can. They're yours. (LEA *jumps up and pulls an old trunk out from under the bed.* CHRISTINE *smiles.* LEA *pulls up the lid. The trunk is overflowing with beautiful white lingerie, under-garments trimmed with lace, nightgowns with fluttering ribbons, delicate ruffled chemises.*)

LEA: *(Gathering it all in her arms.)* All of it! All of it! No one sews like you. (CHRISTINE *stops sewing, watches* LEA.) Oh Christine. I can't believe how beautiful they are. *(She buries her face in the clothing.)*

CHRISTINE: *(Holding up the chemise she was sewing.)* Look, it's almost finished.

LEA: *(Raising her head.)* Already?

CHRISTINE: Yes. Come try it on.

LEA: Now?

CHRISTINE: Don't you want to?

LEA: I want to.

CHRISTINE: Well then. (LEA *comes forward.*) Go ahead. I'll close my eyes. *(She looks at* LEA.) I want to be surprised. *(She closes her eyes.* LEA *takes off her dress and slowly, carefully, puts on the chemise.)*

LEA: Christine . . . you can look now.

CHRISTINE: Can I?

LEA: Yes. (CHRISTINE *opens her eyes.*) It's beautiful.

CHRISTINE: It's you who are beautiful.

LEA: *(Tentatively reaching out her hand.)* I'm cold.

CHRISTINE: *(Going toward her.)* I know.

Scene 7

Light comes up on the empty sitting room. Offstage ISABELLE *is playing "Sur Le Pont D'Avignon" badly on the piano. She hums off key to the music, continuing to make mistakes as she goes along. Abruptly, the music stops.* ISABELLE *peeks her head out into the sitting room. She comes in and goes over to the dining room cabinet. She opens the cabinet and takes out the glass bowl of chocolates. She takes one, unwraps it, and gobbles it up. She takes another, unwraps it, pops it into her mouth.* LEA *comes in, carrying a dusting cloth. She sees* ISABELLE *with the chocolate in her mouth.* ISABELLE *looks away, awkwardly chewing the chocolate.* LEA *begins dusting the couch.* ISABELLE *takes a chocolate from the bowl and, hesitatingly, holds it out to* LEA. LEA doesn't move. ISABELLE continues to hold out the chocolate. LEA *hesitates, cautiously looks around. She looks back at the chocolate, still hesitating. Suddenly she snatches the chocolate and puts the glass bowl back in the cabinet and leaves.* LEA *goes up the staircase to the landing. She takes the chocolate out of her pocket, smiles to herself.* CHRISTINE *comes into the kitchen, holding a mortar and pestle. She starts pounding. Offstage,* ISABELLE *begins playing "Sur Le Pont D'Avignon" with one finger on the piano. She plays quickly, badly.* LEA *begins dusting the banister. Accidentally she hits the pewter pitcher. It rolls off the table and clatters down the stairs. The dried flowers scatter.*

LEA: *(Closing her eyes and screaming.)* CHRISTINE! *(In the kitchen* CHRISTINE *stops pounding instantly. She runs to the stairs.)*

CHRISTINE: What's wrong? What happened?

LEA: *(Frantic.)* The pitcher. The pewter pitcher. Madame will be so angry. Madame will—

CHRISTINE: Shhh. *(She goes down on her knees and apprehensively, picks up the pitcher.)* Look, Lea. Come here. It's not even broken. (LEA, *unbelievingly, opens her eyes, goes down the stairs to* CHRISTINE.) My angel, my dove. *(She pulls* LEA *down beside her.)* Don't be frightened. Look at me. Look. *(The bell rings. The piano stops.* LEA *looks into* CHRISTINE'S *eyes.* CHRISTINE *gathers the dried flowers and puts them back in the pewter pitcher.)* Don't worry. Nothing is broken. Believe me. (ISABELLE *appears and sees* LEA *and* CHRISTINE. LEA *rushes down the hall.* CHRISTINE *puts the pewter pitcher back on the table on the landing. She comes down the stairs, goes to open the front door.* ISABELLE *goes after her.* MADAME DANZARD *comes into the house.* ISABELLE *runs ahead.* CHRISTINE *goes out the hall.)*

ISABELLE: Anything for me, Maman? (MADAME DANZARD *takes off her hat. She smiles delightedly, raises her finger in anticipation. She puts her hat, gloves, coat, bag and package on the dining room table. Smiling with excitement she opens the package.* ISABELLE *leans forward expectantly. Happily,* MADAME DANZARD *holds up a photograph in a frame. It is a picture of herself and* ISABELLE *in their two hats.* ISABELLE *looks at the photograph and grimaces.* MADAME DANZARD *sets the photograph down on the radio table. She turns on the radio, as* ISABELLE *takes the clothing and wrapping paper off the dining room table. "C'est La Saison D'Amour"* blares out over the radio.* MADAME DANZARD *smiles, bursts into song. Blackout.)*

---

*"C'est La Saison D'Amour" Copyright © 1936 by Musikverlag und Bühnenvertrieb Zürich, A.G. Zurich. Reproduit avec l'autorisation de "ROYALTY" Editions Musicales, 25, Rue d'Hauteville, Paris. Musique de Oscar Straus d'après Johann Strauss père. Paroles de Albert Willemetz et Léopold Marchand.

Scene 8

LEA *and* CHRISTINE *stand side by side. They are dressed identically in dark wool dresses. Each dress has a wide yolk of intricate white lace. Their hair is arranged in exactly the same way. Their eyes are wide. They look frightened, shy. They have come to have their photograph taken.*

LEA: *(Whispering.)* Do you really think we should have come?

CHRISTINE: Why not? I wanted a photograph of you—of us together.

LEA: Suppose someone should find out?

CHRISTINE: Suppose they should? We're allowed to have a photograph taken, aren't we?

LEA: It's so expensive.

CHRISTINE: We can afford it.

LEA: I'm nervous.

CHRISTINE: *(Holding her hand for a moment.)* It's all right.

LEA: My hair—is it—

CHRISTINE: It's perfect.

LEA: But did you get it right on top?

CHRISTINE: You look like an angel. I'm going to fix it like that every Sunday.

LEA: I hate that iron.

CHRISTINE: Shhh. He's coming back.

LEA: Oh Christine, I'm frightened.

CHRISTINE: Of what? It's only a photograph. *(For a moment she clasps her hands tightly together. She straightens her dress.)* We should have done it long ago.

PHOTOGRAPHER: *(Voice over.)* I'm sorry that took so long. Now look this way. That's right. You're sisters, aren't you?

CHRISTINE: Yes.

PHOTOGRAPHER: *(Voice over.)* I knew right away. This should make a lovely photograph. Just step a little closer to each other. (CHRISTINE *and* LEA *move very close.)* Not quite so close. *(They move slightly apart.)* That's it. Perfect. Don't move. *(There is a burst of light as he takes the photograph.)* Did your mother always dress you like that? *(They are silent.)* Hmmm?

CHRISTINE: Like what?

PHOTOGRAPHER: *(Voice over.)* In the same clothes.

CHRISTINE: She never did.

PHOTOGRAPHER: *(Voice over.)* You look like twins. (LEA *smiles.*) No, not twins. But sisters. Sisters, certainly. Such a resemblance.

CHRISTINE: We're not twins. I'm six years older than my sister.

PHOTOGRAPHER: *(Voice over.)* Six years? Look up please. *(Again there is a burst of light.)* You look practically the same. But I guess a lot of people have told you that.

CHRISTINE: Some.

PHOTOGRAPHER: *(Voice over.)* Not very talkative, are you? What about your sister? Cat got her tongue?

CHRISTINE: *(Warningly.)* She's shy.

PHOTOGRAPHER: *(Voice over.)* Well, I've always wanted a sister—shy or not. (LEA *looks in the direction of the* PHOTOGRAPHER.) A sister sticks by you. Even when you're in trouble. Isn't that true? (LEA *smiles.)* Can she talk? Such a shy thing. I bet you're your mother's favorite.

LEA: *(Nervously.)* No . . . I . . .

PHOTOGRAPHER: *(Voice over.)* Still a child, isn't she? I can see that. What a sweet smile. Please now, both of you smile. And look at me. (LEA *smiles.* CHRISTINE *looks directly at the* PHOTOGRAPHER.) That's good. *(There is a burst of light, as he takes the final photograph.)* That will be fine. No one would ever know the two of you were servants. At the Danzards, aren't you?

CHRISTINE: *(Nervous.)* Yes.

PHOTOGRAPHER: *(Voice over.)* Excellent people, the Danzards. I've known them for years. Photographed the whole family. Photographed the daughter when she was just a child. *(He pauses.)* I hear she's going to be married soon. (CHRISTINE *and* LEA *are silent.)* Of course I've been hearing that for years. *(He waits. They don't speak.)* Well—seeing is believing I always say. Who knows if it's true. *(They remain silent. He chuckles quietly.)* You two certainly are discreet. They're lucky to have two such discreet young ladies. Especially in this town.

CHRISTINE: Hurry, Lea. I still have the shopping to do. *(She puts on her coat.)*

PHOTOGRAPHER: *(Voice over.)* You've been there a long time, haven't you? *(They are silent.)* How many years is it now?

CHRISTINE: A few.

PHOTOGRAPHER: *(Voice over.)* I'm sure they treat you well. *(They remain silent.)* Very fine people. Excellent people. But of course you know that.

CHRISTINE: Certainly, we know it. Come Lea, don't be so slow. (LEA *turns her back to the* PHOTOGRAPHER *and puts on her coat. It is exactly the same as* CHRISTINE'S).

PHOTOGRAPHER: *(Voice over.)* No need to be shy with me. *(He laughs.)* Madame Danzard makes you work hard enough, I imagine. For the money she pays you. (CHRISTINE, *eager to leave, starts taking out her money.)*

CHRISTINE: You said fifty francs, didn't you?

PHOTOGRAPHER: *(Voice over.)* For you girls, I'll make it twenty-five. You can pay me when you come for the photograph.

CHRISTINE: Fifty is what you said, fifty is what we pay.

PHOTOGRAPHER: *(Voice over.)* I see. Very well. Come back in two weeks.

LEA: *(Smiling.)* Thank you. *(They go out.)*

Scene 9

Before the scene opens, the slap of cards hitting a table is heard. Light comes up on MADAME DANZARD *and* ISABELLE *sitting at the dining room table. They are each armed with a pack of fifty-two cards. They sit facing each other. They are engaged in playing an elaborate game of réussite, a card game similar to double solitaire, the difference being that with réussite, each player secretly asks a question about the future before the game starts. Whether the question is answered affirmatively or not depends on the outcome of the game. When the scene opens,* MADAME DANZARD *and* ISABELLE *are laying out the last row of cards. As all but three cards are used from the very beginning, the cards almost completely cover the table.)*

MADAME DANZARD: *(As she finishes laying out her cards, deftly, neatly, straightening them as she goes along.)* What did you wish for this time? If you don't tell, you won't get it.

ISABELLE: *(Sloppier as she finished laying out her cards.)* That's not true. You don't have to tell what you wish for.

ISABELLE: *(Sloppier as she finished laying out her cards.)* That's not true. You don't have to tell what you wish for.

MADAME DANZARD: Well, I think I can guess. I'm not telling my wish either. Not even if I win.

ISABELLE: Ready Maman?

MADAME DANZARD: I'm ready. But you're not. Look at those cards.

ISABELLE: Which cards?

MADAME DANZARD: Those over there. They're going to fall off the table. (ISABELLE *straightens the last cards.)* Good. Now we're ready. *(She and* ISABELLE *tap their remaining cards on the table three times.)*

ISABELLE: One, two, three . . . begin. Maman—that is not fair.

MADAME DANZARD: What's not fair?

ISABELLE: You started at two.

MADAME DANZARD: I did not. I absolutely did not. However, if you insist, we'll start again.

ISABELLE: One . . . two . . . three . . . start.

MADAME DANZARD: *(Inspecting her cards.)* I don't have anything to start with.

ISABELLE: You always do that. Start first.

MADAME DANZARD: Never. That's your imagination.

ISABELLE: *(Shrieking.)* I saw you.

MADAME DANZARD: Quiet, Isabelle. *(Looking at her cards.)* This is absurd. I can't move a thing. *(She looks over at Isabelle's cards.* ISABELLE *sits pondering.)* Look at you. You have a million things. Don't you see? *(Disgusted.)* Aah.

ISABELLE: Where Maman?

MADAME DANZARD: There. Right there. Right before your eyes. Oh, Isabelle, sometimes you're so slow.

ISABELLE: You think so, Maman?

MADAME DANZARD: Well I'm stuck. Wait a minute. Why didn't I see that seven. Just a minute now. *(She transfers a large block of cards.)* That certainly should make things a little easier. *(Looking at Isabelle's cards.)* What's happening over there? That six is still sitting there.

MADAME DANZARD: *(Directing as* ISABELLE *moves her cards.)* And now the nine. Go ahead.

ISABELLE: What nine?

MADAME DANZARD: The nine of diamonds onto the ten of clubs. What's the matter with you?

ISABELLE: Maman please. I can't concentrate.

MADAME DANZARD: What are you talking about? Of course you can concentrate. This is a game of concentration. You have to concentrate. You have to concentrate on every little detail. Otherwise all will be lost. *(Looking over her own cards like a hawk. Excited.)* Red eight on black nine on red ten on—Perfect! That frees my queen and now I can take all these with the jack—*(She lifts a huge block of cards.)*—put them on the queen and . . . let's see what's under here. What's been hiding from me. *(She turns up a card. Disappointed.)* Three of spades. Now what am I going to do with that? *(Suddenly.)* You got an ace, Isabelle. How did that happen? Clubs. My two is buried under that nine. I'll never get it out.

ISABELLE: I've got it, Maman. Look. And the three.

MADAME DANZARD: How did you get them so fast? *(*ISABELLE *laughs gleefully.)* You're not cheating, are you?

ISABELLE: Maman.

MADAME DANZARD: *(Checking the cards.)* Where is the ace of diamonds? Where is that ace?

ISABELLE: Not the ace of diamonds, Maman. But I've got the ace of spades. And the two, and the—

MADAME DANZARD: Three!

ISABELLE: *(Overlapping and getting there first.)* Three!

MADAME DANZARD: Isabelle! How could you. Blocked again. Incredible.

ISABELLE: What are we having for dinner tonight, Maman?

MADAME DANZARD: Blanquette of veal.

ISABELLE: Veal again?

MADAME DANZARD: *(Looking at her watch.)* They'll be down soon. Ah— there's the four. *(Slapping down the four of spades.)* They never speak anymore. Have you noticed? Not a word. The older one walks by me as if I'm not there. *(*LEA *comes into the upstairs room, lays a delicate, handmade* *white coverlet on their bed, places the photograph of herself and* CHRISTINE *taken at the* PHOTOGRAPHER'S *on the night table, and goes out again.)*

ISABELLE: I have the five. And the six! The older one was always that way.

MADAME DANZARD: *(Slapping down her cards.)* Seven, eight!

ISABELLE: *(Tapping her mother on the hand.)* One hand, Maman!

MADAME DANZARD: Every Sunday—up in that room alone—it's amazing.

ISABELLE: They've always stuck to themselves.

MADAME DANZARD: They haven't seen their mother in years.

ISABELLE: *(Looking at her mother. Quietly.)* That's just as well.

MADAME DANZARD: You know I found the older one in the hallway trying to rub a stain off the door.

ISABELLE: I know that stain. It's been there for years. It'll never come off.

MADAME DANZARD: And she knows it. *(Smacking down three more cards as* ISABELLE *shrieks.)* And the nine, ten, jack! *(She takes a small tidbit from a dish on the table and pops it into her mouth. Making a face.)* What's wrong with her? She's put too much salt in these again.

ISABELLE: *(Laying down a card.)* The queen!

MADAME DANZARD: Have you turned up your three cards yet?

ISABELLE: Not yet. *(She sneaks a card into her lap.)*

MADAME DANZARD: Well, I absolutely refuse to turn— Isabelle! You cheated. I can't believe my eyes.

ISABELLE: I did not.

MADAME DANZARD: You did. You moved that jack of hearts onto the queen of diamonds.

ISABELLE: And—?

MADAME DANZARD: What do you mean—And? You know you can't move red onto red. Move it back.

ISABELLE: It was there before, Maman. I started the whole game that way.

MADAME DANZARD: Isabelle, please stop this lying at once. And just what was happening at the Blanchards the other night?

ISABELLE: Nothing was happening, Maman.

MADAME DANZARD: Nothing? Of course they're so blind—(ISABELLE *sneaks her ace of hearts onto the edge of the table.*) But with a marriage coming, you can't just smile at anyone.

ISABELLE: I wasn't smiling, Maman.

MADAME DANZARD: No? Wait! You put out the ace of hearts without even telling me. Where's my two? Here is it. My two, my three. *(She slaps them down.)* Where's that four?

ISABELLE: Here Maman. I have it. *(She pus it down.)*

MADAME DANZARD: You don't? You do. Well, I'm turning over my three cards. It's finally come to that. *(She turns up one of the three cards.)* Jack of hearts. What use is he? Looks just like Jacques Blanchard, doesn't he? Not a place for him here. *(Looking at her watch again.)* Where are they? Have they forgotten the Flintons are coming? What's wrong with them? Do you know that yesterday, coming back from the Loupins, I saw them sitting in the square. At eleven o'clock in the morning! Can you believe that?

ISABELLE: Unbelievable.

MADAME DANZARD: Eleven o'clock in the morning. I didn't say anything when they came back. But they knew. *(She turns over the second card.)* Four of diamonds. Too soon for that. Should I look at the third one? Yes or no?

ISABELLE: Go ahead Maman. Take a chance. (MADAME *turns over her last card. It is the ace of hearts. She smacks it down in the center.*)

MADAME DANZARD: *(Ecstatic.)* Hearts! Just what I was waiting for.

ISABELLE: *(Slapping down an ace of diamonds.)* Diamonds!

MADAME DANZARD: What?

ISABELLE: My ace, my two, my—

MADAME DANZARD: I can't do a thing till you move that queen.

ISABELLE: Queen? What queen?

MADAME DANZARD: Your queen, your queen. Use your eyes, Isabelle. *(She stands up and moves ISABELLE's queen into the center.)*

ISABELLE: *(Watching her mother.)* There. My queen.

MADAME DANZARD: And *my* king! That frees everything. Now we can really go ahead! *(The game builds to a frenzied finish with ISABELLE feverishly maneuvering her cards, and MADAME DANZARD laughing wildly and madly slapping down card after card with amazing speed. Reaching the end of the game, she triumphantly hugs the despairing* ISABELLE. LEA *comes down the stairs wearing a pale pink sweater. She places a lace cloth on the table in front of the couch.)*

ISABELLE: *(Whispering to her mother.)* Maman, do you see? *(LEA looks up, aware they are whispering about her.)*

MADAME DANZARD: Of course I see. What do you think I am—blind? What in heaven's name allows her to think she can wear a sweater like that in this house. *(LEA clumsily finished laying down the lace cloth and goes to the kitchen. In the kitchen, CHRISTINE is preparing dough for a tart. She stops when she sees LEA.)*

LEA: You told me I could wear it.

CHRISTINE: When I gave it to you, I never told you to wear it in this house, did I? I never told you to wear it downstairs. *(LEA is silent. CHRISTINE goes back to kneading the dough.)*

MADAME DANZARD: Just where did she think she was going? And how did she have the nerve, the extreme nerve to buy such a thing?

ISABELLE: Maman—

CHRISTINE: *(Wetting the dough too much, her hands getting messy.)* Why did you? Why would you want to wear that sweater anywhere but in our room? What were you thinking?

MADAME DANZARD: What is the world coming to? I couldn't believe my eyes.

ISABELLE: But Maman—

LEA: I wasn't thinking of anything but us. *(Carefully, she takes off the sweater.)*

CHRISTINE: *(Pulling her violently into a corner of the kitchen.)* You're lying.

MADAME DANZARD: There are no buts involved here.

CHRISTINE: Don't think I haven't noticed. I have eyes. I can see. When I come into the dining room, you're polishing the table looking off into nowhere. When you sew, you prick your fingers, when you wax the floor, you get the wax on your shoes. You drop plates, you spill water, you chip cups, you burn yourself with the iron—

LEA: I dropped that plate six weeks ago.

CHRISTINE: What about the cup?

LEA: The cup was chipped when we came here. I do things. I get things done.

CHRISTINE: *(Wiping her dough covered hands on her apron.)* But you look good. That I can see. Your apron neat as a pin. Immaculate. *(She circles* LEA.*)* The collar just right in front. The cuffs folded just so. You keep yourself perfect, don't you? And why?

LEA: I've always dressed this way. Look at me. We've always dressed this way.

CHRISTINE: You're different. Believe me. I know. *(*CHRISTINE *goes out the hall.* LEA *follows her.)*

ISABELLE: Maybe she didn't know, Maman.

MADAME DANZARD: *(Gathering up the cards.)* Of course she knew. She deliberately put it on and wore it. That sweater must have cost—

ISABELLE: *(Interrupting.)* Maybe—

MADAME DANZARD: I wonder if I pay them too much.

ISABELLE: Maybe she didn't buy it, Maman.

MADAME DANZARD: What?

ISABELLE: *(Rising and walking to the staircase.)* Maybe it wasn't her.

MADAME DANZARD: What are you talking about? Make yourself clear, Isabelle.

ISABELLE: Maybe it was her sister who gave her that sweater. Didn't you see? It was handmade.

MADAME DANZARD: *(Softly.)* Oh. Yes. Yes. Now I see. *(Softer yet.)* I believe you're right, Isabelle.

ISABELLE: I think so, Maman.

MADAME DANZARD: Handmade! Of course. And such expensive wool. I saw wool just like that in the Dupin's shop window. You don't think she bought it there, do you?

ISABELLE: Maybe, Maman. I wouldn't be surprised.

MADAME DANZARD: What an extravagance! Can you imagine if someone had seen . . .

ISABELLE: *(Standing up.)* Oh Maman, you go too far. *(She starts up the staircase.)*

MADAME DANZARD: *(Following her.)* Do I? Do I, my dear? You don't know this town like I do. Imagine if the Flintons had been here? Or Madame Blanchard. Or . . . I can't even think of it . . . Madame Castelneuve. You think I go too far. No my dear, you haven't lived here nearly long enough.

Scene 10

It is night. Silence. LEA *moans in the darkness.*

CHRISTINE: Lea.

LEA: I can't breathe.

CHRISTINE: Lea.

LEA: I can't breathe. I can't. *(Light comes up in their room.)* Someone behind me, pulling my coat. Even before I turn around I know. She grabs my hand and starts running. Her hand like iron around mine. I make myself heavy, but she holds me tight and I can feel all her little bones. She snatches me into the house and I run from corner to corner but she gets everywhere first. She grows and grows till she's as big as the room. And then I hear the door open but I can't move, Christine. I can't breathe.

CHRISTINE: *(Rocking LEA.)* Hush. Hush now. It's over. Try and sleep. Go to sleep.

LEA: I can't.

CHRISTINE: *(Sings.)*
Sleep my little sister, sleep
Sleep through darkness
Sleep so deep

LEA: You won't ever leave me, will you, Christine?

CHRISTINE: *(Sings.)*
All the rivers find the sea
My little sister
Sleep for me.

LEA: *(Touching CHRISTINE's face.)* You won't, will you?

CHRISTINE: *(Holding LEA close.)* Never.

LEA: I don't think I could bear it—being alone in this house. In any house. (MADAME DANZARD *appears at the top of the stairs. She is wearing a bathrobe and slippers and is carrying a kerosene lamp. She comes down the stairs on tiptoe and goes into the dining room.)*

CHRISTINE: *(Sings.)*
Dream my little sister, dream
Dream I'm here now
Dream your dreams

LEA: Do you hear me, Christine?

CHRISTINE: *(Sings.)*
All the things you want to be
My little sister
Dream for me.
(Softly, MADAME DANZARD *moves across the floor to the cabinet, opens it quietly, takes out a long black box, on top of which lies the white glove, opens it, and silently begins counting the silverware.)*

LEA: I was so scared when Madame was waiting when we came back from the square. Weren't you scared, Christine?

CHRISTINE: Madame doesn't speak to us anymore. She hasn't said a word in months.

LEA: She never did, Christine. Oh Christine, she never did.

CHRISTINE: Shhh. Sleep now. Sleep my angel. *(Continues the song.)*
Somewhere there are meadows
Somewhere there are hills
Somewhere horses run
And sheep are still

*(*MADAME DANZARD *closes the box, lays the white glove carefully on top, returns the box to the cabinet, picks up the kerosene lamp, and quietly goes up the staircase.)*

(Sings.)
Sleep my little sister, sleep
Cows will moo
And lambs will bleat
I will never leave your side
My little sister
Close your eyes.

(As the light dims, LEA'S *eyes remain wide open, staring into the darkness.)*

S c e n e   II

The sound of a 1930s song, "Chez Moi" is heard on the radio.* Light
comes up on an empty house. A door fans open and shut to the music.
ISABELLE *dances out into the sitting room, carrying a hairbrush and an ivory*
mirror. In a 1930s pose, she brushes her hair and gazes at herself in the
mirror. She puts the hairbrush and mirror down on the table, flings herself
onto the couch and plucks an imaginary cigarette out of the air. She dances
over to the staircase, tests the banister for imaginary dust. She goes quickly
to the cabinet and takes out a chocolate. She throws the wrapper on the
table and pops the chocolate into her mouth. CHRISTINE *comes down the*
hallway on her hands and knees, dusting the moulding of the staircase.
ISABELLE *puts on* MADAME DANZARD'S *hat, plunges in the hatpin, and dances*
over to the bottom of the stairs. CHRISTINE *sees* ISABELLE *and stands up.*
ISABELLE *stops dancing immediately. They stare at each other.* ISABELLE
turns off the radio. A soft drip of water begins. CHRISTINE *starts polishing*
the banister. ISABELLE *stands in the sitting room.* LEA *appears carrying a*
silver centerpiece. She puts it on the dining room table, not noticing CHRIS-
TINE *on the staircase.* ISABELLE *looks at* CHRISTINE. *She picks up the hair-*
brush and the mirror. She holds out the brush to LEA. LEA *hesitates. Finally*
she takes the brush from ISABELLE *and starts brushing her hair.* ISABELLE
smiles, luxuriating in LEA'S *brushing her hair.* CHRISTINE *watches them.*
MADAME DANZARD *appears at the top of the stairs. She sees* CHRISTINE
polishing the banister, the same spot over and over again. CHRISTINE *sees*
MADAME DANZARD, *stops, and goes into the kitchen. She begins to struggle*
with the cover of a canister. She cannot get it off. MADAME DANZARD *comes*
all the way down the stairs and stands watching LEA *brush* ISABELLE'S *hair.*
ISABELLE *sees* MADAME DANZARD *and takes the hairbrush from* LEA. *She*
goes out. LEA, *finally seeing* MADAME DANZARD *follows her.* ISABELLE *closes*
the door in LEA'S *face.* LEA *comes back, stands still, nervously watching*
MADAME DANZARD. MADAME DANZARD *takes the chocolate wrapper from*
the table and flicks it onto the floor. She looks at LEA. *Confused,* LEA *doesn't*
move. Pinching LEA'S *arm,* MADAME DANZARD *drags her over to where the*
chocolate wrapper has fallen. She pushes LEA *down on her knees.* LEA *picks*
up the wrapper. There is a loud banging sound. In the kitchen, CHRISTINE
is struggling desperately with the canister. She bangs it several times on the
table. MADAME DANZARD, *hearing the noise, goes into the kitchen. Seeing*
her, CHRISTINE *places the canister carefully on the table. The sound of the*
drip grows louder. MADAME DANZARD *checks a pot, opens the door of a*
cabinet and closes it. Holding the chocolate wrapper, LEA *goes out the hall.*

*"Chez Moi" (Venez Donc Chez Moi) Copyright © 1935. Fox-trot avec refrain chanté
(P. Misraki—J. Feline)

MADAME DANZARD *turns off the dripping faucet.* CHRISTINE *watches her.* MADAME DANZARD *looks at* CHRISTINE, *leaves the kitchen and goes down the hall, the light dims.*

S c e n e   12

ISABELLE *stands on a stool in the middle of the sitting room. She is trying on a drab, mauve dress, much too large on her.* CHRISTINE *is on her knees, pinning up the hem of the dress. Around her neck hangs a large pair of tailor scissors.* LEA *holds the pins and hands them to* CHRISTINE. MADAME DANZARD *stands looking up at* ISABELLE. *Throughout the scene,* CHRISTINE *makes adjustments on the dress—hem, sleeves, waist, bodice. Never, during any point in the scene, is a word addressed to* CHRISTINE *or* LEA.

MADAME DANZARD: What did I tell you? It's perfect.

ISABELLE: Yes Maman. *(After a pause.)* Do you really think so?

MADAME DANZARD: Of course I think so. You're always so difficult when it comes to clothes.

ISABELLE: I'm not difficult. *(Looking down at the dress.)* I just didn't like it.

MADAME DANZARD: Well you see—you were wrong. You really should trust me, Isabelle. Have I ever chosen anything you didn't like? *(ISABELLE is silent.)* Eventually?

ISABELLE: It looks better at home. *(CHRISTINE starts taking in the right sleeve of Isabelle's dress.)*

MADAME DANZARD: Of course it does. Everything always looks better at home. I want you to wear it Friday when we go to the Flintons'.

ISABELLE: But it won't be ready in—

MADAME DANZARD: *(Interrupting.)* It will be ready. She hardly has anything to do.

ISABELLE: Must we go, Maman? The Flintons are so—

MADAME DANZARD: We're going. And put your arm down, Isabelle. Remember how long she took the last time. *(She touches the bodice of the dress.)* You know my dear, I think it's too tight around the chest. *(CHRISTINE moves to Isabelle's right side and undoes the pins around her chest.)* Yes, I really think so. You don't want to wear these things too tight. Though they are wearing them tight these days. I saw Mademoiselle Loupin on the Rue Mafort just yesterday. I couldn't believe my eyes.

ISABELLE: Oh you can't count her. Everything looks tight around her chest. (CHRISTINE *moves behind* ISABELLE.)

MADAME DANZARD: *(Barely restraining a laugh.)* Isabelle! How unlike you. I never even thought you'd noticed Mademoiselle Loupin.

ISABELLE: Of course I've noticed her. Who hasn't? (CHRISTINE *moves to* ISABELL'S *left side.)*

MADAME DANZARD: She's getting married in September Monsieur Bouttier told me at the pharmacy. The date is definitely set.

ISABELLE: *(Smiling.)* So they say.

MADAME DANZARD: Why—do you have any reason to doubt it?

ISABELLE: None.

MADAME DANZARD: You sounded so . . . Anyway I know one marriage that's going to take place. *(She smiles to herself.* CHRISTINE *trembles suddenly, holds the pins out to* LEA *who is not paying attention to her. The pins fall to the floor in front of the footstool.* CHRISTINE *and* LEA *bend down to pick up the pins.* CHRISTINE'S *hands are shaking.* MADAME DANZARD *watches.)* Those first few months of being married, my dear. *(Looking at* CHRISTINE *and* LEA.*)* Some people will never know.

ISABELLE: *(Smiling.)* Maman. (LEA *looks up at* ISABELLE. CHRISTINE *stands up, and looks down at* LEA. LEA *moves to* CHRISTINE. ISABELLE *watches her.* MADAME DANZARD *and* CHRISTINE *look at each other.)*

MADAME DANZARD: *(Moving closer.)* Now how am I going to take you to the Flintons' with a crooked hem. Hmmm? Just tell me that. (ISABELLE *tries to look down at the hem. Glaring at* CHRISTINE.) Don't move, Isabelle. Don't budge. *(Hastily,* CHRISTINE *starts redoing the hem. Watching her.)* Incredible how long it takes to do a simple hem. (CHRISTINE *continues to fix the hem.* MADAME DANZARD *suddenly moves in and rips the bottom of the dress out of Christine's hands. She points to the neck of the dress.)* The neck should be lower. Definitely lower. (CHRISTINE *takes the tailor scissors and slowly begins cutting away the fabric around the neck. Stepping forward.)* Impossible. *(She takes the scissors from* CHRISTINE, *with them gestures her away, and begins cutting the fabric around the neck herself.* CHRISTINE *starts up the stairs. Loudly, as she cuts.)* Really. And with crepe going for seven francs a yard. Next time we'll go to the dressmaker's. *(On the stairs,* CHRISTINE *stops. She continues up.* LEA *follows her.) (Taking a few steps back from* ISABELLE.) Your grandmother's pearls will look just right. You shall have them as a present.

ISABELLE: Maman! *(In their room,* CHRISTINE *sits down on the bed, facing out.* LEA *stands behind her.)*

MADAME DANZARD: I can already see you. And those pearls. A perfect match. *(The light dims slowly on* MADAME DANZARD *and* ISABELLE.)

CHRISTINE: There was nothing wrong with that hem. Nothing. You saw it. That hem was perfectly straight. *(LEA is silent.)* Wasn't it?

LEA: Of course it was.

CHRISTINE: She sees things. Things that aren't even there. Her and her daughter. *(She pauses.)* You won't go, will you?

LEA: Go where? Where would I go?

CHRISTINE: Even if she goes, you won't go. *(LEA is silent.)* Lea! You're thinking about it all the time, aren't you? That's why you're always dreaming. Why you're always off in that other world.

LEA: There is no other world, Christine. *(Coming closer.)* Christine—darling. Don't be upset.

CHRISTINE: You heard Madame. You heard what she said.

LEA: What did she say?

CHRISTINE: You heard her. Don't pretend you didn't.

LEA: I didn't hear anything.

CHRISTINE: Nothing about her daughter.

LEA: Mademoiselle Isabelle, you mean?

CHRISTINE: *(Turning on her.)* Who else?

LEA: *(Drawing back.)* Don't be like that, Christine. You sound just like Maman.

CHRISTINE: You smiled at her. I saw you.

LEA: I didn't smile—

CHRISTINE: *(Interrupting.)* She makes you do everything for her. You're always with her.

LEA: I—

CHRISTINE: *(Cutting in.)* Promise me you won't go. When she goes.

LEA: If she goes. She may never go. We've been over this a hundred times, Christine. She may never get marrie—

CHRISTINE: *(Overlapping.)* Answer me!

LEA: Christine.

CHRISTINE: *(Breaking in.)* Answer me! Don't just keep saying Christine. *(Anguished.)* Sometimes . . . every morning . . . I think of—I imagine— things . . . that you . . .

LEA: Christine.

CHRISTINE: You're all I have, little Lea. All I'll ever have. *(Holding* LEA.*)* Sometimes I think we'll never have enough time. Do you think we'll have enough time, Lea? The days seem to be getting longer. And the nights, ah Lea—the nights—*(Jumping up suddenly.)* There'll never be enough time for us. *(She starts pacing the room.)*

LEA: Come and sit with me.

CHRISTINE: In a minute.

LEA: When you walk like that it reminds me of Sister Veronica. I used to hear her when I went to sleep. And when—

CHRISTINE: What?

LEA: She was angry when Maman took me away.

CHRISTINE: Angry?

LEA: I tried to talk to her. I followed her after morning mass. Remember the garden, Christine? Remember the path? *(CHRISTINE is silent, watching her.)* My shoes . . . my shoes kept clicking on the stone. I followed her all the way to her room. She was walking so fast her habit moved like a wind was blowing it. I got so close I almost tripped on it. But she wouldn't stop. She wouldn't turn around. She never turned around.

CHRISTINE: You never told me.

LEA: *(After a moment.)* Christine.

CHRISTINE: Yes?

LEA: I . . . um . . .

CHRISTINE: What is it?

LEA: *(Swallowing.)* I want you to . . . Would you . . .

CHRISTINE: What? *(Softly.)* Tell me. *(Watching her.)* Tell me.

LEA: Let's . . . Oh Christine, let's . . . let's pretend you're her.

CHRISTINE: Her?

LEA: Just be her.

CHRISTINE: Sister Veronica.

LEA: Yes.

CHRISTINE: I—*(Turning away. Smiling.)* Idiot!

LEA: Christine. Please.

CHRISTINE: Now?

LEA: Yes, now.

CHRISTINE: All right. *(Hesitating.)* Close your eyes. *(LEA closes her eyes.)*

LEA: Can I look yet?

CHRISTINE: Wait a second. *(She unties her long apron from around her waist.)*

LEA: What are you doing?

CHRISTINE: Just a minute. You'll see. Don't be so impatient. *(She ties the apron around her head, so that it falls in front of her face, then slips it back so that it resembles a nun's habit.)* Now look.

LEA: You're ready?

CHRISTINE: *(Turning toward LEA.)* I'm ready. *(LEA opens her eyes, looks at CHRISTINE. The light dims.)*

Scene 13

Sunday morning. Church bells are ringing. ISABELLE *is downstairs, ready to go out.*

ISABELLE: *(Picking up a calling card.)* Maman. Look. Madame Castelneuve was here.

MADAME DANZARD: *(Coming down the stairs.)* No!

ISABELLE: *(Picking up another calling card.)* And Madame Richepin.

MADAME DANZARD: How did they get in? When? The new curtains aren't even here yet. What's the matter with those two? They didn't even tell me.

(Irritated, tapping ISABELLE *on the back.)* Don't slump, Isabelle. You know how I hate that. She asked me for another blanket yesterday.

ISABELLE: Incredible. Why should they complain about the cold? They're hardly ever in their room.

MADAME DANZARD: *(Taking two heavy prayer books, one for her, one for* ISABELLE.*)* No one in this town has a radiator in the maid's room. It's unheard of. Have you ever heard of such a thing?

ISABELLE: Never.

MADAME DANZARD: *(Putting on her gloves.)* They're in the kitchen from six in the morning till ten at night. They have the stove to keep them warm.

ISABELLE: You worry too much, Maman.

MADAME DANZARD: As if I don't make life easy for them in every way.

ISABELLE: You do everything for them. You're too good to them. *(*CHRISTINE *and* LEA *come running into the house, laughing. They are dressed in their identical coats and hats, and wear white gloves. They stop when they see* MADAME DANZARD *and* ISABELLE. *Quietly they go up the stairs into their room.)* Did you see them? Coming back from church.

MADAME DANZARD: Spotless—with their white gloves. They don't even look like maids anymore. *(Softly* LEA *closes the door. She laughs and whirls* CHRISTINE *around.* CHRISTINE *puts her hand over Lea's mouth.* LEA *begins pulling off* CHRISTINE'S *gloves.)* But they're losing their looks, my dear. Have you noticed? Have you seen how thin they've become? Especially the younger one. *(*LEA *takes off Christine's hat.* CHRISTINE *sits still, watching her.* LEA *smiles, takes a few steps back.)* And those circles under their eyes.

ISABELLE: They look like they never sleep. *(*LEA *takes of her gloves. She turns and looks at* CHRISTINE.*) (Suddenly touching the banister.)* Look at this, Maman.

MADAME DANZARD: At what?

ISABELLE: Don't you see? *(Pointing.)* There. Right there.

MADAME DANZARD: *(Turning back.)* What is it? *(*ISABELLE *points again. Looking carefully.)* Oh yes. I see. Yes. They're getting careless. *(*LEA *takes off her hat. The* DANZARDS *go out. The heavy front door slams.* LEA *undoes her hair. It falls around her. Slowly, she unbuttons her coat, pulls it open. She is wearing the elaborate white chemise with the wide shoulder straps* CHRISTINE *sewed for her.* LEA *begins to move around the room. Her movements have a strange grace of their own. She moves all over the small room,* *her hair flying.* CHRISTINE *watches her. Suddenly, she pulls* LEA *down to her. The light dims.)*

S c e n e   14

The sound of water dripping. Slowly CHRISTINE *comes down the stairs. She goes into the kitchen and turns off the faucet. From the cabinet she takes a tray and places it on the kitchen table. From the sink she takes four drying wine glasses. She polishes them, places them on the tray. The fourth glass breaks in her hand. She draws her cut hand to her mouth, licking away the blood. She wraps her hand in a napkin. With the other hand, she puts the broken pieces of glass in the sink. She takes the tray with the polished wine glasses to the cabinet. Upstairs, in their room, the lights go out.*

LEA: *(Voice over. Screaming.)* Christine!

CHRISTINE: *(Almost dropping the tray.)* What is it?

LEA: *(Screaming.)* Oh no, no! Christine!

CHRISTINE: *(Running to the bottom of the stairs.)* What is it? What happened? *(*LEA *comes down the stairs to the landing.)*

LEA: The iron. It blew the fuse.

CHRISTINE: Oh no.

LEA: What will Madame do to us? What will she do? *(*CHRISTINE *goes to the kitchen cabinet and takes out a candle and matches.* LEA *comes down the stairs.)* I was right in the middle of her satin blouse.

CHRISTINE: *(Whirling around, the candle in her hand.)* Did you burn it?

LEA: It's the second time something's gone wrong with that iron.

CHRISTINE: Answer me, Lea. Did you?

LEA: First Mademoiselle's dress and now—

CHRISTINE: Did you burn it?

LEA: Madame will be so angry. Madame will be furious.

CHRISTINE: How can Madame be angry? It's not your fault. She can't be angry. *(She starts up the stairs with the candle.)* Let me see the blouse. *(*LEA *grabs at her arm.)* Let me see it. *(She goes up the stairs.)*

LEA: *(Frozen on the staircase.)* Is it all right?

CHRISTINE: *(Voice over.)* Just a minute.

LEA: *(Nervous.)* Is it? *(Panicked, running up the stairs.)* Is it? *(CHRISTINE comes into their room, spent. LEA comes in after her.)*

CHRISTINE: Don't worry.

LEA: Are you sure?

CHRISTINE: It's all right, Lea.

LEA: *(Sitting down on the bed.)* I'm so tired. That was the last thing left. And what will happen now, Christine? What will happen now?

CHRISTINE: Nothing will happen. There's nothing we can do. Don't worry, Lea. They've gone to the Blanchards for dinner. They'll play cards all night. We just have to wait.

LEA: Christine—now much money do we have saved?

CHRISTINE: Not enough.

LEA: I know it's not enough. But it will be one day. *(CHRISTINE is silent.)* It will be, won't it?

CHRISTINE: Hush, hush. Rest. Rest now.

LEA: And then—then we'll go away from here and—*(CHRISTINE is still.)* And—

CHRISTINE: *(Quietly.)* Yes. Yes my Lea. *(She begins to undo LEA's long braid.)* Someday. *(There is a pause.)*

LEA: *(Devastated, beginning to cry.)* I burned it, didn't I? Didn't I? Tell me.

CHRISTINE: My angel. My love. It's all right. *(CHRISTINE puts her arms around LEA. On the bed they undo each other's hair. There is the sound of hairpins falling on the floor. There is a pause. The sound of a key turning in a lock. MADAME DANZARD and ISABELLE enter downstairs. They are carrying several small packages tied with string. In one hand, MADAME DANZARD holds a set of heavy keys.)*

MADAME DANZARD: *(Impatient.)* Where is she?

ISABELLE: How do I know?

MADAME DANZARD: Don't answer me like that. Go and find her. *(ISABELLE doesn't move. There is something ominous about the house.)* *(Putting down her package and gloves.)* Did you hear what I said? This is absurd. She should be here to take these packages. She should have been here to open the door. At five thirty in the afternoon—what time is it anyway?

ISABELLE: *(Looking at her watch.)* Five forty-five.

MADAME DANZARD: *(Looking at her watch.)* Five forty-five. I mean really. Five forty-five and not a sign of them. I never heard of anything like it. Go into the kitchen, Isabelle. They must be there. (ISABELLE *goes into the kitchen. On the bed upstairs,* LEA *and* CHRISTINE *are in shadow.* ISABELLE *finds the broken glass and a dish in the sink.)*

CHRISTINE: *(Sitting up.)* Lea! Listen. (LEA *sits up.* ISABELLE *comes back from the kitchen.)*

MADAME DANZARD: Well? What took you so long?

CHRISTINE: It's them.

LEA: *(Her eyes wide with terror.)* Oh no.

ISABELLE: They're not there, Maman. And—(LEA *and* CHRISTINE *sit huddled together.)*

MADAME DANZARD: Impossible. *I'll* look. They must be there . . . And what?

ISABELLE: There's a dish in there . . . And a glass. Broken.

MADAME DANZARD: *(Going to the kitchen and picking up the broken glass in the sink.)* Broken. Nerve. What can they be doing?

LEA: Maybe they'll go away.

MADAME DANZARD: *(Listening.)* Shhh. Listen.

CHRISTINE: Shhh.

MADAME DANZARD: *(Looking out into the audience.)* Maybe they're upstairs.

LEA: What will we do, Christine?

CHRISTINE: Lea.

LEA: What will we do?

CHRISTINE: Little Lea. Wait, let me think.

MADAME DANZARD: I'm going up there this minute. (CHRISTINE *stands up.)*

CHRISTINE: I have to go down.

ISABELLE: Maman—wait.

LEA: Wait.

MADAME DANZARD: Wait? What for?

CHRISTINE: Do you want them to come up here?

ISABELLE: I don't think you should.

MADAME DANZARD: This is my house. Of course I'm going upstairs. Right now. *(She starts up the stairs.)*

CHRISTINE: If I don't go down, they'll come up.

MADAME DANZARD: You don't have to come if you don't want to. *(ISABELLE follows her slowly.)*

LEA: I'm frightened, Christine. I'm frightened. *(MADAME DANZARD stops.)*

MADAME DANZARD: *(Looking up.)* What's this? The lights are off up here. *(CHRISTINE leaves.)*

LEA: *(Terrorized.)* Don't leave me!

MADAME DANZARD: *(Quietly but furiously.)* This is really something. *(She and ISABELLE start down the staircase. CHRISTINE appears at the top of the stairs, her hair loose for the first time.)*

CHRISTINE: Madame *(ISABELLE lets out a little shriek.)* Madame has come back.

MADAME DANZARD: What is this? How dare you expect me to come back to a dark house?

CHRISTINE: *(Coming down the stairs, putting her right foot first on each step.)* It was the iron, Madame.

MADAME DANZARD: *Again?* Unbelievable. That's the second time. That iron was just repaired. What about my satin blouse?

ISABELLE: She came back to change into it.

MADAME DANZARD: Your sister didn't burn it, did she? She didn't burn my blouse?

CHRISTINE: Madame's blouse isn't finished yet.

MADAME DANZARD: *(Interrupting.)* Not finished? I'm wearing it to the Blanchards. What's the matter with your sister? *(CHRISTINE is silent.)* And why weren't you downstairs? Where's your apron?

CHRISTINE: *(Covering her uniform with her hands.)* I finished early, Madame.

ISABELLE: There's a dish in there. A glass. Broken.

MADAME DANZARD: Don't lie to me. I won't have a liar in this house.

CHRISTINE: Madame knows I don't lie.

ISABELLE: She is lying. I can tell.

MADAME DANZARD: You disappoint me. Send your sister down with my satin blouse at once. (CHRISTINE *doesn't move.*) Did you hear me? Go.

CHRISTINE: Madame can't see my sister now.

MADAME DANZARD: What?

ISABELLE: Are you going to let her speak to you like that?

MADAME DANZARD: I will see your sister this instant. And she will explain how she ruined my iron for the second time.

CHRISTINE: I already explained to Madame about the iron.

MADAME DANZARD: You call that an explanation?

CHRISTINE: It wasn't our fault, Madame.

MADAME DANZARD: Not your fault? No? Whose fault was it then? (*She turns to* ISABELLE.) Did you hear that?

ISABELLE: I heard. Who knows what else they've done.

CHRISTINE: We haven't done anything.

MADAME DANZARD: How dare you? How dare you speak to my daughter like that?

CHRISTINE: If Madame can't trust us, if she suspects anything—

MADAME DANZARD: (*Interrupting.*) Suspect what?

CHRISTINE: (*Quickly.*) We'll leave this house.

MADAME DANZARD: You'll leave? And just where do you think you'll go?

CHRISTINE: We'll find another house. (MADAME DANZARD, *clenching her fists, is silent for a moment.*)

MADAME DANZARD: Will you? Not with the recommendation you get from me. Don't think you'll get out so easily. Not after what I've seen tonight.

CHRISTINE: (*Breaking in.*) Madame has seen nothing.

MADAME DANZARD: Nothing? (*Snorting.*) That face, that hair. You smell of it, my dear.

CHRISTINE: Madame, stop. Madame. Please.

MADAME DANZARD: *(Pushing* CHRISTINE *down and going up to the landing.)* Not another word out of your mouth. Breaking my iron. The house in darkness.

CHRISTINE: *(Looking up at her.)* I told Madame. It wasn't our fault.

MADAME DANZARD: *(Looking down at* CHRISTINE, *starting to yell.)* Going to church every Sunday. Thinking you were a child of God. *(Raging, crossing herself.)* Forgive me God for what I have harbored here.

CHRISTINE: Madame. You have no right. *(LEA leaves their room.)*

MADAME DANZARD: *(Shrieking.)* No right? You must be mad.

ISABELLE: She is mad. Just look at her.

MADAME DANZARD: *You* have no rights, Christine. *(LEA appears at the top of the stairs.* ISABELLE *gasps.)*

ISABELLE: *(Grabbing her mother's arm.)* Maman! *(CHRISTINE runs up the stairs to LEA.)*

MADAME DANZARD: Look at that sister of yours. Dirt. *(She spits at them.)* Scum. Scum sisters. *(Her face twitching,* CHRISTINE *holds onto LEA.)*

CHRISTINE: *(Continuously.)* Not my sister, not my sister. *(She steps forward.* LEA *comes down the stairs.)*

MADAME DANZARD: You'll never work with your sister again.

ISABELLE: *(Trying to push past her mother.)* No one will take you. *(LEA tries to push past* CHRISTINE *toward* ISABELLE.*)*

CHRISTINE: *(Overlapping.)* Not my sister, not my sister.

LEA: *(Lifting the pewter pitcher high above* ISABELLE'S *head.)* CHRISTINE! *(At the same moment, in a violent gesture,* CHRISTINE *leaps toward* MADAME DANZARD'S *face. Blackout.)*

CHRISTINE: NOT MY SISTER!

ISABELLE: *(Overlapping.)* MAMAN! *(MADAME DANZARD screams wildly. Certain gestures may be made clear, others not. In the darkness are sounds of footsteps, screams, the thump of pewter on flesh. The screams gradually turn into moans in the quiet black house.)*

S c e n e   15

Light comes up on CHRISTINE *and* LEA, *standing separately.*

MEDICAL EXAMINER: *(Voice over. A flat anonymous voice.)* On the last step of the staircase, a single eye was found, intact, complete with optic nerve. The eye had been torn out without the aid of an instrument. *(He pauses.)* The bodies of Madame and Mademoiselle Danzard were found on the landing. On the ground were fragments of bone and teeth, a yellow diamond earring, two eyes, hair pins, a pocketbook, a set of keys, a coat button. The walls and doors were covered with splashes of blood reaching a height of seven feet.

JUDGE: *(Voice over.)* Is this the pewter pitcher with which you struck them down? (LEA *looks up.*)

MEDICAL EXAMINER: *(Voice over.)* Madame Danzard's body lay face up, Mademoiselle Danzard's body face down, the coat pulled up, the skirt pulled up, the underpants pulled down, revealing deep wounds on the buttocks and multiple slashes on the calves. Madame Danzard's eyes had been torn out of their sockets.

JUDGE: *(Voice over.)* The carving knife with which you slashed them? (CHRISTINE *looks up. They are silent.*) What did you have against Madame and Mademoiselle Danzard? *(He pauses.)* Was Madame good to you? *(He pauses.)* Did anything abnormal happen between you and your sister? *(He pauses.)* You understand me, don't you? Was it simply sisterly love? *(He pauses.)* How did you tear out their eyes? With your fingers? (CHRISTINE *clasps herself and rocks back and forth.*) Speak! You are here to defend yourselves. You will be judged.

CHRISTINE: Lea. I want Lea. Please. I beg you. Forgive me. I'll be good. I promise. I won't cry anymore. Give me Lea. Give me my sister. *(With a terrible, long drawn out cry.)* LEA! (LEA *moves to the center. Her face is pale, her eyes vacant.*)

JUDGE: *(Voice over.)* Lea Lutton. You will perform ten years of hard labor. You are refused the right to enter the town of Le Mans for twenty years. *(He pauses.* CHRISTINE *stands beside* LEA.) Christine Lutton. You will be taken barefoot, wearing a chemise, your head covered by a black veil, to a public place in the town of Le Mans. And there, before your fellow citizens, your head will be severed from your body.

LEA: *(Gazing straight out, sings brokenly.)*
Sleep my little sister, sleep
Sleep through darkness

Sleep so deep
All the rivers find the sea
My little sister
Sleep for me.

(CHRISTINE *looks directly out.* LEA *gazes vaguely into the distance. They stand as if framed in a photograph.*)

END

COYOTE
UGLY

Lynn Siefert

Coyote Ugly was originally presented as a staged reading at the 1982 National Playwrights Conference at the Eugene O'Neill Memorial Theatre Center. Subsequently presented at the Yale Repertory Theatre (Lloyd Richards, Artistic Director) as part of Winterfest 1983. *Coyote Ugly* was presented by the Steppenwolf Theatre Company in Chicago in April 1985 and later in Washington, D.C., at the Kennedy Center.

After 12 years in various undergraduate programs in Ohio, Colorado, and Maine, I inadvertently graduated. When I graduated I considered myself a painter. I wrote poems on the side. I got a job painting backdrops for a children's theater. One day I thought I'd write a play for kids. Bingo. Playwriting seemed to be the perfect marriage between painting and poetry. So, I went back to school. I got my MFA in playwriting from the Yale School of Drama, where I wrote *Coyote Ugly,* moved to New York, and rubbed elbows with my fellow Susan Smith Blackburn Prize recipients.

My other plays include *Little Egypt* for which I received a grant from the National Endowment of the Arts and *Hysterica Passio,* written in collaboration with Dare Clubb, which won a New York Foundation of the Arts grant.

LYNN SIEFERT
1990

Characters

SCARLET PEWSY—*Twelve years old. Crooked necked. Wiley. A survivor.*

ANDREAS PEWSY—*Scarlet's mother. Hardened beauty. Cornered. Ferociously funny.*

RED PEWSY—*Married to Andreas. Unrequited in all things. Harmlessly horny. Sweet tempered. Family man.*

DOWD PEWSY—*Gentrified son of Andreas and Red. Non-athletic gym teacher. Nervous suppressor.*

PENNY PEWSY—*Dowd's young bride. A suburban landscape. Manicured. Optimist. Desire to please. Sun-sensitive.*

Scene 1

Dawn. Outside. SCARLET *strikes a stone against a bleached bone. Inside.* ANDREAS *snores on her hide-a-bed.*

SCARLET: For a stone and a stone for a bone and a bone for a stone and a stone for a bone and a bone for a stone and a. *(She looks in through the window at* ANDREAS. *She strikes the stone more insistently.)* And a bone for a stone and a stone for a bone and a bone for a stone and a stone for a bone. *(Silence.)* There. There. She can't move. Every bone of hers is busted. Her leg-bones and her finger-bones and her knee-bones and her nose-bones and her bones holding her eyes together and her voice-bones and her ear-bones and the bones that shrink and grow with her brains. Smashed. Broke to bits. Small as sand. *(In mock alarm.)* What'll I do? What'll I do? Fold her up in the hide-a-bed! *(She goes inside.)* "Where's your mama?" "I don't know, Sheriff." "What's your hide-a-bed doing snoring that-a-way?" CRACK! *(The snoring stops.)* "I don't hear nothing, Sheriff." *(The snoring resumes.* SCARLET *takes a half gallon of milk out of the refrigerator. Leaving the refrigerator door open, she goes outside holding the milk overhead triumphantly. The phone rings.)*

ANDREAS: *(Snapping up in bed.)* WHO'S THERE? *(Looks in the direction of the phone.)* SCARLET? *(The phone continues ringing.)* It's the phone! *(Pause.)* SCARLET? RED? SOME GODDAMNBODY ANSWER THE JESUS H. CHRIST. I CAN'T. I BEEN ASLEEP ON MY HANDS. MY SON-OF-A-GOD-DAMN-IT-TO-HELL-BITCH-HANDS ARE ASLEEP. *(She rises.)* WHERE IS EVERYBODY? ON THE TOILET? IS EVERYBODY ON THE TOILET? *Using her elbows like salad forks,* ANDREAS *picks up the receiver. She struggles with it. It falls to the floor.* SCARLET *enters dragging a heavy bag.)* Hello? SCARLET. ANSWER THE PHONE. HELLO. *(SCARLET picks up the phone.)*

SCARLET: Arf. Arf. Arf.

ANDREAS: Give that here.

SCARLET: Grrrrrrr. (SCARLET *holds the receiver upside down in* ANDREAS' *face.)*

ANDREAS: THE RIGHT WAY. Do it the right way. (SCARLET *holds it the right way but at a distance.)* Hello. Hello. Hello. Hello. Hello? Red? Red? Red? Is that you, Red? Hello. Hello? I can't hear you! I CAN'T MAKE YOU OUT.

LOUDER YOU SON OF A BITCH. WHEN'RE YOU COMING HOME? (SCARLET *hangs up the phone.*)

SCARLET: It wasn't Red on that phone. (*She drags her bag toward her room.*)

ANDREAS: HUP! HUP! YOU MARCH YOUR LITTLE HIND-END OVER HERE. DON'T YOU GO WALTZING PAST YOUR MAMA LIKE YOU WAS THE QUEEN OF SHEBA. I'LL DO THAT WALTZING. WHERE AND WHAT. WHERE HAVE YOU BEEN AND WHAT'S IN THE BAG? (*Pause.*) Waltzing like the Queen of god-damn Sheba past your mama like she's a cowpie. Where's your daddy? I'll tell you where he is. Down to Heber eating pancakes and pinching butts is where. Waltzing by your mama. Carrying some half dead . . . some . . . in a bag. What's in it? Answer me. (*Pause.*) Oh. I get it. You're all talked out this morning from your little chitchat with God. Talking to Mr. God, was you. Well let me tell you something about old God. GOD IS A BUTT PINCHER TOO. He's no different. He's a butt pincher from way back. (*Pause.*) Looks like another day of just me and Mr. Icebox. (*She looks in the refrigerator.*) Where's the milk? Did you take the milk? I want it. I don't want you feeding it to your critters. I want the milk. (SCARLET *slams her bedroom door in* ANDREAS*'s face.*) I WANT IT. I WANT IT. I WANT THE MILK. (*Pause.*) I'm coming in I said, and I'm coming in, DID YOU HEAR ME? (*She doesn't move.*) GET OUT HERE. (SCARLET *bursts out of her room.*) I have seen you. (*Pause.*) Blowing up rabbits. Shooting them from a distance so they think they're blowing up of their own choice. (*Pause.*) KERBLAM! (*Pause.*) I am going to the bathroom. (*Pause.*) I have to pee so bad I can taste it. (*Pause.*) Quit it! (*Pause.*) Quit staring like you think I can't see you. I ain't one of the rabbits. You can't scope me from no distance. (*Pause.*) Awwwwww. Baby. Baby baby baby. Your eyes are working someplace outside the kitchen. They're crying but there's no tears because your true eyes is off someplace else. C'mere. You know she loves you. You know it . . . that . . . but she. C'mere. (*She inches toward* SCARLET.) Tell Mama. Tell Mama what's in the bag. (SCARLET *evades her.*) YOUR LITTLE NECK. YOUR FUNNY LITTLE BURIED ALIVE HEAD ON ITS BURIED ALIVE NECK. DON'T IT YEARN TO COME LOOSE? HOW ABOUT WE PRY IT LOOSE? LOOSEN IT TOGETHER. AS A TEAM. (*She lunges at* SCARLET. SCARLET *spits in her face.*) Ugliness. Don't be uglier than you are.

SCARLET: You want to know what's in the bag you go on and touch me. It's something wild. It's something hungry. It eats *old meat.*

Scene 2

ANDREAS *shakes up a can of Ready Whip. She tilts it into her mouth and sprays, filling her mouth with whipped cream.* RED *enters, giddy.*

RED: You awake?

ANDREAS: You're no dreamboat.

RED: Look what I brung you back from Phoenix.

ANDREAS: What?

RED: That's a car deodorant.

ANDREAS: What am I supposed to do with it?

RED: Come over here. Shut your eyes. There's something I want you to see. (ANDREAS *shuts her eyes. She runs into furniture.*) Open them up.

ANDREAS: What?

RED: Look there.

ANDREAS: I can't see nothing. There's a car blocking the view.

RED: That's it.

ANDREAS: Who's is it?

RED: I own it.

ANDREAS: You heard of brain death? You got it.

RED: *(To* ANDREAS*)* Don't you like it?

ANDREAS: Where'd it come from? (SCARLET *enters from outside.*)

RED: Green, ain't it.

ANDREAS: Where'd it come from?

SCARLET: Don't tell her, Red.

ANDREAS: *Slap* that child.

RED: It's got its own radio.

ANDREAS: I'll radio you if you don't tell me where it came from.

RED: Four on the floor. (SCARLET *humps Red's leg.*)

ANDREAS: Make her stop that.

RED: Remember the first time you rode in a car like that and you knew you had to have one? "Drive me," it says, "Drive, drive."

ANDREAS: *(To* SCARLET.*)* Why don't you go rub yourself on an appliance for awhile.

RED: Soft seats. Beige.

ANDREAS: Tell that child to stop hanging on you and go hump the icebox awhile.

RED: *(To* SCARLET.*)* Simmer down.

ANDREAS: Where'd you find car money? You don't have car money. Where'd you find car money?

RED: Didn't.

ANDREAS: Bought it with your looks?

RED: Maybe. Could be.

SCARLET: Take me somewheres

RED: *(Pushing* SCARLET *aside.)* I'm going to drive us to the supermarket. I'm going to buy us some *food!*

ANDREAS: Is that a hot car?

SCARLET: Supermarket?

RED: Some chicken noodle. Some light bulbs.

ANDREAS: IS THAT CAR HOT?

RED: Hot enough to steam wieners.

ANDREAS: I knew it. Give it back.

RED: *I* didn't steal it.

ANDREAS: You said it was hot.

RED: Some-other-body stole it! Down to Phoenix.

ANDREAS: And they give it to you.

RED: That's what I'm trying to tell you.

SCARLET: *(Motioning* RED *outside.)* Hey.

RED: Guy I know comes into the Texaco. "I got this hot car," he says, "Want it?"

SCARLET: Hey. Hey. Hey.

RED: "Damn right I want it." He says, "What you got in trade?"

SCARLET: *(Warning him.)* Red.

RED: We worked something out.

ANDREAS: That is not Red to you. That is your d-a-d-d-y daddy.

RED: That is all I am going to divulge.

ANDREAS: What'd you give?

RED: Something. *(Pause.)* Nothing. *(Pause.)* Nothing of yours. *(Pause.)* You want to go to the supermarket or do you want to stand there picking your nits.

SCARLET: She ain't in this. Hey.

RED: Make you feel sixteen. Driving driving driving down a hot and dusty road. *(He cruises Andreas' erogenous zones.)* Driving through the hot zone. Doing some of this. And some of this. And some of this.

ANDREAS: Clear off!

RED: *(Doing a dance of his own creation.)* I feel good. I feel like warm spit on hot concrete.

SCARLET: Let's go now, Red. You said we'd go somewheres.

RED: Sure babydoll.

ANDREAS. *(Planting herself between* RED *and* SCARLET.) YOUR HANDS. You want to put'm there. Put'm there. *(She puts both his hands on both her breasts.)* Tell'm to look for some lost thing.

SCARLET: Get your hands off her. (ANDREAS *laughs.)* GET YOUR HANDS OFF HER. (ANDREAS *laughs.* SCARLET *kicks* RED.) GET YOUR HANDS OFF THAT SLUT. (SCARLET *runs into her room.* ANDREAS *throws off* RED'S *hands.* RED *hits his thigh with his fist.)*

RED: Goddamnit. I *brang* you that car. Don't that car turn you on? Don't it make you want to go places?

ANDREAS: No. It don't.

RED: There's the difference between you and me!

ANDREAS: Yeah. You're all pecker and feet.

RED: And you're a cold cunt in house shoes.

ANDREAS: *(With exaggerated gestures.)* Wasn't you going to go someplace? I thought you was. Now, where was it. Someplace where a man can be a manhood man. I know. It was the supermarket. You was going to drive down the aisles showing off to the frozen food. Then you was going to let the lucky day check-out girl at the check-out counter check you out. That was it. Then you was going to drive a hundred miles in that direction. Or a hundred miles in that direction, and you was going to see that a hundred miles in that and that direction was the same. So, maybe you better drive two hundred miles. But two hundred miles is the same as one hundred is the same as setting here. Looks like you got some serious driving to do if you want to see a change.

RED: I'll go. You watch me. I'll go. (SCARLET *marches out of her room directly to the sink. Opens a flour canister. Throws a handful of flour at* ANDREAS' *face. Moves off, furious.*)

SCARLET: IT'S DEAD.

RED: What, babydoll?

SCARLET: STILL IN THE BAG.

ANDREAS: I've about had it with her dragging her mauled-up animals through my house.

SCARLET: STIFF IN THE BAG.

ANDREAS: Hear me, Crippleneck? Hear?

SCARLET: It died from breathing the same air as her.

ANDREAS: I am going to bust you. And I am going to bust both my arms doing it so I know how bad it hurts.

SCARLET: Keep her off me.

ANDREAS: I am going to bust your ugliness in two.

SCARLET: KEEP HER OUT.

RED: Your ma gets angry in her mouth. I get angry in my hands.

SCARLET: I'd ruther be whupped by you than spoke to by her. Remember what you promised. Remember what you said.

RED: Remember what's important. What's important is coolness. Cool. Ness.

ANDREAS: If you and me are going to go somewheres, let's you and me get there.

RED: *(To* SCARLET.) This is a family car.

SCARLET: There's something dead in my bed and I'm going to bury it.

Scene 3

Outside. SCARLET *stands beside a hole in the earth where she has buried her bobcat. She furiously draws in the sand with a stick.*

SCARLET: AND SHE HAS GOT A TONGUE LIKE A SNAKE. HER TONGUE HAS ITS OWN HEAD. CALLING YOU BUTT PINCHER. OLD GOD SHE SAID. YOU SHOULD HAVE PUNCHED HER TONGUE IN THE FACE. I just did what you told me to. I chewed the insides of my cheeks. I spit blood at her. *(Pause.)* We got that Buick. Only except now Red's changed his tune. He's laughing and grabbing behinds and singing FAMILY car now. He better shape up and fly right. I'd never of done what I did for a family car. I wouldn't of delivered for that. *(Pause.)* This bobcat walked into one of my traps. I thought for awhile it was Somebody. I had it in my room but it stayed a cat the whole time. Then it died. When you send me this person he's going to be all mine. He's going to pick me up like a present. I'm going to be wearing a dress. One of them no color dresses that don't seem to be no color at all. And this Somebody is going to pick me up and he's going to say, "Who's this girl? Who's this pretty dressy girl?" And I'm going to say, "It's me." *(Pause.)* Hush! *(She listens.)* Somebody! *(We hear the offstage voices of* PENNY *and* DOWD. SCARLET *sets her leghold trap and places it in their path. She runs off. She runs back on and grabs her rifle. She starts off again.* DOWD *enters wearing gym shorts and a brightly colored pullover. He is lean. He might have been beamed down from another planet.* SCARLET *turns, mid-flight, and they stare at each other for a long time.* SCARLET, *excited, runs off.* PENNY *enters, equally alien, carrying shopping bags and an overnight case.)*

DOWD: This is it.

PENNY: Your roots!

DOWD: Funny after twelve years I still call it going home.

PENNY: Are they having a yard sale?

DOWD: This is the decor.

PENNY: What's this?

DOWD: That? That's just an old engine block.

PENNY: Oh? I like it. No, I do.

DOWD: My old man's a garage mechanic. That's where all this junk comes from. He couldn't afford a car of his own so he'd bring home parts of cars. Figured someday they'd all add up.

PENNY: You told me he was a cowboy.

DOWD: Who?

PENNY: Your father.

DOWD: Oh. Well, see, he moonlights as a cowboy.

PENNY: Where are they then?

DOWD: What?

PENNY: The cows.

DOWD: Yeah. Well, you may not see any today but cows are unpredictable. You can be without cows for years and then one day when you least expect them WHAMMO! Cows everywhere. There! There's one now! (PENNY *looks out.* DOWD *moos. They laugh together.)* Penny?

PENNY: Hm?

DOWD: Honk if you love me.

PENNY: I love you.

DOWD: I knew it. First time I laid eyes on you I said, Dowd Pewsy, there stands a girl weak minded enough to marry you. *(Pause.)* Are you sure you want to stay?

PENNY: We came all this way!

DOWD: Okay. Heads we go. Tails we stay. *(He tosses a coin.)* Tails. Best out of three. *(He tosses the coin.)* Tails. Double or nothing. *(He tosses the coin.)*

PENNY: Tails?

DOWD: We could find a motel. Come back. It means giving up the Grand Canyon. We only have a few days.

PENNY: I want to meet your mother and your father. I want to see where you grew up.

DOWD: I grew up here.

PENNY: I know. I always dreamed I'd live somewhere like this. In the middle of something. On the edge of something. Looking out over something. Surrounded by something. This is everything I've ever dreamed of only smaller. Oh, look! How cute! A little thing! (PENNY *nudges the trap with her foot. It snaps shut on her foot. She screams.)*

DOWD: Penny! What happened!

PENNY: My foot!

DOWD: Okay. Be calm. Stay calm. I can't get it off. The worst thing you can do is panic. Don't move. Stay where you are. I'll find an implement. Don't move.

PENNY: Hurry!

DOWD: Try this.

PENNY: No! Where's your father? He'll know what to do.

DOWD: I can handle this problem.

PENNY: I only thought he might have a better tool.

DOWD: He might have the tool but I can get the job done. *(He removes the trap.* PENNY'S *shoe comes off with it.)*

PENNY: There!

DOWD: Can you walk?

PENNY: Yes. *(She hobbles on her feet and hands.)*

DOWD: Does it hurt?

PENNY: *(Whimpering.)* A little.

DOWD: Okay, ma'am. Mount up. Ready? *(He gathers the bags and helps her onto his back.)*

PENNY: Giddyap!

DOWD: WHOOP WHOOP WHOOPEEEEE! LET THE COWERIN' VARMINT NAME OF RED PEWSY SHOW HIS FACE! WHOOP WHOOP WHOOPEEEEE! *(He gallops into the house, depositing* PENNY *on the hide-a-bed.)* LET THE COWERIN' VAR-MINT NAME OF RED PEWSY SHOW HIS FACE! T'IS DOWD PEWSY COME HOME WITH HIS BRIDE. OH WHO IS THAR LOVELIER THAN PENNY PEWSY. SHOW ME THE FEMALE MORE ENTRANCIN' AND LET ME DROP DEAD AT HER FEET. *(He drops. They look around eagerly.)* Mom? Dad?

SCARLET: *(Revealing herself in homemade wolf mask; puffing up.)* Who the hell are you and what do you want? (DOWD *and* PENNY *back off, hands raised.)* You looking for Red he's gone. You looking for something else it ain't here. What's that?

PENNY: This? This is my shoe. It belongs to me.

SCARLET: Straighten up.

PENNY: Who are you?

SCARLET: My name is Listener. Eye-killer. I live off rabbits.

PENNY: Really? *(Opening her purse.)* Would you like us to take your picture?

SCARLET: Don't. I hate cameras. And I hate picture takers.

PENNY: But Dowd is one of you. He's from the area.

SCARLET: Dowd? Dowd who?

DOWD: T'IS DOWD PEWSY COME HOME WITH HIS.

SCARLET: Why'd you stay gone so long? Why'd you come back?

PENNY: She knows you.

DOWD: No she doesn't.

SCARLET: *(Exiting coyly.)* You left the place a mess.

PENNY: Wait!

DOWD: Let her go.

PENNY: But she knew who you were. *(She crosses to the door.)*

DOWD: No she didn't. She was just some crazy, you know, kid.

PENNY: She lives on rabbits!

DOWD: You don't believe that.

PENNY: Oh. Well, I thought maybe.

DOWD: Why don't you sit down.

PENNY: *(Continuing to stare out the door.)* I will.

DOWD: Stand up, then. Whatever. *(He goes to* SCARLET's *door.)* Nervy wasn't she. Came right in.

PENNY: Where does that go?

DOWD: My old room.

PENNY: Going in?

DOWD: Sure. *(He doesn't.)*

PENNY: Want me to come with you?

DOWD: Don't be silly. I can go into my own old room. *(He doesn't.)*

PENNY: What?

DOWD: I don't know.

PENNY: Bogeyman?

DOWD: Hm?

PENNY: Is there a bogeyman in your old room? *(They open door. Cat scream. They leap and fall onto the hide-a-bed, laughing and tickling each other.* RED *and* ANDREAS *enter with boxes of groceries.)*

DOWD: Hi, Mom. Hi, Dad. I brought you my wife. (PENNY *waves weakly.)*

S c e n e   4

The floor is strewn with wrapping paper and ribbon. RED *pulls on a new red pullover that is several sizes too small. It is so small it won't stretch over his belly. The sleeves should stop at the elbows.* ANDREAS *tries on an apron that says* "HOME ON THE RANGE." DOWD *is wedged between* SCARLET *and* PENNY.

PENNY: Do you have a Bloomingdale's in Heber? If you have a Bloomingdale's you can exchange the shirt. If you'd like.

RED: Shirt's perfect.

PENNY: Yes! I only thought if the color or the sleeves.

RED: What do you say, Dowd?

DOWD: It looks great, Dad. That's the way they wear them.

ANDREAS: Should of told us you was coming. You and Penny Pewsy. We'd of had a chance to warn you you had a sister here. Little Miss Sunshine-Bucket-On-Her-Head.

DOWD: I thought we'd surprise, we thought.

ANDREAS: Surprise surprise. Everybody's surprised.

PENNY: Here we go. I found something for Scarlet. *Mammals of the Southwest.* All the way from Philadelphia. It's a little dog-eared but. (SCARLET *eyes* PENNY *menacingly.)*

DOWD: If we'd known. We didn't know.

RED: Didn't know the old man had it in him. Didn't know the old man could still produce. I pumped your mama full of hi-test and she came racing out.

DOWD: Honey, why don't we go look at the luggage.

ANDREAS: NOBODY LEAVES THIS ROOM UNTIL WE'VE HAD SOME CONVERSATION.

RED: You could say I've set an example. Girls down at the Pancake House tell me they always believed a man dried up around fifty. I point to Scarlet there and they got living proof. Some guys believe it too. Hit fifty and they clog up. *(He grabs his crotch.)* Clog right up.

DOWD: So! I thought I'd take Penny fishing in the reservoir tomorrow. Any fish left in the San Carlos, Dad? Did you leave any fish?

RED: *(To* PENNY.*)* Small ones. Suckers.

DOWD: I thought I'd take Penny fishing. Penny's never been fishing. Have you, Penny?

PENNY: Only in supermarkets! (DOWD *and* PENNY *laugh a little hysterically.)*

ANDREAS: God she's fun.

DOWD: I'll take you. Fishing. In the morning. (PENNY'S *hands move like happy puppies.)*

ANDREAS: *(Looking at* SCARLET.*)* I'm putting you and Penny Pewsy in your room, Dowd.

DOWD: Scarlet's room, now.

ANDREAS: *(Looking at* SCARLET, *speaking to* DOWD.*)* I'm putting you in there. *(Pause.)* Scarlet. Go over there and give Penny Pewsy a kiss. Give her one. (PENNY *rises in anticipation.* SCARLET *doesn't move.)*

DOWD: You should have told me about her.

RED: We figured you'd be back this way.

DOWD: Twelve years?

RED: Time flies. You forget what you've said. What you haven't.

ANDREAS: *(Still looking at* SCARLET.*)* That's a cold child. You kiss that child on the cheek your lip will *stick* to it.

PENNY: *(To* SCARLET.*)* Do you go to school?

ANDREAS: HEY THERE DOWD! STAND OVER HERE A MINUTE. LET YOUR MOTHER HAVE A LOOK.

PENNY: Let your mother have a look, Dowd.

DOWD: *(Standing.)* I'm standing.

ANDREAS: Come over here a minute.

DOWD: *(Staying where he is.)* Here I am.

ANDREAS: Haven't grown much in twelve years.

DOWD: I stopped.

PENNY: He stopped.

RED: Scarlet here just grows and grows.

ANDREAS: Like mold. (SCARLET *rises.*) You set back down until you say something or kiss somebody. (SCARLET *exits into her bedroom.*) LITTLE BONECRUSHER. LITTLE CANNIBAL. (ANDREAS *rushes* SCARLET'S *door.*) I AM PUTTING DOWD AND PENNY PEWSY IN THERE. YOU PUT THEM ANIMAL PARTS IN A BOX. *(She turns to see everyone staring at her. Sweetly.)* I am going to kiss my son. You don't mind if I kiss my son. *(She doesn't move.)*

PENNY: Heavens! Heavens no!

RED: She was kissing him and everything else way before. Little stinker.

ANDREAS: *(Not moving.)* You still think your mother's pretty, don't you?

DOWD: You're *older!*

ANDREAS: *Years* don't make a woman ugly.

RED: Hey, Penny.

ANDREAS: Should of told me you was coming.

PENNY: Yes?

RED: You like that Buick Skylark out there?

DOWD: Is that your car, Dad?

RED: *(To* PENNY.) That car turn you on?

DOWD: What would you call that color, Dad?

PENNY: It's a very sexy car, Mr. Pewsy.

RED: *(Closing in on* PENNY.) Red.

PENNY: It's green.

RED: Red Pewsy.

PENNY: Oh! You mean. He meant and I thought he meant.

DOWD: We don't drive much in Philadelphia.

PENNY: We live two blocks from our high school.

DOWD: Lafayette High.

PENNY: Lafayette High School.

RED: *(To* DOWD.) I'd of thought you'd of finished up by now.

DOWD: I teach. I teach there.

PENNY: Dowd's head of the P.E. Department. I teach biology.

ANDREAS: Did you always have that game leg?

PENNY: Game leg?

ANDREAS: I was wondering if you was crippled up that way when my son found you.

RED: Biology.

PENNY: That's right. (RED *leads* PENNY *away from the group.)*

RED: Biology. I have heard it said that a biologist can keep a frog alive and cut it open at the same time. *(He performs the dissection on* PENNY'S *chest.)* Cut away the walls of the heart cavity so you can see the parts of the heart and the tubes that go to it and leave it. There. Still pumping. Wide open. *(He squeezes her breasts with the tips of his fingers as if they were bicycle horns.)* The heart.

PENNY: *(After a miserable silence.)* That's very beautiful, Mr. Pewsy.

DOWD: *(Not having seen* RED'S *hands in action.)* They're anaesthetized. *(Pause.)* They don't *feel* anything.

PENNY: *(Tripping backwards as* RED *pursues her.)* This is a beautiful house in a beautiful place to live compared to Philadelphia buses and breathing other people's trash.

ANDREAS: Tell it to Dowd. Hear that Dowd?

PENNY: I do. I have. I do.

RED: I never thought you'd of growed up to be a schoolteacher.

DOWD: What did you think I'd growed up into?

ANDREAS: Red thought you'd grow up into exactly what he is.

PENNY: A mechanic!

ANDREAS: A butt pincher.

PENNY: Aha.

ANDREAS: Isn't that so? Some wandering butt pincher looking for a butt to pinch.

RED: Your ma's went nuts. *(Pause.)* I'll go. I still got places inside me to go to.

ANDREAS. Then go! (RED *slumps out the door. On the porch, he drops to his knees and crawls back to the edge of the door.)*

RED: *(In falsetto.)* RED! RED! COME BACK! COME BACK! WE DIDN'T MEAN IT, RED! COME BACK! *(In normal voice.)* Okay. *(He hops back into the house.)* I ain't so bad. *(Pause.)* Hey, Penny! Watch this! Want to see me hold my breath? Want to see how long I can hold it for? *(He sucks air deep into his body. Holds it.)*

ANDREAS: Penny and Dowd. Bound and gagged in marriage. Seems like only yesterday it was me marching down the aisle in front of the eyes of everybody I'd ever known, screwed, or owed money to. The thing was that during the excitement I had got my wedding gown hem stuck up inside my lime green girdle. There I go. Marching to the music. Purely serious in front while all hell had broke loose in the rear. I'd like to of died.

DOWD: I wish I'd been there.

ANDREAS: You was. Red's ma was horrified by this. Took it as an ill omen. She was Christian Scientist. We called her Batface, though. One time Red got a piece of barb'wire stuck through his foot and she pulled it out with her teeth. Never called no doctor. Didn't believe in them. Only thing she believed in was ointments and prayer. Ointments she made from MOON-BLOOD she'd say. IT AIN'T LATIN AND RUBBER GLOVES GOING TO HEAL YOU, she'd say. Fortunately she died. (RED *is blue.)* While Batface was dying she made me rub that putrid-smelling ointment on her eyes so she wouldn't lose her sight at the last minute. It didn't work though. She couldn't see shit with that moon crap on her face!

RED: *(Exploding.)* DID YOU SEE IT?

ANDREAS: "I'M BLIND!," she screamed.

RED: DID YOU SEE IT? DID YOU SEE IT?

ANDREAS: "I'M BLIND! I'M BLIND!" And then she died.

RED: I got to check the car. *(He stays.)*

ANDREAS: You got kids?

PENNY: We have cats.

ANDREAS: You on birth contraptions?

PENNY: No.

ANDREAS: You don't like kids?

PENNY: We can't.

ANDREAS: Easiest thing in the world.

PENNY: We're seeing a specialist.

ANDREAS: There's your problem. Try doing it alone.

PENNY: Dowd's impotent.

RED: Hear that? He's clogged up. Some guys start losing sperm around thirty.

PENNY: Sperm doesn't matter, Mr. Pewsy.

RED: What do you think holds it up? AIR?

ANDREAS: His pecker was in working order till the day he left.

DOWD: My pecker is none of your business.

PENNY: She's your mother.

RED: Speaking of peckers. I was driving the Buick through the Metro-Mart when this whusmobile pulls alongside and the wiener that's driving rolls down his window so his air conditioner slaps me in the face and he says in one of them accents, PARDON ME, SIR, he says, pointing to the intersection, CAN YOU MAKE A U-TURN? NO, I SAYS, BUT I CAN MAKE HER EYES BULGE. *(He laughs alone.)* That's a true story. *(Pause.* PENNY *grins halfheartedly.)* You sure are pretty when you smile, Penny. Come on out. I'll show you my car.

PENNY: Actually. I'm tired. I'm very. If you'll excuse me I'm very tired. And hot. I'm very hot. It's been a long day and my foot. I'd like to lie down. Would you mind? If I lie down awhile?

ANDREAS: SCARLET.

PENNY: She may be sleeping.

ANDREAS: Scarlet don't sleep.

PENNY: Why don't I just curl up on the sofa.

ANDREAS: No you don't. I sleep there. Nowhere but. Besides. It's got a busted spring. You got to know exactly how to curve around it or you'll pierce your belly.

RED: I'd consider it a favor if you'd layed down on my bed. It ain't had nothing soft that smells good in it in awhile. I'd consider it a favor.

ANDREAS: SCARLET!

DOWD: We could go to a motel. We could do that.

ANDREAS: NOBODY LEAVES.

RED: Hey, Dowd. I'll show you my car.

ANDREAS: Stay put, Dowd. Stay here awhile.

RED: You still a mama's boy, Dowd?

DOWD: I'll take a look at your car, Dad. (DOWD *takes* PENNY *aside. Confidential. Reassuring.*) I'm going to take a look at Dad's car. I won't be long. I'll be right back. I'll just take a look.

ANDREAS: *Go ahead then.*

DOWD: What do you say, Dad? Let's stretch out, you know, legs. (DOWD *and* RED *go out.* RED *runs back in.* DOWD *exits.*)

RED: I'm going to take you fishing in the morning, Penny.

ANDREAS: SCARLET. I AM PUTTING PENNY PEWSY IN THERE. YOU HAVE GOT THREE SECONDS TO CLEAR OUT.

PENNY: Don't bother, really. I like animals.

ANDREAS: ONE.

RED: *(Pursuing* PENNY.) I'm going to take you fishing. I know the spot.

ANDREAS: TWO.

RED: I know where they bite. *(He pinches* PENNY *who jumps. He exits.)*

ANDREAS: THREE. (SCARLET *bursts out of her room in wild animal regalia and growls the moment* RED *pinches* PENNY. PENNY *stifles a scream.)*

S c e n e   5

Middle of the same night. SCARLET *flicks a Bic in the dark before the lights come up.* ANDREAS *is asleep inside on the hide-a-bed.*

SCARLET: WHAT'S THE BIG IDEA? WHO ASKED HER? That room is my room and Dowd's room. I should be in there. Not her. What are you going to do about it? Nothing, prob'ly. You're a welsher same as Red, prob'ly. WHO

CARES. I DON'T NEED YOU. I DON'T NEED NOBODY. I can arrange MY OWN EVENTS. Ease her out of the picture. He'd like me like crazy if he got to know me. If I was to introduce myself. Maybe I will. Maybe I won't. Thing is, he don't give me a second glance with her around. *Mammals of the Southwest*. I'll show her mammals. (SCARLET *rips pages out of* Mammals of the Southwest. *She puts the pages into a can or old pot and sets them on fire. She holds* PENNY'S *shoe over the flame. She holds a makeshift doll over the flame. She chants.*) Straight lightning from the east.

ANDREAS: Scarlet?

SCARLET: Zigzag lightning from the west.

ANDREAS: What are you doing?

SCARLET: Step from east to west.

ANDREAS: I got real people here now.

SCARLET: Step from west to east.

ANDREAS: I don't want you playing near the house.

SCARLET: Sunray at north.

ANDREAS: Creating an impression.

SCARLET: Sunray at south.

ANDREAS: I don't want you in my vicinity.

SCARLET: CREATE THE FOOT.

ANDREAS: He come home to his mother.

SCARLET: ERASE THE FOOT.

ANDREAS: Not you. *(She rises. She sneaks out and stands on the edge of the porch.)*

SCARLET: PLUCK. BREATH. BLOOD ENTRAILS.

ANDREAS: YOU MIND YOUR P'S AND Q'S!

SCARLET: *(Arching like a cat.)* KH! KH! TH! TH!

ANDREAS: DON'T YOU STARE AT ME WITH THEM JUNKY EYES LITTLE FERRET. (SCARLET *backs her into the house with her rifle.*) DOWD? DOWD? IT'S YOUR MOTHER. LET ME IN. I'M HAVING NIGHTMARES. (PENNY *enters in her nightgown; still sleeping.*)

PENNY: I'm hungry.

ANDREAS: NOW YOU DID IT. YOU WOKE UP PENNY PEWSY.

PENNY: Close. Close. Close. Close. Close. (PENNY *leaps on the hide-a-bed and shakes the pillow in her teeth.*)

SCARLET: (*Enters.*) She's dreaming! She's chasing rabbits. (ANDREAS *takes* SCARLET'S *rifle.*)

ANDREAS: NOT ON MY HIDE-A-BED. (*She fires. Everybody comes running.*)

DOWD: What's wrong? Where's Penny?

RED: (*From offstage.*) HEY! HEY! WHO'S SHOOTING? WHO'S AFTER MY BUICK?

PENNY: Everybody's awake?

DOWD: I woke up and she was gone!

ANDREAS: She ate my pillow.

PENNY: I couldn't find my shoe!

RED: (*Sitting on the hide-a-bed.*) Hey, sleepwalker. Was you sleepwalking to me? (*He comforts her.*) Pretty Penny. There.

DOWD: (*Extracting her from* RED.) You go back to bed, honey. I'll clean up. (RED *and* DOWD *help her up.* RED'S *hands move like magnets to her buttocks.*)

PENNY: Stranger house. Strange bed. I was hungry. I was so hungry. (*Pause.*) Nitey-night!

ALL FOUR: NITEY-NIGHT!

S c e n e 6

Dawn. SCARLET *aims her rifle in the direction of* RED'S *car.* RED *blocks it with his body.*

RED: HEY! PUT DOWN THAT RIFLE A MINUTE. I WANT TO ASK YOU A QUESTION.

SCARLET: I got it in my hands. Not my ears.

RED: You wasn't considering incapacitating the Buick, was you? (SCARLET *lowers her rifle.*) I want to ask you a question. What'd you do to Penny?

SCARLET: I didn't touch her.

RED: I'm thinking of driving her down to emergency. Down to the John C. Lincoln.

SCARLET: AIN'T LATIN AND RUBBER GLOVES GOING TO HEAL HER!

RED: Techy this morning. Put down that rifle. You mind what your daddy tells you. You do what he says. Don't you say no to your daddy. (SCARLET *aims the rifle at the Buick.*) No! No! Babydoll, no!

SCARLET: I thought we were going to go somewheres. Get lost somewheres together.

RED: It takes time to get lost.

SCARLET: YOU SAID ALL IT TOOK WAS A BUICK.

RED: I know what I said. I know.

SCARLET: You never meant to go noplace.

RED: That ain't so babydoll.

SCARLET: You know anybody wears a blue suit?

RED: Who with a blue suit?

SCARLET: Big guy. Nine, ten feet tall, wears a blue suit. You know him?

RED: No.

SCARLET: Because him and three other guys was looking over the Buick this morning.

RED: Was they carrying guns?

SCARLET: Course. Anybody wearing suits is either carrying guns or Bibles or both.

RED: Aw no. What was they doing to it. What was they doing to my Buick?

SCARLET: Jerking it off.

RED: I don't want you talking that way about the family car.

SCARLET: How should I know. I was standing there. You was sleeping in it.

RED: Aw no.

SCARLET: Alls I know is there's a nine or ten-foot guy wearing a blue suit looking over the Buick.

RED: Touching it?

SCARLET: They was touching your family car.

RED: Aw no. Maybe we better get going out of here.

SCARLET: I'm not going nowhere with you. You better push your family car into the reservoir.

RED: *(Whimpering.)* That's my car. That's my Buick Skylark car!

SCARLET: Half that car's mine. Half that's mine I want setting on the bottom of the San Carlos. (SCARLET *exits.* RED *punches the air she left behind.)*

RED: Only way that car sets on the bottom of the San Carlos is with me setting in it. No. I'm going to hide it. Me and the Buick will go lie low for awhile. Out onto the desert for awhile. *(He moves into the house.)* I'm going. *(He quickly, quietly gathers supplies. In his haste he leaves the refrigerator door open. The refrigerator light glares.)* Flashlight. Knife. Can opener. Fork. (ANDREAS *sits up in the hide-a-bed.)* Matches. Kerosene.

ANDREAS: Where's the picnic?

RED: What?

ANDREAS: Where are you going with matches and kerosene?

RED: Oh. Down to the Texaco.

ANDREAS: Going to blow it up?

RED: No.

ANDREAS: When you coming back?

RED: Twenty. Twenty-five.

ANDREAS: Texaco closes half the week.

RED: I better hurry then.

ANDREAS: This is the half it's closed.

RED: I'm going down there. I'm taking the car with me.

ANDREAS: You ain't leaving me alone with that child.

RED: Dowd's come home. *(Pause.)* I said I was going to the Texaco and I'm going to the Texaco. Have some dinner with the boys.

ANDREAS: You can't get out that easy. There's more to getting out than leaving. (RED *starts for the door.)* HOLD IT. (RED *stops.)* Walk out facing me. Your back has that permanent expression. Walk out facing me. (RED *exits backwards with slow, exaggerated steps. Once out, he makes a dash for the car.* ANDREAS *rises. She goes to the door. She suddenly notices the refrigerator staring at her.)* What are *you* staring at?

S c e n e   7

Following morning. Bright early sun. SCARLET *appears leading the blind-folded and bound* PENNY *by a rope.* PENNY *is a good sport. She is trying to enjoy herself but is overwhelmed by fatigue and her natural clumsiness.* SCARLET *carries a handmade knapsack containing the doll, the shoe, rubber snakes.*

PENNY: Children have a lot of energy. And imagination. They also have a lot of imagination. *(Pause.)* Slow down.

SCARLET: Can't.

PENNY: How much farther?

SCARLET: Little bit.

PENNY: Then it'll be your turn to be the captive.

SCARLET: You can't be the trapper because you don't know the way. JUMP!

PENNY: *(Jumping.)* What was that?

SCARLET: Pygmy cow.

PENNY: Incredible.

SCARLET: Watch out! Thousand foot drop on both sides. Careful. Careful. (SCARLET *winds the rope around* PENNY.) LOOK OUT! *(She pulls on the rope and* PENNY *spins out like a top. Both scream.)* That was close. Landslide.

PENNY: We should think about going back.

SCARLET: Uh-oh.

PENNY: Dowd likes me to be punctual.

SCARLET: Uh-oh.

PENNY: What?

SCARLET: Black Snoot.

PENNY: *(Looking up.)* Black Snoot?

SCARLET: Snake.

PENNY: *(Looking down; after a pause.)* Is it still there?

SCARLET: More of them. A family of Black Snoots.

PENNY: Do they see us?

SCARLET: More. Coming out of nowhere. Dropping out of the sky. Black Snoots raining all over. Scooting around. Pushing. Crawling on top of each other. Nothing but Black Snoots as far as you can see. (SCARLET *falls down.*)

PENNY: No. *(Pause.)* There couldn't be that many snakes.

SCARLET: *(Rising; jerking the rope.)* Let's go.

PENNY: Take it easy! Somebody could get hurt.

SCARLET: Move!

PENNY: Well, I just think we should go home now.

SCARLET: Hurry up.

PENNY: I can't have too much sun.

SCARLET: You don't even know the sun. You're Philadelphia. You ain't been introduced. You seen it from across the room. The sun in person will cook you up and eat you before you can say jack *rabbit.* You meet the sun up close it'll first stare you in the squinty eyes till they pop. Then you'll notice your tongue swelling. Your belly swelling. Your brain swelling. You insides swelling inside. Your outsides swelling outside, then BANG! You pop like popcorn!

PENNY: I'll bet you're a riot at parties.

SCARLET: No parties. Okay. Stop. We're there.

PENNY: Where? Where are we?

SCARLET: Where I took you. Where I do my talking.

PENNY: Well, why don't you talk a little and then we'll go home.

SCARLET: First I got a surprise.

PENNY: I don't like this.

SCARLET: Remember your shoe you lost? I found it. I found it for you.

PENNY: Where did you find it?

SCARLET: Right here. Where you left it.

PENNY: Where I left it?

SCARLET: When you was chasing rabbits.

PENNY: Oh.

SCARLET: Remember?

PENNY: Not really.

SCARLET: Now I got to surprise you some more.

PENNY: How long have we been out here?

SCARLET: Picture this good.

PENNY: It's getting hot.

SCARLET: Ma and Dowd had hot sex on the hide-a-bed and that's why he got out quick and that's why he's been downhill on sex ever since and that's why you got cats.

PENNY: That's not so!

SCARLET: His pecker konked out after that.

PENNY: That is a horrible thing to say.

SCARLET: You think it's horrible saying it, you try doing it. Poking that old pig. Your pecker'd konk out too.

PENNY: Scarlet. You don't have to invent awful stories to impress me. I like you. Dowd likes you, too. I like children. That's why I'm a schoolteacher. That's why—

SCARLET: SHUT UP.

PENNY: Do you know what we do to children who say that? We wash your mouths out with soap. That's what we do. (SCARLET *taps her stone and bone.*) What's that? What are you doing?

SCARLET: Dusting your shoe. It's dusty.

PENNY: Give it to me.

SCARLET: Want it?

PENNY: Yes.

SCARLET: Say please.

PENNY: Please.

SCARLET: Say pretty please.

PENNY: Pretty please.

SCARLET: (*She brushes* PENNY'S *outstretched hand with the bone.*) Naw. You don't want shoes. You're a desert dweller now, Mammal of the Southwest. Fast runner. Loose skinned. Flat skulled. Untouchable.

PENNY: I want the shoe.

SCARLET: You live off rabbits and kangaroo rats. You dig them out with your fingers. With your claws.

PENNY: I WANT MY SHOE.

SCARLET: Your name is Listener. Eye-killer.

PENNY: It's mine and I want it. (SCARLET *pounds the stone with the bone.*) I WANT IT. I WANT MY SHOE.

SCARLET: Okay. I'll give it to you. *(Pause.)* Put out your paw. (PENNY *slides her foot forward.* SCARLET *smashes the* PENNY-*doll with a large rock.* PENNY *opens her mouth. No sound comes out.* SCARLET *rises.*) Come on over, sun! I got somebody I want you to meet!

S c e n e   8

Later the same morning. DOWD *is practicing casting with his Popeil Pocket Fisherman.* ANDREAS *sits on the porch eating an apple.*

ANDREAS: Hot enough for you?

DOWD: Any hotter the fish won't bite.

ANDREAS: Looks like another scorcher.

DOWD: They go down too deep. Down where it's dark and cool.

ANDREAS: Hot enough to fry meat.

DOWD: Can't get to them. They disappear.

ANDREAS: This is the hot month. The hot time of the year.

DOWD: I forgot how hot it got.

ANDREAS: But you remember hot now.

DOWD: It's a different kind of heat.

ANDREAS: This is your *hot* heat.

DOWD: Dry heat.

ANDREAS: No humidity.

DOWD: It's hot.

ANDREAS: No two ways about it. *(Pause.)* I THINK YOU GOT A BITE! *(Pause.)* Just kidding. Heat's got to my brain. Best if you don't move. Best if you keep still. Keep the hot blood low. You never used to mind it. Like you was part Frigidaire.

DOWD: I mind it now.

ANDREAS: Must of broke. Must of lost your freon. *(Pause.)* Did you miss me?

DOWD: No.

ANDREAS: Well, I missed you. You cut a hole so big in my brain the wind blows through it.

DOWD: I was your big joke. So I left.

ANDREAS: Where to? What doing?

DOWD: Hitched a twelve-year ride. Joined up.

ANDREAS: The army?

DOWD: The human race.

ANDREAS: DON'T YOU SASS ME. I AM STILL YOUR MOTHER. NOT SOME.

DOWD: You have never been a mother.

ANDREAS: *(Slightly pleased.)* There may be some truth to that.

DOWD: Got another apple?

ANDREAS: Got this one. *(Tosses it to him.)* Nature's toothbrush. *(Pause.)* Dowd and Penny. Going fishing. Going in a boat.

DOWD: That's right.

ANDREAS: Everybody goes. In a car. In a boat. Not me. Can't drive a house. I stick around all day like Goodwill underpants.

DOWD: Want to try it?

ANDREAS: What?

DOWD: My Popeil Pocket Fisherman. Want to try it? *(He gives her his Popeil Pocket Fisherman.)*

ANDREAS: Me?

DOWD: Sure. It's all in the wrist. Push that little button and let her rip. That's all there is to it. A good Popeil man can put it anywhere. Get the feel of it. Relax. Okay, let her rip.

ANDREAS: *(After letting her rip.)* Now what?

DOWD: What you want to do is call the fish. Go ahead. Here fish.

ANDREAS: Here fish. *(She continues calling.)*

DOWD: Keep it up. There's a big fat lazy catfish sleeping on the bottom or watching TV. He hears you calling. He can't believe his ears. He's mesmerized by the sweetness of that voice. Slowly, in a fish trance, he rises toward the surface. You feel a slight tug as he brushes the hook, but you don't react. You're disinterested. You act like you don't want him. This drives him crazy. He can't think of anything else. He circles back. He sends out a row of bubbles like a string of pearls. His hackles quiver. You start reeling in the line. You pretend to think he's lost his appetite. But you know he hasn't. You know he wants it. He wants it so bad. He rushes the bait. STRIKE. *(Pause. He goes to the bucket of water. He takes off his shirt. He splashes himself. He stands still.)* You pull him in. You check to see how far he's taken the hook. You have to pull out half his guts to remove it. You don't want the mess. You snip the line. You throw him back. *(Pause.)* Why'd you throw him back?

ANDREAS: Ain't you going to dry off?

DOWD: Too hot.

ANDREAS: Ain't you going to put on your shirt?

DOWD: Too wet.

ANDREAS: YOU PUT ON YOUR SON-OF-A-BITCH SHIRT. THIS AIN'T PARIS FRANCE. (DOWD *puts on his shirt.* SCARLET *enters running, out of breath, wound up tight. She bounces off* DOWD *and runs back to him. She's all energy and purpose.)*

DOWD: WHOA!

SCARLET: *(Fast and laughing.)* Penny's changed her mind! She's playing biology in the desert! She said for me to tell you I should go fishing with you! She said for you not to worry! She said she didn't care if we was gone all day!

DOWD: She's out there in this heat?

SCARLET: I give her some hot tips! She said she'd meet us back at the house!

DOWD: Okay, sport. Get your gear. (SCARLET *runs into the house.)*

ANDREAS: Ever since you come she's been a Demolition Derby. You got her all revved up. (SCARLET *runs back out with her hat.)*

SCARLET: I'M GOING TO BRING MY CRITTER. *(She runs back into the house.)*

ANDREAS: THIS AIN'T NO RACE TRACK. She's trouble.

DOWD: I know how to handle kids. First you get their attention. Then you wear them out.

ANDREAS: She's a trapper and a healer. She traps animals, fixes them up, lets them go. An animal that's been mended, been fixed up by somebody, has seen the last of freedom. (SCARLET *runs out with her bag.*) There she is. Your teeny tiny little baby sweet sister.

SCARLET: The fish are getting antsy.

DOWD: Let's get this show on the road. You get the pan hot. We're going to catch our limit.

ANDREAS: Like I was saying. I'd love to come along but I got other things. Like I said to Red when he asked me to come down to the Texaco with him. Now, what am I going to do at the Texaco, I said.

SCARLET: Don't have to go fishing to hear a fish *story. (They exit.)*

S c e n e   9

Late afternoon of the same day. Outside. DOWD *and* SCARLET *clean fish near the house. Iridescent scales fly. They work awhile in silence.*

SCARLET: I was named after Scarlet O'Hara.

DOWD: It fits.

SCARLET: Frankly, my dear, I don't give a damn. That's from the book, *Gone With the Wind.*

DOWD: So, you read it.

SCARLET: Read that page. *(Pauses.)* You think I'm ugly.

DOWD: Don't be silly.

SCARLET: You never look at me.

DOWD: That's because you're so ugly.

SCARLET: Yeah? Well any kid *you* had would be crazy.

DOWD: Yeah?

SCARLET: And stupid.

DOWD: Yeah?

SCARLET: And mean.

DOWD: Yeah?

SCARLET: AND ugly.

DOWD: Is that so.

SCARLET: Just like you.

DOWD: Is that so.

SCARLET: That's so all right. *(Pause.)* Tomorrow I'll take you up to a place where the fish leap right up out of the water right up into your arms scaled clean and ready to eat.

DOWD: You should have taken me there today.

SCARLET: I didn't know if I liked you or not. *(Pause.)* These fish? They got no bones neither. Because they're so young.

DOWD: Jellyfish.

SCARLET: Huh-uh. No jellofish in the San Carlos. Mystery fish. They got squirmy no-bone bodies. *(Pause.)* Do you remember being born?

DOWD: Nobody remembers being born.

SCARLET: I do.

DOWD: Nobody but you. *(Drawing with her stick,* SCARLET *illustrates her story in the sand and in the air.)*

SCARLET: I blame my whole life on that hide-a-bed. I was produced on it after one night of hot sex. Who knows. Ma tried to get rid of me but I was too serious about living. She took ice showers and sat out late waiting for the chill. She beat me with her fist while I was still inside her and that's why she can't lay a hand on me now. There was this creep had pink hair and one eye name of Danny Dog used to drive Red around before he worked for a living. This one eye of his was glass. Just some old marble he'd stuck in. He didn't have no brakes so he'd pick Red up by punching it from the road, coasting to the house, sliding into a three-sixty, swinging Red into the rear, then gunning it fast back to the road. One day he gunned it so hard his marble eye popped out and he drove up onto the porch. Ma come running out screaming and hollering all pooched out with me inside her. HEY YOU WHAT ARE YOU UP TO YOU GO ON HOME NOW, Ma said. Danny Dog pointed to the eye in the palm of his hand. Ma give the pickup a shove. Danny Dog beat it to the road without a look back. Right then. When she was least expecting me, I popped out like Danny Dog's eyeball. Ma fell down kicking and cussing with me still hooked up to her. I hated her already to I bit her.

I bit her and I bit her. She started running. She ran dragging me behind her
all the way to Phoenix. You want to know what happened to my neck. That's
what happened to my neck. She ran and I flew out behind. She felt like
nothing by then but she was driven driven driven. She ran up the front steps
of a man's house. Man's name was Keeper. Sign on the porch said SCISSORS
SHARPENED. Ma rang the bell. I bit her feet. She pulled on the front door.
She pulled so hard the whole house came off in her hand. That's all I remember.

DOWD: Mom says you came packed in a box.

SCARLET: That's *her* story. Red says I come naturally deformed to hold a
rifle. That's his story.

DOWD: What's yours?

SCARLET: I told you. *(Pause.)* You think I'm rotten.

DOWD: I don't think you're rotten. I think you're dramatic.

SCARLET: I'd ruther be rotten. When you're rotten you can shove a fish down
somebody's THROAT. When you're dramatic you have to eat it yourself.

DOWD: Is that so.

SCARLET: That's so all right.

DOWD: I'll show you how so that is. *(He picks up a fish head and attempts
to shove it down* SCARLET'S *throat.)* SO! SO! SO! SO! SO! (SCARLET *frees
herself. She goes after* DOWD *with a fish head in one hand and a scaling
knife in the other.)*

SCARLET: I got a whole world inside me wants to be born, Dowd. Bite it.
(She bites the fish.)

DOWD: That's disgusting.

SCARLET: It's not disgusting. It's dramatic. Bite it. *(She slices the air with
the knife.)* Bite it bite it bite it bite it bite it. *(She nicks his face.)*

DOWD: HEY!

SCARLET: Scairdy cat! *(She runs out of reach, laughing. Puts her knife in
her belt-pouch. Challenges him.)*

DOWD: Me? I'm a coach! Give me the knife before you hurt somebody. *(He
moves cautiously toward her. She stays just out of reach. He lunges at her.
They fight. Finally,* DOWD *pins her and straddles her. She giggles.* DOWD
holds on until she seems to give up. He releases her.) I'm not playing

anymore. *(In one motion,* SCARLET *yanks him back down by the neck of his shirt and applies the knife to his neck. She laughs.)*

SCARLET: I never was.

DOWD: So, put down the knife.

SCARLET: I will. After.

DOWD: After what?

SCARLET: A couple of things. Kiss me. Do it.

DOWD: Christ. Okay. *(He pecks her forehead.)*

SCARLET: Lips.

DOWD: Okay. *(He pecks her lips.)*

SCARLET: Harder. And better.

DOWD: What do you say we call it a day little doggie.

SCARLET: Open your mouth. *(She applies pressure.)* Open it. *(He does.* SCARLET *kisses him thoroughly.)*

DOWD: There. Finished? Up we go.

SCARLET: I said a couple things. Take off my shirt.

DOWD: You're a little.

SCARLET: Take off my shirt I said. So. Take off my shirt. Knives bite. Tits don't.

DOWD: Little sis. You don't have any tits.

SCARLET: Got a knife. *(She begins unbuttoning her shirt.)* There's a tiny part of you wants to do it. The fourth part of you wants to do it.

DOWD: Wouldn't you rather play softball?

SCARLET: Don't give me words. *(Pause.)* You think I'm ugly.

DOWD: I think you're a kid.

SCARLET: Is that so.

DOWD: That's so all right.

SCARLET: I'll show you how so that is. *(She rolls on top of him. She pulls herself away. Pause. He pulls her to him.)*

Scene 10

Late afternoon of the same day. ANDREAS *lights the gas stove and pours oil in a frying pan.* PENNY *crawls on. She is brilliant red. Redder than anyone would believe possible. Her skin should make people wince to look at it. This is an Arizona desert high noon sunburn. Her clothes are torn and filthy from her long crawl home.*

PENNY: YOO HOO!

ANDREAS: Who's there?

PENNY: It's me. Penny.

ANDREAS: Penny?

PENNY: Down here.

ANDREAS: Little shorter than I remembered.

PENNY: I'm thirsty. It's been a long day. I'm beat. (ANDREAS *gets her a glass of water.*) Just put it down in front of me. (PENNY *laps the water with her tongue.*)

ANDREAS: I could put it in a bowl if you want. *(She fills a bowl with water.)* Where've you been?

PENNY: Looking for my shoe.

ANDREAS: On the desert?

PENNY: That's where I left it. When I was chasing rabbits.

ANDREAS: You brain's still cooking.

PENNY: I fell down. Scarlet was eaten by Black Snoots.

ANDREAS: Nothing's going to eat Scarlet. They'd puke.

PENNY: I couldn't find my way back.

ANDREAS: *(Puts the bowl in front of* PENNY.) Here you go.

PENNY: DO YOU SEE IT?

ANDREAS: What?

PENNY: I was followed. (ANDREAS *crosses to door.*)

ANDREAS: There's nobody there.

PENNY: I can hear it. Same as before. Same quiet. Perfectly quiet. No sounds. And then I see it!

ANDREAS: YOUR SHOE?

PENNY: THE SUN! ZOOMING THE AIR. BUZZING MY HEAD. CRASH LANDING ON MY FACE. *(She rolls over.)* For a long time I just lay there. Where I fell down. Thinking about the way things were going. I thought I could stay there indefinitely. Not moving. But after awhile my clothes got hot. Fortunately I remembered reading about a woman whose car ran out of gas on the desert. She was a survivor. She was from Dayton. She drank water from her radiator and when that ran out she drank her body fluids. Her blood and urine. Someone found her. She was never the same. I didn't have a radiator but I knew it was cooler just beneath the surface. I started digging. Slowly at first. Then faster and faster. Hot sand to cool sand. I was digging like crazy. My hands were a blur. I had cartoon hands. The hole they were digging got bigger and bigger and deeper and deeper. My hands were still digging but I was tired so I crawled in and went to sleep. In my sleep I see the hide-a-bed and go to sleep. I'm sleeping in my sleep. While I'm sleeping I hear it. The sun comes crashing in. Sinking on top of me. I pretend not to notice. I lay perfectly still. I don't move. I don't even breathe. And then it burns into me. Its tongue pierces my belly. Burning things all the way up to my brain. Pushing through my eyesockets. I'm looking at the sun with its own tongue!

ANDREAS: *(Pushing* PENNY's *head into the bowl.)* Dunk!

PENNY: *(Gasping for breath.)* I know what I'm talking about. My fingers are still sore from digging.

ANDREAS: You're going to want to squeeze out of your skin later on. I know this.

PENNY: Don't be surprised if I have little hot sunbabies.

ANDREAS: It don't seem bad now, but you wait. This kind of burn only gets worse. You don't stop cooking, even in the dark. Sun fever's going to take you places you've never been. You see a shape moving at you. You don't know what to make of it. Maybe you recognize it, maybe you don't. Maybe you're related to it. Maybe not. You pull it on top of you and hope not. It don't matter. You don't know when you've had too much till it's too late. All the hurt comes later. Your skin explodes. That's what's left. Exploding skin. Pretty soon you're unrecognizable. I've seen this first hand. *(She cups her hands and dips them into the water.)* I know what to do for you. I understand it. I been there myself. I can give you what you need. *(She lifts her hands to* PENNY's *face.* PENNY *drinks.)* That's it. That's it. (DOWD *enters, cocky, with* SCARLET *on his back and fish in his hands.)*

DOWD: *(Singing, laughing, joking.)* OH, BASS AND CRAPPIES AND BLUEGILL AND CATFISH! IT WAS LIKE STANDING AT A FISH COUNTER. I'LL TAKE ONE

OF THOSE. AND ONE OF THOSE. ONE OF THOSE AND ONE OF THOSE. I GOT A
FLATHEAD ON MY LINE THAT WAS SO BIG IT PULLED ME OUT OF THE BOAT.
I CUT IT LOOSE AND IT SWAM BACK! (DOWD *dances into the house with*
SCARLET *singing raucously. They see* PENNY. SCARLET *stops midsong.* DOWD
and PENNY *look at each other for a long time.*) Who. Is. This?

PENNY: I'm incognito!

DOWD: I brought you some fish.

SCARLET: SHE'S HOT! SHE'S A SCORCHER!

ANDREAS: KEEP AWAY.

SCARLET: Tell her, Dowd. Tell her I love you and you love me back because
you do else you wouldn't of smiled so much in the boat. *(She skips into her
room, picking up her song where she left off.)*

ANDREAS: I got the pan hot. But it sounds like fish are frying in somebody's
pants. (DOWD *edges toward* PENNY.) Treat her easy. She don't feel too
good.

DOWD: How's it going? Hey, honey? How's it going? *(Pause.)* It's your
fisherman, Penny.

ANDREAS: Be gentle with her. She's scairt. She's scairt.

DOWD: It's your fisherman, Penny. Your old fisherman's home.

PENNY: DON'T COME IN HERE!

ANDREAS: See what I mean?

DOWD: What's the matter with her?

ANDREAS: She might not recognize you. The sun punched her lights out.
(DOWD *moves in on* PENNY *too quickly.* PENNY *barks.)*

DOWD: What did you say?

PENNY: *(Holding her runaway throat.)* I don't know!

ANDREAS: Penny's got a vagueness about her today.

DOWD: Penny?

PENNY: Grrrrrrrrr.

DOWD: It's your Dowd, Penny.

ANDREAS: She won't bite. I don't think she'll bite. You got to move slow.
Let her know she trusts you.

DOWD: What's going on here? What did you do to her?

ANDREAS: Don't bark up *my* tree.

DOWD: Honey? Honey, what do you say. Sweetheart? Let's pack up the Toyota and get ourselves out of here. What do you think? This is no place for us. For people like us. What do you say, Penny. (PENNY *barks.*) She's barking. WHY IS MY WIFE BARKING? WILL SOMEBODY PLEASE EXPLAIN THAT TO ME? (PENNY *continues barking.*) Stop it. STOP IT. PENNY. YOU ARE *FROM* PHILADELPHIA. (*He gathers her up in his arms. She barks in great pain.*) I told you we shouldn't come here. I told you it was no good. I told you nothing we found here was going to help. Come on. Come on. I'll get you into the car.

ANDREAS: YOU CAN'T TAKE HER AWAY FROM HERE NOW. I'M FAMILIAR WITH THE SITUATION. I CAN TAKE CARE OF HER. I GOT HOME REMEDIES.

DOWD: You're in my way. (*He pushes past her and exits. She runs to the door.*)

ANDREAS: YOU THINK YOU CAN WALK IN AND WALK OUT AGAIN LEAVING YOUR MESS TO CLEAN UP AFTER ITSELF. THEY'RE LEAVING ME! THEY'RE GONE! (SCARLET *runs out of her room carrying her bag.*)

SCARLET: I'M PACKED!

ANDREAS: YOU GET THAT STINKING THING OUT OF HERE.

SCARLET: EVERYTHING THAT'S MINE THAT'S IMPORTANT IS IN THIS BAG. WHERE IS HE? DOWD? WAIT FOR ME!

DOWD: (*Comes back on with* PENNY *still in his arms whimpering.*) Where are the keys?

ANDREAS: Give her to me! Give me my poor baby!

DOWD: (*Holding onto* PENNY.) They're not in the car.

SCARLET: Toyota keys? (*She jangles* DOWD'S *keys at arm's length.* DOWD *puts* PENNY *into* ANDREAS'S *arms.* ANDREAS *cradles* PENNY *on the porch.* DOWD *goes in.*)

DOWD: Hey. Come on, knucklehead. Come on, sweetheart. Scarlet.

SCARLET: I thought I was going away with you.

DOWD: I got to go now. I got to go, babydoll.

SCARLET: See, Red was going to take me somewheres but he went there by himself. So, I'm going away with you.

DOWD: Give me the keys, little buddy.

SCARLET: You're all I got.

DOWD: Scarlet.

SCARLET: I got to have you.

DOWD: I've been through this before. You and your mother. You're no different. You're both the same.

SCARLET: Just like you. You think you're a whole nother breed of dog but you ain't.

DOWD: Now, I live in the city. Now, I work. Now, I jog in the park. Now, I have regular dental checkups. Every morning my trash disappears.

SCARLET: The world that's inside me is yours too.

DOWD: You can have it. I don't want it.

SCARLET: There's places you ain't explored. You ain't been nowhere yet. *(She wraps herself around him. He struggles to peel her off.)*

DOWD: NO THANKS. I'M A STRANGER HERE. I'M ON MY WAY OUT. *(He squeezes her neck until she falls off of him.)*

SCARLET: Please. Please. Please. Please. Please. (DOWD *tries to pry the keys out of her hand. She bites him.)*

DOWD: SHIT! SHIT! *(Pause.)* I'm bleeding. You broke the skin. I'm bleeding.

SCARLET: WHAT ABOUT ME?

DOWD: Look what you did with your rabid little mouth.

SCARLET: See, Batface told me nobody liked me yet because there was this one certain somebody that was going to like me enough for the whole world. That this somebody had picked me. That he was coming. First, she said, he might come as a critter. Might be a bobcat. Might be a coyote. Might be a badger. Might be a wild dog. Me and her used to set out nights waiting.

DOWD: SHE WAS A FRUITCAKE. *(Pause.)* Look. Do yourself a favor. Get this straight. I didn't come here for you. Get it through your skull. I wasn't sent. I don't want you. I don't even like you. So get it straight. The old lady made it up. There's nobody coming. (SCARLET *screams over* DOWD's *voice.)* THERE'S NOBODY COMING. SHE MADE IT UP. *(Pause.)* Look at you. Look at yourself. What would I want with you? Now. Give me the keys.

SCARLET: No, she didn't. She didn't make it up.

DOWD: GIVE ME THE KEYS.

SCARLET: RIP MY ARM OFF.

DOWD: I'll do it. I will do it. (SCARLET *moves over to the stove.*) I mean it.

SCARLET: I hate you.

DOWD: Hand them over. (SCARLET *tosses the keys in the pan of frying fish.*)

SCARLET: I HATE YOU. (*She pushes her hand into the hot pan and holds it there, never taking her eyes off* DOWD.) I HATE YOU. I HATE YOU DOWD PEWSY. (*She goes to* DOWD *holding her arm stiff and brands his face with her burning palm.*) YOU'RE MINE. (*He falls. She falls with him. Holds on tight. Cries.* RED *enters badly beaten.*)

RED: Looks like you and your big brother got real tight real quick. Good. That's good. That's what family's for. I lost the Buick. I need to set down someplace. (*He falls flat.*)

Scene II

Later that night. ANDREAS *props* PENNY *up on the kitchen table. She sloshes cool white milk from a half-gallon container over* PENNY's *red hot limbs.*

ANDREAS: (*Joyfully.*) This is more like it! Don't it feel good? Don't it take the sting out? I picked this technique up from Red's ma. She had a way with the sick. (*She gulps milk from the carton.*) Nothing like a mother's milk, she'd say. MOON BLOOD, she called it. AIN'T LATIN AND RUBBER GLOVES GOING TO HEAL YOU, she'd say. (*She drinks and pours freely.*) Do you like it? If you like it, blink your eyes. SHE LIKES IT! (*She dumps the remaining milk over* PENNY.) I'm good at this. Mothering things that ain't related to me. I took care of a bunch of runts once. Lady in Heber dropped a litter of five. Didn't know what to do with them. Couldn't think up names for them all neither. She gave two of them names and the rest numbers. There was Bob. There was Bob Junior. And there was Three, Four and Five. (ANDREAS *gathers* PENNY *up in her arms.*) I'll do this to you each and every night before I put you to bed. Would you like that? SHE LIKES IT! And when I tuck you in, I'll tell you my other secrets. Do you like me? Do you like me? I BELIEVE SHE LIKES ME! I BELIEVE SHE DOES!

Scene 12

A few moments later. DOWD *and* RED *are outside.* RED *chugs beers. He would chug two at once if he could.* DOWD *is concentrated, silent, cool desperation.*

RED: SO. (RED *laughs.*) So, it come down to it being between him or me. (RED *laughs.*) Big old Bluesuit. Nine feet tall. I thought I was a dead man. OH! he wanted that car. No other car would do. It was the interior he couldn't live without. Soft seats. Beige. *(He laughs and opens a beer.)* Him and them others found me out there nowhere where I knew where I was. They recommended I get out of the car and lay down someplace more comfortable. But. As I am scooting my ass across the seat the goddamn can opener I got in my back pocket catches and RIIIIIIP! I bring the interior to the exterior. When I hear this I turn around I see about a million dollar bills growing up out of the beige seat and when I see this my eyes light up and when my eyes light up big old nine-foot Bluesuit grabs me by my can opener and my balls and he goes, CLOSE YOUR EYES CLOSE THEM. ONLY WAY I WANT YOUR EYES OPEN IS IF I OPEN THEM WITH THIS. And he graaaaazes my eyelids with my can opener. Shit. So. Him and the boys sock me around and then they call a meeting to discuss what they are going to do with my remains. But while they are discussing, I douse them and the Buick with kerosene and BOOOOM! Them and the Buick have seen the world. (RED *laughs.*) Guy that give me the Buick name of Keeper is dead. Ice pick. Now the thing about ice picks is they leave no hole. *(He laughs.)* If he wasn't dead already I'd kill him. *(Pause.)* No strings, my ass. Even exchange, my ass. *(He laughs.)* It was a bad situation that went worse. *(He laughs.)* A man's luck just goes.

DOWD: What happened to it?

RED: What?

DOWD: The Buick.

RED: Oh, set too long in the sun. Evaporated. *(Pause.)* It was repossessed. *(Long pause.)* You are looking at a man without a car. (RED *sobs uncontrollably.*) Where's Andreas? ANDREAS? Where is she in my time of need? *(Pause.)* Plenty of guys they see the world. Don't make them no happier. I'm home. Here I am. No reason to go nowhere. *(Pause.)* ANDREAS! *(Pause.)* Too bad you're going off.

DOWD: Well, you know. The Grand Canyon.

RED: THE GRAND CANYON! *(He breaks wind.)* The Grand Canyon's nothing. You're paying for a name.

DOWD: I've never seen it.

RED: You've seen the Statue of Liberty, ain't you? The Grand Canyon is zip after the Statue of fucking Liberty. That big arm. Holding up that big whaddayacallit. I couldn't mind crawling up into her. But the Grand Canyon! *(He breaks wind again.)* Little string of river. Bunch of women in muu-muus. Course, I always figured on seeing it someday. You can't live nowhere forever and never see the Grand Canyon. (SCARLET *enters.)* There's my babydoll. *(She ignores* RED *and goes to where* DOWD *is sitting.)* Come over here a minute. Your daddy's home.

SCARLET: *(Without looking at him.)* I thought you was never coming back, Red.

RED: Come on over to your d-a-d-d-y, Daddy. (SCARLET *straddles* DOWD's *shoulders.* DOWD *remains impassive.)* Oh. Is that it? *(Pause.)* Things have been reorganizing themselves around here while I was gone. *(He opens a beer.* SCARLET *struts into the house.)* Have a beer, son.

DOWD: Don't want one, dad.

RED: Have one.

DOWD: Don't want one.

RED: Your pucker string's showing. (RED *laughs. He punches the air around* DOWD's *face.* DOWD *doesn't move.)* Come on, son. Come on. Come on. Come on. Hey! You must be driving these women nuts you being a neutered bull like Penny says. Have to take you down to the Pancake house. Get you some pancake therapy.

DOWD: You never had a pancake girl.

RED: I'll knock your goddamn nose off.

DOWD: You never even had a pancake.

RED: I'll send your nose to the moon. *(He offers* DOWD *an arm wrestle arm.)* Always was a whus.

DOWD: You want it?

RED: A whus. And a mama's boy.

DOWD: Scarlet and I went fishing. *(He and* RED *arm wrestle.)*

RED: A whus. A mama's boy. And a fairy.

DOWD: She made me an offer.

RED: A whus. A mama's boy. A fairy. And a BOOGE-WAH.

DOWD: Something.

RED: *(Veins popping, losing.)* A whus. A mama's boy. Wait. A whus. A whus. A fairy.

DOWD: Something exceptional.

RED: Wait. A whus. A whus. (DOWD *wins.*)

DOWD: How could I refuse? *(He rises.)* Like I said, Dad. I don't want a beer.

RED: You know what you are? YOU ARE THE SHIT ON MY SHORTHAIRS. *(He yells into* DOWD'S *back.)* DO YOU KNOW WHAT IT SAYS IN THE BIBLE ABOUT FUCKING YOUR OWN SISTER? It says DON'T.

DOWD: What does it say, Dad?

RED: YOU STAY OUT OF THIS.

DOWD: What does it say, Dad, about a man who couldn't find his butt with both hands in broad daylight. (RED *dives at* DOWD'S *knees. They fight. When* DOWD *seems to be winning,* RED *runs into the house, whimpering.* DOWD *follows him and pummels him into the hide-a-bed. He carries him by the seat of his pants to the stove and, using* RED'S *head as a battering ram, rams him into the oven door repeatedly. They both collapse.* RED *crawls to the refrigerator, opens it, and hollers from inside. He emerges, frothing beer in hand.)*

RED: Lord I missed your Mama and her turkey meat arms. *(He sobs. As he tells his story he finds it increasingly sad and his sobs increase proportionately until he is wailing pathetically. He finds himself embracing himself, clinging to himself, weeping in his own lonely arms.)* There's noplace like the home. No sir. Plenty of guys they see the world. Don't make them no happier. I'm home. Here I am. No reason to go nowhere. *(Pause.)* Naw. I never squoze no pancake girls. I went down there is all. One time. It was one time I went down there and I ordered my usual. One of the girls, she brung it over. She set the plate down in front of me and I couldn't help it. I started crying to beat the band. I was bawling like a baby into my usual. So she. This waitress. She put both her arms around me. That's all. She put her arms around me. *(Pause. He looks at* DOWD *who is still lying face down.)* 'Course, you done it right, son. You done it exactly right. What I *would* of done. You know, I never have been east of the Southwest. Never have. Stuck right here. I don't move. You move. I pretend I'm moving. You done it right.

DOWD: *(Not moving.)* I move.

RED: You move.

Scene 13

Middle of the same night. Inside, ANDREAS *sits on the hide-a-bed with* PENNY *in her arms. Outside,* SCARLET *draws forms in the sand, slowly, with her foot. She wears a boxshaped no color dress. It is in no way beautiful. She occasionally spins experimentally.* DOWD *comes out of* SCARLET'S *room carrying his overnight case. He moves through the house without looking at* PENNY *and* ANDREAS. *He walks down the steps, off the porch and is heading in the direction of his car when he sees* SCARLET.

DOWD: *(Nervous; tight-voiced.)* Who is this girl? Who's this pretty, dressy girl?

SCARLET: It's me.

DOWD: What are you doing out here?

SCARLET: Waiting.

DOWD: Waiting for what?

SCARLET: What I wait for. Nothing. *(She does a spin.)* Red's took your car.

DOWD: I'll walk. *(He sits on the porch.)*

SCARLET: Want to hear something sickening?

DOWD: Sure.

SCARLET: You're my pa. *(Long pause.)*

DOWD: Nice night. *(Pause.)* You don't get stars like this in the city. Like they're all racing down at you. Sometimes at home we used to sit in the yard. We have a yard. It's small. Well, we share it. But sometimes we sit out there, not talking or anything. Just looking up. I keep seeing myself back there. Not immediately. I'll go to some places first. But I keep seeing myself in that yard.

SCARLET: You staged an event. I'm the souvenir *(She does a spin.)*

DOWD: Is that a true story?

SCARLET: Scooch down. I'll show you. Close your eyes. *(She pulls his face into hers.)* Open them up. What do you see?

DOWD: An eye.

SCARLET: How many?

DOWD: One.

SCARLET: That's right. You see one. I see one. Your eye. My eye. Two eyes. One face. My face is you. See it?

DOWD: *(Without emotion.)* I see it.

SCARLET: Remember that fishing place where the fish leap right up out of the water? I'm going to take you there.

DOWD: Is that so?

SCARLET: Shhhhhhh. Put your ear against the top of my head. *(She pulls his ear down onto the top of her head. She presses his head into the top of hers.)* There. Listen. Everything you hear that comes off the top of my head is the truth. Are you listening, Dowd? I am going to be with you forever. Where you are, I am going to be. Hear it? Saying you. And me. And me. And you. And you and me and me and you and you and me and me and you and. (SCARLET *rises.* DOWD *stays very still.* SCARLET *draws with her hand in the sand. She draws faster and faster. She draws in the air. Neither of them makes a sound. She draws her whole life in the air. She hoots for joy and throws herself into a full throttle spin.)*

END

PAINTING CHURCHES

Tina Howe

Painting Churches was first produced by The Second Stage in 1983 under the direction of Carole Rothman. It moved to the Lamb's Theater the following year, once again under Rothman's direction. This production was presented by Elizabeth I. McCann, Nelle Nugent, Ray Larsen, Lee Guber, and Shelly Gross.

Painting Churches won an Outer Critics Circle Award, an Obie, and a Rosamond Gilder Award. The play was televised on *American Playhouse* in 1986 under the direction of Jack O'Brien.

Why on earth does a person become a playwright? In my case it was because I was so tall and goofy-looking as a child, and because of Aunt Helen, my father's hilarious sister, who was a monologist on the order of Ruth Draper. She performed at the White House, the Blue Angel, and at ladies' clubs all across the country. Helen Howe and I had the exact same face. I mean, *identical*—the same wide mouth and the same deep-set blue eyes. It was spooky—except she was 4 foot 11 inches and I was almost 6 feet tall. Well, you can imagine, here I was, this enormous ungainly girl yearning to be accepted, and here was my tiny twin Aunt Helen cracking them up from coast to coast. So I decided to become a mimic like her. It's the ultimate defense: Get them to laugh *with* you before they laugh *at* you. So all through school and college I was the class clown. In fact, I almost signed up to study with the great mime Etienne Decroux. But his students were all beautiful dancers, not baggy clowns, so I retreated in panic.

What turned me around was writing a little one-act play my senior year at Sarah Lawrence. If I was too awkward to get up on stage, I'd have others do it in my stead. When the audience burst into applause at the end of the show and started yelling, "Author, author," I was hooked.

People often ask me where my characters come from. This is a pathetic confession, but they're simply all the voices I yearn to perform if only I had the talent.

TINA HOWE
1990

Characters

FANNY SEDGWICK CHURCH, a Bostonian from a fine old family, in her
sixties.
GARDNER CHURCH, her husband, an eminent New England poet from a
finer family, in his seventies.
MARGARET CHURCH (MAGS), their daughter, a painter, in her early thir-
ties.

Time

Several years ago.

Place

Boston, Massachusetts.

ACT ONE
Scene 1

The living room of the Churches' townhouse on Beacon Hill one week before everything will be moved to Cape Cod. Empty packing cartons line the room and all the furniture has been tagged with brightly colored markers. At first glance it looks like any discreet Boston interior, but on closer scrutiny one notices a certain flamboyance. Oddities from secondhand stores are mixed in with the fine old furniture, and exotic handmade curios vie with tasteful family objets d'art. What makes the room remarkable, though, is the play of light that pours through three soaring arched windows. At one hour it's hard edged and brilliant; the next, it's dappled and yielding. It transforms whatever it touches, giving the room a distinct feeling of unreality. It's several years ago, a bright spring morning.

FANNY is sitting on the sofa, wrapping a valuable old silver coffee service. She's wearing a worn bathrobe and fashionable hat. As she works, she makes a list of everything on a yellow legal pad. Gardner can be heard typing in his study down the hall.

FANNY *(Picks up a coffee pot)*: God, this is good-looking! I'd forgotten how handsome Mama's old silver was! It's probably worth a fortune. It certainly weighs enough! *(Calling)* GARRRRRRRRRRRRRRRRRRRDNERRRRRRRRRRRRR? . . . Well, it should bring us a pretty penny, that's for sure: *(Wraps it, places it in a carton, and then picks up the tray that goes with it. She holds it up like a mirror and adjusts her hat. Louder in another register)* OH, GARRRRRRRRRRRRRRRRRRRDNERRRRR?

(GARDNER continues typing. She then reaches for a small box and opens it with reverence) Grandma's Paul Revere teaspoons! . . . *(She takes out several and fondles them)* I don't care how desperate things get, these will never go! One has to maintain some standards! *(She writes on her list)* Grandma's Paul Revere teaspoons, Cotuit! WASN'T IT THE AMERICAN WING OF THE METROPOLITAN MUSEUM OF ART THAT WANTED GRANDMA'S PAUL REVERE TEASPOONS SO BADLY? . . . *(She looks at her reflection in the tray again)* This is a very good-looking hat, if I do say so. I was awfully smart to grab it up. *(Silence)*

DON'T YOU REMEMBER A DISTINGUISHED-LOOKING MAN COMING TO THE HOUSE AND OFFERING US FIFTY THOUSAND DOLLARS FOR GRANDMA'S PAUL REVERE TEASPOONS? . . . HE HAD ON THESE MARVELOUS SHOES! THEY WERE SO POINTED AT THE ENDS WE COULDN'T IMAGINE HOW HE EVER GOT THEM ON AND THEY WERE SHINED TO WITHIN AN INCH OF THEIR LIVES AND I

REMEMBER HIM SAYING HE CAME FROM THE . . . AMERICAN WING OF THE
METROPOLITAN MUSEUM OF ART! . . . HELLO? . . . GARDNER? . . . ARE YOU
THERE! *(The typing stops)* YOO-HOOOOOOO . . . *(Like a foghorn)*
GARRRRRRRRRRRDNERRRRRRR?

GARDNER *(Offstage; from his study):* YES, DEAR . . . IS THAT YOU?

FANNY: OF COURSE IT'S ME! WHO ELSE COULD IT POSSIBLY BE? . . . DARLING,
PLEASE COME HERE FOR A MINUTE. *(The typing resumes)* FOR GOD'S SAKE,
WILL YOU STOP THAT DREADFUL TYPING BEFORE YOU SEND ME STRAIGHT TO
THE NUT HOUSE? . . . *(In a new register)* GARRRRRRRRRRRRDNERRRRRR?

He stops.

GARDNER *(Offstage):* WHAT'S THAT?   FANNY: I SAID . . . Lord, I hate this
MAGS IS BACK FROM THE NUT   yelling. . . . PLEASE . . . COME . . .
HOUSE?   HERE!

Brief silence.

GARDNER *(Offstage):* I'LL BE WITH   FANNY: It's a wonder I'm not in a
YOU IN A MOMENT, I DIDN'T HEAR   straightjacket already. Actually, it
HER RING. *(Starts singing)* "Noth-   might be rather nice for a change
ing could be finer than to be in Car- . . . peaceful. DARLING . . . I WANT
olina."   TO SHOW YOU MY NEW HAT!

Silence. GARDNER *enters, still singing. He's wearing mismatched tweeds and
is holding a stack of papers which keep drifting to the floor.*

GARDNER: Oh, don't you look nice! Very attractive, very attractive!

FANNY: But I'm still in my bathrobe.

GARDNER *(Looking around the room, leaking more papers):* Well, where's
Mags?

FANNY: Darling, you're dropping your papers all over the floor.

GARDNER *(Spies the silver tray):* I remember this! Aunt Alice gave it to us,
didn't she? *(He picks it up)* Good Lord, it's heavy. What's it made of?
Lead?!

FANNY: No, Aunt Alice did *not* give it to us. It was Mama's.

GARDNER: Oh, yes . . . *(He starts to exit with it)*

FANNY: Could I have it back, please?

GARDNER *(Hands it to her, dropping more papers):* Oh, sure thing. . . .
Where's Mags? I thought you said she was here.

FANNY: I didn't say Mags was here, I asked *you* to come here.

GARDNER *(Papers spilling):* Damned papers keep falling . . .

FANNY: I wanted to show you my new hat. I bought it in honor of Mags' visit. Isn't it marvelous?

GARDNER *(Picking up the papers as more drop):* Yes, yes, very nice . . .

FANNY: Gardner, you're not even looking at it!

GARDNER: Very becoming . . .

FANNY: You don't think it's too bright, do you? I don't want to look like a traffic light. Guess how much it cost?

GARDNER *(A whole sheaf of papers slides to the floor; he dives for them):* OH, SHIT!

FANNY *(Gets to them first):* It's all right, I've got them, I've got them. *(She hands them to him)*

GARDNER: You'd think they had wings on them . . .

FANNY: Here you go . . .   GARDNER: . . . damned things won't hold still!

FANNY: Gar . . . ?

GARDNER *(Engrossed in one of the pages):* Mmmmm?

FANNY: HELLO?

GARDNER *(Startled):* What's that?

FANNY *(In a whisper):* My hat. Guess how much it cost.

GARDNER: Oh, yes. Let's see . . . ten dollars?

FANNY: Ten dollars . . . IS THAT ALL?

GARDNER: Twenty?

FANNY: GARDNER, THIS HAPPENS TO BE A DESIGNER HAT! DESIGNER HATS START AT FIFTY DOLLARS . . . SEVENTY-FIVE!

GARDNER *(Jumps):* Was that the door bell?

FANNY: No, it wasn't the door bell. Though it's high time Mags were here. She was probably in a train wreck!

GARDNER *(Looking through his papers):* I'm beginning to get fond of Wallace Stevens again.

FANNY: This damned move is going to kill me! Send me straight to my grave!

GARDNER *(Reading from a page):*
"The mules that angels ride come slowly down
The blazing passes, from beyond the sun.
Descensions of their tinkling bells arrive.
These muleteers are dainty of their way . . ."
(Pause) Don't you love that! "These muleteers are *dainty* of their way"!?

FANNY: Gar, the hat. How much? *(GARDNER sighs)* Darling . . . ?

GARDNER: Oh, yes. Let's see . . . fifty dollars? Seventy-five?

FANNY: It's French.

GARDNER: Three hundred!

FANNY *(Triumphant):* No, eighty-five cents.

GARDNER: Eighty-five cents! . . . I thought you said . . .

FANNY: That's right . . . eighty . . . five . . . *cents!*

GARDNER: Well, you sure had me fooled!

FANNY: I found it at the thrift shop.

GARDNER: I thought it cost at least fifty dollars or seventy-five. You know, designer hats are very expensive!

FANNY: It was on the markdown table. *(She takes it off and shows him the label)* See that? Lily Daché! When I saw that label, I nearly keeled over right into the fur coats!

GARDNER *(Handling it):* Well, what do you know, that's the same label that's in my bathrobe.

FANNY: Darling, Lily Daché designed hats, not men's bathrobes!

GARDNER: Yup . . . Lily Daché . . . same name . . .

FANNY: If you look again, I'm sure you'll see . . .

GARDNER: . . . same script, same color, same size. I'll show you. *(He exits)*

FANNY: Poor lamb can't keep anything straight anymore. *(Looks at herself in the tray again)* God, this is a good-looking hat!

GARDNER *(Returns with a nondescript plaid bathrobe. He points to the label):* See that? . . . What does it say?

FANNY *(Refusing to look at it):* Lily Daché was a *hat* designer! She designed ladies' *hats!*

GARDNER: What . . . does . . . it . . . say?

FANNY: Gardner, you're being ridiculous.

GARDNER *(Forcing it on her):* Read . . . the label!

FANNY: Lily Daché did *not* design this bathrobe, I don't care what the label says!

GARDNER: READ! *(FANNY reads it)* ALL RIGHT, NOW WHAT DOES IT SAY?

FANNY *(Chagrined):* Lily Daché.

GARDNER: I told you!

FANNY: Wait a minute, let me look at that again. *(She does; then throws the robe at him in disgust)* Gar, Lily Daché never designed a bathrobe in her life! Someone obviously ripped the label off one of her hats and then sewed it into the robe.

GARDNER *(Puts it on over his jacket):* It's damned good-looking. I've always loved this robe. I think you gave it to me. . . . Well, I've got to get back to work. *(He abruptly exits)*

FANNY: Where did you get that robe anyway? . . . I didn't give it to you, did I . . . ?

Silence. GARDNER *resumes typing.*

FANNY *(Holding the tray up again and admiring herself):* You know, I think I *did* give it to him. I remember how excited I was when I found it at the thrift shop . . . fifty cents and never worn! *I* couldn't have sewn that label in to impress him, could I? . . . I can't be that far gone! . . . The poor lamb wouldn't even notice it, let alone understand its cachet. . . . Uuuuuuh, this damned tray is even heavier than the coffee pot. They must have been amazons in the old days! *(Writes on her pad)* "Empire tray, Parke-Bernet Galleries," and good riddance! *(She wraps it and drops it into the carton with the coffee pot)* Where *is* that wretched Mags? It would be just like her to get into a train wreck! She was supposed to be here hours ago. Well, if she doesn't show up soon, I'm going to drop dead of exhaustion. God, wouldn't that be wonderful? . . . Then they could just cart me off into storage with all the old chandeliers and china . . .

The doorbell rings.

FANNY: IT'S MAGS, IT'S MAGS! (*A pause. Dashing out of the room, colliding into* GARDNER) GOOD GOD, LOOK AT ME! I'M STILL IN MY BATHROBE!

GARDNER (*Offstage*): COMING, COMING . . . I'VE GOT IT . . . COMING! (*Dashing into the room, colliding into* FANNY) I'VE GOT IT . . . HOLD ON . . . COMING . . . COMING . . .

FANNY (*Offstage*): MAGS IS HERE! IT'S MAGS. . . . SHE'S FINALLY HERE!

GARDNER *exits to open the front door.* MAGS *comes staggering in carrying a suitcase and an enormous duffel bag. She wears wonderfully distinctive clothes and has very much her own look. She's extremely out of breath and too wrought up to drop her heavy bags.*

MAGS: I'm sorry. . . . I'm sorry I'm so late. . . . Everything went wrong! A passenger had a heart attack outside of New London and we had to stop. . . . It was terrifying! All these medics and policemen came swarming onto the train and the conductor kept running up and down the aisles telling everyone not to leave their seats under any circumstances. . . . Then the New London fire department came screeching down to the tracks, sirens blaring, lights whirling, and all these men in black rubber suits started pouring through the doors. . . . *That* took two hours . . .

FANNY (*Offstage*): DARLING . . . DARLING . . . WHERE ARE YOU?

MAGS: *Then,* I couldn't get a cab at the station. There just weren't any! I must have circled the block fifteen times. Finally I just stepped out into the traffic with my thumb out, but no one would pick me up . . . so I walked . . .

FANNY (*Offstage*): Damned zipper's stuck . . .

GARDNER: You walked all the way from the South Station?

MAGS: Well actually, I ran . . .

GARDNER: You had poor Mum scared to death.

MAGS (*Finally puts the bags down with a deep sigh*): I'm sorry. . . . I'm really sorry. It was a nightmare.

FANNY *reenters the room, her dress over her head. The zipper's stuck; she staggers around blindly.*

FANNY: Damned zipper! Gar, will you please help me with this?

MAGS: I sprinted all the way up Beacon Hill.

GARDNER (*Opening his arms wide*): Well come here and let's get a look at you. (*He hugs her*) Mags!

MAGS *(Squeezing him tight):* Oh, Daddy . . . Daddy!

GARDNER: My Mags!

MAGS: I never thought I'd get here! . . . Oh, you look wonderful!

GARDNER: Well, you don't look so bad yourself!

MAGS: I love your hair. It's gotten so . . . white!

FANNY *(Still lost in her dress, struggling with the zipper):* This is *so* typical . . . just as Mags arrives, my zipper has to break! *(She grunts and struggles)*

MAGS *(Waves at her):* Hi, Mum . . .

FANNY: Just a minute, dear, my zipper's . . .

GARDNER *(Picks up* MAGS' *bags):* Well, sit down and take a load off your feet . . .

MAGS: I was so afraid I'd never make it . . .

GARDNER *(Staggering under the weight of the bags):* What have you got in here? Lead weights?

MAGS: I can't believe you're finally letting me do you.

FANNY *flings her arms around* MAGS, *practically knocking her over.*

FANNY: OH, DARLING . . . MY PRE-CIOUS MAGS, YOU'RE HERE AT LAST.

GARDNER *(Lurching around in circles):* Now let's see . . . where should I put these . . . ?

FANNY: I was sure your train had derailed and you were lying dead in some ditch!

MAGS *(Pulls away from* FANNY *to come to* GARDNER'S *rescue):* Daddy, please, let me . . . these are much too heavy.

FANNY *(Finally noticing Mags):* GOOD LORD, WHAT HAVE YOU DONE TO YOUR HAIR?!

MAGS *(Struggling to take the bags from* GARDNER*):* Come on, give them to me . . . please? *(She sets them down by the sofa)*

FANNY *(As her dress starts to slide off one shoulder):* Oh, not again! . . . Gar, would you give me a hand and see what's wrong with this zipper. One minute it's stuck, the next it's falling to pieces.

GARDNER *goes to her and starts fussing with it.*

MAGS *(Pacing):* I don't know, it's been crazy all week. Monday, I forgot to keep an appointment I'd made with a new model. . . . Tuesday, I overslept and stood up my advanced painting students. . . . Wednesday, the day of my meeting with Max Zoll, I forgot to put on my underpants . . .

FANNY: GODDAMMIT, GAR, CAN'T YOU DO ANYTHING ABOUT THIS ZIPPER?!

MAGS: I mean, there I was, racing down Broome Street in this gauzy Tibetan skirt when I tripped and fell right at his feet . . . SPLATTT! My skirt goes flying over my head and there I am . . . everything staring him in the face . . .

FANNY: COME ON, GAR, USE A LITTLE MUSCLE!

MAGS (Laughing): Oh, well, all that matters is that I finally got here. . . . I mean . . . there you are . . .

GARDNER (Struggling with the zipper): I can't see it, it's too small!

FANNY (Whirls away from GARDNER, pulling her dress off altogether): OH, FORGET IT! JUST FORGET IT! The trolley's probably missing half its teeth, just like someone else I know. (To MAGS) I grind my teeth in my sleep now, I've worn them all down to stubs. Look at that! (She flings open her mouth and points) Nothing left but the gums!

GARDNER: I never hear you grind your teeth . . .

FANNY: That's because I'm snoring so loud. How could you hear anything through all that racket? It even wakes me up. It's no wonder poor Daddy has to sleep downstairs.

MAGS (Looking around): Jeez, look at the place! So, you're finally doing it . . . selling the house and moving to Cotuit year round. I don't believe it. I just don't believe it!

GARDNER: Well, how about a drink to celebrate Mags' arrival?

MAGS: You've been here so long. Why move now?

FANNY: Gardner, what are you wearing that bathrobe for?

MAGS: You can't move. I won't let you!

FANNY (Softly to GARDNER): Really, darling, you ought to pay more attention to your appearance.

MAGS: You love this house. *I* love this house . . . the room . . . the light.

GARDNER: So, Mags, how about a little . . . (He drinks from an imaginary glass) to wet your whistle?

FANNY: We can't start drinking now, it isn't even noon yet!

MAGS: I'm starving. I've got to get something to eat before I collapse! *(She exits towards the kitchen)*

FANNY: What *have* you done to your hair, dear? The color's so queer and all your nice curl is gone.

GARDNER: It looks to me as if she dyed it.

FANNY: Yes, that's it. You're absolutely right! It's a completely different color. She dyed it bright red!

MAGS *can be heard thumping and thudding through the icebox.*

FANNY: NOW, MAGS, I DON'T WANT YOU FILLING UP ON SNACKS. . . . I'VE MADE A PERFECTLY BEAUTIFUL LEG OF LAMB FOR LUNCH! . . . HELLO? . . . DO YOU HEAR ME? . . . *(To* GARDNER*)* No one in our family has *ever* had red hair, it's so common looking.

GARDNER: I like it. It brings out her eyes.

FANNY: WHY ON EARTH DID YOU DYE YOUR HAIR *RED,* OF ALL COLORS?!

MAGS *(Returns, eating Saltines out of the box):* I didn't dye my hair, I just added some highlight.

FANNY: I suppose that's what your arty friends in New York do . . . dye their hair all the colors of the rainbow!

GARDNER: Well, it's damned attractive if you asked me . . . damned attractive!

MAGS *unzips her duffel bag and rummages around in it while eating the Saltines.*

FANNY: Darling, I told you not to bring a lot of stuff with you. We're trying to get rid of things.

MAGS *(Pulls out a folding easel and starts setting it up):* AAAAAHHHHHH, here it is. Isn't it a beauty? I bought it just for you!

FANNY: Please don't get crumbs all over the floor. Crystal was just here yesterday. It was her last time before we move.

MAGS *(At her easel):* God, I can hardly wait! I can't believe you're finally letting me do you.

FANNY: *Do* us? . . . What *are* you talking about?

GARDNER *(Reaching for the Saltines):* Hey, Mags, could I have a couple of those?

MAGS *(Tosses him the box):* Sure! *(To* FANNY*)* Your portrait.

GARDNER: Thanks. *(He starts munching on a handful)*

FANNY: You're planning to paint our portrait now? While we're trying to move . . . ?

GARDNER *(Sputtering Saltines):* Mmmmm, I'd forgotten just how delicious Saltines are!

MAGS: It's a perfect opportunity. There'll be no distractions; you'll be completely at my mercy. Also, you promised.

FANNY: I did?

MAGS: Yes, you did.

FANNY: Well, I must have been off my rocker.

MAGS: No, you said, "You can paint us, you can dip us in concrete, you can do anything you want with us just so long as you help us get out of here!"

GARDNER *(Offering the box of Saltines to* FANNY): You really ought to try some of these, Fan, they're absolutely delicious!

FANNY *(Taking a few):* Why, thank you.

MAGS: I figure we'll pack in the morning and you'll pose in the afternoons. It'll be a nice diversion.

FANNY: These *are* good!

GARDNER: Here, dig in . . . take some more.

MAGS: I have some wonderful news . . . amazing news! I wanted to wait till I got here to tell you.

GARDNER *and* FANNY *eat their Saltines, passing the box back and forth as* MAGS *speaks.*

MAGS: You'll die! Just fall over into the packing cartons and die! Are you ready? . . . BRACE YOURSELVES . . . OKAY, HERE GOES. . . . I'm being given a one-woman show at one of the most important galleries in New York this fall. Me, Margaret Church, exhibited at Castelli's, 420 West Broadway. . . . Can you believe it?! . . . MY PORTRAITS HANGING IN THE SAME ROOMS THAT HAVE SHOWN RAUSCHENBERG, JOHNS, WARHOL, KELLY, LICHTENSTEIN, STELLA, SERRA, ALL THE HEAVIES. . . . It's incredible, beyond belief . . . I mean, at my age. . . . Do you know how good you have to be to get in there? It's a miracle . . . an honest-to-God, star-spangled miracle!

Pause.

FANNY *(Mouth full):* Oh, darling, that's wonderful. We're so happy for you!

GARDNER *(Mouth full):* No one deserves it more, no one deserves it more!

MAGS: Through some fluke, some of Castelli's people showed up at our last faculty show at Pratt and were knocked out . . .

FANNY *(Reaching for the box of Saltines):* More, more . . .

MAGS: They said they hadn't seen anyone handle light like me since the French Impressionists. They said I was this weird blend of Pierre Bonnard, Mary Cassatt and David Hockney . . .

GARDNER *(Swallowing his mouthful):* I told you they were good.

MAGS: Also, no one's doing portraits these days. They're considered passé. I'm so out of it, I'm in.

GARDNER: Well, you're loaded with talent and always have been.

FANNY: She gets it all from Mama, you know. Her miniature of Henry James is still one of the main attractions at the Atheneum. Of course no woman of breeding could be a professional artist in her day. It simply wasn't done. But talk about talent . . . that woman had talent to burn!

MAGS: I want to do one of you for the show.

FANNY: Oh, do Daddy, he's the famous one.

MAGS: No, I want to do you both. I've always wanted to do you and now I've finally got a good excuse.

FANNY: It's high time somebody painted Daddy again! I'm sick to death of that dreadful portrait of him in the National Gallery they keep reproducing. He looks like an undertaker!

GARDNER: Well, I think you should just do Mum. She's never looked handsomer.

FANNY: Oh, come on, I'm a perfect fright and you know it.

MAGS: I want to do you both. Side by side. In this room. Something really classy. You look so great. Mum with her crazy hats and everything and you with that face. If I could just get you to hold still long enough and actually pose.

GARDNER *(Walking around, distracted):* Where are those papers I just had? Goddammit, Fanny . . .

MAGS: I have the feeling it's either now or never.

GARDNER: I can't hold on to anything around here. *(He exits to his study)*

MAGS: I've always wanted to do you. It would be such a challenge.

FANNY *(Pulling MAGS onto the sofa next to her)*: I'm so glad you're finally here, Mags. I'm very worried about Daddy.

MAGS: Mummy, please. I just got here.

FANNY: He's getting quite gaga.

MAGS: Mummy . . . !

FANNY: You haven't seen him in almost a year. Two weeks ago he walked through the front door of the Codman's house, kissed Emily on the cheek and settled down in the maid's room, thinking he was home!

MAGS: Oh, come on, you're exaggerating.

FANNY: He's as mad as a hatter and getting worse every day! It's this damned new book of his. He works on it around the clock. I've read some of it, and it doesn't make one word of sense, it's all at sixes and sevens . . .

GARDNER *(Pokes his head back in the room, spies some of his papers on a table and grabs them)*: Ahhh, here they are. *(He exits)*

FANNY *(Voice lowered)*: Ever since this dry spell with his poetry, he's been frantic, absolutely . . . frantic!

MAGS: I hate it when you do this.

FANNY: I'm just trying to get you to face the facts around here.

MAGS: There's nothing wrong with him! He's just as sane as the next man. Even saner, if you ask me.

FANNY: You know what he's doing now? You couldn't guess in a million years! . . . He's writing criticism! Daddy! *(She laughs)* Can you believe it? The man doesn't have one analytic bone in his body. His mind is a complete jumble and always has been!

There's a loud crash from GARDNER'S *study.*

GARDNER *(Offstage)*: SHIT!

MAGS: He's abstracted. . . . That's the way he is.

FANNY: He doesn't spend any time with me anymore. He just holes up in that filthy study with Toots. God, I hate that bird! Though actually they're quite cunning together. Daddy's teaching him Gray's *Elegy*. You ought to see them in there, Toots perched on top of Daddy's head, spouting out verse after verse . . . Daddy, tap-tap-tapping away on his typewriter. They're quite a pair.

GARDNER *(Pokes his head back in):* Have you seen that Stevens' poem I was reading before?

FANNY *(Long-suffering):* NO, I HAVEN'T SEEN THAT STEVENS' POEM YOU WERE READING BEFORE! . . . Things are getting very tight around here, in case you haven't noticed. Daddy's last Pulitzer didn't even cover our real estate tax, and now that he's too doddery to give readings anymore, that income is gone . . . *(Suddenly handing* MAGS *the sugar bowl she'd been wrapping)* Mags, *do* take this sugar bowl. You can use it to serve tea to your students at that wretched art school of yours . . .

MAGS: It's called Pratt! The Pratt Institute.

FANNY: Pratt, Splatt, whatever . . .

MAGS: And I don't serve tea to my students, I teach them how to paint.

FANNY: Well, I'm sure none of them has ever seen a sugar bowl as handsome as this before.

GARDNER *(Reappearing again):* You're sure you haven't seen it?

FANNY *(Loud and angry):* YES, I'M SURE I HAVEN'T SEEN IT! I JUST TOLD YOU I HAVEN'T SEEN IT!

GARDNER *(Retreating):* Right you are, right you are. *(He exits)*

FANNY: God!

Silence.

MAGS: What do you have to yell at him like that for

FANNY: Because the poor thing's as deaf as an adder!

MAGS *sighs deeply; silence.* FANNY, *suddenly exuberant, leads her over to a lamp.*

FANNY: Come, I want to show you something.

MAGS *(Looking at it):* What is it?

FANNY: Something I made. *(MAGS is about to turn it on)* WAIT, DON'T TURN IT ON YET! It's got to be dark to get the full effect. *(She rushes to the windows and pulls down the shades)*

MAGS: What *are* you doing?

FANNY: Hold your horses a minute. You'll see . . . *(As the room gets darker and darker)* Poor me, you wouldn't believe the lengths I go to to amuse myself these days . . .

MAGS *(Touching the lampshade):* What is this? It looks like a scene of some sort.

FANNY: It's an invention I made . . . a kind of magic lantern.

MAGS: Gee . . . it's amazing . . .

FANNY: What I did was buy an old engraving of the Grand Canal . . .

MAGS: You *made* this?

FANNY: . . . and then color it in with crayons. Next, I got out my sewing scissors and cut out all the street lamps and windows . . . anything that light would shine through. Then I pasted it over a plain lampshade, put the shade on this old horror of a lamp, turned on the switch and . . . *(She turns it on)* VOILÀ . . . VENICE TWINKLING AT DUSK! It's quite effective, don't you think . . . ?

MAGS *(Walking around it):* Jeez . . .

FANNY: And see, I poked out all the little lights on the gondolas with a straight pin.

MAGS: Where on earth did you get the idea?

FANNY: Well you know, idle minds . . . *(She spins the shade, making the lights whirl)*

MAGS: It's really amazing. I mean, you could sell this in a store!

GARDNER *(Enters):* HERE IT IS. IT WAS RIGHT ON TOP OF MY DESK THE WHOLE TIME. *(He crashes into a table)* OOOOOWWWWW!

FANNY: LOOK OUT, LOOK OUT!

MAGS *(Rushes over to GARDNER):* Oh, Daddy, are you all right?

FANNY: WATCH WHERE YOU'RE GOING, WATCH WHERE YOU'RE GOING!

GARDNER *(Hopping up and down on one leg):* GODDAMMIT! . . . I HIT MY SHIN.

FANNY: I was just showing Mags my lamp . . .

GARDNER *(Limping over to it):* Oh, yes, isn't that something? Mum is awfully clever with that kind of thing. . . . It was all her idea. Buying the engraving, coloring it in, cutting out all those little dots.

FANNY: Not "dots" . . . lights and windows, lights and windows!

GARDNER: Right, right . . . lights and windows.

FANNY: Well, we'd better get some light back in here before someone breaks their neck. *(She zaps the shades back up)*

GARDNER *(Puts his arm around* MAGS*)*: Gee, it's good to have you back.

MAGS: It's good to be back.

GARDNER: And I like that new red hair of yours. It's very becoming.

MAGS: But I told you, I hardly touched it . . .

GARDNER: Well, something's different. You've got a glow. So . . . how do you want us to pose for this grand portrait of yours . . . ? *(He poses self-consciously)*

MAGS: Oh, Daddy, setting up a portrait takes a lot of time and thought. You've got to figure out the background, the lighting, what to wear, the sort of mood you want to—

FANNY: OOOOH, LET'S DRESS UP, LET'S DRESS UP! *(She grabs a packing blanket, drapes it around herself and links arms with* GARDNER, *striking an elegant pose)* This *is* going to be fun. She was absolutely right! Come on, Gar, look distinguished!

MAGS: Mummy, please, it's not a game!

FANNY *(More and more excited):* You still have your tuxedo, don't you? And I'll wear my marvelous long black dress that makes me look like that fascinating woman in the Sargent painting! *(She strikes the famous profile pose)*

MAGS: MUMMY?!

FANNY: I'm sorry, we'll behave, just tell us what to do.

FANNY *and* GARDNER *settle down next to each other.*

GARDNER: That's right, you're the boss.

FANNY: Yes, you're the boss.

MAGS: But I'm not ready yet; I haven't set anything up.

FANNY: Relax, darling, we just want to get the hang of it . . .

FANNY *and* GARDNER *stare straight ahead, trying to look like suitable subjects, but they can't hold still. They keep making faces, lifting an eyebrow, wriggling a nose, twitching a lip. Nothing big and grotesque, just flickering changes; a half-smile here, a self-important frown there. They steal glances at each other every so often.*

GARDNER: How am I doing, Fan?

FANNY: Brilliantly, absolutely brilliantly!

MAGS: But you're making faces.

FANNY: *I'm* not making faces. *(Turning to* GARDNER *and making a face)* Are *you* making faces, Gar?

GARDNER *(Instantly making one)*: Certainly not! I'm the picture of restraint!

Without meaning to, FANNY *and* GARDNER *get sillier and sillier. They start giggling, then laughing.*

MAGS *(Can't help but join in)*: You two are impossible . . . completely impossible! I was crazy to think I could ever pull this off! *(Laughing away)* Look at you . . . just . . . look at you!

Blackout.

S c e n e   2

Two days later, around five in the afternoon. Half of the Church household has been dragged into the living room for packing. Overflowing cartons are everywhere. They're filled with pots and pans, dishes and glasses, and the entire contents of two linen closets. MAGS *has placed a stepladder under one of the windows. A pile of tablecloths and curtains is flung beneath it. Two side chairs are in readiness for the eventual pose.*

   MAGS *has just pulled a large crimson tablecloth out of a carton. She unfurls it with one shimmering toss.*

MAGS: PERFECT . . . PERFECT!

FANNY *(Seated on the sofa, clutches an old pair of galoshes to her chest)*: Look at these old horrors; half the rubber is rotted away and the fasteners are falling to pieces. . . . GARDNER? . . . OH, GARRRRRRRRRRRDNERRRRR?

MAGS *(Rippling out the tablecloth with shorter snapping motions)*: Have you ever seen such a color?

FANNY: I'VE FOUND YOUR OLD SLEDDING GALOSHES IN WITH THE POTS AND PANS. DO YOU STILL WANT THEM?

MAGS: It's like something out of a Rubens!

MAGS *slings the tablecloth over a chair and then sits on a footstool to finish the Sara Lee banana cake she started. As she eats, she looks at the table-cloth, making happy grunting sounds.* FANNY *lovingly puts the galoshes on over her shoes and wiggles her feet.*

FANNY: God, these bring back memories! There were real snowstorms in the old days. Not these pathetic little two-inch droppings we have now. After a particularly heavy one, Daddy and I used to go sledding on the Common. This was way before you were born. . . . God, it was a hundred years ago! . . . Daddy would stop writing early, put on these galoshes and come looking for me, jingling the fasteners like castanets. It was a kind of mating call, almost . . . *(She jingles them)* The Common was always deserted after a storm; we had the whole place to ourselves. It was so romantic. . . . We'd haul the sled up Beacon Street, stop under the State House, and aim it straight down to the Park Street Church, which was much further away in those days. . . . Then Daddy would lie down on the sled, I'd lower myself on top of him, we'd rock back and forth a few times to gain momentum and then . . . WHOOOOOOOOOSSSSSSSHHHHH . . . down we'd plunge like a pair of eagles locked in a spasm of lovemaking. God, it was wonderful! . . . The city whizzing past us at ninety miles an hour . . . the cold . . . the darkness . . . Daddy's hair in my mouth . . . GAR . . . REMEMBER HOW WE USED TO GO SLEDDING IN THE OLD DAYS? . . . Sometimes he'd lie on top of me. That was fun. I liked that even more. *(In her foghorn voice)* GARRRRRRRRRDNERRRRR?

MAGS: Didn't he say he was going out this afternoon?

FANNY: Why, so he did! I completely forgot. *(She takes off the galoshes)* I'm getting just as bad as him. *(She drops them into a different carton—wistful)* Gar's galoshes, Cotuit.

A pause. MAGS *picks up the tablecloth again, holds it high over her head.*

MAGS: Isn't this fabulous? . . . *(She then wraps* FANNY *in it)* It's the perfect backdrop. Look what it does to your skin.

FANNY: Mags, what *are* you doing?

MAGS: It makes you glow like a pomegranate . . . *(She whips it off her)* Now all I need is a hammer and nails . . . *(She finds them)* YES! *(She climbs up the stepladder and starts hammering a corner of the cloth into the molding of one of the windows)* This is going to look so great! . . . I've never seen such color!

FANNY: Darling, what is going on . . . ?

MAGS: Rembrandt, eat your heart out! You seventeenth-century Dutch has-been, you. *(She hammers more furiously)*

FANNY: MARGARET, THIS IS NOT A CONSTRUCTION SITE. . . . PLEASE . . . STOP IT . . . YOO-HOOOOO . . . DO YOU HEAR ME?

GARDNER *suddenly appears, dressed in a raincoat.*

GARDNER: YES, DEAR, HERE I AM. I JUST STEPPED OUT FOR A WALK DOWN CHESTNUT STREET. BEAUTIFUL AFTERNOON, ABSOLUTELY BEAUTIFUL! . . . WHY, THAT LOOKS VERY NICE, MAGS, very nice indeed . . .

FANNY *(To MAGS)*: YOU'RE GOING TO RUIN THE WALLS TO SAY NOTHING OF MAMA'S BEST TABLE-CLOTH. . . . MAGS, DO YOU HEAR ME? . . . YOO-HOO! . . . DARLING, I MUST INSIST YOU STOP THAT DREADFUL . . .

MAGS *(Steps down; stands back and looks at the tablecloth)*: That's it. That's IT!

FANNY *(To GARDNER, worried)*: Where have *you* been?

MAGS *kisses her fingers at the backdrop and settles back into her banana cake.*

GARDNER *(To FANNY)*: You'll never guess who I ran into on Chestnut Street . . . Pate Baldwin!

GARDNER *takes his coat off and drops it on the floor. He sits in one of the posing chairs.*

MAGS *(Mouth full of cake)*: Oh, Daddy, I'm nowhere near ready for you yet.

FANNY *(Picks up GARDNER'S coat and hands it to him)*: Darling, coats do *not* go on the floor.

GARDNER *(Rises, but forgets where he's supposed to go)*: He was in terrible shape. I hardly recognized him. Well, it's the Parkinson's disease . . .

FANNY: You mean, Hodgkin's disease . . .

GARDNER: Hodgkin's disease . . . ?

MAGS *(Leaves her cake and returns to the tablecloth)*: Now to figure out exactly how to use this gorgeous light . . .

FANNY: Yes, Pate has Hodgkin's disease, not Parkinson's disease. Sammy Bishop has Parkinson's disease. In the closet . . . your coat goes . . . in the closet!

GARDNER: You're absolutely right! Pate has Hodgkin's disease. *(He stands motionless, the coat over his arm)*

FANNY: And Goat Davis has Addison's disease.

GARDNER: I always get them confused.

FANNY *(Pointing towards the closet)*: That way . . .

GARDNER *exits to the closet;* FANNY *calls after him.*

FANNY: Grace Phelps has it too, I think. Or, it might be Hodgkin's, like Pate. I can't remember.

GARDNER *(Returns with a hanger)*: Doesn't The Goat have Parkinson's disease?

FANNY: No, that's Sammy Bishop.

GARDNER: God, I haven't seen The Goat in ages! *(The coat still over his arm, he hands* FANNY *the hanger)*

FANNY: He hasn't been well.

GARDNER: Didn't Heppy . . . *die?!*

FANNY: What are you giving me this for? . . . Oh, Heppy's been dead for years. She died on the same day as Luster Bright, don't you remember?

GARDNER: I always liked her.

FANNY *(Gives* GARDNER *back the hanger)*: Here, I don't want this.

GARDNER: She was awfully attractive.

FANNY: Who?

GARDNER: Heppy!

FANNY: Oh, yes, Heppy had real charm.

MAGS *(Keeps adjusting the tablecloth)*: Better . . . better . . .

GARDNER: Which is something The Goat is short on, if you ask me. He has Hodgkin's disease, doesn't he? *(Puts his raincoat back on and sits down)*

FANNY: Darling, what *are* you doing? I thought you wanted to hang up your coat!

GARDNER *(After a pause)*: OH, YES, THAT'S RIGHT!

GARDNER *goes back to the closet; a pause.*

FANNY: Where were we?

GARDNER *(Returns with yet another hanger):* Let's see . . .

FANNY *(Takes both hangers from him):* FOR GOD'S SAKE, GAR, PAY ATTENTION!

GARDNER: It was something about The Goat . . .

FANNY *(Takes the coat from* GARDNER*):* HERE, LET ME DO IT! . . . *(Under her breath to* MAGS*)* See what I mean about him? You don't know the half of it!

FANNY *hangs the raincoat up in the closet.*

FANNY: Not the half.

MAGS *(Still tinkering with the backdrop):* Almost . . . almost . . .

GARDNER *(Sitting back down in one of the posing chairs):* Oh, Fan, did I tell you, I ran into Pate Baldwin just now. I'm afraid he's not long for this world.

FANNY *(Returning):* Well, it's that Hodgkin's disease . . . *(She sits on the posing chair next to him)*

GARDNER: God, I'd hate to see him go. He's one of the great editors of our times. I couldn't have done it without him. He gave me everything, everything!

MAGS *(Makes a final adjustment):* Yes, that's it! *(She stands back and gazes at them)* You look wonderful!

FANNY: Isn't it getting to be . . . *(She taps at an imaginary watch on her wrist and drains an imaginary glass) cocktail time?!*

GARDNER *(Looks at his watch):* On the button, on the button! *(He rises)*

FANNY: I'll have the usual, please. Do join us, Mags! Daddy bought some Dubonnet especially for you!

MAGS: Hey. I was just getting some ideas.

GARDNER *(To* MAGS, *as he exists for the bar):* How about a little . . . Dubonnet to wet your whistle?

FANNY: Oh, Mags, it's like old times having you back with us like this!

GARDNER *(Offstage):* THE USUAL FOR YOU, FAN?

FANNY: I wish we saw more of you. . . . PLEASE! . . . Isn't he darling? Have you ever known anyone more darling than Daddy?

GARDNER *(Offstage; hums Jolson's "You Made Me Love You")*: MAGS, HOW ABOUT YOU? . . . A LITTLE . . . DUBONNET?

FANNY: Oh, *do* join us!   MAGS *(To* GARDNER): No, nothing, thanks.

FANNY: Well, what do you think of your aged parents picking up and moving to Cotuit year round? Pretty crazy, eh what? . . . Nothing but the gulls, oysters and us!

GARDNER *(Returns with* FANNY'S *drink)*: Here you go . . .

FANNY: Why thank you, Gar. *(To* MAGS) You sure you won't join us?

GARDNER *(Lifts his glass towards* FANNY *and* MAGS): Cheers!

GARDNER *and* FANNY *take that first lifesaving gulp.*

FANNY: Aaaaahhhhh!   GARDNER: Hits the spot, hits the spot!

MAGS: Well, I certainly can't do you like that!

FANNY: Why not? I think we look very . . . *comme il faut!*

FANNY *slouches into a rummy pose;* GARDNER *joins her.*

FANNY: WAIT . . . I'VE GOT IT! I'VE GOT IT! *(She whispers excitedly to* GARDNER)

MAGS: Come on, let's not start this again!

GARDNER: What's that? . . . Oh, yes . . . yes, yes . . . I know the one you mean. Yes, right, right . . . of course.

A pause.

FANNY: How's . . . *this?!*

FANNY *grabs a large serving fork and she and* GARDNER *fly into an imitation of Grant Wood's* American Gothic.

MAGS: And I wonder why it's taken me all these years to get you to pose for me. You just don't take me seriously! Poor old Mags and her ridiculous portraits . . .

FANNY: Oh, darling, your portraits aren't *ridiculous!* They may not be all that one *hopes* for, but they're certainly not—

MAGS: Remember how you behaved at my first group show in Soho? . . . Oh, come on, you remember. It was a real circus! Think back. . . . It was about six year ago. . . . Daddy had just been awarded some presidential medal of achievement and you insisted he wear it around his neck on a bright red ribbon, and you wore this . . . *huge* feathered hat to match! I'll never forget it! It was the size of a giant pizza with twenty-inch red turkey feathers shooting straight up into the air. . . . Oh, come on, you remember, don't you?

FANNY *(Leaping to her feet):* HOLD EVERYTHING! THIS IS IT! THIS IS REALLY IT! Forgive me for interrupting, Mags darling, it'll just take a minute. *(She whispers excitedly to GARDNER)*

MAGS: I had about eight portraits in the show, mostly of friends of mine, except for this old one I'd done of Mrs. Crowninshield.

GARDNER: All right, all right . . . let's give it a whirl.

A pause; then they mime Michelangelo's Pietà *with* GARDNER *lying across Fanny's lap as the dead Christ.*

MAGS *(Depressed):* The *Pietà*. Terrific!

FANNY *(Jabbing* GARDNER *in the ribs):* Hey, we're getting good at this.

GARDNER: Of course it would help if we didn't have all these modern clothes on.

MAGS: AS I WAS SAYING . . .

FANNY: Sorry, Mags . . . sorry . . .

Huffing and creaking with the physical exertion of it all, FANNY *and* GARD-NER *return to their seats.*

MAGS: As soon as you stepped foot in the gallery you spotted it and cried out, "MY GOD, WHAT'S MILLICENT CROWNINSHIELD DOING HERE?" Everyone looked up, what with Daddy's clanking medal and your amazing hat which I was sure would take off and start flying around the room. A crowd gathered. . . . Through some utter fluke, you latched on to *the* most important critic in the city, I mean . . . Mr. Modern Art himself, and you hauled him over to the painting, trumpeting out for all to hear, "THAT'S MILLICENT CROWNINSHIELD! I GREW UP WITH HER. SHE LIVES RIGHT DOWN THE STREET FROM US IN BOSTON. BUT IT'S A VERY POOR LIKENESS, IF YOU ASK ME! HER NOSE ISN'T NEARLY THAT LARGE AND SHE DOESN'T HAVE SOMETHING QUEER GROWING OUT OF HER CHIN! THE

CROWNINSHIELDS ARE REALLY QUITE GOOD-LOOKING, STUFFY, BUT GOOD-LOOKING NONETHELESS!''

GARDNER (*Suddenly jumps up, ablaze*): WAIT, WAIT . . . IF IT'S MICHELANGELO YOU WANT . . . I'm sorry, Mags. . . . One more . . . just one more . . . please?

MAGS: Sure, why not? Be my guest.

GARDNER: FANNY, *prepare yourself!*

More whispering.

FANNY: But I think *you* should be God.

GARDNER: Me? . . . Really?

FANNY: Yes, it's much more appropriate.

GARDNER: Well, if you say so . . .

FANNY *and* GARDNER *ease down to the floor with some difficulty and lie on their sides,* FANNY *as Adam,* GARDNER *as God, their fingers inching closer and closer in the attitude of Michelangelo's* The Creation. *Finally they touch.* MAGS *cheers, whistles, applauds.*

MAGS: THREE CHEERS . . . VERY GOOD . . . NICELY DONE, NICELY DONE!

FANNY *and* GARDNER *hold the pose a moment more, flushed with pleasure; then rise, dust themselves off and grope back to their chairs.*

MAGS: So, there we were . . .

FANNY: Yes, *do* go on!

MAGS: . . . huddled around Millicent Crowninshield, when you whipped into your pocketbook and suddenly announced, ''HOLD EVERYTHING! I'VE GOT A PHOTOGRAPH OF HER RIGHT HERE, THEN YOU CAN SEE WHAT SHE REALLY LOOKS LIKE!'' . . . You then proceeded to crouch down to the floor and dump everything out of your bag, and I mean . . . *everything!* . . . leaking packets of sequins and gummed stars, seashells, odd pieces of fur, crochet hooks, a monarch butterfly embedded in plastic, dental floss, antique glass buttons, small jingling bells, lace . . . I thought I'd die! Just sink to the floor and quietly die! . . . You couldn't find it, you see. I mean, you spent the rest of the afternoon on your hands and knees crawling through this ocean of junk, muttering, ''It's *got* to be here somewhere; I know I had it with me!'' . . . Then Daddy pulled me into the thick of it all and said, ''By the way, have you met our daughter Mags yet? She's the one who did all these pictures . . . paintings . . . portraits

. . . whatever you call them.'' *(She drops to her hands and knees and begins crawling out of the room)* By this time, Mum had somehow crawled out of the gallery and was lost on another floor. She began calling for me . . . ''YOO-HOO, MAGS . . . WHERE ARE YOU? . . . OH, MAGS, DARLING . . . HELLO? . . . ARE YOU THERE?'' *(She reenters and faces them)* This was at my *first* show.

Blackout.

S c e n e   3

Twenty-four hours later. The impact of the impending move has struck with hurricane force. FANNY *has lugged all their clothing into the room and dumped it in various cartons. There are coats, jackets, shoes, skirts, suits, hats, sweaters, dresses, the works. She and* GARDNER *are seated on the sofa, going through it all.* FANNY, *wearing a different hat and dress, holds up a ratty overcoat.*

FANNY: What about this gruesome old thing?

GARDNER *is wearing several sweaters and vests, a Hawaiian holiday shirt, and a variety of scarves and ties around his neck. He holds up pair of shoes.*

GARDNER: God . . . remember these shoes? Pound gave them to me when he came back from Italy. I remember it vividly.

FANNY: *Do* let me give it to the thrift shop! *(She stuffs the coat into the appropriate carton)*

GARDNER: He bought them for me in Rome. Said he couldn't resist; bought himself a pair too since we both wore the same size. God, I miss him! *(Pause)* HEY, WHAT ARE YOU DOING WITH MY OVERCOAT?!

FANNY: Darling, it's threadbare!

GARDNER: But that's my overcoat! *(He grabs it out of the carton)* I've been wearing it every day for the past thirty-five years!

FANNY: That's just my point: it's had it.

GARDNER *(Puts it on over everything else):* There's nothing wrong with this coat!

FANNY: I trust you remember that the cottage is an eighth the size of this place and you simply won't have room for half this stuff! *(She holds up a sports jacket)* This dreary old jacket, for instance. You've had it since Hector was a pup!

GARDNER *(Grabs the jacket and puts it on over his coat):* Oh, no, you don't . . .

FANNY: And this God-awful hat . . .

GARDNER: Let me see that.

GARDNER *stands next to* FANNY *and they fall into a lovely tableau.* MAGS *suddenly pops out from behind a wardrobe carton with a flash camera and takes a picture of them.*

MAGS: PERFECT!

FANNY *(Hands flying to her face):* GOOD GOD, WHAT WAS THAT . . . ?

GARDNER *(Hands flying to his heart):* JESUS CHRIST, I'VE BEEN SHOT!

MAGS *(Walks to the center of the room, advancing the film):* That was terrific. See if you can do it again.

FANNY: What *are* you doing . . . ?

GARDNER *(Feeling his chest):* Is there blood?

FANNY: I see lace everywhere . . .

MAGS: It's all right, I was just taking a picture of you. I often use a Polaroid at this stage.

FANNY *(Rubbing her eyes):* Really, Mags, you might have given us some warning!

MAGS: But that's the whole point: to catch you unawares!

GARDNER *(Rubbing his eyes):* It's the damndest thing. . . . I see lace everywhere.

FANNY: Yes, so do I . . .

GARDNER: It's rather nice, actually. It looks as if you're wearing a veil.

FANNY: I *am* wearing a veil!

The camera spits out the photograph.

MAGS: OH GOODY, HERE COMES THE PICTURE!

FANNY *(Grabs the partially developed print out of her hands):* Let me see, let me see . . .

GARDNER: Yes, let's have a look.

GARDNER *and* FANNY *have another quiet moment together looking at the photograph.* MAGS *tiptoes away from them and takes another picture.*

MAGS: YES!

FANNY: NOT AGAIN! PLEASE, DAR-   GARDNER: WHAT WAS THAT? . . .
LING!   WHAT HAPPENED?

FANNY *and* GARDNER *stagger towards each other.*

MAGS: I'm sorry, I just couldn't resist. You looked so—

FANNY: WHAT ARE YOU TRYING TO DO . . . *BLIND* US?!

GARDNER: Really, Mags, enough is enough . . .

GARDNER *and* FANNY *keep stumbling about kiddingly.*

FANNY: Are you still there, Gar?

GARDNER: Right as rain, right as rain!

MAGS: I'm sorry; I didn't mean to scare you. It's just a photograph can show you things you weren't aware of. Here, have a look. *(She gives them to* FANNY*)* Well, I'm going out to the kitchen to get something to eat. Anybody want anything? *(She exists)*

FANNY *(Looking at the photos, half-amused, half-horrified):* Oh, Gardner, have you ever . . . ?

GARDNER *(Looks at the photos and laughs):* Good grief . . .

MAGS *(Offstage; from the kitchen):* IS IT ALL RIGHT IF I TAKE THE REST OF THIS TAPIOCA FROM LAST NIGHT?

FANNY: IT'S ALL RIGHT WITH ME. How about you, Gar?

GARDNER: Sure, go right ahead. I've never been that crazy about tapioca.

FANNY: What are you talking about, tapioca is one of your favorites.

MAGS *(Enters, slurping from a large bowl):* Mmmmmmmm . . .

FANNY: Really, Mags, I've never seen anyone eat as much as you.

MAGS *(Takes the photos back):* It's strange. I only do this when I come home.

FANNY: What's the matter, don't I feed you enough?

GARDNER: Gee, it's hot in here! *(Starts taking off his coat)*

FANNY: God knows, you didn't eat anything as a child! I've never seen such a fussy eater. Gar, what *are* you doing?

GARDNER *(Shedding clothes to the floor):* Taking off some of these clothes. It's hotter than Tophet in here!

MAGS *(Looking at her photos):* Yes, I like you looking at each other like that . . .

FANNY *(To* GARDNER): Please watch where you're dropping things; I'm trying to keep some order around here.

GARDNER *(Picks up what he dropped, dropping even more in the process):* Right, right . . .

MAGS: Now all I've got to do is figure out what you should wear.

FANNY: Well, I'm going to wear my long black dress, and you'd be a fool not to do Daddy in his tuxedo. He looks so distinguished in it, just like a banker!

MAGS: I haven't really decided yet.

FANNY: Just because you walk around looking like something the cat dragged in, doesn't mean Daddy and I want to, do we Gar?

GARDNER *is making a worse and worse tangle of his clothes.*

FANNY: HELLO . . . ?

GARDNER *(Looks up at* FANNY): Oh, yes, awfully attractive, awfully attractive!

FANNY *(To* MAGS): If you don't mind me saying so, I've never seen you looking so forlorn. You'll never catch a husband looking that way. Those peculiar clothes, that God-awful hair . . . really, Mags, it's very distressing!

MAGS: I don't think my hair's so bad, not that it's terrific or anything . . .

FANNY: Well, I don't see other girls walking around like you. I mean, girls from your background. What would Lyman Wigglesworth think if he saw you in the street?

MAGS: Lyman Wigglesworth?! . . . Uuuuuuughhhhhhh! *(She shudders)*

FANNY: All right then, that brilliant Cabot boy . . . what *is* his name?

GARDNER: Sammy.

FANNY: No, not Sammy . . .

GARDNER: Stephen . . . Stanley . . . Stuart . . . Sheldon . . . Sherlock . . . Sherlock! It's *Sherlock!*

MAGS: Spence!

FANNY: SPENCE, THAT'S IT! HIS   GARDNER: THAT'S IT . . . SPENCE!
NAME IS SPENCE!   SPENCE CABOT!

FANNY: Spence Cabot was first in his class at Harvard.

MAGS: Mum, he has no facial hair.

FANNY: He has his own law firm on Arlington Street.

MAGS: Spence Cabot has six fingers on his right hand!

FANNY: So, he isn't the best-looking thing in the world. Looks isn't everything. He can't help it if he has extra fingers. Have a little sympathy!

MAGS: But the extra one has this weird nail on it that looks like a talon. . . .
It's long and black and . . . *(She shudders)*

FANNY: No one's perfect, darling. He has lovely handwriting and an absolutely saintly mother. Also, he's as rich as Croesus! He's a lot more prom-
ising than some of those creatures you've dragged home. What was the name
of that dreadful Frenchman who smelled like sweaty socks? . . . Jean Duke
of Scripto?

MAGS *(Laughing):* Jean-Luc Zichot!

FANNY: And that peculiar little Oriental fellow with all the teeth! Really,
Mags, he could have been put on display at the circus!

MAGS: Oh, yes, Tsu Chin. He was strange, but very sexy . . .

FANNY *(Shudders):* He had such tiny . . . feet! Really, Mags, you've got to
bear down. You're not getting any younger. Before you know it, all the nice
young men will be taken and then where ill you be? . . . All by yourself in
that grim little apartment of yours with those peculiar clothes and that bright
red hair . . .

MAGS: MY HAIR IS NOT BRIGHT RED!

FANNY: I only want what's best for you, you know that. You seem to go
out of your way to look wanting. I don't understand it. . . . Gar, what *are*
you putting your coat on for? . . . You look like some derelict out on the
street. We don't wear coats in the house. *(She helps him out of it)* That's
the way. . . . I'll just put this in the carton along with everything else . . .
(She drops it into the carton, then pauses) Isn't it about time for . . . *cock-
tails!*

GARDNER: What's that?

FANNY *taps her wrist and mimes drinking.*

GARDNER *(Looks at his watch):* Right you are, right you are! *(Exists to the bar)* THE USUAL . . . ?

FANNY: *Please!*

GARDNER *(Offstage):* HOW ABOUT SOMETHING FOR YOU, MAGS?

MAGS: SURE, WHY NOT? . . . LET'ER RIP!

GARDNER *(Offstage):* WHAT'S THAT . . . ?

FANNY: SHE SAID YES. SHE SAID   MAGS: I'LL HAVE SOME DUBONNET!
YES!

GARDNER *(Poking his head back in):* How about a little Dubonnet?

FANNY: That's just what she said. . . . She'd like some . . . Dubonnet!

GARDNER *(Goes back to the bar and hums another Jolson tune):* GEE, IT'S GREAT HAVING YOU BACK LIKE THIS, MAGS . . . IT'S JUST GREAT! *(More singing)*

FANNY *(Leaning closer to MAGS):* You have such *potential,* darling! It breaks my heart to see how you've let yourself go. If Lyman Wigglesworth . . .

MAGS: Amazing as it may seem, I don't *care* about Lyman Wigglesworth!

FANNY: From what I've heard, he's quite a lady killer!

MAGS: But with whom? . . . Don't think I haven't heard about his fling with . . . Hopie Stonewall!

FANNY *(Begins to laugh):* Oh, God, let's not get started on Hopie Stonewall again . . . ten feet tall with spots on her neck . . . *(To GARDNER)* OH, DARLING, DO HURRY BACK! WE'RE TALKING ABOUT PATHETIC HOPIE STONEWALL!

MAGS: It's not so much her incredible height and spotted skin; it's those tiny pointed teeth and the size eleven shoes!

FANNY: I love it when you're like this!

MAGS *starts clomping around the room making tiny pointed-teeth nibbling sounds.*

FANNY: GARDNER . . . YOU'RE MISSING EVERYTHING! *(Still laughing)* Why is it Boston girls are always so . . . tall?

MAGS: Hopie Stonewall isn't a Boston girl; she's a giraffe. *(She prances around the room with an imaginary dwarf-sized Lyman)* She's perfect for Lyman Wigglesworth!

GARDNER *(Returns with* FANNY'S *drink, which he hands her):* Now, where were we . . . ?

FANNY *(Trying not to laugh):* HOPIE STONEWALL . . . !

GARDNER: Oh, yes, she's the very tall one, isn't she?

FANNY *and* MAGS *burst into gales.*

MAGS: The only hope for us . . . ''Boston girls'' is to get as far away from our kind as possible.

FANNY: She always asks after you, darling. She's very fond of you, you know.

MAGS: Please, I don't want to hear!

FANNY: Your old friends are *always* asking after you.

MAGS: It's not so much how creepy they all are, as how much they remind me of myself!

FANNY: But you're not '' 'creepy,'' darling . . . just . . . shabby!

MAGS: I mean, give me a few more inches and some brown splotches here and there, and Hopie and I could be sisters!

FANNY *(In a whisper to* GARDNER): Don't you love it when Mags is like this? I could listen to her forever!

MAGS: I mean . . . look at me!

FANNY *(Gasping):* Don't stop, don't stop!

MAGS: Awkward . . . plain . . . I don't know how to dress, I don't know how to talk. When people find out Daddy's my father, they're always amazed. . . . ''Gardner Church is YOUR father?! Aw, come on, you're kidding?!''

FANNY *(In a whisper):* Isn't she divine . . . ?

MAGS: Sometimes I don't even tell them. I pretend I grew up in the Midwest somewhere . . . farming people . . . we work with our hands.

GARDNER *(To* MAGS): Well, how about a little refill . . . ?

MAGS; No, no more thanks.

Pause.

FANNY: What did you have to go and interrupt her for? She was just getting up a head of steam . . .

MAGS *(Walking over to her easel):* The great thing about being a portrait painter, you see, is it's the *other* guy that's exposed; you're safely hidden behind the canvas and easel. *(Standing behind it)* You can be as plain as a pitchfork, as inarticulate as mud, but it doesn't matter because you're completely concealed: your body, your face, your intentions. Just as you make your most intimate move, throw open your soul . . . they stretch and yawn, remembering the dog has to be let out at five. . . . To be so invisible while so enthralled . . . it takes your breath away!

GARDNER: Well put, Mags. Awfully well put!

MAGS: That's why I've always wanted to paint you, to see if I'm up to it. It's quite a risk. Remember what I went through as a child with my great masterpiece . . . ?

FANNY: You painted a masterpiece when you were a child . . . ?

MAGS: Well, it was a masterpiece to me.

FANNY: I had no idea you were precocious as a child. Gardner, do you remember Mags painting a masterpiece as a child?

MAGS: I didn't paint it. It was something I made!

FANNY: Well, this is all news to me! Gar, *do* get me another drink! I haven't had this much fun in years! *(She hands him her glass and reaches for* MAGS'S*)* Come on, darling, join me . . .

MAGS: No, no more, thanks. I don't really like the taste.

FANNY: Oh, come on, kick up your heels for once!

MAGS: No, nothing . . . really.

FANNY: Please? Pretty please? . . . To keep me company?!

MAGS *(Hands* GARDNER *her glass):* Oh, all right, what the hell . . .

FANNY: That's a good girl!   GARDNER *(Existing):* Coming right
                                             up, coming right up!

FANNY *(Yelling after* GARDNER*)*: DON'T GIVE ME TOO MUCH NOW. THE LAST ONE WAS AWFULLY STRONG . . . AND HURRY BACK SO YOU DON'T MISS ANYTHING! . . . Daddy's so cunning, I don't know what I'd do without him. If anything should happen to him, I'd just . . .

MAGS: Mummy, nothing's going to happen to him . . . !

FANNY: Well, wait till you're our age, it's no garden party. Now . . . where were we . . . ?

MAGS: My first masterpiece . . .

FANNY: Oh, yes, but *do* wait till Daddy gets back so he can hear it too. . . . YOO-HOO . . . GARRRRRRDNERRRRRR? . . . ARE YOU COMING? *(Silence)* Go and check on him will you?

GARDNER *enters with both drinks. He's very shaken.*

GARDNER: I couldn't find the ice.

FANNY: Well, *finally!*

GARDNER: It just up and disappeared . . . *(Hands* FANNY *her drink)* There you go. *(*FANNY *kisses her fingers and takes a hefty swig)* Mags. *(He hands* MAGS *her drink)*

MAGS: Thanks, Daddy.

GARDNER: Sorry about the ice.

MAGS: No problem, no problem.

GARDNER *sits down; silence.*

FANNY *(To* MAGS*)*: Well, drink up, drink up! *(*MAGS *down it in one gulp)* GOOD-GIRL! . . . Now, what's all this about a masterpiece . . . ?

MAGS: I did it during that winter you sent me away from the dinner table. I was about nine years old.

FANNY: We sent you from the dinner table?

MAGS: I was banished for six months.

FANNY: You *were?* . . . How extraordinary!

MAGS: Yes, it *was* rather extraordinary!

FANNY: But why?

MAGS: Because I played with my food.

FANNY: You did?

MAGS: I used to squirt it out between my front teeth.

FANNY: Oh, I remember that! God, it used to drive me crazy, absolutely . . . crazy! *(Pause)* "MARGARET, STOP THAT OOZING RIGHT THIS MINUTE, YOU ARE NOT A TUBE OF TOOTHPASTE!"

GARDNER: Oh, yes . . .

FANNY: It was perfectly disgusting!

GARDNER: I remember. She used to lean over her plate and squirt it out in long runny ribbons . . .

FANNY: That's enough, dear.

GARDNER: They were quite colorful, actually; decorative almost. She made the most intricate designs. They looked rather like small, moist Oriental rugs . . .

FANNY (*To* MAGS): But why, darling? What on earth possessed you to do it?

MAGS: I couldn't swallow anything. My throat just closed up. I don't know, I must have been afraid of choking or something.

GARDNER: I remember one in particular. We'd had chicken fricassee and spinach. . . . She made the most extraordinary—

FANNY (*To* GARDNER): WILL YOU PLEASE SHUT UP?! (*Pause*) Mags, what *are* you talking about? You never choked in your entire life! This is the most distressing conversation I've ever had. Don't you think it's distressing, Gar?

GARDNER: Well, that's not quite the word I'd use.

FANNY: What word *would* you use, then?

GARDNER: I don't know right off the bat, I'd have to think about it.

FANNY: THEN, THINK ABOUT IT!

Silence.

MAGS: I guess I was afraid of making a mess. I don't know; you were awfully strict about table manners. I was always afraid of losing control. What if I started to choke and began spitting up over everything . . . ?

FANNY: All right, dear, that's enough.

MAGS: No, I was really terrified about making a mess; you always got so mad whenever I spilled. If I just got rid of everything in neat little curlicues beforehand, you see . . .

FANNY: I SAID: THAT'S ENOUGH!

Silence.

MAGS: *I* thought it was quite ingenious, but you didn't see it that way. You finally sent me from the table with, "When you're ready to eat like a human being, you can come back and join us!" . . . So, it was off to my room with a tray. But I couldn't seem to eat there either. I mean, it was so strange

settling down to dinner in my *bedroom.* . . . So I just flushed everything
down the toilet and sat on my bed listening to you: clinkity-clink, clatter
clatter, slurp, slurp . . . but that got pretty boring after a while, so I looked
around for something to do. It was wintertime, because I noticed I'd left
some crayons on top of my radiator and they'd melted down into these
beautiful shimmering globs, like spilled jello, trembling and pulsing . . .

GARDNER *(Overlapping; eyes closed):*
"This luscious and impeccable fruit of life
Falls, it appears, of its own weight to earth . . ."

MAGS: Naturally, I wanted to try it myself, so I grabbed a red one and
pressed it down against the hissing lid. It oozed and bubbled like raspberry
jam!

GARDNER:
"When you were Eve, its acrid juice was sweet,
Untasted, in its heavenly, orchard air . . ."

MAGS: I mean, that radiator was really hot! It took incredible will power not
to let go, but I held on, whispering, "Mags, if you let go of this crayon,
you'll be run over by a truck on Newberry Street, so help you God!" . . .
So I pressed down harder, my fingers steaming and blistering . . .

FANNY: I had no idea about any of this, did you, Gar?

MAGS: Once I'd melted one, I was hooked! I finished off my entire supply
in one night, mixing color over color until my head swam! . . . The heat,
the smell, the brilliance that sank and rose . . . I'd never felt such exhila-
ration! . . . Every week I spent my allowance on crayons. I must have
cleared out every box of Crayolas in the city!

GARDNER *(Gazing at MAGS):* You know, I don't think I've ever seen you
looking prettier! You're awfully attractive when you get going!

FANNY: Why, what a lovely thing to say.

MAGS: AFTER THREE MONTHS THAT RADIATOR WAS . . . SPECTACULAR! I
MEAN, IT LOOKED LIKE SOME COLOSSAL FRUITCAKE, FIVE FEET TALL . . . !

FANNY: It sounds perfectly hideous.

MAGS: It was a knockout; shimmering with pinks and blues, lavenders and
maroons, turquoise and golds, oranges and creams. . . . For every color, I
imagined a taste . . . YELLOW: lemon curls dipped in sugar . . . RED: glazed
cherries laced with rum . . . GREEN: tiny peppermint leaves veined with
chocolate . . . PURPLE:—

FANNY: That's quite enough!

MAGS: And then the frosting . . . ahhhh, the frosting! A satiny mix of white and silver . . . I kept it hidden under blankets during the day. . . . My huge . . . *(She starts laughing)* looming . . . teetering sweet—

FANNY: I ASKED YOU TO STOP! GARDNER, WILL YOU PLEASE GET HER TO STOP!

GARDNER: See here, Mags, Mum asked you to—

MAGS: I was so . . . *hungry* . . . losing weight every week. I looked like a scarecrow what with the bags under my eyes and bits of crayon wrapper leaking out of my clothes. It's a wonder you didn't notice. But finally you came to my rescue . . . if you could call what happened rescue. It was more like a rout!

FANNY: Darling . . . *please!*   GARDNER: Now, look, young lady—

MAGS: The winter was almost over. . . . It was very late at night. . . . I must have been having a nightmare because suddenly you and Daddy were at my bed, shaking me. . . . I quickly glanced towards the radiator to see if it was covered. . . . *It wasn't!* It glittered and towered in the moonlight like some . . . gigantic Viennese pastry! You followed my gaze and saw it. Mummy screamed . . . "WHAT HAVE YOU GOT IN HERE? . . . MAGS, WHAT HAVE YOU BEEN DOING?" . . . She crept forward and touched it, and then jumped back. "IT'S FOOD!" she cried . . . "IT'S ALL THE FOOD SHE'S BEEN SPITTING OUT! OH, GARDNER, IT'S A MOUNTAIN OF ROTTING GARBAGE!"

FANNY *(Softly):* Yes . . . it's coming back . . . it's coming back . . .

MAGS: Daddy exited as usual; left the premises. He fainted, just keeled over onto the floor . . .

GARDNER: Gosh, I don't remember any of this . . .

MAGS: My heart stopped! I mean, I knew it was all over. My lovely creation didn't have a chance. Sure enough . . . out came the blowtorch. Well, it couldn't have *really* been a blowtorch, I mean, where would you have ever gotten a blowtorch? . . . I just have this very strong memory of you standing over my bed, your hair streaming around your face, aiming this . . . flame-thrower at my confection . . . my cake . . . my tart . . . my strudel. . . . "IT'S GOT TO BE DESTROYED IMMEDIATELY! THE THING'S ALIVE WITH VER-MIN! . . . JUST LOOK AT IT! . . . IT'S PRACTICALLY CRAWLING ACROSS THE ROOM!" . . . Of course in a sense you were right. It *was* a monument of my castoff dinners, only I hadn't built it with food. . . . I found my own ma-terials. I was languishing with hunger, but oh, dear Mother . . . I FOUND MY OWN MATERIALS . . . !

FANNY: Darling . . . *please?!*

MAGS: I tried to stop you, but you wouldn't listen. . . . OUT SHOT THE FLAME! . . . I remember these waves of wax rolling across the room and Daddy coming to, wondering what on earth was going on. . . . Well, what did you know about my abilities? . . . You see, I had . . . I mean, I *have* abilities . . . *(Struggling to say it)* I have abilities. I have . . . strong abilities. I have . . . very strong abilities. They are very strong . . . very, very strong . . .

MAGS *rises and runs out of the room overcome as* FANNY *and* GARDNER *watch, speechless. The curtain falls.*

ACT TWO
Scene 1

Three days later. Miracles have been accomplished. Almost all of the Churches' furniture has been moved out, and the cartons of dishes and clothing are gone. All that remains are odds and ends. Mags's tableau looms, impregnable. FANNY *and* GARDNER *are dressed in their formal evening clothes, frozen in their pose. They hold absolutely still.* MAGS *stands at her easel, her hands covering her eyes.*

FANNY: All right, you can look now.

MAGS (*Removes her hands*): Yes! . . . I told you you could trust me on the pose.

FANNY: Well, thank God you let us dress up. It makes all the difference. Now we really look like something.

MAGS (*Starts to sketch them*): I'll say . . .

A silence as she sketches.

GARDNER (*Recites Yeats's "The Song of Wandering Aengus" in a wonderfully resonant voice as they pose*):
"I went out to the hazel wood,
Because a fire was in my head,
And cut and peeled a hazel wand,
And hooked a berry to a thread,
And when white moths were on the wing,
And moth-like stars were flickering out,
I dropped the berry in a stream
And caught a little silver trout.

When I had laid it on the floor
I went to blow the fire a-flame,
But something rustled on the floor,
And someone called me by my name:
It had become a glimmering girl
With apple blossoms in her hair
Who called me by my name and ran
And faded through the brightening air.

Though I am old with wandering
Through hollow lands and hilly lands,
I will find out where she has gone,
And kiss her lips and take her hands;
And walk among long dappled grass,
And pluck till time and times are done,
The silver apples of the moon,
The golden apples of the sun.''

FANNY: That's lovely, dear. Just lovely. Is it one of yours?

GARDNER: No, no, it's Yeats. I'm using it in my book.

FANNY: Well, you recited it beautifully, but then you've always recited beautifully. That's how you wooed me, in case you've forgotten. . . . You must have memorized every love poem in the English language! There was no stopping you when you got going . . . your Shakespeare, Byron, and Shelley . . . you were shameless . . . *shameless*!

GARDNER *(Eyes closed):*
"I will find out where she has gone,
And kiss her lips and take her hands . . .''

FANNY: And then there was your own poetry to do battle with; your sonnets and quatrains. When you got going with them, there was nothing left of me! You could have had your pick of any girl in Boston! Why you chose me, I'll never understand. I had no looks to speak of and nothing much in the brains department. . . . Well, what did you know about women and the world? . . . What did any of us know . . . ?

Silence.

FANNY: GOD, MAGS, HOW LONG ARE WE SUPPOSED TO SIT LIKE THIS? . . . IT'S AGONY!

MAGS *(Working away):* You're doing fine . . . just fine . . .

FANNY *(Breaking her pose):* It's so . . . boring!

MAGS: Come on, don't move. You can have a break soon.

FANNY: I had no idea it would be so boring!

GARDNER: Gee, I'm enjoying it.

FANNY: You would . . . !

A pause.

GARDNER *(Begins reciting more Yeats, almost singing it):*

"He stood among a crowd at Drumahair;
His heart hung all upon a silken dress,
And he had known at last some tenderness,
Before earth made of him her sleepy care;
But when a man poured fish into a pile,
It seemed they raised their little silver heads . . ."

FANNY: Gar . . . PLEASE! *(She lurches out of her seat)* God, I can't take this anymore!

MAGS *(Keeps sketching GARDNER)*: I know it's tedious at first, but it gets easier . . .

FANNY: It's like a Chinese water torture! *(Crosses to MAGS and looks at GARDNER posing)* Oh, darling, you look marvelous, absolutely marvelous! Why don't you just do Daddy!?

MAGS: Because you look marvelous too. I want to do you both!

FANNY: Please! . . . I have one foot in the grave and you know it! Also, we're way behind in our packing. There's still one room left which everyone seems to have forgotten about!

GARDNER: Which one is that?

FANNY: You know perfectly well which one it is!

GARDNER: I do . . . ?

FANNY: Yes, you do!

GARDNER: Well, it's news to me.

FANNY: I'll give you a hint. It's in . . . *that* direction. *(She points)*

GARDNER: The dining room?

FANNY: No.

GARDNER: The bedroom?

FANNY: No.

GARDNER: Mags' room?

FANNY: No.

GARDNER: The kitchen?

FANNY: *Gar?!*

GARDNER: The guest room?

FANNY: Your God-awful study!

GARDNER: Oh, shit!

FANNY: That's right, "Oh, shit!" It's books and papers up to the ceiling! If you ask me, we should just forget it's there and quietly tiptoe away . . .

GARDNER: My study . . . !

FANNY: Let the new owners dispose of everything . . .

GARDNER *(Gets out of his posing chair):* Now, just one minute . . .

FANNY: You never look at half the stuff in there!

GARDNER: I don't want you touching those books! They're mine!

FANNY: Darling, we're moving to a cottage the size of a handkerchief! Where, pray tell, is there room for all your books?

GARDNER: I don't know. We'll just have to make room!

MAGS *(Sketching away):* RATS!

FANNY: I don't know what we're doing fooling around with Mags like this when there's still so much to do . . .

GARDNER *(Sits back down, overwhelmed):* My study . . . !

FANNY: You can stay with her if you'd like, but one of us has got to tackle those books! *(She exits to his study)*

GARDNER: I'm not up to this.

MAGS: Oh, good, you're staying!

GARDNER: There's a lifetime of work in there . . .

MAGS: Don't worry, I'll help. Mum and I will be able to pack everything up in no time.

GARDNER: God . . .

MAGS: It won't be so bad . . .

GARDNER: I'm just not up to it.

MAGS: We'll all pitch in . . .

GARDNER *sighs, speechless. A silence as* FANNY *comes staggering in with an armload of books, which she drops to the floor with a crash.*

GARDNER: WHAT WAS THAT?!   MAGS: GOOD GRIEF!

FANNY *(Sheepish):* Sorry, sorry . . . *(She exits for more)*

GARDNER: I don't know if I can take this . . .

MAGS: Moving is awful . . . I know . . .

GARDNER *(Settling back into his pose):* Ever since Mum began tearing the house apart, I've been having these dreams. . . . I'm a child again back at 16 Louisberg Square . . . and this stream of moving men is carrying furniture into our house . . . van after van of tables and chairs, sofas and love seats, desks and bureaus . . . rugs, bathtubs, mirrors, chiming clocks, pianos, iceboxes, china cabinets . . . but what's amazing is that all of it is familiar . . .

FANNY *comes in with another load, which she drops on the floor. She exits for more.*

GARDNER: No matter how many items appear, I've seen every one of them before. Since my mother is standing in the midst of it directing traffic, I ask her where it's all coming from, but she doesn't hear me because of the racket . . . so finally I just scream out . . . "WHERE IS ALL THIS FURNITURE COMING FROM?" . . . Just as a moving man is carrying Toots into the room, she looks at me and says, "Why, from the land of Skye!" . . . The next thing I know, *people* are being carried in along with it . . .

FANNY *enters with her next load; drops it and exits.*

GARDNER: People I've never seen before are sitting around our dining-room table. A group of foreigners is going through my books, chattering in a language I've never heard before. A man is playing a Chopin polonaise on Aunt Alice's piano. Several children are taking baths in our tubs from Cotuit . . .

MAGS: It sounds marvelous.

GARDNER: Well, it isn't marvelous at all because all of these perfect strangers have taken over our things . . .

FANNY *enters, hurls down another load and exits.*

MAGS: How odd . . .

GARDNER: Well, it *is* odd, but then something even odder happens . . .

MAGS *(Sketching away):* Tell me, tell me!

GARDNER: Well, our beds are carried in. They're all made up with sheets and everything, but instead of all these strange people in them, *we're* in them . . . !

MAGS: What's so odd about that?

GARDNER: Well, you and Mum are brought in, both sleeping like angels . . . Mum snoring away to beat the band . . .

MAGS: Yes . . .

FANNY *enters with another load, lets it fall.*

GARDNER: But there's no one in mine. It's completely empty, never even been slept in! It's as if I were dead or had never even existed . . .

FANNY *exits.*

GARDNER: "HEY . . . WAIT UP!" I yell to the moving men . . . "THAT'S MY BED YOU'VE GOT THERE!" But they don't stop; they don't even acknowledge me. . . . "HEY, COME BACK HERE . . . I WANT TO GET INTO MY BED!" I cry again and I start running after them . . . down the hall, through the dining room, past the library. . . . Finally I catch up to them and hurl myself right into the center of the pillow. Just as I'm about to land, the bed suddenly vanishes and I go crashing down to the floor like some insect that's been hit by a fly swatter!

FANNY *staggers in with her final load; she drops it with a crash and then collapses in her posing chair.*

FANNY: THAT'S IT FOR ME! I'M DEAD!

Silence.

FANNY: Come on, Mags, how about you doing a little work around here.

MAGS: That's all I've been doing! This is the first free moment you've given me!

FANNY: You should see all the books in there . . . and papers! There are enough loose papers to sink a ship!

GARDNER: Why is it we're moving, again . . . ?

FANNY: Because life is getting too complicated here.

GARDNER: *(Remembering):* Oh, yes . . .

FANNY: And we can't afford it anymore.

GARDNER: That's right, that's right . . .

FANNY: We don't have the . . . *income* we used to!

GARDNER: Oh, yes . . . *income!*

FANNY *(Assuming her pose again):* Of course, we have our savings and various trust funds, but I wouldn't dream of touching those!

GARDNER: No, no, you must never dip into capital!

FANNY: I told Daddy I'd be perfectly happy to buy a gun and put a bullet through our heads so we could avoid all this, but he wouldn't hear of it!

MAGS (*Sketching away*): No, I shouldn't think so.

Pause.

FANNY: I've always admired people who kill themselves when they get to our stage of life. Well, no one can touch my Uncle Edmond in that department . . .

MAGS: I know, I know . . .

FANNY: The day before his seventieth birthday he climbed to the top of the Old North Church and hurled himself face down into Salem Street! They had to scrape him up with a spatula! God, he was a remarkable man . . . state senator, president of Harvard . . .

GARDNER (*Rises and wanders over to his books*): Well, I guess I'm going to have to do something about all of these . . .

FANNY: Come on Mags, help Daddy! Why don't you start bringing in his papers . . .

GARDNER *sits on the floor; he picks up a book and soon is engrossed in it.* MAGS *keeps sketching, oblivious. Silence.*

FANNY (*To* MAGS): Darling? . . . HELLO? . . . God, you two are impossible! Just look at you . . . heads in the clouds! No one would ever know we've got to be out of here in two days. If it weren't for me, nothing would get done around here . . . (*She starts stacking Gardner's books into piles*) There! That's all the maroon ones!

GARDNER (*Looks up*): What do you mean, *maroon* ones?!

FANNY: All your books that are maroon are in *this* pile . . . and your books that are green in *that* pile! . . . I'm trying to bring some order into your life for once. This will make unpacking so much easier.

GARDNER: But, my dear Fanny, it's not the color of a book that distinguishes it, but what's *inside* it!

FANNY: This will be a great help, you'll see. Now what about this awful striped thing? (*She picks up a slim, aged volume*) Can't it go . . . ?

GARDNER: No!

FANNY: But it's as queer as Dick's hatband! There are no others like it.

GARDNER: Open it and read. Go on . . . open it!

FANNY: We'll get nowhere at this rate.

GARDNER: I said . . . READ!

FANNY: Really, Gar, I—

GARDNER: Read the dedication!

FANNY (*Opens and reads*): "To Gardner Church, you led the way. With gratitude and affection, Robert Frost." (*She closes it and hands it to him*)

GARDNER: It was published the same year as my *Salem Gardens*.

FANNY (*Picking up a very worn book*): Well, what about this dreadful thing? It's filthy. (*She blows off a cloud of dust*)

GARDNER: Please . . . *please?!*

FANNY (*Looking through it*): It's all in French.

GARDNER (*Snatching it away from her*): André Malraux gave me that . . . !

FANNY: I'm just trying to help.

GARDNER: It's a first edition of Baudelaire's *Fleurs du mal*.

FANNY (*Giving it back*): Well, pardon me for living!

GARDNER: Why do you have to drag everything in here in the first place . . . ?

FANNY: Because there's no room in your study. You ought to see the mess in there! . . . WAKE UP, MAGS, ARE YOU GOING TO PITCH IN OR NOT?!

GARDNER: I'm not up to this.

FANNY: Well, you'd better be unless you want to be left behind!

MAGS (*Stops her sketching*): All right, all right . . . I just hope you'll give me some more time later this evening.

FANNY (*To* MAGS): Since you're young and in the best shape, why don't you bring in the books and I'll cope with the papers. (*She exits to the study*)

GARDNER: Now just a minute . . .

FANNY (*Offstage*): WE NEED A STEAM SHOVEL FOR THIS!

MAGS: Okay, what do you want me to do?

GARDNER: Look, I don't want you messing around with my—

FANNY *enters with an armful of papers, which she drops into an empty carton.*

GARDNER: HEY, WHAT'S GOING ON HERE?!

FANNY: I'm packing up your papers. COME ON, MAGS, LET'S GET CRACKING! *(She exits for more papers)*

GARDNER *(Plucks several papers out of the carton):* What is this . . . ?

MAGS *(Exits into his study):* GOOD LORD, WHAT HAVE YOU DONE IN HERE?!

GARDNER *(Reading):* This is my manuscript.

FANNY *enters with another batch, which she tosses on top of the others.*

GARDNER: What *are* you doing?!

FANNY: Packing, darling . . . PACKING! *(She exits for more)*

GARDNER: SEE HERE, YOU CAN'T MANHANDLE MY THINGS THIS WAY!

MAGS *enters, staggering under a load of books, which she sets down on the floor.*

GARDNER: *I* PACK MY MANUSCRIPT! I KNOW WHERE EVERYTHING IS!

FANNY *(Offstage):* IF IT WERE UP TO YOU, WE'D NEVER GET OUT OF HERE! WE'RE UNDER A TIME LIMIT, GARDNER. KITTY'S PICKING US UP IN TWO DAYS . . . TWO . . . DAYS! *(She enters with a larger batch of papers and heads for the carton)*

GARDNER *(Grabbing Fanny's wrist):* NOW, HOLD IT! . . . JUST . . . HOLD IT RIGHT THERE!

FANNY: OOOOOWWWWWWWW!

GARDNER: *I* PACK MY THINGS!

FANNY: LET GO, YOU'RE HURTING ME!

GARDNER: THAT'S MY MANUSCRIPT! GIVE IT TO ME!

FANNY *(Lifting the papers high over her head):* I'M IN CHARGE OF THIS MOVE, GARDNER! WE'VE GOT TO GET CRACKING!

GARDNER: I said . . . GIVE IT TO ME!

MAGS: Come on, Mum, let him have it.

FANNY *and* GARDNER *struggle.*

GARDNER *(Finally wrenches the pages from* FANNY*):* LET . . . ME . . . HAVE IT! . . . THAT'S MORE LIKE IT!

FANNY *(Soft and weepy):* You see what he's like? . . . I try and help with his packing and what does he do . . . ?

GARDNER (*Rescues the rest of his papers from the carton*): YOU DON'T JUST THROW EVERYTHING INTO A BOX LIKE A PILE OF GARBAGE! THIS IS A BOOK, FANNY. SOMETHING I'VE BEEN WORKING ON FOR TWO YEARS! (*Trying to assemble his papers, but only making things worse, dropping them all over the place*) You show a little respect for my things. . . . You don't just throw them around every which way. . . . It's tricky trying to make sense of poetry; it's much easier to write the stuff . . . that is, if you've still got it in you . . .

MAGS: Here, let me help . . . (*Taking some of the papers*)

GARDNER: Criticism is tough sledding. You can't just dash off a few images here, a few rhymes there . . .

MAGS: Do you have these pages numbered in any way?

FANNY (*Returning to her posing chair*): HA!

GARDNER: This is just the introduction.

MAGS: I don't see any numbers on these.

GARDNER (*Exiting to his study*): The important stuff is in my study . . .

FANNY (*To* MAGS): You don't know the half of it . . . *not the half* . . . !

GARDNER (*Offstage; thumping around*): HAVE YOU SEEN THOSE YEATS POEMS I JUST HAD . . . ?

MAGS (*Reading over several pages*): What is this? . . . It doesn't make sense. It's just fragments . . . pieces of poems.

FANNY: That's it, honey! That's his book. His great critical study! Now that he can't write his own poetry, he's trying to explain other people's. The only problem is, he can't get beyond typing them out. The poor lamb doesn't have the stamina to get beyond the opening stanzas, let alone trying to make sense of them.

GARDNER (*Thundering back with more papers, which keep falling*): GODDAMMIT, FANNY, WHAT DID YOU DO IN THERE? I CAN'T FIND ANYTHING!

FANNY: I just took the papers that were on your desk.

GARDNER: Well, the entire beginning is gone. (*He exits*)

FANNY: I'M TRYING TO HELP YOU, DARLING!

GARDNER (*Returns with another armload*): SEE THAT? . . . NO SIGN OF CHAPTER ONE OR TWO . . . (*He flings it all down to the floor*)

FANNY: Gardner . . . PLEASE?!

GARDNER (*Kicking through the mess*): I TURN MY BACK FOR ONE MINUTE AND WHAT HAPPENS? . . . MY ENTIRE STUDY IS TORN APART! (*He exits*)

MAGS: Oh, Daddy . . . don't . . . please . . . Daddy . . . *please?!*

GARDNER (*Returns with a new batch of papers, which he tosses up into the air*): THROWN OUT! . . . THE BEST PART IS THROWN OUT! . . . lost . . . (*He starts to exit again*)

MAGS (*Reads one of the fragments to steady herself*):
"I have known the inexorable sadness of pencils,
Neat in their boxes, dolor of pad and paperweight,
All the misery of manila folders and mucilage . . . "
They're beautiful . . . just beautiful.

GARDNER (*Stops*): Hey, what's that you've got there?

FANNY: It's your manuscript, darling. You see, it's right where you left it.

GARDNER (*To* MAGS): Read that again.

MAGS:
"I have known the inexorable sadness of pencils,
Neat in their boxes, dolor of pad and paperweight,
All the misery of manila folders and mucilage . . . "

GARDNER: Well, well, what do you know . . .

FANNY (*Hands him several random papers*): You see . . . no one lost anything. Everything's here, still intact.

GARDNER (*Reads*):
"I knew a woman, lovely in her bones,
When small birds sighed, she would sigh back at them;
Ah, when she moved, she moved more ways than one:
The shapes a bright container can contain! . . . "

FANNY (*Hands him another*): And . . .

GARDNER (*Reads*): Ahh . . . Frost . . .
"Some say the world will end in fire,
Some say in ice.
From what I've tasted of desire
I hold with those who favor fire."

FANNY (*Under her breath to* MAGS): He can't give up the words. It's the best he can do. (*Handing him another*) Here you go, here's more.

GARDNER:
"Farm boys wild to couple

With anything   with soft-wooded trees
With mounds of earth   mounds
Of pinestraw   will keep themselves off
Animals by legends of their own . . .''

MAGS *(Eyes shut):* Oh, Daddy, I can't bear it . . . I . . .

FANNY: Of course no one will ever publish this.

GARDNER: Oh, here's a marvelous one. Listen to this!
''There came a Wind like a Bugle—
It quivered through the Grass
And a Green Chill upon the Heat
So ominous did pass
We barred the Windows and the Doors
As from an Emerald Ghost—
The Doom's electric Moccasin . . .''
SHIT, WHERE DID THE REST OF IT GO . . . ?

FANNY: Well, don't ask *me*.

GARDNER: It just stopped in mid-air!

FANNY: Then go look for the original.

GARDNER: Good idea, good idea! *(He exits to his study)*

FANNY *(To* MAGS): He's incontinent now, too. He wets his pants, in case
you haven't noticed. *(She starts laughing)* You're not laughing. Don't you
think it's funny? Daddy needs diapers. . . . I don't know about you, but I
could use a drink! GAR . . . WILL YOU GET ME A SPLASH WHILE YOU'RE OUT
THERE . . . ?

MAGS: STOP IT!

FANNY: It means we can't go out anymore. I mean, what would people
say . . . ?

MAGS: Stop it. Just stop it.

FANNY: My poet laureate can't hold it in! *(She laughs harder)*

MAGS: That's enough . . . STOP IT . . . Mummy . . . I beg of you . . . *please
stop it!*

GARDNER *enters with a book and indeed a large stain has blossomed on his
trousers. He plucks it away from his leg.*

GARDNER: Here we go . . . I found it . . .

FANNY *(Pointing at it):* See that? See? . . . He just did it again! *(Goes off into a shower of laughter)*

MAGS: *(Looks, turns away):* SHUT . . . UP! . . . *(Building to a howl)* WILL YOU PLEASE JUST . . . SHUT . . . UP!

FANNY: *(To* GARDNER): Hey, what about that drink?

FANNY: Never mind, I'll get it, I'll get it.

FANNY *exits, convulsed. Silence.*

GARDNER: Well, where were we?

MAGS *(Near tears):* Your poem.

GARDNER: Oh yes . . . the Dickinson. *(He shuts his eyes, reciting from memory, holding the book against his chest)*
"There came a Wind like a Bugle—
It quivered through the Grass
And a Green Chill upon the Heat
So ominous did pass
We barred the Windows and the Doors
As from an Emerald Ghost—"
(Opens the book and starts riffling through it) Let's see now, where's the rest? . . . *(He finally finds it)* Ahhh, here we go . . . !

FANNY *(Reenters, drink in hand):* I'm back! *(Takes one look at* GARDNER *and bursts out laughing again)*

MAGS: I don't believe you! How you can laugh at him?!

They all speak simultaneously as MAGS *gets angrier and angrier.*

FANNY: I'm sorry, I wish I could stop, but there's really nothing else to do. Look at him . . . just . . . look at him . . . !

MAGS: It's so cruel. . . . You're so . . . incredibly cruel to him. . . . I mean, YOUR DISDAIN REALLY TAKES MY BREATH AWAY! YOU'RE IN A CLASS BY YOURSELF WHEN IT COMES TO HUMILIATION!

GARDNER *(Reading):*
"The Doom's electric Moccasin
That very instant passed—
On a strange Mob of panting Trees
And Fences fled away
And Rivers where the Houses ran
Those looked that lived—that Day—
The Bell within the steeple wild

The flying tidings told—
How much can come
And much can go,
And yet abide the World!''
(He shuts the book with a bang, pauses and looks around the room, confused) Now, where was I . . . ?

FANNY: Safe and sound in the middle of the living room with Mags and me.

GARDNER: But I was looking for something, wasn't I . . . ?

FANNY: Your manuscript.

GARDNER: THAT'S RIGHT! MY MANUSCRIPT! My manuscript!

FANNY: And here it is all over the floor. See, you're standing on it.

GARDNER *(Picks up a few pages and looks at them):* Why, so I am . . .

FANNY: Now all we have to do is get it up off the floor and packed neatly into these cartons!

GARDNER: Yes, yes, that's right. Into the cartons.

FANNY *(Kicks a carton over to him):* Here, you use this one and I'll start over here . . . *(She starts dropping papers into a carton nearby)* BOMBS AWAY! . . . Hey . . . this is fun!

GARDNER *(Picks up his own pile, lifts it high over his head and flings it down into the carton):* BOMBS AWAY . . . This *is* fun!

FANNY: I told you! The whole thing is to figure out a system!

GARDNER: I don't know what I'd do without you, Fan. I thought I'd lost everything.

FANNY *(Makes dive-bomber noises and machine-gun explosions as she wheels more and more papers into the carton):* TAKE THAT AND THAT AND THAT!

GARDNER *(Joins in the fun, outdoing her with dips, dives, and blastings of his own):* BLAM BLAM BLAM BLAM! . . . ZZZZZZZZRAAAAAA FOOM! . . . BLATTY-DE-BLATTY-DE-BLATTY-DE-KABOOOOOOOOM! . . . WHAAAAAAA . . . DA-DAT-DAT-DAT-DAT-DAT . . . WHEEEEEEEE AAAAAAAAAAAAA . . . FOOOOOO . . .

They get louder and louder as papers fly every which way.

FANNY *(Mimes getting hit with a bomb):* AEEEEEEEIIIIIIIIIIII! YOU GOT ME RIGHT IN THE GIZZARD! *(She collapses on the floor and starts going through death throes, having an absolute ball)*

GARDNER: TAKE THAT AND THAT AND THAT AND THAT . . . *(A series of explosions follow)*

MAGS *(Furious)*: This is how you help him? . . . THIS IS HOW YOU PACK HIS THINGS?

FANNY: I keep him company. I get involved . . . which is a hell of a lot more than you do!

MAGS *(Wild with rage)*: BUT YOU'RE MAKING A MOCKERY OF HIM. . . . YOU TREAT HIM LIKE A CHILD OR SOME DIMWITTED SERVING BOY. HE'S JUST AN AMUSEMENT TO YOU!

FANNY *(Fatigue has finally overtaken her. She's calm, almost serene)*: And to you who see him once a year, if that . . . what is he to *you*? . . . I mean, what do you give him from yourself that costs you something? . . . Hmmmmmm? . . . *(Imitating* MAGS*)* "Oh, hi Daddy, it's great to see you again. How have you been? . . . Gee, I love your hair. It's gotten so . . . *white!*" . . . What color do you expect it to get when he's this age? . . . I mean, if you care so much how he looks, why don't you come and see him once in a while? . . . But oh, no . . . you have your paintings to do and your shows to put on. You just come and see us when the whim strikes. *(Imitating* MAGS*)* "Hey, you know what would be really great? . . . To do a portrait of you! I've always wanted to paint you, you're such great subjects!" . . . *Paint* us?! . . . What about opening your eyes and really *seeing* us? . . . Noticing what's going on around here for a change! It's all over for Daddy and me. This is it! "Finita la commedia!" . . . All I'm trying to do is exit with a little flourish; have some fun. . . . What's so terrible about that? . . . It can get pretty grim around here, in case you haven't noticed . . . Daddy, tap-tap-tapping out his nonsense all day; me traipsing around to the thrift shops trying to amuse myself. . . . He never keeps me company anymore; never takes me out anywhere. . . . I'd put a bullet through my head in a minute, but then who'd look after him? . . . What do you think we're moving to the cottage for? . . . So I can watch him like a hawk and make sure he doesn't get lost. Do you think that's anything to look forward to? . . . Being Daddy's nursemaid out in the middle of nowhere? I'd much rather stay here in Boston with the few friends I have left, but you can't always do what you want in this world! "L'homme propose, Dieu dispose!" . . . If you want to paint us so badly, you ought to paint us as we really are. There's your picture."

FANNY *points to* GARDNER, *who's quietly playing with a paper glide.*

FANNY: Daddy spread out on the floor with all his toys and me hovering over him to make sure he doesn't hurt himself! *(She goes over to him)* YOO-HOO . . . GAR? . . . HELLO?

GARDNER *(Looks up at her):* Oh, hi there, Fan. What's up?

FANNY: How's the packing coming . . . ?

GARDNER: Packing . . . ?

FANNY: Yes, you were packing your manuscript, remember? *(She lifts up a page and lets it fall into a carton)*

GARDNER: Oh, yes . . .

FANNY: Here's your picture, Mags. Face over this way . . . turn your easel over here . . . *(She lets a few more papers fall)* Up, up . . . and away . . .

Blackout.

Scene 2

The last day. All the books and boxes are gone. The room is completely empty except for Mags's backdrop. Late afternoon light dapples the walls; it changes from pale peach to deeper violet. The finished portrait sits on the easel, covered with a cloth. MAGS *is taking down the backdrop.*

FANNY *(Offstage to* GARDNER): DON'T FORGET TOOTS!

GARDNER *(Offstage; from another part of the house):* WHAT'S THAT?

FANNY *(Offstage):* I SAID: DON'T FORGET TOOTS! HIS CAGE IS SITTING IN THE MIDDLE OF YOUR STUDY!

Silence.

FANNY *(Offstage):* HELLO? . . . ARE YOU THERE?

GARDNER *(Offstage):* I'LL BE RIGHT WITH YOU; I'M JUST GETTING TOOTS!

GARDNER *(Offstage):* WHAT'S THAT? I CAN'T HEAR YOU?

FANNY *(Offstage):* I'M GOING THROUGH THE ROOMS ONE MORE TIME TO MAKE SURE WE DIDN'T FORGET ANYTHING . . . KITTY'S PICKING US UP IN FIFTEEN MINUTES, SO PLEASE BE READY. . . . SHE'S DROPPING MAGS OFF AT THE STATION AND THEN IT'S OUT TO ROUTE 3 AND THE CAPE HIGHWAY . . .

GARDNER *(Enters, carrying Toots in his cage):* Well, this is it. The big moment has finally come, eh what, Toots? *(He see* MAGS) Oh, hi there, Mags, I didn't see you . . .

MAGS: Oh, hi, Daddy, I'm just taking this down . . . *(She does and walks over to* TOOTS*)* Oh, Toots, I'll miss you. *(She makes little chattering noises into his cage)*

GARDNER: Come on, recite a little Gray's *Elegy* for Mags before we go.

MAGS: Yes, Mum said he was really good at it now.

GARDNER: Well, the whole thing is to keep at it every day. *(Slowly to Toots)*
 ''The curfew tolls the knell of parting day,
 The lowing herd wind slowly o'er the lea . . .''
Come on, show Mags your stuff! *(Slower)*
 ''The curfew tolls the knell of parting day,
 The lowing herd wind slowly o'er the lea . . .''

Silence; GARDNER *makes little chattering sounds.*

GARDNER: Come on, Toots, old boy . . .

MAGS: How does it go?

GARDNER *(To* MAGS*)*:
 ''The curfew tolls the knell of parting day,
 The lowing herd wind slowly o'er the lea . . .''

MAGS *(Slowly to Toots)*:
 The curfew tolls for you and me,
 As quietly the herd winds down . . .

GARDNER: No, no, it's ''The curfew tolls the knell of parting *day* . . .''*!*

MAGS *(Repeating after him)*: ''The curfew tolls the knell of parting day . . .''

GARDNER: ''The lowing herd wind slowly o'er the lea . . .''

MAGS *(With a deep breath)*:
 The curfew tolls at parting day,
 The herd low slowly down the lea . . . no, *knell!*
 They come winding down the *knell!*

GARDNER: Listen, Mags . . . *listen!*

A pause.

TOOTS *(Loud and clear with* GARDNER'S *inflection)*:
 ''The curfew tolls the knell of parting day,
 The lowing herd wind slowly o'er the lea,
 The ploughman homeward plods his weary way,
 And leaves the world to darkness and to me.''

MAGS: HE SAID IT. . . . HE SAID IT! . . . AND IN YOUR VOICE
. . . OH, DADDY, THAT'S AMAZING!

GARDNER: Well, Toots is very smart, which is more than I can say for a lot
of people I know . . .

MAGS *(To* TOOTS): Polly want a cracker? Polly want a cracker?

GARDNER: You can teach a parakeet to say anything; all you need is patience . . .

MAGS: But *poetry* . . . that's so hard . . .

FANNY *enters carrying a suitcase and Gardner's typewriter in its case. She's
dressed in her traveling suit, wearing a hat to match.*

FANNY: WELL, THERE YOU ARE! I THOUGHT YOU'D DIED!

MAGS *(To* FANNY): HE SAID IT! I FINALLY HEARD TOOTS RECITE GRAY'S *EL-
EGY. (She makes silly clucking sounds into the cage)*

FANNY: Isn't it uncanny how much he sounds like Daddy? Sometimes when
I'm alone here with him, I've actually thought he *was* Daddy and started
talking to him. Oh, yes, Toots and I have had quite a few meaty conversations together!

FANNY *wolf-whistles into the cage; then draws back.* GARDNER *covers the
cage with a traveling cloth. Silence.*

FANNY *(Looking around the room):* God, the place looks so bare.

MAGS: I still can't believe it . . . Cotuit, year round. I wonder if there'll be
any phosphorus when you get there?

FANNY: What on earth are you talking about? *(She carries the discarded
backdrop out into the hall)*

MAGS: Remember that summer when the ocean was full of phosphorus?

GARDNER *(Taking* TOOTS *out into the hall):* Oh, yes . . .

MAGS: It was a great mystery where it came from or why it settled in Cotuit.
But one evening when Daddy and I were taking a swim, suddenly it was
there!

GARDNER *(Returns):* I remember.

MAGS: I don't know where Mum was . . .

FANNY *(Reentering):* Probably doing the dishes!

MAGS *(To* GARDNER): As you dove into the water, this shower of silvery
green sparks erupted all around you. It was incredible! I thought you were

turning into a saint or something; but then you told me to jump in too and the same thing happened to me . . .

GARDNER: Oh, yes, I remember that . . . the water smelled all queer.

MAGS: What *is* phosphorus, anyway?

GARDNER: Chemicals, chemicals . . .

FANNY: No, it isn't. Phosphorus is a green liquid inside insects. Fireflies have it. When you see sparks in the water it means insects are swimming around . . .

GARDNER: Where on earth did you get that idea . . . ?

FANNY: If you're bitten by one of them, it's fatal!

MAGS: And the next morning it was still there . . .

GARDNER: It was the damndest stuff to get off! We'd have to stay in the shower a good ten minutes. It comes from chemical waste, you see . . .

MAGS: Our bodies looked like mercury as we swam around . . .

GARDNER: It stained all the towels a strange yellow green.

MAGS: I was in heaven, and so were you for that matter. You'd finished your day's poetry and would turn somersaults like some happy dolphin . . .

FANNY: Damned dishes . . . why didn't I see any of this?!

MAGS: I remember one night in particular. . . . We sensed the phosphorus was about to desert us; blow off to another town. We were chasing each other under water. At one point I lost you, the brilliance was so intense . . . but finally our foot appeared . . . then your leg. I grabbed it! . . . I remember wishing the moment would hold forever; that we could just be fixed there, laughing and iridescent. . . . Then I began to get panicky because I knew it would pass; it was passing already. You were slipping from my grasp. The summer was almost over. I'd be going back to art school; you'd be going back to Boston. . . . Even as I was reaching for you, you were gone. We'd never be like that again.

Silence. FANNY *spies Mags's portrait covered on the easel.*

FANNY: What's that over there? Don't tell me we forgot something!

MAGS: It's your portrait. I finished it.

FANNY: You finished it? How on earth did you manage that?

MAGS: I stayed up all night.

FANNY: You did? . . . *I* didn't hear you, did you hear her, Gar . . . ?

GARDNER: Not a peep, not a peep!

MAGS: Well, I wanted to get it done before you left. You know, see what you thought. It's not bad, considering . . . I mean, I did it almost completely from memory. The light was terrible and I was trying to be quiet so I wouldn't wake you. It was hardly an ideal situation. . . . I mean, you weren't the most cooperative models . . . *(She suddenly panics and snatches the painting off the easel. She hugs it to her chest and starts dancing around the room with it)* Oh, God, you're going to hate it! You're going to hate it! How did I ever get into this? . . . Listen, you don't really want to see it . . . it's nothing . . . just a few dabs here and there. . . . It was awfully late when I finished it. The light was really impossible and my eyes were hurting like crazy. . . . Look, why don't we just go out to the sidewalk and wait for Kitty so she doesn't have to honk—

GARDNER *(Snatches the painting out from under her grasp):* WOULD YOU JUST SHUT UP A MINUTE AND LET US SEE IT?

MAGS *(Laughing and crying):* But it's nothing, Daddy . . . *really!* . . . I've done better with my eyes closed! It was so late I could hardly see anything and then I spilled a whole bottle of thinner into my palette . . .

GARDNER *(Sets the portrait down on the easel and stands back to look at it):* THERE!

MAGS: *(Dancing around them in a panic):* Listen, it's just a quick sketch. . . . It's still wet. . . . I didn't have enough time. . . . It takes at least forty hours to do a decent portrait . . .

Suddenly it's very quiet as FANNY *and* GARDNER *stand back to look at the painting. More and more beside herself,* MAGS *keeps leaping around the room wrapping her arms around herself, making little whimpering sounds.*

MAGS: Please don't . . . no . . . don't . . . oh, please! . . . Come on, don't look. . . . Oh, God, don't . . . please . . .

An eternity passes as FANNY *and* GARDNER *gaze at their portrait.*

GARDNER: Well . . .

FANNY: Well . . .

More silence.

FANNY: I think it's perfectly dread-   GARDNER: Awfully clever, awfully
ful!   clever!

FANNY: What on earth did you do to my face . . . ?

GARDNER: I particularly like Mum!

FANNY: Since when do I have purple skin?!

MAGS: I told you it was nothing, just a silly—

GARDNER: She looks like a million dollars!

FANNY: AND WILL YOU LOOK AT MY HAIR . . . IT'S BRIGHT ORANGE!

GARDNER *(Views the painting from another angle):* It's really very good!

FANNY *(Pointing):* That doesn't look anything like me!

GARDNER: First-rate!

FANNY: Since when do I have purple skin and bright orange hair?

MAGS *(Trying to snatch the painting off the easel):* Listen, you don't have to worry about my feelings . . . really . . . I—

GARDNER *(Blocking her way):* NOT SO FAST . . .

FANNY: And look at how I'm sitting! I've never sat like that in my life!

GARDNER *(Moving closer to the painting):* Yes, yes, it's awfully clever . . .

FANNY: I HAVE NO FEET!

GARDNER: The whole thing is quite remarkable!

FANNY: And what happened to my legs, pray tell? . . . They just vanish below the knees! . . . At least my dress is presentable. I've always loved that dress.

GARDNER: It sparkles somehow . . .

FANNY *(To GARDNER):* Don't you think it's becoming?

GARDNER: Yes, very becoming, awfully becoming . . .

FANNY *(Examining it at closer range):* Yes, she got the dress very well, how it shows off what's left of my figure . . . My smile is nice too.

GARDNER: Good and wide . . .

FANNY: I love how the corners of my mouth turn up . . .

GARDNER: It's very clever . . .

FANNY: They're almost quivering . . .

GARDNER: Good lighting effects!

FANNY: Actually, I look quite . . . *young,* don't you think?

GARDNER (*To* MAGS): You're awfully good with those highlights.

FANNY (*Looking at it from different angles*): And *you* look darling . . . !

GARDNER: Well, I don't know about that . . .

FANNY: No, you look absolutely darling. Good enough to eat

MAGS (*In a whisper*): They like it. . . . They like it!

A silence as FANNY *and* GARDNER *keep gazing at their portrait.*

FANNY: You know what it is? The wispy brush stroke makes us look like a couple in a French Impressionist painting.

GARDNER: Yes, I see what you mean . . .

FANNY: A Manet or Renoir . . .

GARDNER: It's very evocative.

FANNY: There's something about the light . . .

They back up to survey the picture from a distance.

FANNY: You know those Renoir café scenes . . . ?

GARDNER: She doesn't lay on the paint with a trowel; it's just touches here and there . . .

MAGS: They *like* it . . . !

FANNY: You know the one with the couple dancing? . . . Not that we're dancing. There's just something similar in the mood . . . a kind of gaiety, almost. . . . The man has his back to you and he's swinging the woman around. . . . OH, GAR, YOU'VE SEEN IT A MILLION TIMES! IT'S HANGING IN THE MUSEUM OF FINE ARTS! . . . They're dancing like this . . .

FANNY *goes up to* GARDNER *and puts an arm on his shoulders.*

MAGS: They like it. . . . They like it!

FANNY: She's got on this wonderful flowered dress with ruffles at the neck and he's holding her like this. . . . That's right . . . and she's got the most rhapsodic expression on her face . . .

Getting into the spirit of it, GARDNER *takes* FANNY *in his arms and slowly begins to dance around the room.*

GARDNER: Oh, yes . . . I know the one you mean. . . . They're in a sort of haze . . . and isn't there a little band playing off to one side . . . ?

FANNY: Yes, that's it!

KITTY'S *horn honks outside.* MAGS *is the only one who hears it.*

MAGS: There's Kitty! *(She's torn and keeps looking towards the door, but finally gives in to their stolen moment)*

FANNY: And there's a man in a dark suit playing the violin and someone's conducting, I think. . . . And aren't Japanese lanterns strung up . . . ?

FANNY *and* GARDNER *pick up speed, dipping and whirling around the room. Strains of a faraway Chopin waltz are heard.*

GARDNER: Oh, yes! There are all these little lights twinkling in the trees . . .

FANNY: And doesn't the woman have a hat on? . . . A big red hat . . . ?

GARDNER: . . . and lights all over the dancers, too. Everything shimmers with this marvelous glow. Yes, yes . . . I can see it perfectly! The whole thing is absolutely extraordinary!

The lights become dreamy and dappled as FANNY *and* GARDNER *dance around the room.* MAGS *watches them, moved to tears as slowly the curtain falls.*

END

OURSELVES ALONE

Anne Devlin

For Chris Parr with love

Ourselves Alone was coproduced at the Liverpool Playhouse Studio on October 24, 1985, and at the Royal Court Theatre Upstairs, London, on November 20, 1985.

In the autumn of 1982, after the broadcast of my first radio play, I met the Artistic Director of the Liverpool Playhouse, Bill Morrison, who offered me a theater commission. The only proviso was that the play have main parts for women. I readily accepted, because I wanted to write a stage play and because I wanted to write about the women who lived in Andersonstown, the Catholic ghetto in West Belfast where I had grown up. In the two years following the end of my first marriage in 1979, I had been living alone and spending a great deal of my time in the company of women. I was suddenly aware of what it was like to live without men. I noticed too, in my frequent trips to Belfast, where I was born, that there was a whole generation of women who were also living without men, alone with their children and each other for support, against a backdrop of political violence. The men, of course, were in prison or on the run. The characters in *Ourselves Alone* were conceived as a trinity of women: the mother (DONNA), the mistress (JOSIE), and the career woman (FREIDA). I found the three women representative of the three paths available at different stages of life, my own essentially. I have been all three women, both political (JOSIE) and nonpolitical (FREIDA), yet when I began writing this play (I began in the summer of '83 and finished in April 1985) I had never been a mother. At the end of Act One of the first draft, I found myself pregnant and the baby was born in October 1984. This fact of motherhood changed my whole perspective on the script. Because I had given life, I couldn't take it away; not even on paper. So no one dies in this play. Mother, or the absence of her, became, in the face of the violence, a major force for good. Josie and Freida have no mother; their friend Donna is a mother substitute. My own personal journey had been toward the maternal. At the time of writing *Ourselves Alone* I grew another heart—because I had a son, I had, for a time, within a female body, a male and a female heart.

This gave me a new politics, which was not separatist feminism. The womb does not discriminate.

My other plays are screen plays. *The Way-Paver,* a book of short stories, was published in 1986 by Faber & Faber.

ANNE DEVLIN
1990

Author's Note

I began this play with two women's voices—one funny and one serious—and then I found I had a third—the voice of a woman listening. And all the women were in some ways living without men. And then the father and a stranger came into the room. And I found myself wondering who the stranger was and what he was doing there. And I set the play in Andersonstown because once, I used to live there—and I still do.

August 1985

Characters

FRIEDA	Sister to Josie, under 25 years
JOSIE	Sister to Frieda, under 29 years
DONNA	Friend to both sisters, Liam's common-law wife, under 30
MALACHY	Father to Frieda, Josie and Liam
LIAM	Malachy's son, Donna's common-law husband
GABRIEL	Cousin to Frieda, Josie and Liam
JOE CONRAN	The Englishman
CATHAL O'DONNELL	Josie's lover, a member of the Provisional IRA
JOHN MCDERMOT	A member of the Workers' Party
DANNY MCLOUGHLIN	A musician
FIRST MAN	A helper in the club
SECOND MAN	In the fight outside the club
FIRST POLICEMAN	In the park, and in Donna's house
SECOND POLICEMAN	In the park
FIRST SOLDIER	In Donna's house
SECOND SOLDIER	In Donna's house

Time: Act One is set in late summer; Act Two autumn into winter.
Duration: eight months.
Setting: mainly Andersonstown, West Belfast; but also Dublin, a hotel room, and JOHN MCDERMOT's house in South Belfast, near the university and the Botanic Gardens.

ACT ONE
Scene 1

FRIEDA, DANNY, GABRIEL, FIRST MAN. *The setting is a club, the center of Republican activity, political and social, in West Belfast. The period of Republicanism in the post-hunger-strike days is set by the wall hangings; the traditional prominence of Pearse and Connolly has given way to the faces in black and white of ten men: Sands, Hughes, McCreesh, O'Hara, McDonnell, Hurson, Lynch, Doherty, McElwee, Devine.*
It is early evening, the lights in the club are down, the surroundings are not so visible. FRIEDA, *a singer, and* DANNY, *a musician, are rehearsing.*

FRIEDA: *(Sings.)*

Armored cars and tanks and guns
came to take away our sons
every man should stand beside
the men behind the wire.

(Throws the paper down.)
I don't want to sing this any more!
(Behind them and around them two men are coming in and out with boxes and stacking them in every available space.)

DANNY: *(Stops playing.)* Why not?

FRIEDA: Because it's about a man.

DANNY: The song's about Internment, Frieda!

FRIEDA: I'm fed up with songs where the women are doormats!

DANNY: It's a Republican classic!

FRIEDA: I want to sing one of my own songs.

DANNY: But your songs are—not as popular as this one.

FRIEDA: You told me the next time we got a job here you'd let me sing one of my own songs! Just one.

DANNY: *(Sighs.)* Which one did you want to sing?

FRIEDA: I've rewritten "The Volunteer."
  (She starts getting a paper out of her bag by the piano.)
234

DANNY: All right. I'll look at it when we've rehearsed this.

FRIEDA: Oh Danny. I knew you would.

DANNY: OK. Let's go again.

FRIEDA: *(She sings the first verse of "The Men Behind the Wire.")*

Armored cars and tanks and guns
came to take away our sons—

DANNY: *(Stops.)* Frieda! Do you have to sound so pleased about it? Armored cars and tanks and guns!

FRIEDA: But the tempo's fast and lively.

DANNY: Absolutely. You have to work hard against that tempo. Again! *(She sings. She stops. The men carrying boxes are now piling them nearer FRIEDA.)* Just a minute . . . Are you going to be much longer shifting that stuff around?

GABRIEL: Nearly finished.

FRIEDA: *(Looking into the box GABRIEL has put down)* What is it anyway?

GABRIEL: Bandages.

FRIEDA: In all of them?

GABRIEL: *(Nods.)* I think so. *(The FIRST MAN comes in with a larger box, his last.)*

FRIEDA: What are you trying to do—start a fight? *(Calls out.)* Hey wee fella, what have you got in your box?

FIRST MAN: *(Reading off the lid)* Cotton wool balls.

FRIEDA: I always thought there was something funny about you.

FIRST MAN: *(On his way out)* See you wee girl, come the revolution, you'll be the first one up against the wall!

FRIEDA: Well, I hope it's in the nicest possible way.

GABRIEL: What were you looking for?

FRIEDA: Sugar.

GABRIEL: Maybe next week.

DANNY: Frieda!

(She clears her throat, takes up her position. The men depart. She sings the song again completely.)

Scene 2

DONNA, JOSIE, FRIEDA, MALACHY, JOE. JOSIE *is sitting in the dark in a room. Footsteps quickly approach the door.* DONNA *comes in and turns on the light.*

DONNA: Josie! What are you doing sitting in the dark? You've let the fire out.
*(*JOSIE *laughs.)*
What's so funny?

JOSIE: My daddy used to say, well close the door quickly and keep it in.

DONNA: Used to say? *(Takes her coat off and sits down.)* You couldn't wait to get away from him.

JOSIE: I know.

DONNA: Is everything all right? You were sleepwalking again last night.

JOSIE: Was I?

DONNA: It's the third time this week. I opened my eyes and there you were. Standing over the cot, looking at Catherine.

JOSIE: Was I?

DONNA: You gave me an awful fright.

JOSIE: I'm sorry.

DONNA: I wouldn't have said anything, but I'm afraid of you waking Catherine. It takes so long to get her to sleep these days.

JOSIE: I think I was dreaming about my mother.

DONNA: Was she quiet for you?

JOSIE: Who?

DONNA: Catherine. Was she quiet while I was out?

JOSIE: Yes.

DONNA: I'll just take a wee look in.

JOSIE: She's asleep! I wish I could sleep like that.

DONNA: What's wrong?

JOSIE: I feel sick all the time now.

DONNA: Is it him?

JOSIE: I can't live like this any more. I sit here night after night wondering will he come tonight.

DONNA: We're all waiting on men, Josie.

JOSIE: If he has to go away for any other reason but her I can stand it.

DONNA: Have you told him this?

JOSIE: No. Of course not. I don't want him to think I care.

DONNA: Aye, but it strikes me that if you were the one with a wife, he might care. Has he ever talked about her?

JOSIE: No.

DONNA: Well I expect she waits too, Josie.

JOSIE: Thanks.

DONNA: At least you have his love.

JOSIE: Love? It's such a silly word. We've never spoken it. It's just that when I'm totally me and he's totally him we swop. Do you know what I mean? *(Pause.)* His arrival is the best time. It's his mouth on my neck, his cool fingers touching me—I make it last right up until he has to leave. And then I row, I fight, I do everything I can to keep him with me and when I hurt him I hurt myself. It's as if we're driven, that bed is like a raft and that room is all the world to us.

DONNA: You're lucky you can feel like that, you might not if you had to live with him.

JOSIE: Live with him? I've dreamt of nothing else.

DONNA: He frightens me Josie—he's not like any man I know.

JOSIE: No he's not.

DONNA: The things I've heard about him. He's a spoiled priest.

JOSIE: Sure I wanted to be a nun once.

DONNA: Aye when you were ten years old. But he's actually been trained as a priest. *(Pause.)* They told him when they blew up the police station near the cemetery that morning that some of our people might get hurt as well. And he asked—how many?

JOSIE: You don't know what you're talking about. Our force is defensive!

DONNA: I'm looking at you but it's him who's talking. I wish I didn't know any of this. I wish I hadn't walked into the room that night and seen you both. I wish you hadn't left the door open.

JOSIE: But you approved of us. You made me come and live with you so it was easier for us to meet. You got me away from my daddy.

DONNA: I was afraid for you if they found out. And because you have Liam's eyes. When I woke last night I thought it was Liam who was standing there, that he'd come back. But when I saw it was you, I knew it was only because I hadn't been with him for so long I was wanting him again.

JOSIE: Don't talk to me about wanting, my body's like armor. The nerve ends are screeching under my skin. I need him back so I can stretch out again.

DONNA: How long since you've seen him?

JOSIE: Five weeks.

DONNA: I wonder does she know. *(Pause.)* Women have a way of knowing these things. I knew with my ex-husband when he was seeing somebody else. I knew the minute he put his hand on me. Once when we were in bed together a woman's name came into my head and I thought, he's not making love to me, he's making love to Margaret—I asked him afterwards, who's Margaret? He froze. He was, you see.

JOSIE: Sometimes when we make love I pretend I'm somebody else.

DONNA: Who?

JOSIE: Not someone I know. Someone I make up—from another century. Sometimes I'm not even a woman. Sometimes I'm a man—his warrior lover, fighting side by side to the death. Sometimes we're not even on the same side.

DONNA: That's powerful, Josie! *(Pause.)* What will you do if he doesn't come back?

JOSIE: Why do you say that?

DONNA: The man is still married to someone else. He has known you all these years—but he has never left his wife.

JOSIE: But she's not important to him!

DONNA: Wives are always important.

JOSIE: You only say that because you're so anxious to marry my brother.

DONNA: I must have struck home!

JOSIE: I'm sorry. *(She suddenly stops. Footsteps clattering in the alley towards the door.)* Listen.

DONNA: You've ears like a cat.

JOSIE: It's Frieda. She always walks as if her feet don't belong to her.

DONNA: Here. *(Offers her a hanky.)* Blow your nose.
(The door bursts open. FRIEDA *arrives, breathing deeply. Leans against the closed door.)*

FRIEDA: Oh God!

DONNA: What's wrong?

FRIEDA: I was nearly gang-raped at the club.

JOSIE: Is that all?

DONNA: Don't do that again. You gave us the fright of our lives. The way you came down that alley.

FRIEDA: I was rehearsing at the club for the Prisoners' Dependents ''do.'' It was dark and there was only Danny and myself. Danny's a friend of mine, he's a musician.

DONNA: Yes. We know.

FRIEDA: I'd been singing for about an hour when I suddenly looked around and the room was full of men. There'd been one of those meetings upstairs. They must have heard my singing and come down.

JOSIE: Like a siren.

FRIEDA: I'll ignore that. Anyway, Danny sent me home. I was the only woman in the room.

JOSIE: No doubt you made the most of it.

DONNA: Strange there was a meeting and you weren't there.

JOSIE: I'm going out later.

FRIEDA: You'll never guess what I was singing when they came down to listen!

DONNA: I'll never guess.

FRIEDA: My own song. We were rehearsing a song I had written myself.

DONNA: It was that bad, was it? *(Pause.)* I'm only joking. That's great Frieda. That's a break for you.

FRIEDA: Must have been something important going on. Cathal O'Donnell was there. He stopped to talk to me on my way out. He said I'd a great voice. He had that doe-eyed look about him; you know the one—I'm married, please rescue me. I could hardly get away from him.

JOSIE: O'Donnell's in the north?

FRIEDA: I think he's been here for a while. I thought I saw him there last week as well. You know how distinctive he looks. He's so lean and dark and brooding.

DONNA: Are you going to wash your hair tonight? There's plenty of hot water.

FRIEDA: I am, then I'll do yours.

DONNA: Good. My roots are beginning to show.

FRIEDA: *(To* JOSIE*)* Are you all right?

DONNA: She's got a bit of a cold. Why don't you take your things and go and do your hair now.

FRIEDA: There's no rush.

DONNA: There is—I want an early night.

FRIEDA: She's just said she's got to go out.

DONNA: I still want an early night.

FRIEDA: What's wrong with you?

JOSIE: I've got earache and a sore throat; I haven't had a good night's sleep for a long time.

FRIEDA: *(Pause.)* Do you know what I thought you said? I haven't had a man to sleep with for a long time.

DONNA: Frieda! While the water's warm!

FRIEDA: I'm going. I'm going.
(FRIEDA *exits.)*

DONNA: Why don't you go and have a sleep before you go out?

JOSIE: He's here, Donna. He talked to her!

DONNA: Quick, before she comes back. Sleep in my room. Then you won't have to listen to Frieda all evening.

JOSIE: Why doesn't he come? Is it her? She says he wants her.

DONNA: Oh stop it. It's all in Frieda's mind. She doesn't know who to be at!

JOSIE: I don't know if I could share him.

DONNA: You're already sharing him! Stop tormenting yourself. Why don't you have a wee sleep before you go out?

JOSIE: I can't, not now. I'm going to see him in a few hours.
(In the distance the faint sound of bin lids hammering on the pavement.)

DONNA: Bin lids.

JOSIE: Quite far off.

DONNA: Somebody's been lifted.

JOSIE: No doubt.
(They listen again. It seems to get louder.)

DONNA: Is it getting closer?

JOSIE: No. It's the wind. It's changed direction.
(It stops.)

DONNA: It makes me nervous. Nights like this. I'm glad Liam's in prison—God forgive me—it means I don't have to lie awake waiting for them to come for him. Listening to every sound. I wouldn't go through that again for anything.
(Sound of helicopter faintly in the background.)

JOSIE: My mother spent her life listening. My father was picked up four times.

DONNA: Oh, I hope they're not going to raid us. I only got the carpets down at Christmas. I'll never get the doors to close. That happened the last time they came. They pulled up the carpets and half the floorboards. That was after your brother'd been arrested, and I'd no one to help me put them back.
(Bin lids begin faintly again. FRIEDA opens the door. She is wearing a tinfoil turban.)

FRIEDA: Well, girls, what do you think—Miss Andersonstown second year running.
(JOSIE motions her to be quiet. She listens.)
What is it, a raid? It's far enough away. *(They all listen.)* Do you remember the last time you were raided?

DONNA: I was just talking about that.

FRIEDA: It was hardly worth their while. They only found a couple of rounds of ammunition. I remember this place the morning after, though. It was a shambles.

DONNA: Don't remind me.
(The bin lids die.)

JOSIE: It's stopped.

DONNA: I wish you didn't have to go out again tonight.

FRIEDA: I must say you don't look very well.

JOSIE: I don't look well?

DONNA: *(Eyeing* FRIEDA *also)* What's the tinfoil for?

FRIEDA: They use tinfoil at the salon, I'll be blonde in ten minutes.

DONNA: Why do hairdressers think they always have to be blonde!

FRIEDA: It's not that. It's for my act. Marlene Dietrich was blonde.

JOSIE: If you spent as much time on your mind as you do on your appearance you'd be better equipped.

FRIEDA: For what? I want to be a singer, not an academic.

JOSIE: A few exam passes might help.

FRIEDA: How did it help you? You went to university, but you still live in Andersonstown.

JOSIE: I live here because I choose to.

FRIEDA: I don't believe you—anyway, Marilyn Monroe didn't pass any exams.
(DONNA and JOSIE laugh.)

DONNA: What did I tell you? Monroe! Dietrich! She's a head about herself.

JOSIE: Why do you always want to be somebody else?

FRIEDA: I don't always want to be somebody else. I just want to be somebody.

JOSIE: Be yourself.

FRIEDA: When did I ever have a chance to be myself? My father was interned before I was born. My brother's in the Kesh for bank robbery. You mention the name McCoy in this neighborhood, people start walking away from you backwards. I'm fed up living here, this place is a hole!

JOSIE: If it's a hole, it's a hole for all of us.

FRIEDA: Yeah, but there's this voice in my head which says—"Nobody knows you. Nobody knows you exist. You've got to make yourself known."

JOSIE: Is that why you've attached yourself to the Workers' Party?

DONNA: Have you?

JOSIE: She was seen with them at a dance at Queen's last week.

FRIEDA: I was talking to John McDermot.

JOSIE: You were also seen coming out of Maguire's pub on Saturday.

FRIEDA: I thought that was Gabriel driving off when I waved.

JOSIE: Maguire's is where the Officials hang out.

FRIEDA: You ought to apply to the SAS, Josie. They could use somebody with your intelligence.

JOSIE: You may be my sister, but it won't save you! You're in and out of the Club all the time. You could be carrying information to the Officials.

FRIEDA: I've nothing to do with the Officials. I was talking to John McDermot.

JOSIE: I know you wouldn't talk; but there's others who might point the finger at you. You'll put all of us under suspicion.

DONNA: Josie's right. They're paranoid about informers now. You'll get your family a bad name.

FRIEDA: Could we sink any lower?

JOSIE: I give up with you. Liam's getting out of the Kesh next month; talk to him about it.

FRIEDA: I don't know why you're making such a fuss. John McDermot is an old friend. You used to like him yourself when he was Liam's mate.

JOSIE: Not these days, my girl. The only loyalties you are allowed are ideological.

FRIEDA: Baloney! Look at her! She's not living with an ideology. My brother's changed his political line three times at least since 'sixty-nine. He joined the Officials when they split with the Provos, then the INLA when they split from the Officials; the last time he was out on parole he was impersonating votes for the Sinn Fein election. And I hear lately while he's in the Kesh he's joined the Provos! Now what does that tell us—apart from the fact that he's a relentless political opportunist?

JOSIE: Liam's always been confused!

FRIEDA: Wrong answer. The Provos are big in this area. My daddy's a big fella in the Provos, so when the son gets out after five years inside, guess who's the young pretender? Meanwhile, she still writes her twenty-two page letters to him every night and has done since the beginning. Not that he's worth it, but you have to admire her tenacity for sticking with him. That's the only loyalty I know or care about. Loyalty to someone you love, regardless! I'd like to think if I loved someone I'd follow that person to hell! Politics has nothing to do with it!

JOSIE: One day you will understand, when you come to the limits of what you can do by yourself, that this is not dogma, that there are no personal differences between one person and another that are not political.

FRIEDA: You can't believe that.

JOSIE: I do. I do.

DONNA: I wish you two would give over. You're like chalk and cheese, you always have been.

JOSIE: Do you know what they did when they divided this country—

FRIEDA: Oh, here we go again. Mystical alienation.

JOSIE: They gave us political amnesia.

FRIEDA: Jargon.

DONNA: (*Getting up*) Would anyone like a drink? I'm going to open a bottle.

FRIEDA: Do you mean to tell me you've got booze in this house?

DONNA: Did you get me any sugar?

FRIEDA: (*Waves her hand.*) Oh, apart from the Château Lenadoon.

DONNA: (*Hurt*) What's wrong with it?

FRIEDA: I think the French do it better.

DONNA: Do you not want any?

FRIEDA: I will if there's nothing else.

DONNA: Will you have a drink, Josie? It'll relax you?

JOSIE: I shouldn't.

DONNA: (*Disappearing to the kitchen*) I'll bring three glasses.

FRIEDA: When does Liam actually get out?

JOSIE: Two weeks.

FRIEDA: What will you do? Stay on here?

JOSIE: No. Probably move back to my daddy's.

FRIEDA: After all this time? You'll enjoy that.

JOSIE: I don't see any alternative.

FRIEDA: I'm glad it's not me. I wouldn't want to be his housekeeper.

JOSIE: It's purely economic.

FRIEDA: Oh, now. We never do anything we don't want to do.

JOSIE: But we do! Often.

DONNA: *(Returning)* It looks a bit cloudy, but I expect it'll settle.

FRIEDA: When do you want me to do your hair?

DONNA: I've changed my mind.

FRIEDA: Why?

DONNA: If I go up to the prison tomorrow with dyed hair Liam'll think I'm running after somebody.

FRIEDA: So what?

DONNA: So it's not worth the fights.

FRIEDA: That's ridiculous.

(Doorbell)

JOSIE: Who's that at this time?

(DONNA moves cautiously to look out of the window. She turns out the light and pulls back the curtain, rattling the venetian blind as she looks out without being seen from the outside.)

DONNA: It's two men. Jesus Christ! It's your daddy!
(She switches the light on again. JOSIE lifts the bottle and glasses and runs into the kitchen. FRIEDA does not move. The doorbell rings again as JOSIE returns.)
What'll I do?

JOSIE: Wait a minute. *(To FRIEDA)* Get rid of that ashtray! And open the back door.

FRIEDA: *(Unmoved)* What for?

JOSIE: To let fresh air in.

FRIEDA: The whole place stinks. He'll know.

(Doorbell, more urgently)

JOSIE: *(To* DONNA*)* All right, open it.

*(*DONNA *exits to open the front door.* JOSIE *rushes into the kitchen with the three glasses and the bottle of wine, while* FRIEDA *refuses to co-operate.)*

FRIEDA: What are you tidying up for? Why don't you be yourself?

*(*DONNA *lets two men quickly into the room. One of them is* MALACHY MCCOY, JOSIE*'s and* FRIEDA*'s father. The other is* JOE CONRAN *a younger man whom the women have never seen before.)*

MALACHY: *(Reacting to the smoke-filled room; he waves his arm in front of his face.)* In the name a'Jesus! Is this how you spend your time? Who's been smoking in here?

FRIEDA: I have!

MALACHY: Oh yes. *(Coughing violently)* It would be you. You think because you're living round at your auntie's you can do what you like. I'll bring you home one of these days if you're not careful.

FRIEDA: Suits me. I wouldn't have to look after them.

MALACHY: What have you got on your head?

FRIEDA: Tinfoil.

MALACHY: I can see that! *(*JOSIE *returns, he puts his arm round her to draw her near in a bear hug.)* How's my mate! Hey!

JOSIE: *(Resisting the embrace)* I'm not your mate. I'm your daughter.

MALACHY: *(Angry, releasing her from his grip)* Jesus Christ! What's wrong with you, for God's sake!

FRIEDA: *(Sweetly, to* JOE*)* Don't mind our father. It's just that we don't have a mother any more and he's kinda protective.

MALACHY: That's enough from you.

FRIEDA: Well, are you going to introduce us or do we have to do it ourselves?

MALACHY: This is Joe Conran.

JOE: Hello.

MALACHY: My daughter, Josie.

JOSIE: Hello.

MALACHY: *(Coughs.)* This is Donna, my son's wife.

DONNA: Hello Joe.

MALACHY: And that creature in the tinfoil—for whatever reason—is my other daughter, Frieda.

FRIEDA: Hello Joe Conran.

MALACHY: Joe's going to stop here for a while. Maybe a couple of nights or so.

JOSIE: I wasn't expecting you.

MALACHY: We weren't expecting to be raided at the top end of the estate.

JOSIE: Oh, I see.

MALACHY: Did you not hear them?

JOSIE: Yes, earlier.

MALACHY: What a night. I don't know where they're getting their information from. This is probably the safest place. He's in your care—from now on.

JOSIE: I see.

MALACHY: *(To* DONNA *and* FRIEDA*)* You're not to go asking him any questions about what he's doing here. Do you hear me, Frieda?

(She feigns surprise.)

(To JOE*)* And you're not to answer any questions until the time comes. She's a mouth like the QE2. Josie's responsible for you.

JOE: Fine.

DONNA: Where's he going to sleep?

MALACHY: He can sleep down here on the sofa. Sure, it's only for an odd night.

JOSIE: No, he can't do that. He can have my bed. *(*FRIEDA *is looking wide-eyed at* JOSIE. JOSIE *ignores her.)* He probably needs his sleep. I'll sleep down here.

JOE: Oh, no, I couldn't—I'm used to sleeping—anywhere—and this is very nice. I couldn't put you out.

JOSIE: You're not putting me out.

MALACHY: Well, sort it out between you. I'll be on my way.
(To JOSIE, *taking her aside)* You know what your instructions are. *(*JOSIE *nods.)*

Liam will be out soon . . . you'll be coming home . . . I'll get your room painted.

JOSIE: We'll see.

MALACHY: I'll be glad to have him back—the business is too much for one.

DONNA: Sure I thought Gabriel was helping you.

MALACHY: Gabriel nearly ruined me. He paints everything that moves. A woman rang me up the other day—he'd painted all her windows shut. Nobody paints gloss like Liam.

DONNA: Would you like a cup of tea before you go?

MALACHY: No thanks, I'd better be getting back. *(He turns to go.)*

FRIEDA: Daddy! Will you be at the Prisoners' Dependents "do"?

MALACHY: Why?

FRIEDA: I'm singing one of my own compositions.

MALACHY: I don't know. I'll see. Wait a minute. *(Puts his hand into his pocket.)* Here's a couple of quid. Buy yourselves a bar of chocolate.

JOSIE: Thanks, Daddy.

DONNA: Cheerio, Mr. McCoy.

FRIEDA: Goodbye, Father. *(MALACHY exits.)* Chocolates! Sweeties! What age does he think we are! A bottle of whiskey would be more like it.

JOE: I have one in my travelling bag. I got it on the boat. *(He puts his bag on the floor.)*

FRIEDA: *(Full of admiration)* Good man!

JOSIE: *(Restraining JOE from opening his bag.)* I suggest you keep it in your bag. My sister and a glass of whiskey are quite a combination.

FRIEDA: Am I? That's the nicest thing you've said about me all evening.

JOSIE: The grain and the grape don't mix. Your wine's in the kitchen.

DONNA: *(To JOE)* Would you like a cuppa tea, Joe?

JOE: I don't drink tea.

DONNA: You're joking.

JOE: No, I'm not.

DONNA: Coffee?

JOE: Yes, that would be lovely.

DONNA: Right.

FRIEDA: Why do you not drink tea?

DONNA: Frieda!

FRIEDA: No, I'm interested. Do you not like it?

JOE: No.

FRIEDA: Did something happen to put you off it?

JOE: When I was at school I had to drink tea and I didn't like it, so I've never drunk it since.

FRIEDA: When you were at school?

DONNA: Was that like a boarding school?

JOE: Public school, yes.

FRIEDA: What public school did you go to?

JOE: I went to Eton.

(DONNA *and* FRIEDA *can hardly suppress their disbelief. Only* JOSIE *appears uninterested and even impatient.*)

DONNA: Well, if you'll excuse me for a minute I'll just get you a cup of coffee.
(She exits. FRIEDA *sits down beside* JOE.*)*

JOSIE: Your wine's in the kitchen.

FRIEDA: Donna'll bring it out when she's coming.

JOSIE: We've got some homemade wine, would you like some?

JOE: No, thank you.

FRIEDA: You don't like wine either?

JOE: No, I do, very much. But I prefer to leave it to the experts.

FRIEDA: That's just what I said.

JOE: Would you like a cigarette, Frieda? You smoke, don't you?

FRIEDA: Listen, we all do, but these two are so afraid of my da they won't admit it.

JOE: *(Laughs.)* Oh, I see. Well, help yourselves.
(They take the packet.)

Do you live here as well?

FRIEDA: No, I live round the corner.

JOE: You're a singer?

FRIEDA: You've heard about me?

JOE: You told your father you were singing one of your own compositions.

FRIEDA: I'm a singer/songwriter.

JOSIE: She works in the hairdresser's by the bus depot.

FRIEDA: I still sing.

DONNA: *(Opening the kitchen door)* Do you like it made with milk or water?

JOE: I like it black, thanks.

DONNA: *(To herself)* Black. *(Withdrawing again)*

JOE: Is that what you want to be, a professional singer?

FRIEDA: Och, no—that's only a front. What I really want is to marry some-body rich and live abroad.

JOE: I'm not exactly sure when you're serious and when you're joking.

FRIEDA: Oh, I'm perfectly serious. Do you think I want to end up like my big sister here? Running about like a wee messenger girl for my father and his cronies. No thanks. And if she's not careful she'll finish up like my auntie Cora. Do you know about my father's maiden sisters?

JOE: No.

FRIEDA: I live with them. Cora is blind and deaf and dumb and she has no hands, and she's been like that since she was eighteen. And Bridget, the other one, is a maid because she stayed to look after Cora. And I'm still a maid because I'm looking after both of them.

JOE: What happened to your aunt when she was eighteen?

FRIEDA: Oh, the usual. She was storing ammunition for her wee brother Malachy—my father, God love him—who was in the IRA even then. He asked her to move it. Unfortunately it was in poor condition, technically what you call weeping. So when she pulled up the floorboards in her bed-room—whoosh! It took the skin off her face. Her hair's never really grown properly since and look—no hands! *(She demonstrates by pulling her fists up into her sleeves. DONNA comes into the room with coffee for JOE.)*

DONNA: God forgive you! *(To* JOE*)* I hope this is all right.

FRIEDA: They stick her out at the front of the parades every so often to show the women of Ireland what their patriotic duty should be. But I'll tell you something—it won't be mine!

JOSIE: She was supposed to have been a beautiful girl, my auntie Cora. My father told me that. So I suppose you could say she really had something to sacrifice.

DONNA: We've all got something to sacrifice!

FRIEDA: You're right! And when there's a tricolor over the City Hall, Donna will still be making coffee for Joe Conran, and Josie will still be keeping house for her daddy, because it doesn't matter a damn whether the British are here or not.

JOSIE: That's just your excuse for not doing anything.

FRIEDA: Aye. But it's a good one. *(To* JOE*)* So, Joe Conran, now that you know about us, what are you doing here?

JOE: *(Looking to* JOSIE, *who gives him no help whatsoever)* I'm not supposed to answer any questions.

FRIEDA: Oh come on, this is family.

JOE: My grandfather was Irish. He married a Catholic. My grandmother, Teresa Conran, was a friend of Connolly's.

DONNA: James Connolly?

FRIEDA: You're here because your granny knew Connolly? *(Pause.)* She didn't meet him at the parents' association at Eton, did she?

JOSIE: Frieda?

FRIEDA: What?

JOSIE: How long did you say you had to keep the tinfoil on for?

FRIEDA: *(Touches her head.)* Oh fuck! Ten minutes!
(Dashes out and slams the door.)

DONNA: I think I'd better help her with the head dress.
(She exits.)

JOE: So you're the courier?
*(*JOSIE *nods.)*
What exactly do you do?

JOSIE: I take messages between the commanders, move the stuff from one place to another, or people. I operate at nights mostly, which is why I was offering you my bed. I'm hardly ever in it.

JOE: Your security's not very good on this estate. I'd only just arrived when the Army came up the road. Why did that happen?

JOSIE: There've been a lot of raids recently. Informers using the confidential telephones—it's always the same after a bombing campaign.

JOE: Are the others involved? *(Indicates the kitchen.)*

JOSIE: Donna has a child to look after.

JOE: And Frieda?

JOSIE: Well, you've seen her.

JOE: Can they be trusted?

JOSIE: This is family.

JOE: You must be very brave.

JOSIE: I'm not brave. I just began doing this before I had to think of the consequences. I think I'm more scared than I was ten years ago. But I'm getting better at smiling at soldiers. *(She smiles at him.)*

JOE: You shouldn't do that.

JOSIE: What?

JOE: Smile at soldiers.

JOSIE: Why not?

JOE: If you smile to deceive, how will I know when it's for real?

JOSIE: *(Laughs.)* I think that's the least of your worries.

JOE: Worries? Do I have worries?

JOSIE: Now humor I didn't expect.

JOE: What did you expect?

(She gets up.)

JOSIE: I have to go out for a while.

JOE: Are you married, Josie?

JOSIE: *(Putting on her coat)* No.

JOE: Do you have a boyfriend?

JOSIE: You ask too many questions, Joe Conran.

JOE: I know, but you have such beautiful eyes I can't help wondering.

JOSIE: I'm very puritanical. I wanted to be a nun once—and you're not going to charm your way into this organization.

JOE: Charm? I was interrogated in Amsterdam!

JOSIE: You weren't interrogated, you were questioned. There are still some questions you need to answer before we're satisfied.

JOE: But how long, how long am I going to be here?

JOSIE: For a while.

JOE: So I'm not going to meet anyone tonight?

JOSIE: No. You're going to stay here with me for a while.

*(*FRIEDA*'s voice offstage from the kitchen, singing:* "Oh love is pleasing and love is teasing and love is—")

I suggest you go to bed soon. Then you won't have to tell any more lies. Eton? You surprise me.

*(*JOSIE *exits by the front door.* JOE *sits down. The singing stops as* FRIEDA *enters the room carrying a glass in each hand. She has a towel around her head like a turban and she is dressed only in a long towelling dressing gown, which is tied at the waist.* JOE *pays no attention to her entrance until she speaks.)*

FRIEDA: I'm sorry I was so long.
(She puts the empty glasses down, and begins to rummage through JOE*'s traveling bag.)*

JOE: What are you doing?

FRIEDA: You said you had whiskey. I'm looking for it. *(She takes the bottle out.)* Would you like a glass?

JOE: Thanks. *(She pours whiskey.)*

FRIEDA: Would you have a cigarette?

JOE: I think you have the packet.

FRIEDA: Oh, so I have.
(She sits down on the sofa beside him. JOE *remains obstinately preoccupied, and looking around the room.)*

JOE: I wanted to ask you something.

FRIEDA: Yes?

JOE: Why are you so critical of your family's involvement with the Republican movement?

FRIEDA: Oh, I wouldn't say I was critical exactly. I mean, I respect them all very much. My father's a great man and Josie's so committed. You have to admire her and Liam's dedication. I mean, what the Brits have done to my family would make you weep.

JOE: But you're not an activist?

FRIEDA: No. Well, I used to be. I gave all that up in the seventies. God, I was on more demonstrations than enough.

JOE: So you're not political at all now?

FRIEDA: Well, that's not true either. I sing.

JOE: You sing?

FRIEDA: Yes. That's what I do instead. *(She gets up as she is speaking and walks around the room, finally turning to face him.)* Can you see my pubic hair?

JOE: No.

FRIEDA: Oh good. I was a bit worried in case you could. I'm antinationalist, that's all.

JOE: What do you mean by that?

FRIEDA: Nationalism is always the last resort of people who've failed to achieve anything else. Joe, could we be friends?
(Sits down beside him again, very close.)

JOE: Well, I wouldn't want to argue with you, Frieda.

FRIEDA: Oh, but I love arguing. Before Donna comes in, there's something I've been wanting to tell you—you're disturbing me and I'd like to do something about it. Since you walked in here tonight I thought—yes, him! Let me see your hand. *(She grabs his hand.)* Are you a Scorpio?

JOE: I'm very easily seduced. I'm on a job here—I don't want to get involved.

(DONNA comes in from the kitchen. She has a towel over her shoulders, she has just washed her hair.)

DONNA: I see you've opened the whiskey, Frieda.

(JOE gets up.)

JOE: Can you tell me where you want me to sleep?

DONNA: Oh yes, of course. I'm sorry. I should have said so earlier. Josie's room at the top of the stairs.

JOE: Thank you. Good night.

DONNA: What about your whiskey?

JOE: Please help yourselves. Goodnight.
(He leaves the room. Footsteps heard on the stairs.)

DONNA: Do you have to throw yourself at every man on the run who stays under my roof! What do you think this place is?

FRIEDA: What's wrong, did I get to him first?

DONNA: You watch your tongue!

FRIEDA: You never object to Josie doing it. She threw herself at him as soon as he arrived. He's sleeping in her bed for God's sake. Don't think I don't know why Josie stays here, and not at home with my father. Helping you with Catherine. My God, I've never seen any evidence of it.

DONNA: Josie, whatever she does, is older than you are.

FRIEDA: Josie's older than any of us.

DONNA: That may well be . . .

FRIEDA: At least four hundred years! *(FRIEDA begins to cry.)*

DONNA: You shouldn't drink. Whiskey always makes you cry.

FRIEDA: Nobody seems to care what happens to me. If I died tomorrow—it would be no loss.

DONNA: I care, Frieda.

FRIEDA: Oh yes, I know, but I was talking about love!

DONNA: I love you, Frieda.

FRIEDA: Yes, I know, but I want to be happy with someone! I haven't anyone of my own. Sometimes when I'm walking along the street and I see a couple holding hands I have to look away—I'm so jealous. Other times I look closely at the woman and think, well, I'm more attractive than her, why doesn't that man notice me? And lots of times I just wander around looking at men.

DONNA: Happiness requires all your intelligence. You won't find it just by looking; and the only thing you'll get from a man who looks like Joe Conran is a lot of trouble. But that's only my opinion. You must make up your own mind.

FRIEDA: *(Sniffing)* No. It's all right. I don't fancy him, anyway. I think he's got sexual problems.

DONNA: *(Putting the top on the whiskey bottle)* Oh well, that's all right then. Let's have a look at this hair of yours and see how well it's taken.

FRIEDA: No, wait. I have to dry it first.
(FRIEDA exits.)

S c e n e 3

DONNA, JOSIE.
Several hours later. DONNA *is in bed. A cot stands beside the bed, and a night light by the cot. Slowly the door opens in the dark and light falls across the room. A figure is silhouetted in the doorway; the figure approaches the cot.* DONNA *turns instinctively as the figure approaches.*

DONNA: Who's there?
(The baby murmurs.)
Please don't wake her.

JOSIE: It's all right, she's looking for us.

DONNA: What did you say?

JOSIE: She's looking through her life for us. She'll be back in a minute.

(DONNA gets out of bed quickly and takes JOSIE's arm.)

DONNA: Wake up, Josie. Wake up.

JOSIE: Oh. Oh. *(Shivering)* I'm very cold.

DONNA: Come to bed.
(DONNA helps her into bed.)
Here, I'll make a bucket with my nightdress. It's better than the sofa . . . Do you remember when we were kids we used to do this. You, me and Frieda in a double bed. We all had to face in the same direction or we wouldn't fit in. Except Frieda kept turning the other way and we had to push her out. She'd run off crying to your mammy and we'd to bribe her to keep her quiet . . . What's wrong? Was he not at the meeting?

JOSIE: He knew I was going to be there, but he didn't wait!

DONNA: You're shivering, hold on to me.

JOSIE: He left before I arrived, Donna. Half an hour. He's in this town, he talked to Frieda tonight, but he wouldn't wait for me!

DONNA: Don't abandon yourself like this!

JOSIE: He told me I invaded his life.

DONNA: Invaded. It's not a word I would use.

JOSIE: Oh, Donna, I did make him happy. I did!

DONNA: I know, love. I know.

S c e n e   4

FRIEDA, DANNY, MCDERMOT, MALACHY, GABRIEL, SECOND MAN.
FRIEDA *is sitting on a high stool in a circle of light. The setting is the club. Hanging down from the walls behind her are portraits of the ten dead hunger strikers, visible now that the lights are on.* FRIEDA*'s song is accompanied by* DANNY *at the piano.*

FRIEDA:
When I was young my father
Walked me through the hall to see
Where Connolly, Pearse and Plunkett hung;
A profile against the darkening sky
My father pointed out to me,
Was the greatest name of all,
To be called the Volunteer,
To be called the Volunteer.

When I grew up my first love
Whispered in my ear,
What do you most desire, my love?
What do you most desire?
Lying on a moonlit beach
I held his hand and said
To be a Volunteer, my love,
To be a Volunteer.

(Someone is whistling. DANNY *stops, addressing a young man in the darkness.)*

DANNY: I'm sorry, you can't come in. We're not open till seven. This is a rehearsal.

MCDERMOT: It's not a rehearsal she needs; it's an education!

FRIEDA: *(Covering her eyes from the lights and peering out into the darkness)* Who is that?

MCDERMOT: I came to see what you did in your spare time.

FRIEDA: John McDermot, have you gone mad!

DANNY: Do you know him?

FRIEDA: Could we take a break now?

MCDERMOT: Come back in a hundred years: she needs all the time she can get!

FRIEDA: Go on. *(Pushing the hesitant DANNY out)* It's all right. He really is a friend of mine. *(DANNY exits.)* Why do your jokes always sound like a threat?

MCDERMOT: You think I was joking?

FRIEDA: What are you doing here anyway?

MCDERMOT: You were supposed to be selling papers with me on Saturday. What happened to you?

FRIEDA: You're mad coming in here!

MCDERMOT: What did you do to your hair? Is that a disguise so I wouldn't ever recognize you again!

FRIEDA: Oh, don't you start.

MCDERMOT: On second thoughts, it's just as well you didn't come out on Saturday. I would have had to explain that your appearance was your own idea and in no way reflected the views of the Workers' Party.

FRIEDA: It's for my act.

MCDERMOT: The song you were singing, was that part of your act as well?

FRIEDA: Before you say anything devastating, I wrote that song.

MCDERMOT: I thought you did. *(Pause.)* Do you want to know what I think?

FRIEDA: *(Puts her hands over her ears.)* I don't want to hear. I never listen to criticism.
(FRIEDA has her hands over her ears and she is humming. He pulls her hands away.)

MCDERMOT: Listen, you! It's about time you came out of the closet and stood up for what you believe in. Instead of singing these endless Republican dirges around the clubs! "The greatest name of all, to be a Volunteer!"

FRIEDA: I wrote it after Bobby Sands died. It's very popular here, you know. It's always requested.

MCDERMOT: Listen, kid. You want to be big? You want to lead the tribe, not follow it. This song celebrates militarism. How many times have you been told it's the Party not the Army that is dominant. The political thinker, not the soldier. That's the greatest name of all. You know that—you've known it since you were seventeen. You must use everything you know when you write songs, Frieda.

FRIEDA: There haven't been many moments in my life when I've felt honest; the feeling I had when I wrote that song was one of them. When I feel I can write a song about the Party I'll let you know.

MCDERMOT: He who suffers the most! That's you all over. You weep at Bobby Sands's funeral, but a bomb in a store and the IRA are bastards. You could end up on both sides of the border if you don't think!

FRIEDA: At least I'd see everybody's point of view.

MCDERMOT: If you can see everybody's point of view you can see nothing at all. What you lack is a conceptual framework.

FRIEDA: One of these days, John McDermot, you'll collapse in a conceptual framework.

(A door bangs. GABRIEL *appears.)*

GABRIEL: You're a bit out of your territory, fella.

MCDERMOT: And you're out of your depth—son.

FRIEDA: Look, Gabriel, we don't want any trouble. He's with me. We were just leaving.

GABRIEL: My uncle Malachy won't like it when he hears about this.

FRIEDA: He can say what he likes, I've never been afraid of my father. I'm not about to start because he's drilling the Boy Scouts!

GABRIEL: You can tell him that yourself. *(Door bangs.)* Here he is now.

(MALACHY comes in, followed by the SECOND MAN.)

FRIEDA: Oh fuck!
(FRIEDA takes JOHN's arm and braces herself to confront MALACHY.)

MALACHY: What's he doing here?

FRIEDA: He's with me.

MALACHY: Get him out of here!

FRIEDA: No, no. Wait!

(MCDERMOT *and* FRIEDA *are dragged apart.*)

SECOND MAN: Have you no control over your daughter?

(MCDERMOT *is pushed roughly towards the door by* GABRIEL *and the* SECOND MAN. *They exit.* MALACHY *has caught* FRIEDA *by the wrist to restrain her from following. He now pushes her across the room.*)

MALACHY: You stay—(FRIEDA *is struck on the back of the head by* MALACHY.)—away from him!
(FRIEDA *remains holding her head, momentarily stunned.*)
You'll not make a little boy of me! I'm sick to death of hearing about you . . . All I get is complaints . . . bringing that hood in here.

FRIEDA: (*Recovering*) What do I have to do or say, Father, to get you to leave me alone—

MALACHY: I'll leave you alone all right. I'll leave you so you'll wish you'd never been born.
(He makes a race at her. She pushes a table into his path.)

FRIEDA: Oh, Mammy. Mammy.
(He attempts to punch her in the stomach.)

MALACHY: You'll not make little of me. Siding with the people who condemned Bobby Sands.

FRIEDA: (*Backing away towards the door*) They didn't condemn him. They said he beat his wife! Hard to believe, isn't it?

MALACHY: Get out of my sight.

(Overturned club furniture stands between them.)

FRIEDA: They say when he was dying she was so afraid of him she wouldn't go up to the prison to see him. In fact she wouldn't go near him until she was sure he was definitely dead.

MALACHY: Never let me see your face again.

FRIEDA: (*Still backing out*) You know something, Father? You've been burying your friends since 'sixty-nine. But do you know something else, your friends have been burying you!

MALACHY: Never cross my door again!

FRIEDA: (*Desperation*) We are the dying. Why are we mourning them! (*She points at the portraits of the dead hunger strikers. She exits.*)

S c e n e   5

DANNY, GABRIEL, SECOND MAN, MCDERMOT, FRIEDA. *Outside the club, at the back,* JOHN MCDERMOT *is on the ground trying to protect his ribs and head from the feet of his two attackers.* DANNY *comes rushing in on them.*

DANNY: For Christ's sake, are yous mad?

GABRIEL: What's wrong with you, McLoughlin!

DANNY: There's a foot patrol at the top of the entry—you can hear yous a mile away.

GABRIEL: Beat it!

(The TWO MEN *run off,* DANNY *appears to follow, then stops and returns to* MCDERMOT.*)*
DANNY: Are you OK?

MCDERMOT: *(Beginning to look for his glasses)* I don't know yet. I can't see a thing.

DANNY: *(Stoops to retrieve them.)* I'm afraid they're broken.

MCDERMOT: *(Taking them from him)* Oh shit. I have another pair but— they're not as good. *(He tries to fix them.)* I hope I can remember where I put them.

DANNY: I don't know who you are or where you're coming from but next time they'll kill you . . .
*(*MCDERMOT *doesn't reply.)*
Is she worth it?

MCDERMOT: Did you say the Army were about?

DANNY: Aye, for their benefit.

*(*FRIEDA*'s footsteps are heard coming towards them.)*

FRIEDA: Where's John McDermot?

DANNY: Hey, Frieda! Over here! He's OK, calm down! He'll live.

FRIEDA: *(Gets down on her knees to face* JOHN, *who is propped against the wall.)* You stupid, thoughtless, reckless, insensitive, selfish bastard!

DANNY: Aye, well, I'll head away on.

FRIEDA: I could murder you! You have blown my one chance! Walking in there tonight and brazenly exhibiting yourself.

DANNY: I wouldn't hang about. Those boys might come back.
(DANNY *exits.*)

MCDERMOT: You didn't have to say you were with me.

FRIEDA: Who did you come to talk to—my daddy?

MCDERMOT: I'm sorry.

FRIEDA: *(Getting to her feet)* Well, you're responsible for me now.

MCDERMOT: Don't be silly. Nobody's responsible for you . . . Are you all right?

FRIEDA: No, I'm not. My head aches and my stomach's heaving—I think I'm going to be sick.

MCDERMOT: It's the shock!

FRIEDA: Shock? My life's in ruins. My father thinks I'm in the Workers' Party, and he thinks you and I are lovers. Jesus, when our Liam gets out of the Kesh he'll probably kill both of us.

MCDERMOT: What do you want to do about it?

FRIEDA: I've made a decision.

MCDERMOT: What's that?

FRIEDA: I'd like to join the Party.

MCDERMOT: That's a step in the right direction.

FRIEDA: It's a beginning.

MCDERMOT: Why?

FRIEDA: I have never in my life forgiven anyone who raised their hand to me.

MCDERMOT: I'll try to remember.

FRIEDA: I have another problem. I'm homeless and I don't have any money. Do you think you could find me somewhere to live?

MCDERMOT: I could take in a lodger.

FRIEDA: This is serious.

MCDERMOT: I am serious.

FRIEDA: Would your wife not mind?

MCDERMOT: We separated six months ago.

FRIEDA: In that case, no, I think not. Surely some other member of the Party could help me.

MCDERMOT: There's someone who visits me from time to time. Between you and me would be a business arrangement. I'm hardly ever at home.

FRIEDA: All right. I accept. The other thing is—I really don't have any money at the moment. I packed in my job at the hairdresser's.

MCDERMOT: I think that was wise.

FRIEDA: I want to devote more time to writing songs.

MCDERMOT: Well, I wouldn't depend on making a living from your singing career just yet, Frieda.

FRIEDA: You think not.

MCDERMOT: Your material isn't very commercial.

FRIEDA: I'm trying to get a gig at the Orpheus—or somewhere.

MCDERMOT: Well, I can't do anything about that—but we can come to some arrangement about the money when you've got some. (*Begins to try to struggle to his feet.*) Now, would you like to help me up from here. My back's killing me.

FRIEDA: (*Helping him with her arm*) Why are you doing this?

MCDERMOT: (*In some pain*) Because someone put his boot in my rib cage.

FRIEDA: No. Why are you helping me?

MCDERMOT: Because you're lost, Frieda. You're lost and I'm half blind.

FRIEDA: (*Going off with him*) I'm not lost! I just don't want all those people on my side. Do you?

Scene 6

JOE, JOSIE, O'DONNELL, MALACHY.
The Club. In addition to the portraits of the hunger strikers there are balloons and decorations around the room. It is after closing time and the chairs are upturned on the table tops. JOE follows JOSIE into the room. She switches on a small light above a table and lifts down two chairs, standing them upright on the floor.

JOE: (*Looking around*) This is very festive.

JOSIE: It's our club. My brother's getting out tomorrow and there's to be a party.

JOE: How long's he been away?

JOSIE: Five years.

JOE: The baby's nearly two?

JOSIE: Parole. He gets out on parole.

JOE: And in between she waits?

JOSIE: Of course she waits.

JOE: When was the last time he was out?

JOSIE: He was at the birth.

JOE: Would you wait two years for a man, Josie?

JOSIE: For the right man.

JOE: Are you waiting for the right man?

JOSIE: Sit down.

JOE: You seem nervous.

JOSIE: It's cold in here.

JOE: When do I get to meet O'Donnell?

JOSIE: When you've answered my questions.

JOE: Your questions?

JOSIE: A lot of people want to meet O'Donnell, Joe. The British don't even know what he looks like. We know that.

JOE: All right, but this is the third time I will have been questioned. Amsterdam, Dublin, and now here.

JOSIE: I promise you this will be the last.
(JOE *sits in the chair* JOSIE *has indicated. Taking a file from her shoulder bag and placing it on the table she also sits down.*)
I saw this report on you—I've been dying to meet you since I read it. *(Reads from the file.)* Educated Trinity and Cambridge. First class honors Sociology. PhD. Chairman of the Socialist Society. Revolutionary Socialist Students' Federation. Member of the European International Liberation Group . . . ardent supporter of the Basque Separatist Movement . . . recently brought a group of left-wing German students into talks with the Free Wales Army on anti-technology in industry, or how to prevent, by force if necessary, the replacement of workers by machines. Also set up discussions between the Italian Communist-controlled administrations of several states and the British Left—including some of our people in Britain—on advantages of the local state. Items on the agenda: the control of police, Army and security

systems, also the subsidization of communes. You're a clever fellow. Oh, and something else. You've got a very interesting emotional life. Married: 1971. Several girlfriends. Currently: in Spain, a Basque lawyer; in Germany, Hamburg, a Marxist psychoanalyst; in Italy, a dancer, or was it an actress with a socialist theater company, whose father is a mayor of a Communist town. Now, after all those exotic locations, what brings you to West Belfast?

JOE: You make me sound like a tourist. I do take my politics home with me. *(Pause.)* My wife's an Irish Catholic.

JOSIE: I wouldn't cite loyalty to your wife as a reason for your being here—it's not exactly your most stable characteristic.

JOE: We have an arrangement.

JOSIE: That's very nice. But it doesn't answer my question.

JOE: What exactly do you want to know?

JOSIE: Let me tell you a story, Joe. When I was little my daddy used to say—"When the British withdraw we can be human." I believed that, since the south of Ireland was already free, there I could be human . . . Well, I'd been down south quite a few times, always to Bodenstown to the Wolfe Tone Commemorations and that meant coming back on the coach again as soon as it was over. One year when I was nearly sixteen, instead of coming straight back I stayed on and went to Dublin. I simply wanted to see the capital . . . I had no money and my shoes let in water, and I came back to Belfast at night with very wet feet in the back of a pig lorry. It smelt of pig feed. It dropped me off at seven-thirty in the morning on the Falls Road. I had time to go home and change before going to school at nine . . . There was a girl next to me in assembly. She had long straight fair hair and gleaming white teeth. If you leaned close she smelt of lemon soap. When she went to Dublin it was to buy clothes, she told me. I stood looking down at her beautifully polished shoes and I knew that it was all for her. Dublin existed for her to buy her shoes in . . . All day the smell of pig feed stayed with me . . . From then on I stopped wanting only British withdrawal—to unite Ireland for the shoppers and the shopkeepers of Belfast and Dublin. I became a revolutionary. You see it wasn't the presence of the British that made me feel unclean that morning—it was the presence of money—Irish money as much as English money. Do you understand, Joe? What I want to know is, what are you doing in the ranks of the unhuman? I was born here.

(JOE thinks for a minute, then reaches into his pocket, takes out his wallet, from which he quickly takes all the notes, and thrusts both wallet and notes into JOSIE's hands.)

JOE: Buy them! . . . Buy shoes! . . . You're not a revolutionary, Josie, you're a shoe fetishist. Go out, fill yourself with all the things that make you envious, then when you've got it out of your system—come back and talk to me seriously about revolution . . . You want to know what I'm doing here? It's very simple: I'm taking responsibility for what is made of me.

JOSIE: *(Puts the wallet and the money back on the table between them.)* What is made of you?

JOE: Ascendancy. Anglo-Irish. British Army. I was born there. A prisoner of circumstances you might say; circumstances which found me enrolling in Sandhurst when I was seventeen, before I could think. But I did think—so I changed. I stopped being a soldier. And I've continued to resist circumstances ever since.

JOSIE: Would you die for an impossibility?

JOE: No . . . I don't think so . . . What impossibility?

JOSIE: The thirty-two-county Workers' Republic. Connolly's dream. Some of our people, and I'm one of them, believe it to be an impossibility. A place we will never come into. But we'll die trying to get there, because I suppose this is our country and as it is our lives are meaningless . . . But your life isn't meaningless, Joe, with your international conferences and your international girl friends . . . It's hard to imagine a better life. So, come on, why are you risking so much for us? And this isn't even your country?

JOE: Not for you—for the revolution. I happen to be one of those people who believe that my government's aggression in another country has something to do with me. I also know full well that there cannot be an English revolution unless there is one in Ireland. "A nation that enslaves another . . ."

JOSIE: ". . . can never itself be free." You'll find that slogan on the wall behind the swimming baths. We've come a long way. Ten years ago we wouldn't have dared quote Marx on the gable walls. Now we simply don't bother to attribute it to him . . . But what would make you, with your background, support a revolution? You've too much to lose.

JOE: Absolutely. I have too much to lose. You have to trust my integrity. You put too much emphasis on the weight of experience—I am the sum of all my reading.

JOSIE: Of your reading? Do you mean books? Jesus . . . Your fucking ideas, Joe. I'm trying to find out how you actually feel. The thing is—why would you be a traitor to your own country?

JOE: I'm not a traitor—my father was an Irish Protestant son of a mixed marriage. My grandparents were Southern Unionists. My mother is an English Catholic. I was sent to Ampleforth. I went into the Army as an engineer—yes. My mother's family are all British Army. I left the Army after eighteen months and have had no connections with it since. I went back to university and read sociology and became a believer in revolutionary socialism.

JOSIE: Like many other sons of the bourgeoisie in the sixties. Fascinating generation. God I hated them. Made it all too clear to you who was in and who was out. I imagine you were in, Joe.

JOE: You seem to object to the idea that a person can refuse to render back what their social conditioning will make of them. And yet the history of the world we live in, of change and revolution, suggests we do just that very thing.

JOSIE: I'm objecting to the fact that you refuse to talk about your emotional involvement with the British.

JOE: The question of identity is very complex.

JOSIE: So it is, Joe. *(She waits while he appears to think.)* In fact it's crucial. *(Very quietly, while still awaiting his reply)* We've had a number of volunteers who come to us, usually Catholics married to Protestants, driven out of an area by loyalist intimidation. They get bitter about it and join the Republican movement to hit back. They're the worst type of volunteers as far as I'm concerned. They hit back because all they wanted was to be good Protestants, to be acceptable, like the working class who want to be middle class; blacks who want to be white. This type of volunteer hates the Protestants and the British because they are not Protestant and they are not British. They are not entirely trustworthy either because they will be among the first to back the state should conditions improve; and they will never make good revolutionaries because they are not fighting to be what they are. Until we know what you are; until you know who you are, how can we trust your motives for being here?

JOE: I didn't realize the Republican Movement was so choosey about the conscience of its recruits!

JOSIE: It's a bit like the Catholic Church, Joe; easy if you were born in it, difficult if you try to convert.

JOE: I regard myself as Irish!

JOSIE: There's no need to go that far. The thing is—are you rejecting Mother because Mother's rejecting you?

JOE: This is extraordinary.

JOSIE: You're no ordinary recruit, Joe. And it really doesn't concern us whether you regard yourself as Irish or English. You have already met on your travels a number of English socialists who work for us. If we hesitate it has nothing to do with your nationality; it is merely because we have very strong doubts about your motives.

JOE: You've said that before. What doubts?

JOSIE: Your family?

JOE: My wife's an Irish Catholic.

JOSIE: I was talking about a more binding relationship than that one—your mother's a hard woman to impress, I imagine. Was she impressed by your marriage to Rosa Connelly?

JOE: My mother's not important to me. I hardly ever see her.

JOSIE: Is that right?

JOE: She's retired to South Africa. I've never even visited her there.

JOSIE: But you do see her?

JOE: When she comes to England, yes.

JOSIE: How often? How often does she do that?

JOE: Once or twice a year.

JOSIE: Where? Where in England do you see her? At your house?

JOE: No. Rosa, my wife, doesn't—they don't get on. So my mother's never stayed with us.

JOSIE: So, when you want to see your mother, where do you see her?

JOE: Airports, restaurants, hotels.

JOSIE: And at your sister's?

JOE: My stepsister. My father died, my mother remarried.

JOSIE: Where does she live?

JOE: Sussex. But I haven't seen her for some time.

JOSIE: Christmas two years ago. Where was she living?

JOE: Sandhurst.

JOSIE: And you told us you hadn't been in touch with the Army since you bought yourself out in 1968.

JOE: It was a family matter; my mother was spending Christmas at Sandhurst with Alice.

JOSIE: And six months after that? You went back to Sandhurst but your mother wasn't there.

JOE: I had to visit Alice again. It had to do with my mother's will. I'm an executor.

JOSIE: What rank is your sister's husband?

JOE: He's a colonel.

JOSIE: Your wife was with you.

JOE: Yes, I always took her with me when I went to visit them. I don't really get on with my family and my wife has the facility to talk to anyone.

JOSIE: Except your mother?

JOE: My mother's a difficult woman.

JOSIE: And there was no difficulty with Rosa being Irish?

JOE: My father was Irish.

JOSIE: *(Appears to find this funny, but continues.)* Your wife is a Catholic from Derry.

JOE: Yes.

JOSIE: Your brother-in-law was in Derry in 'sixty-nine. The then Captain Blakemore was attached to the officer responsible there for releasing 350 CS gas canisters to the police in one night for use against the people of the Bogside—where your wife and her family lived at the time.

JOE: You can't lay that decision at the door of an Army officer. That's a political decision!

JOSIE: Not the point of my question. How did your wife get on with the Colonel, given this inconvenient piece of history?

JOE: Rosa, my wife, never talked to the Colonel. She talked to my sister. They never discussed politics.

JOSIE: What did she talk to your sister about?

JOE: Cooking.

JOSIE: Cooking?

JOE: Yes. Rosa loved cooking. Alice hated it. So Rosa did the cooking when we stayed there.

JOSIE: You say you have an arrangement with your wife. I think you mean that she left you.

JOE: We split up.

JOSIE: She left you three months after that last visit to Sandhurst.

JOE: Yes.

JOSIE: Why?

JOE: I don't know. *(Sighs.)*

JOSIE: What reason did she give you?

JOE: None. She couldn't. She didn't say anything.

(JOSIE gets up from the table and walks to the door of the room, as if to leave.)

JOSIE: I don't think you can realize the seriousness of the position you are in. You approached us six months ago offering us your services as a political adviser. We declined because we said we only accept that kind of advice from inside this organization. You then, as we hoped, reapplied to be an active and trained volunteer. Now, at present, as a result of our own investigations, you are under suspicion of attempting to infiltrate us as an agent of British Intelligence. If you don't deal with those suspicions, I am going to walk out of here in a few minutes' time and leave you to your fate.

JOE: But I don't know how to clear myself. You knew about my Army background. I never attempted to hide that. It was partly an asset to you.

JOSIE: Your training, yes. We knew you'd left the Army in 'sixty-eight. But what you never told us was that you visited Sandhurst Military Training Academy on several occasions in the past two years. And previously, Warminster, Bodmin and Osnabruck.

JOE: Exactly where my sister was based each time.

JOSIE: On the last occasion, eighteen months ago, after a visit to Sandhurst your wife left you. At exactly the same time Commander Kitson was also at Sandhurst. I'm sure I don't need to remind you that Kitson is head of Counter Insurgency Operations for the British Army. Now, did your wife leave you because she realized you were working for Counter Insurgency Operations? We think she did. And all you've been able to offer in reply is that your wife spent her visits to Sandhurst happily acting as a kitchen maid for the family of the man who sent CS gas into her family home in Derry.

JOE: It's not true. She was never happy about going there. She hated it. And I did too. But—I gave her no choice. She even used to cry a lot before she went. And then she'd get there and start talking to Alice. It was like a flood. The sun came out. I never knew how she did it. And because she cheered up, I thought she didn't mind in the end. I really believed everything was all right. I have not been recruited by British Intelligence. They never approached me; in fact it's been quite the opposite since I bought myself out of the Army. I met Rosa, as you know, while I was at university in Dublin. My family never approved of my going back to Ireland. My mother saw it as a rejection of her in going there and leaving the Army as I did. She actually complained once to my sister that I married Rosa to spite her, to make her ashamed. A wee hussy from the Bogside, she called her. In marrying Rosa I was also a security risk. My sister even suggested to me that her husband would probably never be made a colonel because of my connections with the wrong side in the Irish War. Not one member of my family came to the wedding. The Army of course refused permission to the Blakemores to attend, something to do with Rosa's part in the Bogside Riots of 'sixty-nine. She was a member of the Citizens' Defense Committee and her name was on the list of conditions which she handed to the Army on their arrival in Derry prior to dismantling the barricades. One of the conditions was a general amnesty for all those people defending their homes in the barricaded area. The barricades came down. However the Army Council and Blakemore's superiors still regarded my wife as a rioter. *(Pause.)* There is one thing you should know. Eighteen months ago at Sandhurst, I did try to meet Kitson. I asked Blakemore to arrange a meeting for me. I had very selfish reasons for doing so. I wanted to interview him for a paper I was giving at a conference in Stockholm on Insecurity and the State. It would have been a great coup. When I suggested a drink with Kitson either at the mess or at the house, Blakemore refused point blank. My brother-in-law doesn't like him—Kitson has no small talk. My family has nothing but. *(Pause.)* When Rosa left me, she said she regarded all her association with me as a betrayal of her tribe. I really didn't know what she meant at the time. I was deeply mortified and ashamed. Because I do believe she was happy with me once.

(A long pause. Then JOSIE comes back to the table.)

JOSIE: Joe.
(JOE looks up.)
It's finished.

(She picks up the file and puts it back in her bag. She holds out her hand to him.)
Welcome. To the tribe.

(JOE gets to his feet half dazed. She walks quickly away, followed by JOE. A door bangs. They have gone, the room is in darkness. Someone strikes a match, and we are alerted to the presence of two men. MALACHY lights a cigarette for CATHAL O'DONNELL.)

MALACHY: Well, Cathal, I think we have a new man.

O'DONNELL: I must stop this. *(Holding the lighted cigarette out for inspection)* Filthy habit. The wife—doesn't approve.

ACT TWO
Scene 1

DONNA, LIAM, JOSIE.

DONNA *is sitting on a straight-backed chair, alone in the living room. There is a light on her face, the rest is darkness.*

DONNA: The devil's back. He was lying with his head on my pillow this morning. When I woke up I recognized him immediately. Even though it's been years. *(Pause.)* The first time I ever saw him, he was standing in the corner of the room. I could feel something watching me. I had the bedclothes tucked up almost to my nose, so that I had to peer carefully round the room—and there he was. He seemed to grow out of the corner until he was towering over me. I panicked because I felt I was suffocating. My first husband was with me at the time. He called a doctor. He said I had asthma. The funny thing was, I really didn't get over my asthma attacks until my husband was interned. And I haven't seen the devil since. *(Pause.)* Until this morning. Liam bent over and kissed me goodbye as he was leaving. The trouble was he blocked my mouth and I couldn't breathe through my nose so I kept having to break away from him. When he'd gone, I closed my eyes and tried to get some sleep before the child woke. That was when I heard the door open. I thought Liam had come back so I opened my eyes, and there he was, the devil. If he had any hair at all it was red. He climbed on top of the bed and put his head on the pillow next to me. I felt so sick at the sight of him because I knew I didn't have the strength to struggle any more. I said: 'Please leave me alone.' I was very surprised when he replied. He's never spoken to me before. He said very quietly, "All right, Donna." And do you know—he vanished. But I don't believe he's really gone. He never really goes away.

(She begins to have an attack. She starts to vomit or choke twice, but nothing happens. Recovers. The door opens into the room, throwing light across the floor. A figure stands in the light of the doorway.)
Who is it?

LIAM: Who were you expecting?
(He switches on the light and closes the door. Almost tripping over luggage he crosses the room.)
What's this? Are you leaving me?

DONNA: I told you—Josie's moving back home.

LIAM: What's the matter with you?

DONNA: I'm tired.

LIAM: You're tired all the time now. I think maybe you're tired of me.

DONNA: Liam, what are you saying?

LIAM: It's been three weeks since I came out of the Kesh, and all I hear is that you're tired.

DONNA: Catherine kept me awake all night. I'm exhausted.

LIAM: You were never exhausted with your husband!

(DONNA *rushes around the room closing the doors.*)

DONNA: Please don't fight with me in front of Josie.

LIAM: *(Raising his voice)* I'm not fighting with you.

DONNA: Please don't shout. She'll hear you. I'll feel so humiliated.

LIAM: But it's true. It's him you want.

DONNA: Please, Liam. Please lower your voice. She'll think you don't love me and then it'll be difficult for me to feel good about myself and I'll have to leave here for shame and I've nowhere else to go.

LIAM: Go on, say it. I revolt you. You can't stand the sight of me.

DONNA: Oh Jesus God, I wish I were dead.

LIAM: It's true, admit it. Admit it. It's him, isn't it?

DONNA: No. No. I've loved only you. I always loved only you.

LIAM: But you married him!

DONNA: You've got to stop tormenting me because I had a husband. I was a girl then!

LIAM: Why don't you love me Donna?

DONNA: I cried all the way up the aisle. I told you that before. I was pregnant, they made me marry him. He was fifteen years older than me. I told him, I didn't love him. He said, 'Try to love me, then one day you will.' But I couldn't, because I'd always loved you. Oh, I did ever since I was a child.
(LIAM *is utterly immobile and unmoved during her entreaty.*)
Oh Liam, remember I used to come and have my bath with Josie and Frieda on Friday nights. And you used to pretend not to notice us. And then one Friday night you came into the parlor and said, "What's happening?" And

we said we were having a party and we were putting our money together for
lemonade and crisps and you said, 'Well, here's some silver towards your
party.' And Josie said you'd never given them a penny before towards anything. It was because I was there. And I blushed and laughed. Oh, I've
loved you since I was nine years old.
(For the first time he turns to her.)

LIAM: But you married him!

DONNA: Oh Liam. Liam! You know why.

LIAM: You had him first.

DONNA: You went away! You went away that summer!

LIAM: I had work to do.

DONNA: But you went away, you went to the Republic.

LIAM: I was wanted. We feared internment.

DONNA: And when you came back you had a girlfriend from Dublin. God,
you had so many. I started going with Peter McNamee after that because I
was lonely and he was kind to me. I left him for you. I gave up my son for
you. As soon as you wanted me, I came. What more can I do?

LIAM: It wasn't just McNamee. There were others. They told me. They'd
all had you. After the dances.

DONNA: Oh Jesus God!

LIAM: In the Kesh they told me about you after the dances. They all had
you. But now you don't want me! Where they better than me, was that it?

(DONNA takes up a knife from the table, and hands it to him.)

DONNA: Take it. Kill me, love. Kill me. Kill me.

LIAM: No!

DONNA: Kill me. You want to kill me. Please.

LIAM: No! *(He throws the knife away.)*

DONNA: I can't do any more. I love you. I have always loved you. I gave
away my only son for you. Because he looked like Peter. If you don't believe
that I love you—I wish I were dead. I wish I were dead.

LIAM: Don't say that, Donna.

DONNA: I wish I were dead.

LIAM: I just had to find out.

(LIAM *ruffles her hair.*)
I love you so much you see. And I can't get enough of you. When I'm away, things prey on my mind. I kept remembering all those years before we went out together and all the other men in your life. And I thought because I'm not around so much you'd find someone else.

DONNA: I won't find anyone else. I promise. You mean everything to me.

LIAM: I'd like to go to bed now.

DONNA: I can't! Josie's upstairs.

LIAM: *(Becoming cold again)* All right. I'll be back in an hour.

DONNA: Liam! Please. Where are you going?

LIAM: I'm going to the club!

(He leaves, slamming the door. DONNA *sinks down, beginning to cry; only* JOSIE*'s rapid footsteps on the stair force her to pull herself together.)*

JOSIE: *(Bursts open the door from the stairway carrying an armful of dresses on hangers.)* Was that our Liam? (DONNA *nods.* JOSIE *leaves the dresses over the cases.)* I was hoping for a lift. He uses this place like a cloakroom. *(Coming back to* DONNA*)* My daddy'll be along later to pick this stuff up.

DONNA: I wish you weren't going.

JOSIE: So do I. I'm dreading it. He treats me like a kid!

DONNA: Why don't you stay?

JOSIE: Three's a crowd. Anyway, I think you and Liam need time together. You should have a wee holiday.

DONNA: Yes, I know. He said he would take us away somewhere hot. Where are you off to now?

JOSIE: Dublin for the weekend—with Joe Conran.

DONNA: Do you see much of him?

JOSIE: We're working together. *(Hurrying)* Bye-bye. *(She kisses* DONNA.*)*

DONNA: Nice perfume. Lemons?

JOSIE: Joe gave it to me. He got it duty free on his last trip to Amsterdam.

DONNA: What are you getting so defensive about? I just said you smelt of lemons.

JOSIE: *(At the door)* What'll I bring you back from Dublin?

DONNA: *(Waving her away)* Yourself.

JOSIE: I'll see you.

(JOSIE *smiles and leaves the room.* DONNA *is smiling as well.*)

Scene 2

MCDERMOT, FRIEDA.

A room in JOHN MCDERMOT*'s house. He is on the telephone. The clasped hands symbol of the Party is on the wall, along with the slogan: "Democracy against Direct Rule." The room reflects that his political commitment is not separate from his domestic arrangements. The telephone cradle stands on a chair.*

MCDERMOT: Well, obviously it's very dangerous, it will set back the cause of Irish unity another—*(Pause.)* You're not interested in Irish unity? Thank you.

(FRIEDA *arrives with a handful of leaflets. She has been outside.* MCDERMOT *puts down the phone.*)

That's the third trade unionist out of seven who refuses to discuss the Petition against the Amendment. It's unbelievable. They've all said the same thing—no interest in the politics of the Republic.

FRIEDA: What's the Petition against the Amendment?

MCDERMOT: *(Going towards her)* Do you mean to tell me that you haven't even read the leaflets you're handing out?

FRIEDA: I was rushing.

MCDERMOT: That's no excuse.

FRIEDA: Och, what is it about? It'll save me reading it. I hate political pamphlets. Anyway, you always explain things better than you write them.

MCDERMOT: I don't think there's anybody who has insulted me more than you have—in my life.

FRIEDA: You're awful easy insulted. I'm the same with everybody.

MCDERMOT: *(Sighs.)* There's to be a referendum in the Republic to decide whether the Constitution should be amended to include an anti-abortion clause. Abortion is already illegal in the South; by putting it into the Constitution it cannot be challenged or even changed. Do you see? It's the Catholic Church barricading itself into the Constitution.

FRIEDA: *(Putting the leaflet down)* I wouldn't sign that petition.

MCDERMOT: You don't agree with abortion as a civil right for Protestants in the South?

FRIEDA: I don't really regard the politics of Southern Ireland as having anything to do with me.

MCDERMOT: Well, that is truly extraordinary.

FRIEDA: It's a foreign country as far as I'm concerned.

MCDERMOT: I think you're taking your rebellion against your father a bit far. Surely you want a united Ireland by democratic consent?

FRIEDA: No, it's not even that, I just don't care if Ireland is united or not.

MCDERMOT: What do you care about?

FRIEDA: I just want to sing my own songs.

MCDERMOT: *(Ironic)* Is that all?

FRIEDA: *(Misunderstanding)* It's everything. When the lights go down and I'm standing in a spotlight. There's a tremor; it starts in my toes and roots me to the floor when the first note comes. I'm pulled away to somewhere else entirely. There's nothing like it. Except that I want to do it again and again.

MCDERMOT: I used to feel like that a long time ago when I made political speeches. But I don't any more. Maybe it's the size of the audience these days. *(Pause.)* Have you ever cared about a person the way you care about singing?

FRIEDA: I don't believe in love, if that's what you mean.

MCDERMOT: What about caring for a friend? A person?
(FRIEDA *shakes her head.*) You see, I'm in politics because I care for people. But I care most of all for one person, and have for some time. Frieda, I care about you.
FRIEDA: Don't say that! I'll only disappoint you.
(*He takes advantage of her confusion and kisses her. She responds momentarily, and then breaks away.*) Oh I hate you!

MCDERMOT: No, you don't.

FRIEDA: I do. You've gone and spoiled everything.

MCDERMOT: You wanted me to spoil it. You were furious when my girlfriend came out of the bathroom the other morning.

FRIEDA: That was because she was having a bath when I wanted a pee.

MCDERMOT: And you were very annoyed when I stayed away last night. All night.

FRIEDA: Ha! The vanity of it!

MCDERMOT: You sulked all through breakfast. In fact you manage to sulk every time I bring a woman into the house. I can't persuade anyone to spend the night any more because your hostility makes them so uncomfortable.

FRIEDA: If that's what you think, there is a solution.

MCDERMOT: I think so, too.

FRIEDA: I'd better move out.

MCDERMOT: Alternatively I could kiss you again, and we could go to bed this afternoon.

FRIEDA: You're smiling.

MCDERMOT: I've been smiling from the beginning. And I've wanted you for a long time. Why do you think I invited you to stay with me?
(He attempts to kiss her again, but she moves away immediately.)

FRIEDA: I can't. You're my friend. You're the only friend I've got now. If I sleep with you, you won't be my friend anymore. And I'll have to find somewhere else to live. And frankly, I don't feel like it.

MCDERMOT: What are you afraid of?

FRIEDA: I'm not afraid. *(Furious)* I've never run away from anything in my life.

MCDERMOT: You've never run away from a fight. But there are other areas of experience. *(Makes another attempt to touch her.)* Frieda, *(very kindly)* I'm very good in bed.

FRIEDA: *(Enraged. Hits him in the chest.)* I hate you, John McDermot.
(She throws the pamphlets across the room and exits.)

MCDERMOT: Frieda! What did I say?
(The phone rings. MCDERMOT *is not sure whether to pick it up.)*
Frieda! Please come back!
(The phone rings until he picks it up.)
Hello? . . . Yes, this is John McDermot . . . yes, I did call you earlier . . . It's about the Petition against the Amendment. I'm collecting signatures from prominent trade unionists and people like yourself. It's for an open letter we want to publish in the *Irish Times* . . . (FRIEDA *arrives with a suitcase. He begins to signal to her while talking on the phone, but she refuses to respond.)*

What's that? . . . Look, can I ring you back? . . . You've caught me at a difficult moment . . . Yes, of course . . . Goodbye. *(Puts the phone down.)*

FRIEDA: Can I use that phone please? I want to ring for a taxi.

MCDERMOT: What are you doing? *(She sits down on her suitcase.)* I thought you didn't want to be homeless.

FRIEDA: I find your confidence both in relation to me, other women, and the rest of the world nothing short of nauseous. You behave as if you had nothing to learn, nothing to discover, no problems, and everybody else was waiting for you to fuck them!

MCDERMOT: I'm sure you're right.

FRIEDA: But what I really hate is the idea of having to trade something for my being here.

MCDERMOT: My intention wasn't to trade. I wanted you. And I didn't repress it. That's all. The house is yours; there's no price.
(She proceeds to pick up the phone book. He seems about to leave the room and give up, when he stops.)
Where will you go?

FRIEDA: As far away from you as possible. I'll resign from the Party.

MCDERMOT: And what reason will you give for that?

FRIEDA: Personal reasons.

MCDERMOT: There are no personal reasons any more. Everything is political.

FRIEDA: I've heard that before!

MCDERMOT: When you joined the Party you promised to secure working class unity—Catholic and Protestant—before the real struggle could begin. I can't see that my personal behavior towards you should make any difference to your commitment to that idea.

FRIEDA: On the contrary, I tend to judge ideas by the people who utter them.

MCDERMOT: *(Sighs.)* That's just the trouble, Frieda. Your standards are so high.
(She is arrested by the remark for a moment. Then she closes the telephone book, puts it down and reaches for the phone. Beginning to dial the number.)
Frieda. *(He stops her.)* Listen to me. I'll miss you. I'll miss you messing up the house. I'll miss you leaving all the dishes for me to wash. Leaving all the lights on. Running up the heating bills. I'll miss you letting the fire go out, and then not being able to relight it. I'll miss your awful singing in the bath. Being rude to my friends, particularly when they're women. Most

of all I'll miss the way you change your mind. You're so much trouble, Frieda, would you do one thing—one thing I wouldn't miss?

FRIEDA: What?

MCDERMOT: Would you stay?

FRIEDA: (*Overcome. Moving towards him*) Do I really annoy you that much?

MCDERMOT: Yes.

FRIEDA: Am I really that much trouble?

MCDERMOT: Yes.
(*They kiss, for a long time.*)

Scene 3

JOSIE, JOE.
Dublin. A hotel bedroom. JOSIE *is sitting up on the bed staring at an eighteenth-century doorway.* JOE *is lying back, listening sleepily.*

JOSIE: It's strange you bringing me here.

JOE: Why?

JOSIE: That time I told you about, when I first came to Dublin, I walked round for hours just looking at the place. I passed this hotel but I didn't notice it. I had my head down against the rain until a glass coach drew up alongside me.

JOE: And a beautiful girl got out wearing glass slippers!

JOSIE: There was a bride and groom in it. They were coming in here. There were some people in gold braid on the steps, they were standing on red carpet, through the window you could see the chandeliers, and above it all a tricolor was flying . . . It was the same flag that one July my father flew from our upstairs window. I'd have braved a baton charge to get that flag back from the police who snatched it. And I did . . . Yet nothing in the world would have induced me to defy the grandness of this place. I felt as if they'd snatched the flag away again . . . That's why it's so strange you bringing me here.

JOE: I can't imagine you lacking in courage, Josie.

JOSIE: Oh, I frequently do . . . Have you ever killed anyone?
(*He begins to sit up.*)

JOE: I can't say that I have.

JOSIE: Not even as a soldier?

JOE: I trained as an engineer.

JOSIE: Oh yes.

JOE: Have you ever killed anyone?

JOSIE: I planted a bomb once. It didn't go off.

JOE: Why?

JOSIE: I don't know, some technical fault.

JOE: No, I mean why did you plant a bomb?

JOSIE: I was fed up being a courier . . . They used women as messengers then. I wanted to show them I could take the same risks as a man. So I planned it, stole the car, and left it outside the law courts. I'm glad it didn't go off.

JOE: You did this entirely on your own?

JOSIE: No. A man I'd have gone to hell for helped me.

JOE: When was this?

JOSIE: In the early seventies. We were all a little bit mad then. Me especially.

JOE: So you wouldn't do it again?

JOSIE: I've lost the killing instinct. Now, I tend to think the crushing of a fetus is a tragedy.

JOE: Well, that's up to you.

JOSIE: Have you ever loved anyone so much you would die for them?

JOE: This is fun, Josie. I want what there is between us to begin and end in this room. And then on another occasion we could go to another room and have some more fun.

JOSIE: Fun! I hate that word.
(He reaches out to stroke her hair.)

JOE: I'm sorry if I offended you.
(He kisses her.)
Do you know him well?

JOSIE: Who?

JOE: O'Donnell.

JOSIE: He taught me how to build a barricade. *(She looks at her watch.)* And he doesn't like to be kept waiting.

(JOE *gets out of bed, goes to the bathroom en suite, leaving the door open. Immediate sound of ablutions.* JOSIE *finds herself entirely alone. The sound of ablutions gradually fades as she begins to speak.)*

(Speaking aloud) Bus stop posts; manhole covers; telephone kiosk doors; traffic signs; corrugated iron fencing; and old doors, wood is best not glass; especially if you don't have an upturned bus or lorry. And a tape measure is useful too, to measure the mouth of the street . . . He held one end of the tape and I had the other. It was the first time I'd ever seen him. He kept shouting at me to hold still. Hurry up. Move quickly. Find the rope, nails, wood. He was so precise. And I kept coming back with what he wanted every time . . . All day we ran about measuring, hammering, securing, until towards evening we needed only two slim posts and it was finished. I remember we rushed off to the park to uproot some young trees, saplings the Corporation planted. We were high up on the bank when a woman passed. She was pushing a pram; a pregnant woman in a headscarf, then she waved. It was my first whole day with him. "It's my wife," he said. Safe. I'm safe from him. The sight of her large and alone, thoughts in her child on the womb and in the pram were battleship enough to keep me away. Until minutes later I slipped, slid down the wet bank after him and came to a halt. "I can't get down," I said. And he reached out his hand . . . I wasn't safe. I was lost.

(JOE *returns, dressed. He watches from the doorway.)*

S c e n e   4

FRIEDA, MCDERMOT, FIRST POLICEMAN, SECOND POLICEMAN.
Two swings. A litter bin. Sounds of a children's playground.
FRIEDA *comes on.*

FRIEDA: This is a good place. *(Looking skyward)*
(MCDERMOT *comes on, also looking skyward.)*
There'll be hundreds here. *(Running with her hands outstretched)*
This one's mine. *(Pause.)* How many have you got?

MCDERMOT: I wasn't counting.

FRIEDA: You've got to count them. That's the whole point.

MCDERMOT: I'm not very good at this. It's not easy.

FRIEDA: Listen . . .

MCDERMOT: It's too calm.

(She looks round. He takes a notebook out of his pocket to write in.)

FRIEDA: Ah you're not going to do that again.
(He walks away to the swing and sits down.)

MCDERMOT: There's not enough wind.

FRIEDA: It won't be long.
(She follows him and sits down on the second swing.)
What is it anyway?

MCDERMOT: A piece for the paper on the by-election in Area H.

FRIEDA: Where's Area H?

MCDERMOT: North Belfast.

FRIEDA: Why can't they call it that? Why do you have to be a computer these days before you get any information?
(Pause. Waiting) How did we do?

MCDERMOT: Four hundred and seventy-four votes out of a total poll of 6,881. Seven per cent of the poll. Not bad. We seem to be a growing force in the north of the city.

FRIEDA: John . . . there was a man following me in the rose gardens. I wasn't taking much notice—and then everywhere I turned he seemed to follow. When I stopped, he stopped. He was blocking the only way out. I had to run through the rose beds to get away from him.

MCDERMOT: Where was I when this was happening?

FRIEDA: I think you were in the Tropical Ravine. My arms are all scratched!

MCDERMOT: I suppose you thought he wanted to assault you? Not everybody does you know.

FRIEDA: He wasn't looking at me like that. He frightened me! His eyes were like ice. It felt as if he were deliberately marking me.

MCDERMOT: Why would he do that?

FRIEDA: Intimidation!

MCDERMOT: Your head's cut! This is a university district. It's always been safe.

FRIEDA: For some people nowhere is safe. *(Suddenly looks up.)* Oh look! We're missing our chance. *(She gets up from the swing and runs forward, looking skyward, her arms outstretched, hands cupped.)* I've got one. *(She*

runs first to the left a little, then to the right, as if chasing something. Claps her hands suddenly.) Missed!
(MCDERMOT *starts up.)*

MCDERMOT: I see one.
(He runs forward, towards it, and then follows it off. Voice off. Claps hands.) Got it!

FRIEDA: Oh, I see another. *(She follows it as before, running about. She claps her hands together.)* Missed it! Damn!
(A Land Rover screeches to a halt. Door slams. A POLICEMAN *in a bullet-proof jacket approaches* FRIEDA, *who is standing with her eyes trained sky-ward.)*

FIRST POLICEMAN: What's going on here?
(FRIEDA *starts to rush off.)*

FRIEDA: There's another gust of wind—
(The POLICEMAN *grabs her arm.)*

FIRST POLICEMAN: I'm speaking to you.

FRIEDA: *(Indignant)* Shit! I've lost it.
(MCDERMOT *appears, holding his head.)*

MCDERMOT: I nearly knocked myself out that time.
(A SECOND POLICEMAN *in a bulletproof jacket approaches. He too is looking skyward. Everyone is looking skyward.)*

SECOND POLICEMAN: Is there something up there?
(Everyone looks at FRIEDA.*)*

FRIEDA: Yes. Leaves.

FIRST POLICEMAN: Leaves?

FRIEDA: Yeah. It's autumn and the leaves are falling. So what you have to do is stand under a really big tree and wait till they fall.

SECOND POLICEMAN: Why?

FRIEDA: You have to try and catch them before they reach the ground. And for every one you catch you have one happy day next year. So I was standing here trying to catch three hundred and sixty-five, before you came along.
(She looks skyward again.)

FIRST POLICEMAN: Are you trying to make a fool of us?

MCDERMOT: No. Look. We're terribly sorry. She was a bit depressed, so we thought we'd come out and catch a few leaves to cheer her up!

FIRST POLICEMAN: You realize you're causing an obstruction.

FRIEDA: *(Looking up)* That's the intention.

FIRST POLICEMAN: We've had a number of complaints from the residents here that you two people have been causing a disturbance.

SECOND POLICEMAN: Do you live around here?

MCDERMOT: We live close by. We didn't realize we'd upset anyone. We'll go home now. Come on, Frieda.
(He begins to take her away. She stops.)

FRIEDA: Wait a minute. Do they not know about catching leaves, the people who complained about us?

SECOND POLICEMAN: Go on home now. Before you cause any more trouble.

MCDERMOT: Come on, Frieda.

FRIEDA: Trouble? Is it trouble to want to be happy? Do you not know about catching leaves? Do you not remember?

(MCDERMOT and FRIEDA go. The FIRST POLICEMAN goes off in the opposite direction. The SECOND POLICEMAN looks up skyward for a moment. Sound of a Land Rover engine starting. He too hurries off. A leaf flutters down.)

Scene 5

DONNA, JOSIE, FIRST SOLDIER, SECOND SOLDIER, POLICEMAN.
Donna's living room. There is a glass of red wine on a low table and a bottle of pills. A small child's toy, a musical ball, is on the floor. DONNA comes into the room followed by JOSIE.

JOSIE: Liam said you were upset.

DONNA: Upset? Catherine fell down the stairs. Her head must have hit every step on the way down. Liam was right behind her. He couldn't stop it.

JOSIE: Is she all right?

DONNA: I sometimes think men don't actually like children—she's all right. She's made of rubber. I feel sick every time I think of it.

JOSIE: What are the pills for?

DONNA: The doctor gave me them—to calm me down.

JOSIE: Donna, I've something to tell you.

DONNA: Has he left his wife for you yet?

JOSIE: She left him ages ago.

DONNA: She's a braver woman than I thought. She's eight months pregnant.

JOSIE: Where did you hear that?

DONNA: Everybody knows Mairead O'Donnell's pregnant.

JOSIE: Not Cathal! I was talking about Joe.

DONNA: I can't keep up with this! Three months ago you had my head turned—you were so passionately in love with Cathal O'Donnell.

JOSIE: I know, but . . . have you ever thought, is this the man who has come to love me?

DONNA: You're not wise.

JOSIE: Oh Donna. I owe him so much. I'm really beginning to feel healed. I even forgot about Cathal. He took all the pain away!

(CATHERINE *begins to cry.* DONNA *goes to the door and listens. It stops. Then crying continues.*)

DONNA: I'm in for a bad night.
(*She exits.* JOSIE *listens also.*)
(*Voice off*) All right, lamb pie. Mammy's coming!
(JOSIE, *very thoughtful, picks up the musical ball. It tinkles gently when lifted, and again as she moves it at her ear.*)

JOSIE: Fuck! (*Drops it.*) Donna! It's the Brits.
(DONNA *runs back into the room.*)

DONNA: Get out! Leave me!

JOSIE: Can you cope?

DONNA: Leave me! The can't take me away if there's nobody to look after the child.
(JOSIE *exits quickly through the front door, which she doesn't have time to close. The sound of Landrovers screeching to a halt and doors slamming, followed by heavily shod feet running.*
DONNA *takes up the bottle of pills in time to face the first of two armed soldiers who come through the open door.*)
Where are the RUC? You're not allowed to raid our houses without a member of the police being present.

FIRST SOLDIER: Don't get smart.
(*A* POLICEMAN *enters, and waits quietly in the background.
The* SECOND SOLDIER *begins to look around.*)
Where is he?
(DONNA *watches the* SOLDIER *who has gone out to search the rooms.*)

DONNA: Don't waken the child. Where's who?

FIRST SOLDIER: Your husband.

DONNA: My husband's in the Crumlin Road Gaol. I haven't seen him for ten years.

POLICEMAN: We're looking for Liam McCoy.

DONNA: I don't know. I haven't seen him.

POLICEMAN: He lives here.

DONNA: Only when it suits him.

FIRST SOLDIER: So where is he?

DONNA: I don't know. You know what it's like. He goes out, gets drunk and forgets to come back. It's not against the law you know.
(*The* SECOND SOLDIER *comes back. He is carrying two small firearms in a towel. He presents it to her.*)
You planted it.

SECOND SOLDIER: (*To the* FIRST SOLDIER) Loose floorboard at the top of the stairs.

FIRST SOLDIER: You could do three years for this.

DONNA: How could I do three years? You won't find my prints on them.

FIRST SOLDIER: (*To the* POLICEMAN) What about that other address? (*The* POLICEMAN *hands him a piece of paper.*) Two-six-two Grosvenor Road. (*They wait for* DONNA*'s reaction.*) Maybe she knows where he is.

SECOND SOLDIER: Must be with Eileen tonight.

FIRST SOLDIER: Have you met Eileen? Dark hair. Slim. Very nice. Sure you don't know her?
(*Bin lids start up.*)

DONNA: Get out! Get out of my house!
(CATHERINE *begins to cry loudly.*)

SECOND SOLDIER: I'm sure Eileen knows where he is?

DONNA: If you don't leave me alone I'll take these pills. I mean it. I'll swallow the lot!
(She puts the bottle to her mouth and begins to swallow the pills. Some fall on the floor, scattering.)

POLICEMAN: *(Coming forward)* Hey, hey.
(The SOLDIERS *withdraw quickly.)*
Now, now. Nobody's going to harm you. It's your man they're after.
(The bin lids die down with the SOLDIERS' *exit.* DONNA *stops, looks round at the policeman.* CATHERINE *cries out again.)*
What age is the baby?

DONNA: Fuck off!
(The POLICEMAN *exits.* DONNA *sits down and pours the rest of the pills into her hand; she looks at the glass of wine.* CATHERINE*'s crying reaches a pitch of screaming. The tin lids get louder. Darkness. Every sound stops.)*

S c e n e   6

JOSIE, O'DONNELL, LIAM, MALACHY, DANNY, DONNA.
The Club. A room off the main bar. CATHAL O'DONNELL *is sitting at a small café table. The scene is similar to the room arrangement when* JOSIE *interrogated* JOE CONRAN. *There is an empty chair opposite* CATHAL; *he seems to be waiting.* JOSIE *comes in. She has not expected to find herself alone with* O'DONNELL.

JOSIE: I was told my brother was here.

O'DONNELL: He's all right.

JOSIE: Donna's house was raided.

O'DONNELL: Yes, we heard.

JOSIE: I think someone should go and see if she's all right. I wasn't able to go back. *(Pause.)* I suppose he realizes that he can't go home. *(She turns to go.)*

O'DONNELL: Josie!

JOSIE: I've got to find Joe—I don't want him walking into a patrol.

O'DONNELL: He's gone home. I want to talk to you.

JOSIE: So I hear.

O'DONNELL: Did Joe tell you about his assignment?

JOSIE: No. Of course not!

O'DONNELL: That's very professional of him.

JOSIE: He is—I cleared him, remember.

O'DONNELL: Oh yes . . . So you think it's an impossibility?
(She looks confused.) The thirty-two-county workers' republic. A place we
will never come into.

JOSIE: You were there!

O'DONNELL: You never said that to me.

JOSIE: You don't trust anyone. Do you Cathal?

O'DONNELL: You do yourself an injustice. I wanted to see him. I thought if
I could see him—I would know.

JOSIE: And do you?

O'DONNELL: Yes. It's really very simple. He's a romantic. Sit down. *(Pause.*
JOSIE *sits reluctantly.* O'DONNELL *immediately gets to his feet.)* I've put
Conran in charge of arms purchasing. The whole operation. And stockpiling
for the period after British Withdrawal. That's why I wanted to talk to you.
He's going to meet the Libyans in Malta next month. The idea is that he
will do the buying abroad but I'd like you to find the locations in Ireland
where the stuff can be kept until it's needed. *(Pause.)* Well, are you happy
about that? Do you see any problems?

JOSIE: Since when has my happiness been a priority of yours?

O'DONNELL: Oh I see. You're going to be vengeful.

JOSIE: I'm not going to be vengeful. My wounds are healed. But I am just
a little surprised and suspicious that I am being consulted about something
I am usually told to do.
(O'DONNELL *sits down again opposite her.)*

O'DONNELL: Are we talking about this assignment or are we talking about
something else? If we're talking about your assignments, you have always
been consulted by me. I have always taken your advice. I have always
trusted your instincts and your judgement. If we're talking about something
else, then I suggest that you say so. But don't infect your political judgement
with emotional considerations!

JOSIE: You were never very keen to separate them before.

O'DONNELL: I did try to talk to you in Dublin, but you ran away from me.

JOSIE: You know damn well what I'm complaining about. Your interest in me was to do with your desires, your appetites, your needs, which were fortunately once coincidental with mine. Now they're clearly not!

O'DONNELL: Once? Once coincidental?

JOSIE: Yes. They ceased to coincide when you let go of me five months ago!

O'DONNELL: Not for me.

JOSIE: Oh please. You cut me off! You sat at meetings ignoring me. You made sure that you and I were never alone. I got my orders through other people all of a sudden. You put the whole power of this organization between us, so I could never get a chance to ask you why. For ten years you have been my only lover, and because it was never publicly acknowledged no one ever understood my grief. *(Pause.)* You came out of that meeting in Dublin and you said, ''Are you around?'' What did you expect me to say? ''Yes.'' For your pleasure?

O'DONNELL: Five months ago I had to leave you and return to my wife. She was pregnant again. As you know, her last pregnancy miscarried. She has no family, unlike you. She has no one to turn to but me. She depends on me totally. And she's tenaciously loyal. Because I was sent word that she'd been so ill, and because of being married to me, she was having a very difficult time—the house was raided twice in a month—I came north to take her back across the border. It was not easy for me to stop seeing you, but there was nothing else for it. Since Mairead and I have been living together again I rediscovered what I'd forgotten—that my wife is not the passion in my life, you are. I once told you that I'd never let you down.

JOSIE: You said you'd never let her down either.

O'DONNELL: I intend to keep my promise. I don't intend to choose between you.

JOSIE: I'm afraid you'll have to.

O'DONNELL: I can't live without you. I have tried. I fought the memory of you every day. But you are the one who is with me in my thoughts all the time, not her; it's your voice I want to hear when she speaks, not hers.

JOSIE: I've begun again with someone else.

O'DONNELL: I can't let you go. It's not over.

JOSIE: *(Almost laughing)* Oh, it's not over. For months there was no one. Until Joe Conran appears. Then suddenly you notice, and it's not over! Well, it is for me.

O'DONNELL: I understand why you're with him. But you also need me. I see no reason why our friendship shouldn't continue. I don't let go of my friends easily.
(JOSIE *gets up from the table.*)

JOSIE: I hope that's not a threat!

O'DONNELL: It's not a threat. How could I threaten you when the whole apparatus of the British State doesn't cause you a hair's turn! Josie, I still love you.

JOSIE: Love? You once told me that to love something was to confer a greater existence on it—you were talking about patriotism—the love of your country. I've only recently realized that you never loved me. You took me. You possessed me. You took my youth and you hid it in a dark corner for a long time. You never draped me with a public celebration. But I'm out of the corner. It's over. The hiding is finished. You are in my thoughts from time to time, I admit; but usually as a prelude to a nightmare. (*Getting up*) If you've nothing else to say, I'd like to go. I've no wish to discuss "other business" with you. You can send your messages through the usual channels.

O'DONNELL: All right, Josie. But it's not over yet!

JOSIE: (*Turning*) Six months ago I'd have died for you. Five weeks ago, even, I might have listened. Now—it's too late.

O'DONNELL: Why is it too late? What has so many weeks got to do with it?

JOSIE: I'm going to have his child.
(*He is visibly devastated.*)
(*Relentless*) I'm pregnant too.
(*He attempts a recovery.*)

O'DONNELL: Congratulations.

JOSIE: Thanks.
(*She walks away to the exit door. Turns again.*)
Goodbye Cathal.

(*She exits. He is left alone sitting at the table. He smiles through his teeth, takes a packet of cigarettes from his pocket, stops smiling, crushes the cigarette packet, goes off, passing* MALACHY *and* LIAM *on his way out.*)

LIAM: Was that Cathal?

MALACHY: Aye.

LIAM: What's he looking so pleased about?

MALACHY: He's not. He's got an ulcer; he always smiles when it hurts. *(He puts his empty glass down.)* Will you take another wee drink? (LIAM *shakes his head.)* What's wrong with you tonight?

LIAM: I'm worried about Josie. I don't know how you could let her do it.

MALACHY: What else could I do? She said: "I want to go and live with him." I said: "Over my dead body." She said: "I'm having his baby." I said: "Fair enough. I'll help you move." What was I supposed to do? I'm no good with wee babies.
(The TWO MEN *move down the table with their pint glasses and set them down.)*

LIAM: She hardly knows him.

MALACHY: Well, she'll get to know him better now!

LIAM: You should never have let her move out of the house in the first place.

MALACHY: Don't you lay that at my door. It was your idea that she moved in with Donna. If you hadn't been so paranoid about your wife running off with somebody while you were in the Kesh, Josie would still be at home with me now.
*(*DONNA *comes in like a ghost, unseen, and waits.)*
At least he's on our side. Not like that other wee bitch running off with a Stickie!

LIAM: We hope he's on our side.

MALACHY: Ah now, don't you start that again. He's off to Malta with four and a half million of our money; you can be sure we checked him out.

LIAM: I just don't trust Conran. It's funny my house being raided.

DONNA: Your house?
(Both men turn.)

LIAM: Donna!

MALACHY: Would you take a wee drink? *(Senses danger.)*
Gabriel's got three tons of sugar.
*(*MALACHY *senses danger and exits quickly.)*

LIAM: *(Pause.)* I'm sorry about what happened.
(She walks up to him and hits him with her fists on the side of the head. The blow stuns him. He reels momentarily. He never takes his eyes off her.)
All right Donna. *(Backing off)* All right.
(He backs away and then turns and hurries off to another part of the club. She turns and walks away towards the door out. She stops, puts her hand

to her chest, breathing deeply. She appears to vomit or choke once, then twice. Nothing happens. DANNY *appears quickly at her side. She is bent double and does not see who it is.)*

DANNY: Donna? Donna?
(She straightens hopefully and discovers him.)
Are you all right?

DONNA: Yes, I'm fine.

DANNY: What's wrong?

DONNA: Nothing. Please go away.

DANNY: You don't look very happy.

DONNA: Life's not a bed of roses.

DANNY: Can I walk you home? Please?

DONNA: If you like.
(They exit.)

S c e n e   7

JOSIE, JOE.
Bedroom. JOE *is packing clothes into a bag.* JOSIE *comes into the room in her nightdress.*

JOE: What is it?

JOSIE: I'm bleeding again.

JOE: What can I do?

JOSIE: *(She gets into bed.)* I have to lie down and put my feet up. Can you put a pillow under my feet? *(He puts a pillow under her feet.)* I have to raise them higher than my head. *(She lies back.)* It happened a few days ago; but it stopped when I lay down. It's such a dangerous time . . . Oh God! I'd be so angry if I lost it.

JOE: You won't lose it, Josie. I know what that's like. My wife miscarried. *(He lies down beside her.)*

JOSIE: If you'd had a child with your wife, would you have stayed with her?

JOE: If, if, if. Who can answer if?

JOSIE: What's wrong?

JOE: *(Pause.)* I was thinking about your brother.

JOSIE: Our Liam?

JOE: He's not happy.

JOSIE: Liam's never happy. He's stupid. He's on the run permanently.

(JOE *sits up.*)

JOE: I think he's resentful because I got the assignment he wanted.

JOSIE: That's right: foreign travel. He promised Donna a continental holiday when he got out of the Kesh.

JOE: I wish O'Donnell hadn't been so brutal with him. He said I spoke five modern languages, which is an absolute must for working abroad, while Liam only had Gaelic. The last thing I want is to make enemies here—

JOSIE: Joe! I want out!

JOE: Out? Out of what?

JOSIE: I'm tired. Tired of this endless night watch. I've been manning the barricades since 'sixty-nine. I'd like to stop for a while, look around me, plant a garden, listen for other sounds; the breathing of a child somewhere outside Andersonstown.

JOE: You constantly surprise me.

JOSIE: Do you know what I spent the last few days worrying about? An incident—the night Donna's house was raided. I was walking back from the club, there was a foot patrol in the street. I should have turned back immediately and warned the men. But I was so preoccupied I wasn't even aware of the Army until I walked right into them and nearly fell over a corporal sitting in a hawthorn hedge with his face blackened. He shouted something stupid after me like: "This is a great place to come for a holiday." And do you know what I was thinking about? Whether my womb would be big enough for the child. Because you're so big and I'm so small. I'm really worried that the baby might get too big too quickly and come out before it's finished.

JOE: You idiot!

JOSIE: I'm so afraid of losing it. It's like a beginning within me. For the first time the possibility of being happy. So I'm going to tell O'Donnell that I won't accept this or any other assignment.

JOE: Perhaps it's something you feel at the moment.

JOSIE: No. I don't want my mother's life!

JOE: Then why? Why are you having a child? You did this without asking me!

JOSIE: It was my decision—it had nothing to do with you.

JOE: It was our decision!

JOSIE: We grew up by the hearth and slept in cots at the fire. We escaped nothing and nothing escaped us . . . I wish I could go back.

JOE: Go back?

JOSIE: Yes, and remember . . . those first moments.

JOE: Remember what?

JOSIE: Back then . . . somehow rid myself of that dark figure which hovered about the edge of my cot—priest or police I can't tell—but the light is so dim in my memory—most of the room is in shadow—and gets dimmer all the time.

JOE: Josie!

JOSIE: I'm trying to tell you why—about the first few moments when I took the wrong way.

JOE: Josie! It's not what we saw through the bars of a cot or heard from the corner of a nursery that made us what we are.

JOSIE: You would say that.

JOE: It won't help you to remember, because it wasn't so individual.

JOSIE: The bleeding's stopped.

JOE: I came to this country because I tried to live the life you seem to want now. I tried it with someone else and it didn't work.

JOSIE: Rosa. That woman's name haunts me. Did she want children very much? And you didn't?
(He gets off the bed quickly and paces the room.)

JOE: I hate tots! Babies! I hate this whole fertility business! I'm not interested in fucking children!

JOSIE: *(Pause.)* I don't ask you for anything but to be with me until the birth.

JOE: Of course I'll be with you. But you mustn't depend on me, Rosa—
(JOSIE *stares.* JOE *realizes.*) Josie.
(He gets into bed beside her) Let me hold you . . . Look, when I come back from Malta, I'll take you away for a while.

(A long pause.)

JOSIE: You don't have to worry about me, Joe. I've got two hearts.

Scene 8

FRIEDA, MCDERMOT.
Bedroom in McDermot's flat in South Belfast.
A cacophony of cymbals, skindrums, tambourines from the street.

FRIEDA: What on earth's that?
(She sits up in bed.)

MCDERMOT: The Chinese restaurants are celebrating their sabbath.

FRIEDA: It's not very harmonious.

MCDERMOT: I think the year of the rat is about to begin.
(She listens again.)

FRIEDA: Stop it!

MCDERMOT: What?

FRIEDA: Don't be so innocent. You know what you are doing.

MCDERMOT: I was just exploring.

FRIEDA: John! . . . I've come seven times already, I can't come any more.

MCDERMOT: But I thought you liked it.

FRIEDA: I'm all confused. I have so many things to think about . . . what I'm going to do with my life . . . where I'm going to go next . . . I have plans to make but every time you make love to me my mind goes blank!

MCDERMOT: You're tired of me.

FRIEDA: Maybe I'm not just what you want, John . . . I want a wee bit of privacy.

MCDERMOT: Marry me?
(Terrifying sound of breaking glass.)

FRIEDA: God!

MCDERMOT: That wasn't a Chinese gong.
(He leaps out of bed quickly and goes to the living room. FRIEDA follows him to the bedroom door, it looks immediately on to the hall.)

FRIEDA: *(Calling out)* It's all your fault, John McDermot! I told you not to put up an election poster in the window.

MCDERMOT: *(Comes back. He is carrying a brick in one hand and a note in the other.)* Don't be such a harpy!

FRIEDA: You called me a harpy!
(She snatches the note from him and reads. He sits down wearily on the bed and watches her.)
I expected this. Now do you believe me?

MCDERMOT: About what?

FRIEDA: The man in the park.

MCDERMOT: Catch yourself on!
(She moves across the bedroom to the hall.)

FRIEDA: Time I was going.

MCDERMOT: Where to?

FRIEDA: Safety.
(She drags a suitcase out of the hall.)

MCDERMOT: I forgot, it's Sunday. You always run away on Sunday.
(She is packing clothes into the case.)
I thought you were banned from the ghetto.

FRIEDA: I'm not going back there. I was thinking of leaving the tribes behind. Both of them!

MCDERMOT: Are you talking about leaving the country again?

FRIEDA: Very definitely.

MCDERMOT: I ought to buy you a season ticket for the Liverpool boat. You pack that suitcase about three times a week. *(She continues packing.)* You'll be very unhappy. The Irish aren't popular where you're going. Thanks to your relatives.

FRIEDA: You think I'm popular here? *(She indicates the brick.)* Whatever England is—it's got to be better than this!

MCDERMOT: Oh, for heaven's sake! You're running away from a couple of drunks!

FRIEDA: A couple of drunks?

MCDERMOT: Yes. A couple of drunks who've had their moment of power over you. Why give in to them?

FRIEDA: I'm not so enamoured with my life here that it's something I could die defending.

MCDERMOT: Who said anything about dying?

FRIEDA: It said in that note that this is a Protestant street! I have no wish to contest that. You have every right to live here. I haven't.

MCDERMOT: Frieda! Nobody in this street knows anything about you. The brick was thrown by a couple of mindless yobbos.

FRIEDA: How do you know?

MCDERMOT: I teach those kids every day.

FRIEDA: Oh please don't try to dismiss it just like that. You wouldn't believe me about the man in the rose gardens. And you wouldn't listen when I told you I felt watched every time I left the house. Now someone has put a brick through the front window! Please don't try to make out there's something wrong with me because I won't treat this as normal.

MCDERMOT: I'm not asking you to treat it as normal.

FRIEDA: What's wrong, John? Are the Prods not allowed to be bad? *(She turns and picks up her case.)* I think you're becoming something of an apologist for your tribe.
(He leaps out of bed and slaps her across the head.)

MCDERMOT: How dare you! *(In a rage, he hits her again.)* How dare you! *(Hits her again.)* I've spent my life fighting sectarianism.
(She falls into the corner, putting up her hands to protect her face and head. He hits out again.)

FRIEDA: Stop it! Please!

(He is standing over her breathing deeply, while she is crouched on the floor holding her head, unable and afraid to look up at him or move. He begins to pace the room.)

MCDERMOT: My father was driven out of the shipyards thirty years ago. He was thrown from the deck of a ship by his workmates. When he plunged into the water he had to swim for his life; they pelted him with rivets, spanners, crowbars, anything they had to hand. His tribe, my tribe, drove him out. And they did so because he tried to set up a union. He was a Protestant and a socialist. He was unemployed most of my life. Don't ever call me an apologist for my tribe again!
(She gets up and runs into the hall, where she bolts the door behind her. She sits down on the floor with her head in her hands and weeps. MCDERMOT comes to the door.)

Frieda! Open the door!

FRIEDA: *(Voice off. Shouts.)* No! I never want to see you again.
(MCDERMOT *begins to bang his head against the door, very hard. Several times. She is so frightened by this that she gets up and opens the door.)*
Stop it! Please! Stop it!

MCDERMOT: Don't shut me out! Don't leave me!

FRIEDA: But I can't stay here any more. I can't!

MCDERMOT: If you leave me, I'll kill myself.

FRIEDA: If I stay, you'll kill me—or they will.
(He gets up and immediately bangs his head against the door again. Alarmed, she pulls him away to restrain him.)
All right. All right. I won't leave. But stop doing that! Please stop it!

MCDERMOT: I love you, Frieda. I'll never let you go. I love you.
(He embraces her. She looks distressed.)

S c e n e   9

DONNA, JOSIE, DANNY, FRIEDA, MALACHY, LIAM.
Donna's living room. The room is empty. JOSIE *comes in, followed by* DONNA
who is wearing only a dressing gown and slippers.)

JOSIE: I haven't seen you for so long I was worried. Were you sleeping?

DONNA: What time is it?

JOSIE: It's not that late. You're not usually in bed at this time. When I was
here we used to sit up all night.

(DANNY *appears.)*

DANNY: Hello, Josie.

JOSIE: Hi.

DANNY: I'll head away on. See you later. Good night.
(He exits.)

DONNA: Are you staying? *(Pause.)* Is something wrong?

JOSIE: I'm not used to this. You might have told me!

DONNA: Like you told me about the baby?

(JOSIE *sits down.)*

JOSIE: I saw Liam at the club.

DONNA: Liam? What does he look like?

JOSIE: It's not his fault that he can't come home!

DONNA: No? But he can see other people.

JOSIE: Oh God. What a mess.

DONNA: *(Lighting a cigarette)* Next time you see him, would you give him a message from me? Would you ask him to leave me alone?

JOSIE: You don't mean that.

DONNA: I do. I'm happy with Danny. He's young, he makes me feel innocent. *(Pause.)* Why didn't you tell me about the baby?

JOSIE: I tried to once. You rushed off.

DONNA: You should have come and told me.
(DONNA *sits.*)
Did you want it?

JOSIE: I was surprised. It was a shock.

DONNA: What about Joe?

JOSIE: He's inscrutable. At first he wanted me to have an abortion so I'd be free.

DONNA: So that he could be free.

JOSIE: But now he's come around. He said he never thought he could make love to a pregnant woman.

DONNA: Is he away?

JOSIE: He's in Malta. He's due back tonight. I was too excited to sit in the house and wait on my own. And there were no women at the club, so—I felt a bit prominent.
(They both laugh.)

DONNA: Josie, I think you look beautiful. You suit a bit of weight on.

JOSIE: You know something, when he first came here, I wasn't sure about his motives. Then I realized that he had come to Ireland to win back his wife. I thought, I'm going to make this man love me.

DONNA: We all do desperate things when we're lonely.

JOSIE: *(Looking at herself)* I'll never be lonely again!

(FRIEDA *puts her head round the door.*)

FRIEDA: I was looking for a party. Did I come to the right place? *(They all stand and stare, then laugh.)*

JOSIE: Frieda!

DONNA: Look who it is! You're a stranger. *(Hugs* FRIEDA.*)*

FRIEDA: Look at you. (FRIEDA *hugs* JOSIE.)

JOSIE: You look great.

FRIEDA: *(To* JOSIE*)* You look different. It's your face; it's fatter. No, it's not—I don't know what it is.

DONNA: She's pregnant.

FRIEDA: *(Pause.)* What did my daddy say?

JOSIE: Nothing.

FRIEDA: As bad as that? He's good at saying nothing.

JOSIE: No, really. He was OK.

(DONNA *excitedly goes off to the kitchen for glasses and a bottle.)*

FRIEDA: Well, tell me this, did you marry well?

JOSIE: Who's married!

FRIEDA: Look, I'm dying to ask. Is there a father?

JOSIE: Joe Conran.

FRIEDA: I always liked him. He's kinda shy.

DONNA: *(Returning)* This calls for a celebration.
(She pours the new wine into a glass for each one.)

FRIEDA: I thought I saw Danny McLoughlin from the top of the street.

DONNA: You just missed him.

FRIEDA: I think I did.

DONNA: So let's have a toast.

FRIEDA: To?

DONNA: To Josie's baby . . . To Frieda's return . . . To my love!
(They clink glasses and drink.)

FRIEDA: Was it an accident?

DONNA: Frieda!

JOSIE: I wanted this.

FRIEDA: Did it matter who the father was?

JOSIE: I wouldn't have wanted it to be Cathal's child.

(DONNA *chokes on her wine, and looks in amazement at* JOSIE.)

JOSIE: It's all right. I can talk about it now.

FRIEDA: Sure everybody knew about you and Cathal O'Donnell. *(Drinks.)* Anyway, he's got nine kids already.

DONNA: Ten. She had a girl.

FRIEDA: She must be worn out.

DONNA: She's my age.

FRIEDA: She looks ten years older.

JOSIE: A child for every year . . . that I knew him.

DONNA: *(To* FRIEDA) What did you start!

JOSIE: I spoke to her once—a long time ago. It was just after I first saw her. She was suffering because of the heat. "He loves children," she said. "He's hoping for a boy this time." I tried to end it then.

(DONNA *pours more wine into* JOSIE*'s glass.)*

DONNA: I don't think you should be drinking in your condition.
(They laugh. There is immediate hammering at the door.)
(Springs to her feet and looks out of the window.) That's your daddy! And you're not supposed to be here.

JOSIE: You could hide in the kitchen.

FRIEDA: No! *(She stands up with her arms folded and waits.* DONNA *lets* MALACHY *into the room. He seems in a hurry. He stops at the sight of* FRIEDA, *then turns to* JOSIE.)

MALACHY: Are you fit to travel?

JOSIE: I'm pregnant, Daddy; I'm not an invalid!

MALACHY: I've come to take you away with me now.

JOSIE: Why?

MALACHY: The *Sea Fern* was met as soon as it entered Irish waters—before the fishing fleet could get to her and before the crew could dump the cargo.

JOSIE: Who met her?

MALACHY: Irish security police—they were tipped off this afternoon by the British Government. Our contact in the Guarda said the shipment was betrayed in Valetta. The British had been following its progress since it left Malta.

JOSIE: *(Suddenly alarmed)* Jesus! God! What's happened to Joe?

MALACHY: Josie! It was Joe who betrayed us! Everybody's saying it. I've come to take you away with me.

JOSIE: Who's saying it?

MALACHY: Ask Liam.

JOSIE: Liam's down on Joe. What does Cathal say?

MALACHY: Cathal is stubborn enough to believe that Joe Conran is coming back—he insists on waiting for him at the rendezvous.

JOSIE: *(Relieved)* Believe Cathal.

MALACHY: Listen. Joe's coming back isn't proof of his innocence.

JOSIE: The capture of the *Sea Fern* is not proof of Joe's guilt. We've lost shipments before!

MALACHY: If Conran is a British agent they'll be looking for us and everyone he's met.

JOSIE: Joe would not betray me! I've lived with him. I know him. I'm carrying his child. Do you not think I would know?

(Hammering at the door. Everyone freezes.)

DONNA: *(Looks out of the window.)* Liam.

MALACHY: Go on, girl. Open the door!
(DONNA moves quickly to the door, admitting LIAM.)
What's happened, son?

LIAM: *(Starts suddenly at the sight of FRIEDA.)* What's she doing here?

MALACHY: Who?

LIAM: Frieda! She's standing right behind you!

MALACHY: I don't see anyone. What's wrong, for Christ's sake!

LIAM: Gabriel drove out of the hospital tonight with a van load of supplies. He was stopped by the police. He showed them his forged security pass and told them he was delivering provisions to the Nurses' Home.

MALACHY: At this time of night?

LIAM: They let him go. He drove the stuff straight to the club as usual.

MALACHY: What—the pin head!

LIAM: Of course, he didn't know the police were following him. They arrested him and everybody on the premises for handling stolen goods. O'Donnell was among the people arrested. *(Slightly turning in* DONNA*'s way and then back.)* So was that musician, Danny McLoughlin. He'd just walked in.

MALACHY: Holy Jesus!

(DONNA *crosses the room to where* JOSIE *is standing.)*

DONNA: How come you got away?

LIAM: I wasn't on the premises.

JOSIE: How do you know all this?

LIAM: Eileen Watterson told me. She's a barmaid at the club.

MALACHY: Now do you believe me?

JOSIE: This is pure chance!

LIAM: It was a cover for a raid.

JOSIE: Joe would not betray me!

LIAM: He's not coming back!

JOSIE: I don't believe it.

LIAM: Josie. He got what he came for. Eileen told me they went straight to O'Donnell. They even had a layout of the club. And they knew what he looked like.

JOSIE: No. No. No!

LIAM: How many months pregnant are you?

JOSIE: Three.

LIAM: Kill it. I want you to kill the child!

JOSIE: Why?

LIAM: The father is a traitor. He did not love you; he used you. It's better that his child should not be born at all.

JOSIE: But it's my baby—it doesn't matter about anything else.

LIAM: It's his child!

DONNA: No. It's not, Liam. It's what you never understood. A child doesn't belong to anyone. It's itself.

(LIAM *grabs* JOSIE*'s arms.*)

LIAM: Do it. Don't force us!

JOSIE: *(In terror)* No!

MALACHY: Take your hands off her!
(LIAM *lets go of* JOSIE*'s arm*)

MALACHY: I'm the father here, son!

LIAM: What's wrong with you? She's carrying Conran's baby!
(MALACHY *puts his arm round* JOSIE.)

MALACHY: My baby now. *(Pause while he looks around.)* Josie's going to
live with me from now on. Isn't that right, love?

JOSIE: *(Hesitant)* Yes.

MALACHY: This baby's my blood. If anyone harms a hair on its head . . . !

LIAM: You're an old man, Malachy.

(MALACHY *begins to move through the room to the door, leading* JOSIE *away
with him.*)

MALACHY: I'll live twice as long as you, son!
(MALACHY *opens the door.*)
Now Josie and I are going to take a wee trip away from all this attention—
I advise you three to do the same. The soldiers will be here before long.
(He leads JOSIE *away.)*

DONNA: Josie!
(She does not turn round. They exit.)

LIAM: I have to make tracks.
(LIAM *prepares to leave.*)

DONNA: Liam!

LIAM: I can't stay, Donna. They'll be looking for me. I couldn't go back in there.

DONNA: I'll be here.

LIAM: I'd prefer if she wasn't!

FRIEDA: I came to say goodbye to my sisters, I wasn't intending to stay.

DONNA: *(To* LIAM) Come back when it's safe.
(LIAM *appears to want to embrace* DONNA, *but she isn't encouraging. He
thinks better of it, and leaves quickly.*)

FRIEDA: Why don't you leave him!

(They sit on the sofa.)

DONNA: *(Mildly surprised)* Why? How?

FRIEDA: You're not happy.

DONNA: I think I may have lost the capacity for happiness. I left my son for him. I thought if I had another it would make it up. But it didn't. As soon as I conceived I noticed the change. I lost my desire. All my life I felt I had to run fast, seek, look, struggle for things and hold on to things or lose them, but as soon as I felt the child inside me again, the baby quickening, I knew that it was coming and there was nothing I could do. I felt for the first time the course of things, the inevitability. And I thought, no, I won't struggle any more, I shall just do. And all that time—longing—was wasted, because life just turns things out as they are. Happiness, sadness, has really nothing to do with it.

(A child begins to cry upstairs. DONNA *listens.* FRIEDA *makes a move to go.)*

DONNA: Don't go yet.

FRIEDA: I'll stay until it's light.
(The crying stops. The room darkens.)

DONNA: She has wee dreams. I'll bring her down if she cries again. *(Pause.)* So you're saying goodbye.

FRIEDA: *(Nods.)* I left him sleeping. I walked out just as I am. If I'd taken a suitcase he'd have known and stopped me.

DONNA: Have you somewhere to go?

FRIEDA: England.

DONNA: Why England?

FRIEDA: Why not? It's my language.

DONNA: Why not go South?

FRIEDA: I'm not that kind of Irish.

DONNA: It didn't work out then?

FRIEDA: No.

DONNA: Any reason?

FRIEDA: Different commitments.

DONNA: It'll be lonely.

FRIEDA: I'd rather be lonely than suffocate.

DONNA: I understand, but it only lasts a little while that feeling. As you get older, companionship is very important. Filling the space in the bed with someone. Preferably a good friend.

FRIEDA: I want to write songs.

DONNA: Write to me.

FRIEDA: If I have anything to say. *(Pause. Looks away from* DONNA *straight ahead.)* I remember a long time ago, a moonlit night on a beach below the Mournes, we were having a late summer barbecue on the shore at Tyrella. Among the faces at the fire were Josie, Donna, Liam, and my father and mother were there too. And John McDermot was a friend of Liam's.

DONNA: I remember.

FRIEDA: We three slipped off from the campfire to swim leaving the men arguing on the beach. And Donna said, "I'm going to marry Liam McCoy one day." And we all laughed. And I said, "Well then, I'll marry John McDermot." And we sank down into the calm water and tried to catch the phosphorescence on the surface of the waves—it was the first time I'd ever seen it—and the moon was reflected on the sea that night. It was as though we swam in the night sky and cupped the stars between our cool fingers. And then they saw us. First Liam and then John, and my father in a temper because we'd left our swimsuits on the beach. And the shouting and the slapping and the waves breaking over us. We raced for cover to another part of the shore. We escaped into the shadows and were clothed again before they reached us. We lay down in the sandhills and laughed.

DONNA: I remember.

FRIEDA: I have not thought of that night for many years.

DONNA: *(Looking out)* The sky's getting lighter.

FRIEDA: Oh, it's not him; it is Ireland I am leaving.

DONNA: How quietly the light comes.
(Darkness.)

SERIOUS MONEY

Caryl Churchill

Serious Money was first performed at the Royal Court Theatre, London, on March 21, 1987.

"Futures Song": words by Ian Dury, music by Micky Gallagher
"Freedom Song": words by Ian Dury, music by Chaz Jankel

The play includes a scene from *The Volunteers, or The Stockjobbers,* by Thomas Shadwell, 1692.

I'd been writing plays for nearly 30 years when I wrote *Serious Money*. I started in 1958 with a play that was done by students, and over the next few years wrote a lot of plays—some had student productions, some were done on radio, some weren't done at all. In 1972 *Owners* was done at the Royal Court Theatre Upstairs in London, and since then I've written fairly constantly for the theater, and occasionally for TV. In 1976 I was asked by Max Stafford-Clarke to work with Joint Stock Theatre Group, whose way of working was to have a three- or four-week workshop to find out about a subject, a ten-or-so-week gap for the writer to write a play, and a six-week rehearsal. *Light Shining in Buckinghamshire, Cloud Nine, Fen,* and *A Mouthful of Birds,* (the first two directed by Max Stafford-Clarke, the second two by Les Waters) were all written for Joint Stock, though meanwhile I wrote other plays, such as *Top Girls*, in the usual way. In 1986 Max Stafford-Clarke set up a two-week workshop at the Royal Court to find out about the City. By chance it was just before Big Bang, the deregulation of the City, which meant that foreign banks could trade in the English stockmarket, and that the distinction between jobbers (who held stock) and brokers (who bought and sold it for their clients) was ended. So we were looking at the City at a time of great upheaval. When I went off to write the play the newspapers went on being full of City news and, in particular, the scandals involving the takeover of Guinness, and Boesky, the American arbitrageur. When I got the idea to write the play in verse, it gave me the theatrical purchase on the material that made it possible to write it.

CARYL CHURCHILL
1990

Characters

SCILLA TODD *a LIFFE dealer*

JAKE TODD *Scilla's brother, a commercial paper dealer*

GRIMES *a gilts dealer*

ZACKERMAN *a banker with Klein Merrick*

MERRISON *a banker, co-chief executive of Klein Merrick*

DURKFELD *a trader, co-chief executive of Klein Merrick*

GREVILLE TODD *Jake and Scilla's father, a stockbroker*

FROSBY *a jobber*

TK *personal assistant to Marylou Baines*

MARYLOU BAINES *an American arbitrageur*

JACINTA CONDOR *a Peruvian businesswoman*

NIGEL AJIBALA *an importer from Ghana*

BILLY CORMAN *a corporate raider*

MRS. ETHERINGTON *a stockbroker*

DUCKETT *chairman of Albion*

MS. BIDDULPH *a white knight*

DOLCIE STARR *a PR consultant*

GREVETT *a DTI inspector*

SOAT *president of Missouri Gumballs*

GLEASON *a Cabinet Minister*

Note on Layout

A speech usually follows the one immediately before IT BUT:

1. When one character starts speaking before the other has finished, the point of interruption is marked /.

e.g. MARYLOU:

> Now Albion's share price has rocketed
> It's time we sold out and pocketed / the profit.

TK:

> We could wait and see what Duckett's planning to do.

2. A character sometimes continues speaking right through another's speech:

e.g. JAKE:

> No, it's just . . . I'm in a spot of bother with the authorities / but it's no problem, I'm sorting it

SCILLA:

> What have you done?

JAKE:

> out, it's more what the sorting might lead to /

3. Sometimes a speech follows on from a speech earlier than the one immediately before it, and continuity is marked *.

e.g. BRIAN:

> How much would it cost to shoot her through the head?*

TERRY:

> You can't get rid of your money in Crete.
> Hire every speedboat, drink till you pass out, eat
> Till you puke and you're still loaded with drachs.

MARTIN:
DAVE: } Drach attack! Drach attack!
VINCE:

> Why's a clitoris like a filofax?

DAVE and OTHERS:

> Every cunt's got one.

BRIAN:

> *And he says five grand.

Where "shoot her through the head?" is the cue to "You can't get rid" and "And he says five grand."

4.Superior numerals appear where several conversations overlap at the same
  time.

e.g. DAVE:

    I've got a certain winner for the 3.30 if anyone's interested.[4]

BRIAN:

    You haven't paid us yesterday's winnings yet.

DAVE:

    Leave it out, Brian, I always pay you.

KATHY:

    [4]Come on gilts. 2 at 4 the gilts.

Where KATHY starts speaking as DAVE finishes his first speech, but BRIAN
  and DAVE continue their dialogue at the same time.

ACT ONE

A scene from The Volunteers, or The Stockjobbers *by Thomas Shadwell.*

HACKWELL, MRS. HACKWELL, *and two jobbers.*

HACKWELL:
Well, have ye been enquiring? What Patents are they
soliciting for, and what Stocks to dispose of?

1ST JOBBER:
Why in truth there is one thing liketh me well, it will go all over England.

MRS. HACKWELL:
What's that, I am resolved to be in it Husband.

1ST JOBBER:
Why it is a Mouse-Trap, that will invite all mice in, nay rats too, whether
they will or no: a whole share before the Patent is fifteen pound; after the
Patent they will not take sixty: there is no family in England will be
without 'em.

2ND JOBBER:
I take it to be great Undertaking: but there is a Patent likewise on foot
for one walking under Water, a share twenty pound.

MRS. HACKWELL:
That would have been of great use to carry messages under the ice this
last frost, before it would bear.

HACKWELL:
Look thee Lamb, between us, it's no matter whether it turns to use or
not; the main end verily is to turn the penny in the way of stock jobbing,
that's all.

1ST JOBBER:
There is likewise one who will undertake to kill all fleas in all the families
in England—

2ND JOBBER:
There is likewise a Patent moved for, of bringing some Chinese Rope-
Dancers over, the most exquisite in the world; considerable men have
shares in it.

IST JOBBER:

But verily I question whether this be lawful or not?

HACKWELL:

Look thee, brother, if it be to a good end and that we ourselves have no share in the vanity or wicked diversion thereof by beholding of it but only use it whereby we may turn the penny, always considered that it is like to take and the said Shares will sell well; and then we shall not care whether the aforesaid dancers come over or no.

2ND JOBBER:

There is another Patent in agitation for flying; a great virtuoso undertakes to outfly any post horse five mile an hour, very good for expresses and intelligence.

MRS. HACKWELL:

May one have a share in him too?

2ND JOBBER:

Thou mayst.

HACKWELL:

Look ye Brethren, hye ye into the city and learn what ye can; we are to have a Consultation at my house at four, to settle matters as to lowing and heightening of Shares: Lamb, let's away, we shall be too late.

Three different dealing rooms simultaneously. All have screens and phones.

Shares—GREVILLE
Gilts—GRIMES *and* OTHERS
Paper—JAKE *and* OTHERS

S h a r e s

GREVILLE *(on phone)*:

It's quite a large placement and what we've done is taken them onto our own books, one of the first deals of this kind we've done since Big Bang, yes . . . It's Unicorn Hotels, whom of course you know, they've acquired a chain of hotels in Belgium, and the main thing is they're a perfect mirror of their hotels here, 70 percent business, 3 and 4 star. They acquired them for sixteen million, the assets are in fact valued at eleven million but that's historic and they're quite happy about that. The key to the deal is there's considerable earnings enhancement. It was a private owner who got into trouble, not bankrupt but a considerable squeeze on his assets, and they were able to get them cheap. I can offer you a million shares, they're 63 to 4 in the market, I can let you have them for 62½ net. At the moment the profits are fourteen million pretax which is eleven million, the shares pay 4.14 with a multiple of 13.3. With the new hotels we expect to see a profit of twenty million next year paying 5.03 with the multiple falling to 12, so it's very attractive. This is only the beginning of a major push into Europe. Essentially the frontiers have been pushed back quite considerably.

The following is heard after the overlapping scenes finish:

I would show them to Joe in New York but it's only five in the morning. He's usually quite yielding when he's in bed but I don't think he'd want to start a whole new story.

Gilts

GRIMES *and his* MATE *in gilts dealing room of Klein Merrick.*

SCILLA *on* LIFFE *floor. Each has two phones.*

GRIMES *(to* MATE*)*:
I'm long on these bastards.

MATE *(to* GRIMES*)*:
3's a nice sell. They'd be above the mark.

GRIMES *(on phone)*:
Scilla? Sell at 3.

SCILLA *(on two phones / others)*:
10 at 3. 10 at 3.
(On phone 2)
That's March is it?

MATE *(phone)*:
6 Bid.

GRIMES *(phone)*:
What you doing tonight?

SCILLA *(to floor)*:
4 for 10. 4 for 10. Are you looking at me?
4 for 10.

GRIMES *(phone)*:
Scilla?

SCILLA *(phone 1)*:
Yes, we sold them.

GRIMES *(phone)*:
What you doing tonight?

SCILLA *(phone 1)*:
Going out later—hang on.
(Phone 2.) 4 for 10 nothing doing. Will he go to 5?
(To floor.) 5 for 10! 5 for 10!

GRIMES *(phone 2)*:
Bid 28 at the figure.

MATE *(to GRIMES)*:
I'm only making a tick.

GRIMES *(to MATE)*:
Leg out of it.

SCILLA *(phone)*:
Grimes?

GRIMES *(to MATE)*:
Futures are up.
(Phone) Champagne bar / at six?

MATE *(phone)*:
Selling one at the figure.
(to GRIMES.) I'm lifting a leg.

SCILLA *(phone 2)*:
We got you 10 for 5 bid, OK?
(Phone 1.) Yes, champagne bar at 6.
(Puts down phone 1, answers phone 2 again.) Yes?

GRIMES *(phone 2)*:
Get off the fucking line, will you please?

MATE *(to GRIMES)*:
01 bid, 01 offered.

SCILLA *(phone 2)*:
No, it's 5 bid at 6. I can't help you, I'm afraid.

GRIMES *(phone 1)*:
Is it a seller or a buyer?
(To MATE.) He don't want to take us because he don't want to pay commission.

MATE *(phone 2)*:
Offered at 4. Thanks very much but nothing done.

GRIMES *(phone 2 to* SCILLA*)*:
  5 March at 28.
  (To MATE.*)* What are we long of?

SCILLA *(phone 1)*:
  No, it's gone to 29.

GRIMES *(to* MATE*)*:
  29 bid.
  (Phone 2.) All right, 9 for 5.

SCILLA *(to floor)*:
  9 for 5! 9 for 5! / Terry!

MATE *(phone 1)*:
  You'd better keep up, I'll be off in a minute.

GRIMES *(phone 1)*:
  I'll make you a price, what do you want to do?

MATE *(to* GRIMES*)*:
  Bid 4.
  (Phone 1.) I'm off, I'm off.

GRIMES *(to* MATE*)*:
  They were offered at 4.
  (Phone 1.) Bid 3.

SCILLA *(phone 2)*:
  Three month sterling opened at 89.27 for March delivery and they've been
  trading in a 4 tick range.

MATE *(phone 2)*:
  Can't help you.
  (to GRIMES.*)* There's a fucking seller trying to make us pay up.

GRIMES *(phone 2)*:
  Bid 3.

MATE *(to* GRIMES*)*:
  I think we should buy them.

GRIMES *(phone 1)*:
  Bid 4, bid 4 at 6.

SCILLA *(phone 2)*:
  No, it's quite quiet.

(Phone 1.) 9 for 5 a deal.

GRIMES:
You're getting good at this. Extra poo tonight.

MATE *(phone 1):*
2 bid at 5.
(To GRIMES.) Am I still cheap?

GRIMES *(to* MATE):
Sold 5 for 9 bid.

SCILLA *(phone 2):*
Looks as if they may finish at 25.

MATE *(to* GRIMES):
What shall we do overnight?

GRIMES *(to* MATE):
I'll be long.

MATE *(to* GRIMES):
You don't want to be too long.

GRIMES *(phone 2):*
Closing out now at 4.
GRIMES *starts going down a list on a piece of paper marking prices.*

MATE *(to* GRIMES):
Doing the long end?

GRIMES *(to* MATE):
How shall I mark these, 2 or 3?

MATE *(to* GRIMES):
3.

GRIMES *(to* MATE):
Does it make a lot of difference to you?

MATE *(to* GRIMES):
Hundred thousand.

GRIMES *(to* MATE):
You must have made that trading in the last half hour.

SCILLA *(to floor):*
If you've lost any cards, Dave, I'm not helping you.

P a p e r

JAKE *and another dealer sitting side by side. Two salespeople who shout from behind. Loud. American sound though they're not.*

SALES 1:
I tell you what else here. Sweden / just called.

SALES 2:
If you want to jump on the Hambro / bandwagon you better hurry.

JAKE *(phone):*
We also have two Japanese. I'll make those 88 6.

SALES 1:
Sweden first 10 has been called. How do we go these days?

DEALER *(phone):*
There's also an issue coming out again.

SALES 2:
The new BFC for World Bank.

DEALER *(to* JAKE):
I've just sold some paper / like that.

SALES 1 *(phone):*
They're not taking. I'll give you a level.

DEALER *(to* JAKE):
Shall we go ahead?

JAKE *(to* DEALER):
Let's wait a few / minutes before we have the whole world crashing down on us.

SALES 2:
Chase Corporation 68 88.
He can bash you in with one arm. He's got a black belt in karate.

SALES 1:
He's a very nice guy.

JAKE *(phone):*
What I suggested was swapping into something longer, threes or whatever.

DEALER *(phone):*
I've been talking to Hong Kong.

JAKE *(phone):*
  Because / it's up to 14.

SALES 1:
  We're waiting on the Bundesbank here.

JAKE *(phone):*
  He doesn't care at the moment, / David.

SALES 2:
  Paris intervention rate / still at 8 percent. Buy 10.

DEALER *(phone):*
  It's done.

JAKE *(phone):*
  Band two are at thirteen-sixteenths. It's a softer tone today.

DEALER *(to* JAKE*):*
  He just said to me 590, I said it's done. He would have said 610 wouldn't
  he?

JAKE *(to* DEALER*):*
  Get back on.

SALES 1:
  We have Frankfurt here, Frankfurt, guys.
  Discount rate remains 3 percent. Lombard 5. Buy twos / twos, twos, twos.

DEALER *(phone):*
  He said to me 595 . . . OK that would be great.

SALES 2:
  Tokyo one month 4.28125.*

DEALER *(phone):*
  Discretion is my middle name. Tell me tell me tell me tell me . . . you
  said you were going to tell me after lunch . . . / What, you bought
  some? . . . It's

SALES 1:
  He broke an arm wrestling with a treasury bond dealer

DEALER:
  going down . . . How fast do you want it to go down? . . . You're in
  profit, / it's 7–8 right.

JAKE *(phone):*
  Listen, guy. Listen listen listen listen listen.
  Lombard Intervention steady at 5.

DEALER:

If it takes at 6 . . . no it's not going to take at 5 . . . if it goes to 7 . . . You're such a sleaze, you're not really a man of honor, you said you'd tell me after lunch . . . / I didn't know that's

SALES 2:

The guy dealt with Citibank but got back to them too late

DEALER:

What your best was   tell me tell me   Futures are crashing off

JAKE *(phone):*

The Mori poll put the Tories four up.

SALES 1:

We're going to lose power any minute, that's official.

DEALER:

What the fuck?

JAKE *(phone):*

So the three month interbank sterling rate—no it's a tick under—

SALES 1:

We have Milan three months 11½.

JAKE *(phone):*

There's a discrepancy between band 2 and band 3 . . . I thought it might give us some arbitrage possibilities.

DEALER *(phone):*

Come on come on come on guy.

SALES 1:

What's with the ECU linked deposits for Nomura?

SALES 2:

Now hurry hurry hurry guys hurry.

Power goes—no screens, no phones.
Outcry.

JAKE:

Marvelous.

DEALER:

If the market moves in a big way we'll get cremated.

JAKE:

They left us a whole lot of orders we're meant to be filling.

DEALER:
  I have to speak to Zurich.

SALES 2:
  So what happens now?

SALES I:
  They go elsewhere, bozo.

Liffe Champagne Bar

SCILLA *(trader with* LIFFE*),* her brother JAKE *(commercial paper dealer),* GRIMES *(gilts dealer) drinking together in the champagne bar.*

GRIMES:
  Offered me sixty right? So next day
  The other lot seventy five. OK,
  So I go to the boss and go "I don't want to trouble
  You," and he goes "All right you cunt,
  Don't mess about, how much do you want?"
  So I go—I mean why not—I go "Double
  What I'm getting now," and he goes "fuck off." Meanwhile
  Zackerman rings and—this'll make you smile—
  He goes, he goes, I'll give you a hundred grand,
  Plus the car and that, and fifty in your hand,
  But no thinking about it, no calling back,
  This is my first and last. I say, Zac,
  A good dealer don't need time to think.
  So there you go. Have another drink.

JAKE:
  So there's twenty-seven firms dealing gilts.

SCILLA:
  Where there used to be two.

GRIMES:
  Half the bastards don't know what to do.

JAKE:
  Those of you that do have got it made.

SCILLA:
  And all twenty seven want ten percent of the trade.

GRIMES:

So naturally there's going to be blood spilt.

JAKE:

Ten per cent? Go in there and get fifty.

SCILLA:

Everyone thinks it's Christmas and it's great to know they love you,
But you mustn't forget there's plenty still above you.
(There's at least two dozen people in the City now getting a million a
year.)
Think of the ones at the top who can afford
To pay us to make them money, and they're on the board.

GRIMES:

They're for the chop.

JAKE *(simultaneously):*

I'm on the board.

SCILLA:

True, you're on the board,
But how many of us will make it to the top?
If we've a Porsche in the garage and champagne in the glass
We don't notice there's a lot of power still held by men of daddy's class.

GRIMES:

No but most of them got no feel
For the market. Jake's the only public schoolboy what can really deal.

JAKE:

That's because I didn't go to university and learn to think twice.

SCILLA:

Yes, but they regard us as the SAS.
They send us in to smash the place up and get them out of a mess.

GRIMES:

Listen, do you want my advice?

SCILLA:

They'll have us on the scrap heap at thirty five,

JAKE:

I've no intention of working after I'm thirty.

SCILLA:

Unless we're really determined to survive
(which I am)

JAKE:

It probably means you have to fight dirty.

GRIMES:

Listen, Nomura's recruiting a whole lot of Sloanes.
Customers like to hear them on the phones
Because it don't sound Japanese.
If you want to get in somewhere big—

SCILLA:

Grimes, don't be such a sleaze.
Daddy could have got me in at the back door
But you know I'd rather be working on the floor.
I love it down with the oiks, it's more exciting.

JAKE:

When Scilla was little she always enjoyed fighting
(better at it than me.)

SCILLA:

But it's time to go it alone and be a local.
I'm tired of making money for other people.

GRIMES:

(Going to make a million a year?

SCILLA:

I might do.)

GRIMES:

I tell you what though, Zackerman can recruit
The very best because he's got the loot.

JAKE:

I told him for what he's getting from my team, why be a meanie,
He got rid of the BMW's and got us each a Lamborghini.
He's quite a useful guy to have as a friend.
So I thought I'd ask him home for the weekend.
He's talking to dad about amalgamation.
Klein needs a broker.

SCILLA:

And daddy needs a banker.

GRIMES:

Won't survive without one, poor old wanker

JAKE:

I told dad/his best bet's a conglomeration.

GRIMES:

Some of them old brokers is real cunts.

JAKE:

But I've got to go to Frankfurt Friday night,
So Scilla, you can drive him down, all right?

SCILLA:

Yes, that's fine. I wonder if he hunts.

JAKE:

JAKE *leaves*.

SCILLA:

I'm beginning to find Zackerman quite impressive.
(I wonder how he got to where he is now?)

GRIMES:

My school reports used to say I was too aggressive
(but it's come in quite useful.)
My old headmaster wouldn't call me a fool again.
I got a transfer fee like a footballer. He thought I was a hooligan.
He goes, you fool boy, you're never going to get to work,
What use is a CSE in metalwork?
I could kiss his boots the day he kicked me out of school.

GRIMES *and* SCILLA *leave*.
ZAC *enters*.

ZAC:

So cut the nostalgia. I'm the guy they're talking about, Zac.
I'm here for my bank, Klein Merrick, to buy up jobbers and brokers.
And turn the best of them into new market makers.
The first time I realized how fast things were changing was something
that happened at Klein's in New York a few years back.

MERRISON, *a banker, co-chief executive officer of Klein Merrick*.
DURKFELD, *a trader, co-chief executive officer of Klein Merrick*.

MERRISON:

So I told them 83 was a great year,
Profits up ten million on 82.
But we can do better than that by far.
Leveraged buyouts are the way to go
(I told them).

Take Krafft, put up three million to acquire Hoffman Clocks,
Borrowed the rest of the fifty million, a year later makes a public offer-
ing, and pockets
—a whole fifty million plus he retains thirty million of stock.
That's eighty million dollars on his initial three.
And that's from taking a risk instead of a fee.
We advise other people on acquisitions.
They make the serious money. Fuck it all.
The company should take its own positions.
Partners should be willing to risk their own capital.
I told them, man is a gambling animal.
Risk is one of our company traditions.
Old Benny Klein took risks, the latest news
Meant profit, they'd say on Wall Street. Let the Jews
Have that one, and he would. Imagine the scene
Guy comes and says I can make flying machines.
Benny puts up the money, doesn't bat an eye.
He says, 'OK, so make the machines fly.
When I was working with Henry under Nixon

DURKFELD:
Jack, I heard this speech before.

MERRISON:
There were quite a few things needed fixing—

DURKFELD:
Jack, I heard it already.

MERRISON:
So, I'm a bore.
Tell me, do you have a problem, Eddie?
I trust you've no more trouble with your wife?
It's a while since you took a good vacation.
None of us gets enough relaxation
    (I never even make it upstairs to the gym get a massage.)
Tell me what you want out of life.

DURKFELD:
I'm a simple guy, Jack. I walk in the woods
And shoot things. I don't talk so good
As you, I'm good on my own, I shoot straight.
I don't say, 'Shall I, shan't I?' You guys deliberate
One hell of a lot. I walk on my own
And I know I could run this show on my own.

MERRISON:

I'm not sure I understand what you're saying.

DURKFELD:

I don't have the same alternatives
A guy like you does. You say Henry
Where I say Kissinger. You want to move?
You've talked about some possibility.
For me, this is enough.
I don't look beyond this company.
You ready to go do that stuff?

MERRISON:

Let me understand what you're saying here.

DURKFELD:

I want to go solo running Klein.
I'm saying I'm suggesting you resign.

MERRISON:

I just promoted you.

DURKFELD:

Should I be grateful?

MERRISON:

I made you my equal.

DURKFELD:

Jack. I hate you.
Didn't you know that? You're not so smart.
You're too important to smell your own fart.

MERRISON:

Eddie. I need to understand your problem.

DURKFELD:

There's guys don't want me in their club.
I don't give a rat's ass.
Those guys would have looked the other way
And let the cattle trucks pass.
   (I don't want to play golf with those bastards. I don't even play golf. I
can walk without hitting a ball.)
I'm good at my job.
I stay on the floor with the guys.
Screw the paneling, screw the Picassos, I am not interested in office size.
   (You like lunch, you have lunch.)

I run the best trading floor in New York City,
And traders make two dollars profit for this company
   for every dollar made by you bankers.
And you treat us like a load of shit.
You make me your equal, I'm meant to say thanks
For that? Thanks, Jack. Come off it.
I make this company eighty million dollars and bankers pocket most of
   that profit.
Bankers get on the cover of Time.

MERRISON:
   Brother, can you spare a dime?

DURKFELD:
   I do OK, sure, I'm not talking greed.
   I'm talking how I mean to succeed.
      (My father came to this country—forget it.)
   Which of us does this company need?
   I'm talking indispensable.

MERRISON:
   And my father? You think I'm some kind of patrician?
   I was sweeping floors in my uncle's delicatessen
   So don't—
   The company needs us both. Be sensible.
   There's two aspects to the institution.
   Nobody means to imply they underestimate your invaluable contribution.
   I need to understand what you're saying here so let's set a time we can
      have a further talk.

DURKFELD:
   You don't seem to get it. You're sitting in my chair. Walk.

ZAC:
   And the guy walked.
      (He walked with twenty million dollars but he walked.)

The financial world won't be the same again
Because the traders are coming down the fast lane.
They don't even know it themselves, they're into fucking or getting a
   Porsche, getting a Porsche *and* a Mercedes Benz.
But you can't drive two cars at once.
If you're making the firm ten million you want a piece of the action.
You know you've got it made the day you're offered stock options.

There are guys that blow out, sure, stick too much whitener up their nose.
Guy over forty's got any sense he takes his golden handshake and goes.
Because the new guys are hungrier and hornier,
They're Jews from the Bronx and spics from South California.
It's like Darwin says, survival of the fit,

Now, here in England, it's just beginning to hit.

The British Empire was a cartel.
England could buy whatever it wanted cheap
And make a profit on what it made to sell.
The empire's gone but the City of London keeps
On running like a cartoon cat off a cliff—bang.
That's your Big Bang.
End of the City cartel.
Swell.
England's been fucking the world with interest but now it's a different scene.
I don't mind bending over and greasing my ass but I sure ain't using my
    own vaseline.

Now as a place to live, England's swell
Tokyo treats me like a slave, New York tries to kill me, Hong Kong
I have to turn a blind eye to the suffering and I feel wrong.
London, I go to the theater, I don't get mugged, I have classy friends,
And I go see them in the country at the weekends.

The meet of a hunt. On horses are ZAC, GREVILLE, *50, stockbroker, his
daughter* SCILLA, *and other hunt members, e.g.,* MRS. CARRUTHERS, LADY
VERE, MAJOR *and* FARMER FROSBY, *jobber, comes in late, on foot to watch.*

MRS. CARRUTHERS:
The hound that I walked goes up front with the best.

FARMER:
The best of the pack is that cunning old bitch.

LADY VERE:
His fetlocks swell up so I'll give him a rest.

MAJOR:
Went over his neck and headfirst in the ditch.

GREVILLE:
Stand still will you dammit, whatever's the matter?

MAJOR:
Bottle of sherry he won in a raffle.

LADY VERE:
Hunt saboteurs made a terrible clatter.

MRS. CARRUTHERS:
You can't hold her, Greville, in only a snaffle.

FARMER:
It's colder today but the going's much quicker.

SCILLA:
Jumped onto the lawn and straight over the vicar.

GREVILLE:
Good morning

MAJOR:
  Good morning

GREVILLE:
   Good morning

MRS. CARRUTHERS:
    Hello

GREVILLE:
Good morning

LADY VERE:
  Good morning

GREVILLE:
   I don't think you know
Mr. Zackerman here, my colleague and guest.

MRS. CARRUTHERS:
The hound that I walked goes up front with the best.

GREVILLE:
Mr. Zackerman wanted to join us of course
And Mrs. Carruthers provided a horse.

MRS. CARRUTHERS:
He's terribly clever, won't put a foot wrong,
When he hears the horn blow he'll be off like a rocket.
His mouth's rather hard and he is very strong,
Don't fight him, he'll pull out your arms by the socket.
There's not a horse safer and not a horse faster,
So don't step on hounds and don't override master.

LADY VERE:
Making the most of the beautiful weather.

GREVILLE:

American fellow, a friend of my daughter,
Colleague of mine, we'll be working together.

SCILLA:

Left behind at the gate and came off in the water.

FARMER:

The best of the pack is that cunning old bitch.

MAJOR:

Went over his neck and headfirst in the ditch.

LADY VERE:

Hunt saboteurs made a terrible clatter.

GREVILLE:

Stand still will you dammit, whatever's the matter?
Priscilla insists upon working for Liffe.
I was terribly doubtful and so was my wife.
  (The London International Financial Futures Exchange, terrible place,
  full of the most frightful yobs)
Hardly the spot for a daughter of mine
But she buys her own horses and takes her own line.

LADY VERE:

We've lost our head gardener, bit of a chore.

MAJOR:

I'm sure Mr. Zimmerman's hunted before.

ZAC:

Not a great deal but I have been out a few times in Ireland with the Galway
Blazers.

LADY VERE:

In that case I'm sure you can give us a lead.

MRS. CARRUTHERS:

The girl's putting far too much oats in his feed.

SCILLA:

Is is true?

ZAC:

Well I saw both the start and the finish.
I was on foot drinking plenty of Guinness.

SCILLA:

There aren't any gates and I'm not waiting for you.

ZAC:

You're so tenderhearted, that's why I adore you.

FARMER:

It's colder today but the going's much quicker.

SCILLA:

Jumped onto the lawn and straight over the vicar.

   (So Klein have taken over Daddy. How long will he last? Five years?)

ZAC:

(He could be lucky.)

GREVILLE:

Not joining us Frosby? Find horses a bore?

MRS. CARRUTHERS:

He's terribly clever, won't put a foot wrong.

LADY VERE:

We've lost our head gardener, bit of a chore.

MRS. CARRUTHERS:

His mouth's rather hard and he is very strong.

FROSBY:

I like a stroll to see the meet.

I'm happier on my own two feet.

Is that chap there the American?

GREVILLE:

Yes, it's Klein's Zac Zackerman.

FROSBY *(to himself)*:

Yanks go home. Yanks are robbers.

GREVILLE:

Zac, I want you to meet a colleague I've done a great deal of business with
over the years, one of the jobbers,
Mr. Frosby, Mr. Zackerman.

ZAC:

Hi Mr. Frosby, I can't really talk.

This horse won't stand still and he won't even walk.

MRS. CARRUTHERS:

When he hears the horn blow he'll be off like a rocket.

Don't fight him, he'll pull out your arms by the socket.

GREVILLE:

No more long lunches for me, Frosby, no more lying in bed.

It's up at six now in the godforsaken
Dark cold mornings. On the bright side
The company does an excellent egg and bacon.

FROSBY:

Some things change, some things don't end.
After all, a friend's a friend.

MRS. CARRUTHERS:

So don't step on hounds and don't override master.

ZAC:

Is this horse going to do what I tell it Priscilla?

MRS. CARRUTHERS:

There's not a horse safer and not a horse faster.

SCILLA:

It's generally known around here as a killer.

ZAC:

(When I end up in bed with a broken leg I only hope you're going to look
after me.)

SCILLA: (Drop dead, bozo.)

The horn blows.
They all go in a rush, leaving FROSBY *alone.*

FROSBY:

The stock exchange was a village street.
You strolled about and met your friends.
Now we never seem to meet.
I don't get asked much at weekends.

Everyone had a special name.
We really had a sense of humor.
And everybody played the game.
You learned a thing or two from rumor.

Since Big Bang the floor is bare,
They deal in offices on screens.
But if the chap's not really there
You can't be certain what he means.

I've been asked to retire early.
The firm's not doing awfully well.
I quite enjoy the hurly burly.
Sitting alone at home is hell.

I can't forgive Greville. He's gone with that Yankee bank buying it's way in, that Yak, Whack, whatsisname, Zac, trying to keep up with his children. His son Jake's one of these so-called marketmakers. Some of us have been making markets for thirty years. And his daughter Scilla works with those barrow boys in Liffe you'd expect to see on a street corner selling Christmas paper and cheap watches, they earn more than I do, they won't last.

I have a constant funny ache,
I can't see straight because of grief.
I really think my heart will break.
Revenge would give me some relief.

So now I'll phone the DTI,
Who want a clean and honest City.
Jake's no better than a thief
And why should I have any pity?
I've cried and now my friends can cry.

I've had the odd tip from Greville, I know he gets it from Jake and there's far more than I ever see. Let the DTI investigate. The City's not mine any more so let it fall.

I love the masters in their pink
I'm glad traditions still exist.
I think I'll go and have a drink.
I love the valley in the mist.
    (I'm very frightened.)

ZAC *phones* TK *and* MARYLOU BAINES *in New York.*

TK:
This is Marylou Baines' personal assistant.

ZAC:
It's Zac, I've got to speak to her this instant.
I know it's 3 a.m. your time, but I know she's awake.
Tell her it's about Jake.

TK:
Hi, Zac, this is TK here. Can I help you? What's the problem? Is it urgent?

ZAC:
Stop talking like a tubful of detergent / .
I got to speak to her now and not now but five minutes ago.

MARYLOU:
Zac, is there something I should know?

ZAC:

Jake's dead. They think it's suicide.

MARYLOU:

Thank you, Zac.
Jake was a nice guy but I haven't heard from him since some time back.

She hangs up and speaks to TK.

MARYLOU:

Put anything from Jake Todd in the shredder.

ZAC *phones* JACINTA CONDOR *in London.*

ZAC:

Jacinta, it's me. / Bad news. Jake's been found shot. /
It looks like suicide because he was in some kind of trouble with the DTI /
though so far nobody seems to know exactly what.

JACINTA:

Zac! What? My God.
He was the English colleague I like the most (except for you.)
I hope I never meet his unhappy ghost.
I look forward to meeting. /

JACINTA *phones* NIGEL AJIBALA.

JACINTA:

Nigel, have you read the newspapers today?

NIGEL:

No, what's the matter?

JACINTA:

Don't panic, OK?

This overlaps with CORMAN *phoning* ZAC.

CORMAN:

Zac, have you seen the fucking *Times* this morning?
Why didn't Todd give us any warning.
Why didn't he tell us about the DTI?
Do you think he's talked?

ZAC:

Deny. Deny. Deny.
(Let them see what they can prove.)

This overlaps with JACINTA *phoning* MARYLOU.

JACINTA:
Marylou, the delivery. You think we should wait a week?

MARYLOU:
Hold off for twenty-four hours, OK? We'll speak.

NIGEL *phones* CORMAN.

NIGEL:
Mr Corman, I'm deeply shocked that anyone associated with your company
should be touched by the slightest breath / of scandal.

CORMAN:
The deal's in no way affected by his death.
 (The deal is the priority.)

This overlaps with MARYLOU *phoning* ZAC.

MARYLOU:
Zac, your news is causing a certain amount of tension.

ZAC:
Can we still rely / on you?

MARYLOU:
          Sure, but never mention.

CORMAN *phones* MARYLOU *and gets tk on answering machine.*

CORMAN:
  TK? MARYLOU?

TK *(on machine):*
Hello, this is the office of Marylou Baines. I'm afraid Ms. Baines is not
available right now to come to the phone,
But if you wish to leave a message for her or for tk, her personal assistant,
please speak for as long as you wish after the tone.

CORMAN:
Fuck.

ZAC:
I went with Scilla to identify her brother Jake's body which was kind of a
    mess.
Then we stopped off for coffee, which was making me late for work, but it
    was a special occasion, I guess.
It'd be good if we could handle this
So you don't get associated with anything too scandalous.
 (Just stick to No comment, and let them make things up.)

SCILLA:

Zac, I told the police I had breakfast with Jake at Klein Merrick yesterday
morning.

Just to say hello. But in fact he gave me a warning.

ZAC:

They know the DTI paid him a visit.

SCILLA:

But it wasn't just that. He was frightened of . . .

ZAC:

Well, what is it?

SCILLA:

What was Jake like? charming, clever, idle.
He won, he lost, he cheated a bit, he treated it all as a game.
Can you really imagine him killing himself for shame?
(He didn't know what honor meant.)
He wasn't telling me he was suicidal,
He was telling me . . . You may think it's absurd, but
I'm certain he must have been murdered.

JAKE *and* SCILLA *at breakfast.*

JAKE:

Don't let me worry you, I'm probably imagining it.

SCILLA:

Have you shared a needle?

JAKE:

Not AIDS, I'm perfectly / healthy.

SCILLA:

At work they ask for tea in an AIDS cup, they mean / a disposable because
the dishwasher

JAKE:

Listen, I've a problem. Listen.

SCILLA:

What?

JAKE:

No, never mind, you know I left my diary at your place last week? / You
haven't got it on you?

SCILLA:

Yes, do you want—?

No, but I could—.

JAKE:

Hold onto it. No, maybe you'd better—No, hold onto it. You can always burn it later. Fine.

SCILLA:

What is this?

JAKE:

No, it's just . . . I'm in a spot of bother with the authorities / but it's no problem, I'm sorting it

SCILLA:

What have you done?

JAKE:

out, it's more what the sorting out might lead to / because once I start—

SCILLA:

Are you going to prison?

JAKE:

No, I'm not going to be in trouble at all by the look of it but that's the problem, I'm going to be very—I'm probably paranoid about this.

SCILLA:

Leave the country. / Are you serious?

JAKE:

They've taken my passport. I just wanted to let you know in case anything—. I haven't mentioned any of this to Dad / but when the shit hits—

SCILLA:

No, don't get Dad started. Can I do anything?

JAKE:

No, it's all under control. I feel better talking to you. I didn't go to bed, you know how you get in the night. / If anything happens to me—

SCILLA:

Have some more coffee.
What? like what?

JAKE:

Shall I get you another croissant?

SCILLA:

So what have they found out?

JAKE:

Jam with it?

SCILLA:

If you've been making a fortune, I think it's very unfair of you not to have let me in on it.

JAKE:

Forget it.

SCILLA:

So you haven't got AIDS. That's great.

SCILLA *and* ZAC *continue.*

SCILLA:

So clearly he was frightened because he'd agreed to tell the DTI who else
   was involved (and they'd want to shut him up.)
If I can find out who they are, the murder's halfway solved.
There's plenty of names and numbers here in his diary
So I'll start by contacting anyone who looks interesting and making my
   own inquiry.

ZAC:

Are you OK?

SCILLA:

Yes, I feel terrific.

ZAC:

You'll just find out a whole lot of colleagues numbers, that won't tell you
anything specific.
My number's probably there for God's sake.

SCILLA:

I'm going to find out who killed Jake.

ZAC:

Take a sedative, have a sleep, and then see how you feel.

SCILLA:

Nobody sleeps in the middle of a deal.

ZAC:

You've always been lucky, Scilla, don't abuse it.
   (I mean, these guys, whoever they are, they could be dangerous.)
You're crazy at the moment, / you're in shock.

SCILLA:

I'm in shock, I might as well use it.

(I'll let you know what happens.)

ZAC:
   Jake's death was a shock for me too, and I kept thinking about a friend
      of his I'd just met.
   She was called Jacinta Condor and we'd all been doing business together
      and I knew she'd be quite upset.

   ZAC *phones.*

ZAC:
   I want to order a number of tropical birds . . . Maybe 20? . . .
   Don't tell me what kinds because I won't have heard . . .
   Yeah, parrots, cockatoos, marmosets (no, is that a monkey?) lovebirds,
      sure; stick in some lovebirds, an assortment in good bright colors, I
      don't care the exact number but plenty . . .
   No not a cage so much as a small aviary . . .
   Deliver it gift wrapped to Jacinta Condor, at the Savoy and the card should
      read, "From Zac, as a small tribute to your beauty and bravery."

SCILLA *and* GREVILLE *at Greville's house.*

SCILLA:
   Pull yourself together, Daddy.
   What does it matter if Jake was a baddy?

GREVILLE:
   Poor boy. Who would have thought? I'd rather he'd been a failure.
   He used to want to emigrate and sheepfarm in Australia.
   He always would rush in. He had no sense of balance.
   He could have done anything, you know, he had so many talents.
   Musician. Politician. No obstacles in his way.
   If he'd done something else, he'd be alive today.

SCILLA:
   What was he up to, Daddy?
   If it was just insider dealing,
   It's not a proper crime like stealing.
   They say it's a crime without a victim.
   He'd hardly kill himself just because the DTI nicked him.

GREVILLE:
   Dammit, why should he die for something that's not a crime?
      (It's not illegal in America, Switzerland, Japan, it's only been illegal
      here the last few years)
   You have to use what you know. You do it all the time
   That used to be the way you made a reputation

By having first class contacts, and first class information
One or two greedy people attracted attention to it
Suddenly we all pretend Englishmen don't do it

SCILLA:

So what was he up to, Daddy?

GREVILLE:

        I've simply no idea.

SCILLA:

Do you know who these people are? I've got Jake's diary here.
Marylou Baines.

GREVILLE:

Marylou Baines
Was originally a poor girl from the plains.
She set out to make whatever she wanted hers
And now she's one of America's top arbitrageurs.
   (second only to Boesky)

SCILLA:

Condor, Jacinta.

GREVILLE:

A very smart lady from South America who comes here every winter.
Europe sends aid, her family says thanks
And buys Eurobonds in Swiss banks.

SCILLA:

Corman.

GREVILLE:

Billy Corman,
William the Conqueror, the great invader,
A very highly-successful dawn raider.
I don't want to hear any more. Did Jake have friends like this?
I wish he was still a baby and giving daddy a kiss.

SCILLA:

Pull yourself together, daddy.
Did he give you information?

GREVILLE:

        Absolutely not.

SCILLA:

I thought you might be in on it.

GREVILLE:

      In on what?

SCILLA:

Then aren't you annoyed he kept it secret from you and didn't share what he'd got?

GREVILLE:

Scilla—

SCILLA:

Jake had powerful friends, that's clear from what you said.
And that means powerful enemies who'd like to see him dead. /
   (He wasn't brave enough to kill himself.)

GREVILLE:

Absolute nonsense.

SCILLA:

I'll start by calling on Corman.

GREVILLE:

      Security's terribly tight /
He'll never agree to see you.

SCILLA:

Don't worry. I'll get in somehow and see if it gives him a fright.

GREVILLE:

Scilla, you don't seem to realize. Newspapers across the nation.
I could easily lose my job if I lose my reputation.
You and the yobs you work with are hardly worth a mention,
   (no one expects them to have any standards)
But I have to keep very quiet, and not attract attention.
Until it's all blown over I think I'll stay in bed.

SCILLA:

You never liked me, Daddy. Jake was always your favorite.

GREVILLE:

I don't like the louts you work with.

SCILLA:

      And now you've got to pay for it.

GREVILLE:

Poor Scilla, are you suffering from feelings of rejection?

SCILLA:

If I find out you were in on it, you're not getting my protection.

GREVILLE:

(In on killing Jakey?)

SCILLA:

(In on anything.)

GREVILLE:

Darling, don't be difficult when I'm so awfully sad. /
I think Jakey was playing in a bigger league than Dad.

SCILLA:

I've always been ashamed of you. Your drink and your pomposity.

GREVILLE:

Scilla, the oiks you work with have made you a monstrosity.

SCILLA:

If I find you're implicated in my investigation / the News of the World can
have you.

GREVILLE:

Darling, you always did have a vivid imagination
(like poor Mummy.)

ZAC:

When I left Scilla I rushed back to work because Corman's bid for Albion
    was just reaching its peak.
He'd been spending the night in the office the whole of that week.
We'd been building to this since the day a few months ago
When Albion started, must one of several deals, easy and slow.
It started like this:

CORMAN, *a corporate raider.* BROWN *and* SMITH, *industrial spies.* ZAC.
MRS ETHERINGTON, *a stockbroker.*

CORMAN:

The analysts report are satisfactory,
Predicting high industrial synergy.
I'll have to close the chocolate biscuit factory.
The management lacks drive and energy.
Tell me what you learnt about the company.

BROWN:

I spent a month posing as a secretary.
The working atmosphere is very pleasant.
A shock to the chairman would be salutary,
His presence at his desk is just symbolic,
He disappears to fish and shoot pheasant.

The managing director's alcoholic,
But still he's everybody favorite,
His drink 'n' driving ends him up in court,
He gets the company to pay for it.
The middle management are sound but lazy,
The details will be found in my report.
The chief of marketing is going crazy.

CORMAN:

Excellent, they'll put up no resistance.
I'll sack them all, put in a new staff, maybe promote a few of their
assistants.
Too late for them to make the company over,
Because I am going to take the company over.
Now to the larger and still more inviting
Albion Products. Fuck the analysts,
What do they know? It's that much more exciting.
Is their chairman gaga too and their managing director always pissed?

SMITH:

No, he's sober and quite competent.
Duckett runs a rather happy ship.
I hear the head of sales is impotent,
A very old director broke his hip,
Apart from that they all seem quite efficient.
Employees feel considerable loyalty.
The factory has been visited by royalty.

CORMAN:

Albion is obviously deficient
In management. Old-fashioned and paternal.
These figures stink. I can make it earn a
lot more for its shareholders, who are
The owners after all. It will be far
Better run, streamlined, rationalized,
When it forms part of Corman Enterprise.
    (And anyway I want it.)
Right. Both targets will be hit.
Now summon my war cabinet.

CORMAN:

Zac, I really like this company.

ZAC:

It'll take some stalking. It's a big confident beast.

CORMAN:

But I'm told you're a takeover artiste.
Can you get it for me?

ZAC:

Corman, you're the buyer./
I pride myself I can acquire any company the client

CORMAN:

Anyway, if it was easy it'd bore me.

ZAC:

may desire.
  (If I was defending Albion you wouldn't stand a chance.)
We're going to need a whole lot of finance from somewhere.

CORMAN:

Zackerman, that's your ride on the funfair.

Now Etherington. I want you to start a stealthy
Purchase of Albion stock. Don't frighten them.
The price must hardly move, just look quite healthy.
We'll put nooses round their necks and suddenly tighten them.

ETHERINGTON:

Albion's price is 310.
I shall acquire twenty million ordinary
Shares on your behalf, imperceptibly.
And I shall let you know of any change.

ZAC:

We've got to get out here and ride the range.

ETHERINGTON:

I don't think you'll find me lacking in assiduity.

CORMAN:

I'm a great admirer of Etherington's ingenuity.
  (Top brokers for fuck's sake, what do you think I am? Brokers to
  royalty.)
When we tell Duckett I own five per cent
  (plus what else I'll control by then)
He'll suddenly wonder where his company went.

DUCKETT.

DUCKETT:

I'm Duckett. I enjoy the *Financial Times*.

It's fun reading about other people's crimes.
My company Albion's price is looking perky.
I think I'll buy that villa in the south of Turkey.

CORMAN, ETHERINGTON, ZAC.

CORMAN:
So what's on the agenda today?
Let's get all the rubbish out of the way.

ETHERINGTON:
We're failing to acquire Mayfield.

CORMAN:
          Except I never fail.
Why don't I suggest we'll leave them alone, provided they pay us greenmail?
    (American term, greenbacks, blackmail, everybody happy?)

ZAC:
If they really want to defend themselves they'll do a leveraged management buyout to get back their shares.

ETHERINGTON:
So we make a hundred million.

CORMAN:
          And the lousy company's still theirs.

ZAC:
    (Plus a whole lot of debt.
    In the US there's an oil company borrowed four billion dollars to fight
    off T. Boone
    Pickens and now they're paying three million a day interest.)

CORMAN:
So that money goes to improving our position
With Albion, my favorite acquisition.
How we doing?

ETHERINGTON:
The Albion share is up to 315
And you now own 4.9 percent/
Not 5 percent, so no need to disclose.

CORMAN:
Excellent.

So now?

ETHERINGTON:

> Now we contact institutions,
> The pension fund managers who hold
> Millions of Corman shares and indicate
> It would be wise to lend us their support.

ZAC:

Can we rely on them?

ETHERINGTON:

> They won't say no,
> For otherwise a succulent new issue
> Next time we have one might not come their way.

CORMAN:

It's their duty to keep our price up after all.
The poor old pensioners won't want it to fall.

ETHERINGTON:

We also intimate it's in their interest
To buy up Albion so that more and more
Albion shares belong to friends of ours./
A fan club and not a concert party.

ZAC:

A concert party.

CORMAN:

> Come on, don't fart
> About, it's a concert party.

ETHERINGTON:

A fan club (of disinterested supporters) is respectable and legal.
A concert party (of people you've induced to support you) reprehensible.
This is a line you may trust us to tread/
(as long as necessary)

CORMAN:

Tread in the shit. Tread where you need to tread.
Now purchases must also be made by Metgee, Upkate,
Battershot, Mountainring

ZAC:

> and Stoneark.

CORMAN:

Five nominee companies registered in the Turks and Caicos Islands, Panama and Sark.

They can each acquire 4.9 percent.

ZACKERMAN:

And one of our problems is solved.

You'll acquire a huge share in Albion without anyone suspecting you're involved.

ETHERINGTON:

We're still left with a cashflow problem.

Albion's more than three times as big as Corman.

CORMAN:

Zac, you understand how a buyer works

Time you stepped in and showed us a few fireworks.

ZAC:

The last couple of years in the United States it's been takeover mania

And I guess the deals there have gotten somewhat zanier

Junk bonds are a quick way of raising cash, but it's kind of a hit 'n' run method, which doesn't go down too well in Britain.

You don't have millions of private investors crazy to gamble on debt.

ETHERINGTON:

No, you wouldn't succeed with junk bonds here just yet.

But the British public's financial education

Is going in leaps and bounds with privatization.

Sid will buy junk soon./Just wait.

ZAC:

Great.

CORMAN:

So no junk. How do we stand with the loan?

Can you show us some tricks?

ZAC:

The money can be supplied from a number of banks here and in the United States led by our own.

I got the rate of interest down a couple of ticks.

In return they want us to mortgage Upkate, Battershot and Stoneark, and form five new nominee companies so we can wind up Albion and redistribute its assets,

Which gives us tax neutral benefits.
We repay the loan and the interest by selling off certain sections of Albion
    after it's been acquired.

CORMAN:

Some people might think I'm a touch overgeared.
Our ratio of debt to equity is—?

ETHERINGTON:

        Four hundred percent.

CORMAN:

Taking into account the billion and a half you've lent.
(But being in debt is the best way to be rich.)

ZAC:

(America's national debt is over a trillion dollars.)

CORMAN:

So we've got the money. [*to* ETHERINGTON.] Get out there and spend it.
We've got Albion.

ZAC:

       No, let's wait and see how Duckett's going to defend it.
(Poison pills? shark repellent?)

ETHERINGTON:

If Albion's shares should fall some of our friends would be n for a shock.

ZAC:

A deposit with us could provide a guarantee.

CORMAN:

And then there's the question of buying Corman stock.
To buy your own shares is illegal and cannot be.

ZAC:

But the bank can buy them, no problem and we'll let you know later about
our fee.

CORMAN:

Zackerman, my very sincere thanks.
This is the kind of service I expect from our banks.
Etherington, I'm sure you've plenty to do.
I'll join you later for a glass of poo.

ETHERINGTON *goes.*

We don't breathe a word of this to anyone.
But someone could breathe a word to Marylou.
I think she could step in here and have some fun.
But I don't want direct contact and nor should you.

ZAC:

No problem.

CORMAN *goes*.

So I called Jake Todd.

ZAC *and* JAKE *drinking in champagne bar. Late night. Both drunk.*

JAKE:

What did you think of the family?

ZAC:

Quite a mansion.

JAKE:

You could buy yourself something equally handsome.
  (Or three.)

ZAC:

Why do the British always want land?
  (In Paris or New York you live in an apartment, why do the English
  need gardens?)

JAKE:

You're not upper class without it, you're too American to understand.

ZAC:

You don't make money out of land, you make money out of money.

JAKE:

It's a dream. Woods. Springtime. Owning the spring.
What's so funny?

ZAC:

Is that your dream?

JAKE:

              I never dream./(I never sleep)

ZAC:

              Because it's come to an end.
Young kids like you making money now—and I mean the ones who've

never had it, not like you—they're going to come up with new ways to spend

Because they're going to come up with new dreams.

JAKE:

I'll tell you, Zac, sometimes it seems . . .

ZAC:

What?

JAKE:

I don't know, what were we saying?

ZAC:

When?

JAKE:

Forget it./

ZAC:

Tell you something, Jake.
Give Albion some attention.

JAKE:

I could get on the blower to
MaryLou/and

ZAC:

Don't tell me.

JAKE:

Tell you something. I fancy the ocean.
Instead of land. I'd like to own a big cube of sea, right down to the bottom, all the fish, weeds, the lot.
There'd be takers for that.

ZAC:

        Sure, it's a great notion.

JAKE:

Or air. Space. A square meter going straight up into infinity.

ZAC:

And a section of God at the top.

JAKE:

        Oh, yes, I'll make you a market in divinity (any day.)

MARYLOU BAINES *and* TK *in New York.*

TK:

There's a message from Jake Todd in London.
He recommends buying shares in Albion.

MARYLOU:

Can I take it this is so far completely secret?

TK:

Yes, when it gets out it'll really move the market.

MARYLOU:

Are you trading in this stock on your own account?

TK:

Not for a very considerable amount.

MARYLOU:

You'll soon be setting up your own show.

TK:

No, Ms Baines, I wouldn't go, you taught me everything I know.
I really admire your style, Miss Baines.
　　(You're a great American.)

MARYLOU:

Sure, arbitrage is a service to the community,
And it's too bad they're prosecuting people you'd have thought would have
　　had immunity.
By buying and selling large amounts of stock we ensure the market's
　　liquidity—
I work twenty-hour days and take pills for stomach acidity—
So companies can be taken over easy,
Which means discharging superfluous workers, discontinuing unprofitable
　　lines, the kind of stuff that makes your lazy inefficient management queasy.
So considering the good we do the US economy,
I reckon we should be treated with a little more respect and bonhomie.

I have a hundred and fifty telephone lines because I depend on information.

TK:

　　(What's the least a person could start with?

MARYLOU:

　　I started small—say twenty?)
You need to know what's going on in businesses all over the nation,

TK:

(And Britain)

MARYLOU:

You take a lot of gambles,/which keeps the adrenalin flowing and is why
it's known as risk arbitrage,

TK:

(Ms Baines, I admire your guts)

MARYLOU:

Though if you know how to get the right information the risk isn't all that
large.

TK:

But since Boesky was caught out—

MARYLOU:

Sure, some of our informants are more cautious,
But information's what it's all about,
So I reckon it's business as usual and only now and then does nervousness
make me nauseous.
You and I both know what it's like to have other guys stepping on your
head,
And you can't get on when you're dead.

TK:

So you think it's worth me giving it a shot?

MARYLOU:

Get out, TK, and give it all you've got.
After all, what happens if you fail?

TK:

I end up broke and in jail.

MARYLOU:

Look, with his own collapse Boesky did the biggest insider deal of all:
The SEC let him unload over a billion dollars worth of shares ahead of
announcing his fall.
So paying a hundred million dollar fine was pretty minimal.
Which is great, because he overstepped some regulations, sure, but the
guy's no criminal.
Like he said about his own amazing wealth.
"Greed is all right. Greed is healthy. You can be greedy and still feel
good about yourself."

Buy twenty million shares in Albion today.
(That's in addition to what you've bought.)
In a few weeks when Corman announces the bid and the price shoots up,
we sell quick, take the profit, and on our way.

DUCKETT, *chairman of* ALBION, *and* MS. BIDDULPH, *a white knight. Both
from the north.*

DUCKETT:
Biddulph, I'm desperate. Corman's going to take over Albion. Shall I pay
him
greenmail and take on half a billion debt? Shall I do one of those American things,
poison pills, shark repellant, make some arrangement so the company
comes to bits
if he gets hold of it? Shall I cash in my Eurobond and emigrate?

BIDDULPH:
Now Duckett, you're under quite serious attack.
It's time to fight back.

DUCKETT:
       I'd like to fight back.

BIDDULPH:
I know you'd give Corman a terrible fright
If you had a white knight.

DUCKETT:
       I'd like a white knight.

BIDDULPH:
Now Corman will throw the top management out
But I'd guarantee that your job would remain.

DUCKETT:
   Say it again?

BIDDULPH:
       Your job would remain.
But Corman would throw the top management out.
That's what it's about.

DUCKETT:
       That's what it's about.
But you'd guarantee that my job would remain.

BIDDULPH:

So if I should step in would I have your support?

DUCKETT:

Would you have my support!

BIDDULPH:

      That's just what I thought.

DUCKETT:

It's very unfair to be attacked like this. I run a highly efficient company. I've sacked the finance director and the chief of marketing who'd both been with the company ten years. I've closed two factories and made five hundred people redundant. No one can say I'm not a hardhitting management.

BIDDULPH:

Hold on, Duckett, you've got it all wrong. Think of it from the PR angle. You're an old-fashioned firm. A good old English firm that has the loyalty of its employees and the support of the local community. You spend a lot of money on research and development.

DUCKETT:

I spend some, I suppose, but I always consider the shareholders' dividend and the short-term—

BIDDULPH:

No no no, you consider the long term. You're the kind of company the CBI likes. Corman means short-term profit. You mean industrial development. Think of Pilkington, Duckett. You're loved locally. Children like you. Dogs.

DUCKETT:

What I dream of you know is cornering the coffee market. Brazil needs to be hammered into the ground and the price kept right down low and—

BIDDULPH:

No, Duckett, not at the moment.

You're a sweet English maiden, all shining and bright.
And Corman's the villain intent upon rape
And I'm the white knight

DUCKETT:

      You're the white knight

BIDDULPH:

And the knight has a fight and the maiden escapes
And when I'm in charge I'll put everything right.
(We can talk about closing Scunthorpe later.)

ZAC.

ZAC:

Jake couldn't have picked a worse time to die if he hated my guts.
Corman hadn't slept for forty-eight hours and was driving himself and
everyone else nuts.
Jake was my one real friend over here. It's not that I don't care,
But the deal could get clinched today and I just don't have the attention
to spare.
(If he's put me in the shit with the DTI I'll worry about that later.)

CORMAN, ZAC, ETHERINGTON *and others of* CORMAN'S *team.*

CORMAN:

Right, you all know the position,
Biddulph's stepped in as a white knight to stop us making the acquisition.
Don't worry, she hasn't a chance, it's just a try on.
We've 15 percent of Albion stock plus 20 percent fan club holdings whose
votes we can rely on.
Two aims:
One. Boost our own share price by getting anyone at all to buy Corman
stock to
increase the value of our offer. Two. Get anyone at all who'll vote for
us to buy up
Albion shares.
So in a word, get anyone you can by any means you can to buy both our
stock and theirs.
From today we're coming to the crunch.
Nobody's going out any more to lunch.
(You can cancel dinner too.)
From today, we're going for the gold.
Put your family life and your sex life on hold.
A deal like this, at the start you gently woo it.
There comes a time when you get in there and screw it.
So you get the stock. And I don't care how you do it.

ETHERINGTON:

My reputation for integrity
Compels me to suggest you should take care.

No point succeeding if that same success
Destroys you and your company forever.
Remember Guinness.

CORMAN:

Thank you, Etherington. Some of us have work to do here.

ZAC:

There's no question there are thin lines and this is definitely a gray area.
And since Guinness it's a whole lot scarier.
You can't play ball if you keep off the grass.
So promise whatever you have to. Peddle your ass.
Let's give it all we've got and worry later.

CORMAN (*to* ETHERINGTON):

Are you standing there as some kind of arbitrator?
You can piss off, I'll get another broker.
The last thing I need in my pack is some tight-arsed joker.
(I thought you were good at this.)

ETHERINGTON:

My duty has been done in speaking out.
And now I'll help in every way I can.
My reputation for integrity
Will reassure our colleagues of their safety
In making any purchase we advise.

CORMAN:

Then let's get on/with it.

ZAC:

Let's get on with it, guys.

OTHERS *on phones.*

This works as a round i.e., each starts at slash in previous speech and continues with all speeches as long as required. At end of each speech, each shouts out the amount of stock the person at the other end of the phone has agreed to buy e.g., twenty thousand, a hundred thousand.

1. If you were interested in acquiring some Corman stock/there is a con-
    siderable sum on deposit with Klein Merrick so/in the event of any
    subsequent fall in the share price you would be guaranteed against loss—
    20,000

2. If you were interested in buying some Albion stock/there would be no question of being unable to dispose of them at a price at least equal to what you gave—100,000

3. If you were able to see your way to supporting the bid/the new Albion under Corman management would naturally look favorably at any tenders for office cleaning that compared favorably with our present arrangements—

4. If you should be interested in following our recommendation to acquire Corman stock, an interest free loan could be arranged at once with which the purchase could be made—

Meanwhile:

ZAC *(on phone):*
Remember me to Vanessa and the boys.
Listen, Corman, this may just be a rumor,
But if it's true it doesn't appeal to my sense of humor.
I've just had a word with a colleague in Atlanta & Gulf.
Marylou's been dealing with Biddulph.
I think it's time you spoke to her yourself.

CORMAN:
Dealing with Biddulph? I just sent her some flowers.
What the fuck does she think—? She's meant to be one of ours.
I tried to call her this morning but I got the machine.
Leave a message after the tone? I'll leave something obscene.

CORMAN *phones* MARYLOU.

CORMAN:
Marylou? You got the flowers? A tragic bereavement.

MARYLOU:
Yes, TK made a real pretty arrangement.

CORMAN:
And our pretty arrangement's still OK?

MARYLOU:
I did dispose of a large holding today.

CORMAN:
You what? Disposed? A large Albion holding?
I gave you that on the clear understanding—

MARYLOU:

No, Corman, don't pursue it.
Anything I do I just happen to do because I want to do it.

CORMAN:

You owe me, Marylou.

MARYLOU:

I owe you?
I'm not even certain that I know you.

Unnoticed by CORMAN *or* ZAC, SCILLA *arrives, explaining herself quietly to one of* CORMAN*'s team.*

Meanwhile CORMAN *and* MARYLOU *continue:*

CORMAN:

How much Albion did you have?

MARYLOU:

15 Percent.

CORMAN:

Can I just ask you where the hell it went?

MARYLOU:

Don't be slow, Bill. That's quite upsetting
I like to think I'm dealing with an equal.

CORMAN:

Marylou, it's not that I'm not smart.
It's just hard to believe you'd break my heart
Biddulph? Biddulph? what? you knew you were getting
Information from me/via Zackerman via Jake Todd

MARYLOU:

You can't predict the sequel.

CORMAN:

But you knew Jake Todd was one of mine.

MARYLOU:

You are slow,/Bill.

CORMAN:

Because he's dead? you didn't want to be connected
With Jake now he's dead in case someone suspected—/
So that's why you sold to Biddulph.

MARYLOU:

I hope these phones are adequately scrambled.

CORMAN:

I don't give a fuck who else is on the line.
You cheated me./I hate you. I'll fucking annihilate you.

MARYLOU:

Corman, you'll get rumbled
If you don't keep your temper. Be glad you're alive,
   (as my very irritating old aunty used to say.)
Don't worry about it. What's 15 percent? Get after the other 85.

MARYLOU *hangs up.*

ZAC:

We need her.

SCILLA:

Kissogram for Mr. Corman.

CORMAN *calls* MARYLOU *back.*

CORMAN:

Marylou? You know how it is. You say things in haste.
Our friendship's far too important/to waste.

MARYLOU:

What do you want, Bill?

CORMAN:

Can you see your way to going back into Albion?
Will you buy Corman and support our price?
Smashing Biddulph would be very nice/
If you've anything—

MARYLOU:

Bill I'd be glad to do something for you/but

CORMAN:

I understand your problem, how can I reassure you?

MARYLOU:

I'm playing with about a billion
But most of that's occupied over here.
If I had another hundred million
In my investment fund,

Then I guess/I'd have a freer hand.

CORMAN:

I think I can probably see my way clear.

This is hardly the moment with so much else on our minds.

But I had been meaning for some time to approach you with a view to becoming a

contributor to your investment fund because I have of course the greatest admiration/for your wide experience and market timing

MARYLOU:

I could have my people send you some documentation.

MARYLOU *hangs up.*
SCILLA *approaches* CORMAN *and sings.*

SCILLA:

Happy takeover day.

Take Albion away.

Happy takeover, Corman.

Happy takeover day.

CORMAN:

What the hell?

SCILLA:

Kissogram from Marylou Baines.

CORMAN:

From Marylou Baines? I'll kill her.

SCILLA:

I'm not really. I'm Jake Todd's sister, Scilla.

ZAC:

What the—

CORMAN:

What?

SCILLA:

Jake Todd's sister.

CORMAN:

Is this a terrorist a—/
ttack?

SCILLA:

I heard you. 'Jake Todd was one of mine.'
Tell me what it's all about./
Did someone kill Jake?

CORMAN:

Will someone please get this lunatic out?

ZAC:

Hold it, hold it, everything's fine.
I know her, it's OK, she's not insane, she won't be armed, don't press
The security button, we'll be held up for hours with water sprinklers and
    the SAS./
(Let's get on with the job here.)

SCILLA:

You killed my brother.

CORMAN:

Zac.

ZAC:

He didn't/he really didn't. I'm certain he didn't.

CORMAN:

Do you work for Marylou Baines?
    (Because you can tell her from me—)

SCILLA:

No, that was a trick to get in./Now will you explain

CORMAN:

(Don't work for her.)

SCILLA:

What 'one of mine' means. One of your what?
He did something illegal. You were frightened of what he'd say
To the DTI and you wanted him out of the way.
Tell me what's going on or I'll tell the press
My brother was acting for you the night he was shot.
Did you kill him yourself or get your broker to pull the trigger?

CORMAN:

After the deal, after the deal I'll confess
To murdering anyone just let me get on with the deal.

SCILLA:

You and Zac got Jake into some mess.

He did little fiddles but this must have been much bigger.
You and Zac got him involved in some corrupt/ring.

CORMAN:

Suppose I had killed Jake, his ghost would have had more sense than walk
in here today
and interrupt./

ZAC:

Can you spare me for five minutes?

CORMAN:

He got on because he knew what was a priority/and he'd have reckoned

SCILLA:

He got on. Doing what exactly?

CORMAN:

That matters of life and death came a poor second.

ZAC:

Can you spare me for five minutes?

CORMAN:

No, not for two./Go on.

SCILLA:

I'm not leaving here/until you

ZAC:

I'll tell you./I'll tell you.

SCILLA:

You will.

CORMAN:

You'll what?

ZAC:

Can I handle this? Can I just handle this please?

ZAC *and* SCILLA *outside* CORMAN's *office.*

SCILLA:

So tell me.

ZAC:

Marylou Baines—we'll make it quick, OK?/
Needs inside information and she's willing to pay.

SCILLA:
You knew all this this morning and you didn't say.

ZAC:
So anyone in London with news would give it to Jake.
And he'd get half a percent/on whatever she'd make.

SCILLA:
Half a percent?
That meant . . .

ZAC:
If she made fifty million—

SCILLA:
                He got two hundred and fifty thousand.
If she made two hundred million—he never told me.

ZAC:
I think little Jakey could have bought and sold me.
So now you know, OK? And now you drop it.

SCILLA:
What do you mean?/I'm just getting started.

ZAC:
I've got work to do.

SCILLA:
Who killed him? Corman? You?

ZAC:
                I'm too tenderhearted
And Corman's too busy. Scilla, stop it.
We have to keep this quiet now. Face the facts.
You're never going to find out all Jake's contacts.
Let it go. I've got work to do. Don't get in a state.

SCILLA:
You knew all along. He never told me. Wait.

ZAC *goes*.

He was making serious money.

SCILLA:
So Zac went back to Corman and I thought I'd better go to work despite
Jake being

dead because Chicago comes in at one twenty and I hate to miss it. I work on the floor
of LIFFE, the London International Financial Futures Exchange.

Trading options and futures looks tricky if you don't understand it.
But if you're good at market timing you can make out like a bandit.
  (It's the most fun I've had since playing cops and robbers with Jake when we were
  children.)
A simple way of looking at futures is take a commodity,
Coffee, cocoa, sugar, zinc, pork bellies, copper, aluminium, oil—
  I always think pork bellies is an oddity.
  (They could just as well have a future in chicken wings.)
Suppose you're a coffee trader and there's a drought in Brazil like last year or suppose
  there's a good harvest, either way you might lose out,
So you can buy a futures contract that works in the opposite direction so you're covered
  against loss, and that's what futures are basically about.
But of course you don't have to take delivery of anything at all.
You can buy and sell futures contracts without any danger of ending up with tens tons of
  pork bellies in the hall.

On the floor of LIFFE the commodity is money.
You can buy and sell money, you can buy and sell absence of money, debt, which used
  to strike me as funny.

For some it's hedging, for most it's speculation.
In New York they've just introduced a futures contract in inflation.
  (Pity it's not Bolivian inflation, which hit forty thousand percent.)

I was terrified when I started because there aren't many girls and they line up to watch
  you walk,
And every time I opened my mouth I felt self-conscious because of the way I talk.
I found O levels weren't much use, the best qualified people are street traders.
But I love it because it's like playing a cross between roulette and space invaders.

LIFFE *canteen.*

SCILLA. JOANNE *a runner.* KATHY *a trader.*

JOANNE:
I said I'm not going to work down there.
It's like animals in a zoo./So then I thought I'll have a bash.

KATHY:
When you start they really stare.

SCILLA:
Don't let them see you care.

JOANNE:
I'll never learn what to do./I'll never learn hand signals.

SCILLA:
I couldn't walk across the floor/my first day

KATHY:
This morning's really a bore,/there's nothing happening.

JOANNE:
I answered a telephone/for the first time.

KATHY:
You really feel on your own.

SCILLA:
Never say hold on/because they don't hold on.

KATHY:
I can manage two phones at once but not three.

SCILLA:
Sometimes I've put the phone down because I don't know what they're
saying.

JOANNE:
You do get used to the noise, I nearly fainted the first day.

KATHY:
I can deal without shouting, most of them like shouting.

SCILLA:
Men are just little boys./Dave had lost twenty slips at the end of yesterday
and
muggins finds them for him.

JOANNE:

Terry asked me out this morning. He was the first person who spoke to
me on my first
day, he was really friendly.
Is it all right going out?/Do they talk about you?

SCILLA:

You do get talked about,/I hear so and so's knocking off so and so.

KATHY:

Just go out for lunch,/then nothing can happen after.

SCILLA:

They're a very chauvinist bunch.

KATHY:

We've all been out with Terry.

SCILLA:

Anyway they're all too knackered/by the end of the day.

KATHY:

It's true, they're all frustrated/because they never have time to do it.

JOANNE:

I'm completely exhausted.
At midnight I'm washing my knickers/because I'm too speedy to sleep.

KATHY:

I get up at half-past five and have a good breakfast.

SCILLA:

Mind you, I like Terry.

TERRY, DAVE, MARTIN, BRIAN *and* VINCE, traders, arrive.

KATHY:

Hello, Terry.

TERRY:

What about Saturday?

JOANNE:

I don't know.

TERRY:

Think about it.

KATHY:

Better be getting back.

MARTIN:
Time we did some work. Nearly time for Chicago.

VINCE:
Coming out with me tonight?

SCILLA:
Leave it out, Vince.

DAVE:
Leave the lady alone.

VINCE (*to* JOANNE):
Coming out with me tonight?

KATHY:
Leave it out, Vince.

Floor of LIFFE. *Four separate companies each with their phones, and a trading pit.*
Klein Merrick has SCILLA *on the phone,* TERRY *and* DAVE *on the floor,* MANDY *as runner.*
2—has SHERILL *on the phone,* MARTIN *and* KATHY *on the floor,* PETE *as runner.*
3—has DICK *on the phone,* BRIAN *and* JILL *on the floor,* JOANNE *as runner.*
4—has MARY *on the phone,* VINCE *and* JOHN *on the floor,* ANNIE *as runner.*
They all start going to their places. As ANNIE, *who is new, walks down the lads cheer and jeer.*

TERRY:
You're in late.

SCILLA:
Trouble at home. My brother's been shot.

TERRY:
You what?

SCILLA:
There's going to be a scandal.

TERRY:
Another one?/Did you say your brother?

SCILLA:

Bigger.

TERRY:

Is it worth trading on?

SCILLA:

There might be a run on sterling if you're lucky.

KATHY:

Ere come the c'nardhes.

BRIAN:

Fuck off, sweaty git.

DICK:

Fuck off, dogbreath.

BRIAN:

Yeh, lovely. I'll feel better when I get rid of these oysters.

SCILLA:

Dave! Dave!

BRIAN:

And how are you this morning?

JILL:

Don't talk to me, I'm all fucked up.

JOANNE:

Do you call him Dick because he's got spots?

JILL:

No, I call him Spot because he's a dick.

VINCE:

Annie, if you sell the front and buy the back,/you'll be short of front and long of back.

BRIAN:

Muff city, no pity.

SCILLA:

Dave, Grimes says Zac's got a ten million rollover for March so sell 10 at 9. If you can't

get it he'll go to 8. And 15 June at your best price.

TERRY:

Are you Annie? Can you find this guy and give him a message.

ANNIE:
Mike who?

TERRY:
Hunt.

KATHY:
I'm tired of making money for other people. I'd like to be a local.

SCILLA:
Oi! Dave! You can't signal with a pencil in your hand.

DAVE:
Just fuckin have, haven't I.

KATHY:
The theoretical spread is too large.[1]

JOANNE:
Did you see that actor from the Bill who was in here yesterday?

KATHY:
I saw him first.

JOANNE:
I saw him first.

KATHY:
I wonder if he'll come back.

JOANNE:
I wonder if he's married.

Trading is now getting going.

JOANNE:
What do you want this morning?

PETE:
She wants 18 at 15.

JOANNE:
All I want is a bacon roll.

PETE (*sings*):
All I want is a bacon roll.

Meanwhile.

DAVE:

Red June is showing 4 bid for 5.

TERRY:

Sterling showing 5 at 3.

DICK (*phone*):

March showing 9.

(*To* BRIAN *on floor.*) 5 at 9. 5 at 9.

(*Another phone call.*) Is that another 5 or the same 5?

(*To* BRIAN.) 5 more at 9. 5 more. 10 at 9. 10 at 9.

BRIAN:

5 at 9 filled.[2]

DICK (*phone*):

Your first 5 at 9 filled.

SHERILL:

We want 20 out of Footsie and into gilts.[3]

(*To* MARTIN.) Sell 20 at 1. 20 at 1.

(*To* KATHY.) Bid 9 for 20, 9 for 20.

MARTIN:

20 at 1.

KATHY:

9 for 20.

MARY:

[2]March gilts 8 rising fast. Do you want to sell now or wait? They might go another two

ticks if you're lucky. (*To floor.*) 5 at 9. 5 at 9.

BRIAN:

[3]Where we going tonight?

TERRY:

The old Chinese?

BRIAN:

Dragon city, no pity.

DAVE:

I'll tell Vince.

BRIAN:

Oi, we're 18 for 15.

TERRY:
18 for 15. Working 20.

DAVE:
Table for 15 please.

JOHN:
10 at 19. 10 at 19.

VINCE:
John John John—just 5 at 19.
You can't trust John's bids.

MARY:
He's had too many beers.

DAVE:
I've got a certain winner for the 3.30 if anyone's interested.[4]

BRIAN:
You haven't paid us yesterday's winnings yet.

DAVE:
Leave it out, Brian, I always pay you.

KATHY:
[4]Come on gilts. 2 at 4 the gilts.

MARTIN:
Sterling showing 5 at 3.

TERRY:
Euro 4 bid now.

SCILLA:
Dave, you're supposed to be looking at me right?

DAVE:
Am I in or am I out?

MANDY:
You gotta listen. If you don't listen we can't get in touch with you.

DAVE:
What?

SCILLA:
If you look at me I won't give you stick.

VINCE:

⁵10 bid for 70. Let's get some stock away.

MARTIN:

Whare the fuck have you been?

PETE:

Oh I see, you're not even allowed to crap.

MARTIN:

If Tony rings tell him I can't get out.

BRIAN:

I'm long on Footsie.

DAVE:

Don't know why I bothered coming in today.

MARTIN:

It's really flying./It's really going somewhere.

SCILLA *(to* MANDY*):*

Find out if Brian bought 20 off Dave at 6.

MANDY *goes to* BRIAN.

MANDY:

Did you buy 20 off Dave at 6?⁶

BRIAN:

Going to the Greenhouse tonight?

DICK (*to* BRIAN):

⁶5 at 9. Have you got that second 5 at 9 filled?

JILL (*to* BRIAN):

Have you got that second 5 to 9 filled?

BRIAN:

Leave me alone, I'm talking to the young lady.⁷

ANNIE *comes up to* BRIAN.

ANNIE:

I'm looking for Mike Hunt.

BRIAN:

She's looking for her cunt.

ANNIE *realizes and starts to cry.* MANDY *takes her back to her trading booth.*

MANDY:
    Don't worry, they do it to everyone when they're new.

SHERILL:
    OUT! OUT! OUT!
    John, phone for you.

MARTIN:
    My car keeps getting stolen.

SAM:
    Dont leave it outside your house.

PETE:
    Then they wont know it's yours.

VINCE:
    Terry! It's a doodle, four hour drive at most.

TERRY:
    It's four hundred, five, it's five hundred miles.

BRIAN:
    I'm not doing that / on a Sunday.

DICK:
    Check your oil the night before and leave at five.

TERRY:
    What's he doing living in a castle?

VINCE:
    He's a fucking iron.

ALL FOUR:
    Iron oof!/

SCILLA:
    Chicago two minutes. Footsie's going to move.

DAVE:
    No, he showed me a picture of his girlfriend once with a carrot in her
    mouth right up to the green bit.

BRIAN:
    Veg city, no pity.

JOHN:
    Dave, the horse! It won!

DAVE *and* JOHN *embrace and jump up and down.*

DAVE:

I fucking won two thousand pounds!

CATHY:

Chicago, Chicago.

Everyone is suddenly quiet, watching the boards, waiting for Chicago to come in. All burst out at once. Furious trading. Everyone flat out. Among the things we hear:

VINCE:

6 for 10. 6 for 10.

JOHN:

10 at 6. 10 at 6.

VINCE:

I'm buying at 6, you cunt.

SHERRILL *(on phone):*

11 coming 10, 11 coming 10, 11 10 11 10, 10! 10 10 10 10 coming 9, 10 coming 9, etc.

BRIAN:

What's your fucking game?

MARTIN:

Oh fuck off.

BRIAN:

I'll fucking break your leg, you fucking cunt.

SCILLA *(to* DAVE):

You'll have to shout louder if you can't signal better.

BRIAN *(to* DAVE):

You're trading like a cunt.

Out of furious trading emerges the song:

FUTURES SONG

Out you cunt, out in oh fuck it
I've dealt the gelt below the belt and I'm jacking up the ackers
My front's gone short, fuck off old sport, you're standing on my knackers
I've spilt my guts, long gilt's gone nuts and I think I'm going crackers

So full of poo I couldn't screw, I fucked it with my backers
  I fucked it with my backers
  I fucked it with my backers

Backups: Out! Buy buy buy! Leave it!
  No! Yes! Cunt!
  4! 5! Sell!
  Quick! Prick! Yes! No! Cunt!

How hard I dredge to earn my wedge, I'm sharper than a knife
Don't fucking cry get out and buy, Chicago's going rife
You're back to front come on you cunt don't give me any strife
You in or out? Don't hang about, you're on the floor of LIFFE!

They call me a tart who can hardly fart when it's bedlam in the pit
I'm the local tootsie playing footsie but I don't mind a bit
Cos my future trusts my money lusts as far as it can spit
And my sterling works on mouthy jerks whose bids are full of shit

I'm a Romford scholar in eurodollars and June is showing four
Botham out nineteen on the Reuters screen is the very latest score
I fucked that runner she's a right little stunner so I pulled her off the floor
I was bidding straight till my interest rate jumped up and asked for more

Money-making money-making money-making money-making
Money-making money-making money-making caper
Do the fucking business do the fucking business do the fucking business
And bang it down on paper

So L.I.F.F.E. is the life for me and I'll burn out when I'm dead
And this fair exchange is like a rifle range what's the price of flying lead?
When you soil your jeans on soya beans shove some cocoa up your head
You can never hide if your spread's too wide, you'll just fuck yourself
  instead.

ACT TWO

JACINTA CONDOR *flying first class.*

JACINTA:

Flight to England that little gray island in the clouds where governments don't fall overnight and children don't sell themselves in the street and my money is safe. I'll buy a raincoat, I'll meet Jake Todd, I'll stay at the Savoy by the stream they call a river with its Bloody Tower and dead queens, a river is too wide to bridge. The unfinished bridge across the canyon where the road ends in the air, waiting for dollars. The office blocks father started, imagining glass, leather, green screens, the city rising high into the sky, but the towers stopped short, cement, wires, the city spreading wider instead with a blur of shacks, miners coming down from the mountains as the mines close. The International Tin Council, what a scandal, thank God I wasn't in tin, the price of copper ruined by the frozen exchange rate, the two rates, and the government will not let us mining companies exchange enough dollars at the better rate, they insist we help the country in this crisis, I do not want to help, I want to be rich, I close my mines and sell my copper on the London Metal Exchange. It is all because of the debt that will never be paid because we have to borrow more and more to pay the interest on the money that came from oil when OPEC had too much money and your western banks wanted to lend it to us because who else would pay such high interest, needing it so badly? Father got his hands on enough of it but what happened, massive inflation, lucky he'd put the money somewhere safe, the Swiss mountains so white from the air like our mountains but the people rich with cattle and clocks and secrets, the American plains yellow with wheat, the green English fields where lords still live in gray stone, all with such safe banks and good bonds and exciting gambles, so as soon as any dollars or pounds come, don't let them go into our mines or our coffee or look for a sea of oil under the jungle, no get it out quickly to the western banks (a little money in cocaine, that's different). Peru leads the way resisting the IMF, refusing to pay the interest, but I don't want to make things difficult for the banks, I prefer to support them, why should my money stay in Peru and suffer? The official closing price yesterday for grade A copper was 878-8.5, three months 900.5-1, final kerb close 901-2. Why bother to send aid so many miles, put it straight into my eurobonds.

Meanwhile the London metal exchange starts quietly trading copper. When JACINTA *finishes speaking the trading reaches its noisy climax.*

ZAC:

There's some enterprising guys around and here's an example.

You know how if you want to get a job in the states you have to give a urine sample?

(this is to show you're not on drugs.)

There's a company now for a fifty dollar fee

They'll provide you with a guaranteed pure, donated by a churchgoer, bottle of pee.

(They also plan to market it dehydrated in a packet and you just add water.)

And AIDS is making advertisers perplexed

Because it's no longer too good to have your product associated with sex.

But it's a great marketing opportunity.

Like the guys opening up blood banks where you pay to store your own blood in case of an accident and so be guaranteed immunity.

(It's also a great time to buy into rubber.)

Anyone who can buy oranges for ten and sell at eleven in a souk or bazaar

Has the same human nature and can go equally far.

The so-called third world doesn't want our charity or aid.

All they need is the chance to sit down in front of some green screens and trade

(They don't have the money, sure, but just so long as they have freedom from

communism so they can do it when they do have the money.)

Pictures of starving babies are misleading and patronizing.

Because there's plenty of rich people in those countries, it's just the masses that's poor,

and Jacinta Condor flew into London and was quite enterprising.

It was the day before Jake Todd was found dead

And the deal was really coming to a head.

Jake was helping us find punters because anyone with too much money and Jake would know them.

You'd just say, Jake, who's in town, what have you got, and he'd bring them in and show them.

ZAC *and* JAKE.

JAKE:

Señora Condor has plenty of cash in her coffer.

She owns mountains and her garden's twice

The size of Wales. What's Corman going to offer?

ZAC:

He hopes she'll be able to help support his price.

JAKE:

She's going to need some kind of incentive.

ZAC:

I think she'll find Corman quite inventive.

JAKE:

Zac, while we're alone.
I didn't want to say this on the phone.
I had a visit from a DTI inspector.

ZAC:

Have you done something not quite correct or/what?

JAKE:

Zac, it's no joke. They didn't say too much/
But once they—

ZAC:

Did they mention me?

JAKE:

      I can't say I don't know
You./(That doesn't tell them anything, knowing you.)

ZAC:

Great.
Sure, no, of course not.

JAKE:

      Don't let's pay too much
Attention to it. OK?/If you like I'll go.

ZAC:

      It could be quite a smash/
Not just for you.

JAKE:

I have been making quite a lot of cash.
When they take your passport you feel surprisingly trapped.
I didn't know I was so fond of travel.

ZAC:

You're the kind of loose thread, Jake, that when they pull you the whole
fucking City could unravel.

JAKE:

Shall we cancel Condor in case it makes things worse?

ZAC:
Just don't give them the whole thing giftwrapped.

JAKE:
I can walk out the door now.

ZAC:
            OK.

JAKE:
            I feel—

JAKE:
What shall I do?

ZAC:
            Jake, I'm not your nurse.

JAKE:
Tell me to walk/and I'll walk.

ZAC:
            And fuck up the deal?

JAKE:
There might be a bug on the light.

ZAC:
            Jake, what the hell.
There might be a microphone under your lapel.
The City's greed or fear, you've got to choose.

JAKE:
Greed's been good to me. Fear's a bitch.

ZAC:
Then be greedy, guy, and let's get this payload home without a hitch.

JAKE:
I can always hit the straight and narrow tomorrow.

            JACINTA CONDOR *arrives.*

This is Zac Zackerman you've heard so much about.
The guy who always knows the latest shout.

ZAC:
How are you enjoying your stay in London, Señora Condor?

JACINTA:
I have been for a walk

In your little saint's park
Where the pelicans eat the pigeons (but I didn't see it).
I have been to the opera (very nice).
I have sold all my copper
For a rather small number of millions.

ZAC:

This is no time to sell copper, the price is lousy.

JAKE:

And when's it ever in season?
She's selling copper she's got to have a reason.

JACINTA:

I lose every quarter,
The cash goes like water,
Is better to close the mine.
I chose very well
The moment to sell,
I benefit from the closures in Surinam because of guerilla activity and also
I leak the
   news I am closing my mines, which puts the price up a little, so it is
fine.

JAKE:

So you've wiped out your mines? That's telling them who's master.
You must feel like a natural disaster.

ZAC:

Hurricane Jacinta.

JACINTA:

If I keep them Jake I have to be derange.
The Minister of Energy says 'Mining is not dead'—
It brings 45 percent of our foreign exchange
But a pound of copper won't buy a loaf of bread.
   (Our mining companies lost a hundred million dollars last year, it is the
   fault of the IMF. I don't like to suffer.)

JAKE:

The dagos always like to blame the gringos.
I suppose the miners want a revolution.
The most amazing lake full of flamingos—
   (I think that was Peru.)

JACINTA:

How can I support ten thousand people? ˙

When I did they weren't even grateful.
The miners all strike
And do what they like,
They want subsidized food, I say get on your bike.

JAKE:

I didn't know they had bikes, I thought they had llamas,/
And woolly hats and trousers like pajamas.

ZAC:

(So are the miners bothering you?

JACINTA:

You come and protect me?)
It's really a pity,
They go to the city (where there's no work)
Or they sit down outside the mine.
Growing coca is nice,
A very good price
    (Ten to thirty times as much as tea or coffee or cocoa)
So I think that's going to be fine.

JAKE:

Great product to grow.
Peru with its mountains covered in snow.
You're not giving up all your Peruvian interests?

JACINTA:

Europe is more interesting. Mr. Corman is fascinating.

Jake, I have asked a friend to this meeting.

ZAC:

I'm not sure a—

JACINTA:

You've heard of Nigel Ajibala?/

ZAC:

I can't say I have.

JAKE:

Listen, don't cross the señora.

JACINTA:

I tell you I've caught a
Big cocoa importer,
Your deal goes without a hitch.

His school was at Eton
Where children are beaten,
He's a prince and exceedingly rich.

JAKE:

Any friend of Jacinta
Will be a good punter.

ZAC:

So where does he operate?

JACINTA:

He has connections in

Ghana and Zambia
Zaire and Gambia
But it's here that he likes to invest.
His enemies are jealous
Because he's so zealous (and makes so much money)/
And at home he faces arrest
   (like the man they tried to kidnap in the trunk?)

JAKE:

You see, I told you, it's great.

JACINTA:

Here he comes now. Be cunning.

ZAC:

I suppose Corman can always meet him.

   NIGEL AJIBALA *arrives.*

JACINTA:

My friend, Jake Todd, and Mr. Zackerman,
A very considerable American.

JAKE:

You spend much time in Zambia and Zaire?

NIGEL:

Yes, but one's mostly based over here.
Africa induces mild hysteria.
Terrible situation in Nigeria.
   (oil earnings down from twenty-five billion dollars to five this year so
   they're
   refusing to make their interest payments.)
And Zaire

Pays the west a hundred and ninety million more than it receives each
year.
So as the last of several last resorts
It's cutting its payments to 10 percent of exports.

JACINTA:
So the IMF
Will turn a deaf
Ear.

NIGEL:
They've just cut off their payments to Zambia.

ZAC:
The IMF is not a charity.
It has to insist on absolute austerity.

NIGEL:
Absolutely. It can't be namby pamby.
These countries must accept restricted diets.
The governments must explain, if there are food riots,
That paying the western banks is the priority.

JAKE:
Bob Geldof was a silly cunt.
He did his charity back to front.
They should have had the concerts in Zaire
And shipped the money to banks over here.

ZAC:
So you're better off out of Africa, I guess.

NIGEL:
The continent is such a frightful mess.
One's based in London so one's operation
Is on the right side of exploitation.
One thing one learned from one's colonial masters,
One makes money from other people's disasters.

ZAC:
Señora Condor tells me you might be interested in Corman Enterprise.

ZAC takes NIGEL aside.

JAKE:
You can't completely pull out of Peru.

JACINTA:

Don't worry, Jake, I don't pull out on you.

I give up all my interests—except the cocaine.

And I keep the houses of course and the airplane.

My country is beautiful, Jake, white mountains, jungle greenery.

My people will starve to death among the scenery.

(Let them rot, I'm sick of it.)

JAKE:

So what's the story?

JACINTA:

The airstrip's rebuilt—

The government feels guilt

So it's always trying to bomb it.

(also they try to destroy my processing plants which is deceitful because they dare

not confront the peasants and stop them growing it.)

And they don't really want

To destroy all the plants.

They are making billions from it (more than all the rest of our exports.)

To keep Reagan our friend

We have to pretend,

But the US pretends and we know it.

Who likes a coke buzz?

America does.

They stop using it, we won't grow it.

JAKE:

So when can we see some action? Let's get going.

JACINTA:

I have to get a little cash flowing.

Maybe Mr. Corman?

JAKE:

I'm curious to see Corman, we've never met,

I'm just a secret compartment in his desk.

He's very bright so be on your best behavior.

He's obsessed with the bid and he'll look on you as a savior.

You can push him quite hard, he likes a risk.

So have you decided what to ask for yet?

JACINTA:

If I buy or I sell

I always do well
So don't worry about it, my pet.
Whatever I get
I look after you
And Corman will too
I expect.
Don't be embarrassed, Jake, you're young and greedy, I like to see it.

ZAC *and* NIGEL *rejoin them.*

JAKE:

I was at Eton myself. This is rather a different ballgame.

NIGEL:

Oh not at all. Did you ever play the wall game?

JAKE *and* NIGEL *talk apart.*

ZAC:

It would be great to see you while you're over here.

JACINTA:

Maybe we could drink some English beer.
I have a meeting at eight,
It won't go on late.
Maybe at half-past nine?

ZAC:

No, I don't think . . .
I'll be stuck with Corman, I can't get out for a drink.
Eleven's probably fine.

JACINTA:

I'm having late supper
With terribly upper-
class people who buy my plantation.

ZAC:

And after that?

JACINTA:

Unfortunately they live in Edinburgh.

ZAC:

How you getting there?

JACINTA:

By helicopter.

ZAC:
I'm beginning to run out of inspiration.

JACINTA:
Breakfast?

ZAC:
Would be great except I have to have breakfast with Corman till this deal goes through.
I suppose I might get away for a minute or two.

JACINTA:
That would be heaven.

ZAC:
Maybe eleven?

JACINTA:
Eleven I see my lawyer.
At twelve—

ZAC:
            No, please.

JACINTA:
I see some Japanese,
Just briefly in the hotel foyer.
So we meet for lunch?

ZAC:
I have to be in Paris for lunch. I'll be back by four.

JACINTA:
That's good!

ZAC:
But I have to go straight to Corman.

JACINTA:
            What a bore.

ZAC:
Maybe we could . . .

JACINTA:
Dinner tomorrow
Much to my sorrow
I have with some eurobond dealers.

ZAC:
Cancel it.

JACINTA:
Business.

ZAC:
Shit.

JACINTA:
Afterward?

ZAC:
Bliss.
No, hang on a minute.
I have as a guest a
Major investor,
I have to put out some feelers.
(The only time he can meet me is after a show.)
I guess I might be through by 1 A.M.

JACINTA:
Zac, I could cry,
There's a nightclub I buy,
And really I must talk to them.
So maybe next morning
You give me a ring?

ZAC:
Maybe I can get out of breakfast with Corman, I'll call you first thing.

JACINTA:
Which day?

ZAC:
Tomorrow.

NIGEL *and* JAKE.

NIGEL:
If you fancy a wolfhound I'll let you have a pup.

JAKE:
If I'm down in Wiltshire I'll certainly look you up.

ZAC *takes* JAKE *aside*.

JACINTA *(to* NIGEL*)*.
That went very well.

They can't possibly tell
You live in one room in a rundown hotel.

I'll buy you a silk shirt in Jermyn Street.

ZAC *and* JAKE.

ZAC:
You've not met Corman before, had you better split?
There may be a good time to meet him but is this it?
If you've actually spoken it gets us in more deep—

JAKE:
What the hell, Zac. Hang for a sheep.

ZAC *joins* CORMAN *and* ETHERINGTON *in Corman's office.*

CORMAN:
Cup of coffee someone. I'm going mental.
So we get these people involved in distribution,
Or supply, whatever, and they make a contribution?

ZAC:
Their involvement should look kind of coincidental.

CORMAN:
Look what? Zac, don't you start talking sin,
It'll look terrific. Show the buggers in.

NIGEL, JACINTA *and* JAKE *come into Corman's office.*

ZAC:
Señora Condor. Mr. Ajibala.

CORMAN:
And this must be the infamous Jake Todd.
I'd begun to think you were a bit like God—
You make things happen but you don't exist.
Etherington, don't look as if you smell something burning.
This is Jake Todd, our invisible earning.

ETHERINGTON:
How do you do, Mr. Todd. Extremely glad.

JAKE:
You're really so looked up to by my dad.

CORMAN:
OK, let's skip the introductions.
How do you do. Let's get on with the ructions.

What's the idea?

NIGEL:

   Albion seems an excellent investment
   Especially under your expert control.
   I assure you that the stag is not my role.
   I'm talking about a long term commitment.

CORMAN:

   So you'd have the company's interests at heart?

NIGEL:

   I'd certainly be glad to play my part.
   I can't imagine why anyone bothers with water
   When Albion produces so many delicious drinks.
   Orange, coffee, chocolate/with cream—

CORMAN:

   I think the product stinks.
   Cocoa? you're a cocoa importer?
   I know fuckall about the cocoa bean.
   Buy the company first and run it later.

NIGEL:

   The London market suits the speculator.
   You really have to know your way around.
   And excellent bargains can be made.

CORMAN:

   You've wide experience have you in the trade?

NIGEL:

   The only job I haven't done is peasant
   Who grows the stuff, which wouldn't be so pleasant.

CORMAN:

   So what's the story with cocoa—
   Anyone know?
   Are Albion having to pay through the nose?

NIGEL:

   There's mistrust between the countries where it grows
   And countries like this where we consume.
   Cocoa is very far from having a boom.
   A new agreement has just been implemented.

ZAC:

   (Hell of a lot of wrangling about the buffer stock.)

NIGEL:

This has driven the price up a little but it's well below the price at which buffer stock

buying is permitted,

And 18% down on a year ago.

We consumers are holding the price low.

CORMAN:

So how can you give me a better price than your rivals?

NIGEL:

Because options and futures are more important than physicals

(In today's market following an unchanged opening futures rallied £15 during the

afternoon before trade profit taking pared the gains on the closing call. With

producers withdrawn physical interest was restricted to forward/consumer

offtake—

JAKE:

He buys a forward contract, sells it later,

And every time he's making money off it.

ZAC:

And you get the benefit of the profit.

JACINTA:

It's thrilling to watch such a skillful operator.

CORMAN:

And funny business with import licenses, Mr. Ajibala? Don't answer that.

Right Zac, let's put cocoa on the back burner.

It looks as if it's a nice little earner.

And you Señora? Are you full of beans?

I suppose you want to sell me some caffeine?

JACINTA:

Coffee's no joke.

It makes me go broke.

No, my interest is distribution.

CORMAN:

I spent a good weekend once in Caracas.

You don't by any chance play the maracas?

JACINTA:

  I'm here to do business, Mr. Corman.

  I wish to obtain an exclusive franchise.

CORMAN:

  Señoritas in Brazil have beautiful eyes./

ZAC:

  Cut it out, Corman.

JACINTA:

  Mr. Corman, you appreciate my country's spirit.

  I appreciate your company's products and I wish to sell it in Peru, Brazil,
    Argentina,

    Venezuela and Chile.

ZAC:

  This could very probably be arranged.

CORMAN:

  Zackerman, I hope you haven't changed.

ZAC:

  The proposal has considerable merit.

CORMAN:

  You wouldn't be suggesting something silly?

  Can't you tell me anything good the present distributors did?

ZAC:

  No, they've shown no interest at all in your bid.

CORMAN:

  That's too bad.

  I think we may be in business, Señora.

JACINTA:

  If you want to set up

  Debt for equity swap

  And have Albion plants in Peru

  It's a way that we get

  To sell some of our debt.

  I ask you, what else can we do?

  Better than selling copper.

CORMAN:

  Zac, do I want to invest in South America?

ZAC:

  South American companies will swap their debt

For dollars you invest in their country, which means you get
Say a hundred million dollars of equity
Paid by the government in local currency
And you've only got to hand over seventy.
It gives you a great advantage over the locals.

JACINTA:

Also you could help to build my hospitals.
I have one for sick and hungry men and women,
One for poor drug-addicted children.
I visit and hold the hands of the poor people.

CORMAN:

This is all extremely admirable,
Don't you think so, Etherington? *(To* JACINTA.*)* If you'll excuse us.

CORMAN *takes* ZAC *and* ETHERINGTON *aside.*

Is this wise?
Hospitals, she's simply trying to use us.
Every penny would go in her own pocket.
Everything she looks at I want to lock it.
You can't help admiring the way she tries.
Etherington?

ETHERINGTON:

       I'm afraid I can't advise.
Questions of supply and distribution
For Albion after you make the acquisition
Are matters of internal management,
So naturally, I haven't liked to listen./
I really don't feel qualified to comment.

CORMAN:

Do you want the money for the deal or not?
Zac?

ZAC:

Swapping debt might come in handy later.
I agree the hospitals/are just a scam.

CORMAN:

Hospitals! what does she think I am?

ZAC:

So we buy his cocoa, give her the franchise and get out the calculator.

CORMAN:

They have got serious money?

ZAC:
          Jake recommends/them.

CORMAN:
   That boy's got very interesting friends.
   Let's keep them sweet.

   CORMAN *returns to others.*

   I'd be delighted to make a small contribution
   To your hospital, Señora. The distribution
   Franchise would of course be contingent
   On my acquiring Albion.

JACINTA:
          I know the arrangement.
   If you get it, I get it. I help you get it.

CORMAN:
   And Mr. Ajibala.
   I'm most impressed. As Albion's sole supplier/
   Of cocoa?

NIGEL:
   I would feel it my duty to acquire/
   An interest in the company.

CORMAN:
   I think a change of supplier is probably indicated,
   Don't you, Zac?
   Right, you can both discuss the exact sum
   With my banker here, Mr. Zackerman.

NIGEL:
   There's a small problem.
   I was hoping to buy five-million poundsworth of Albion stock but I have
      a holdup in
      cash liquidity.

CORMAN:
   That is a problem.

NIGEL:
   I suppose it is a matter of some urgency?
   If my involvement could be postponed, ten days, or eight?

CORMAN:
   That's too late.

NIGEL:

If I had an extra two million now a five million purchase could be made by several
small companies under various names registered in various places not traceable to
anyone alive.

ZAC:

Maybe if he buys three million now/and two—

CORMAN:

Zack, I want five. Five!

NIGEL:

I don't have five at my immediate disposal.

CORMAN:

Mr. Ajibala, if you're happy with my proposal/about the cocoa

NIGEL:

Perfectly.

CORMAN:

I could make a downpayment of two million in advance.
(We're going to need a hell of a lot of cocoa beans.)

NIGEL:

That way nothing would be left to chance.

CORMAN:

Zackerman will write a check.
And Señora Condor, if you see my lawyer.

JACINTA:

The deal is exciting,
I get it in writing?

CORMAN:

I can't be bothered with all these trivalities.
We've got the money. Fuck the personalities.
Etherington will see you all right for stock.

CORMAN *and* ETHERINGTON *leave, followed by* ZAC.

ZAC:

I'll call you first thing.

JACINTA, NIGEL *and* JAKE:

NIGEL:

I've got the money!/Two million!

JACINTA:

For Albion?

NIGEL:

I want a better return,
Albion won't earn,

JACINTA:

Put up your stake,
Get it doubled/by Jake.

NIGEL:

Doubled?

JACINTA:

He's a good dealer, let him play with it.

JAKE:

No problem. Give me a week.

NIGEL:

I'll go and get the check from Zackerman.

NIGEL *goes.*

JACINTA:

Two million. What are you going to do?

JAKE:

I thought I might invest it in Peru.

JACINTA *phones* MARYLOU BAINES.

JACINTA:

Hello? Marylou?
Four million, repeat four,
Arrives Thursday, the usual way.

MARYLOU:

But the CIA
Won't help it through
Unless we agree to give/
    another 10% to the Contras.

JACINTA:

But Marylou, already we pay—

MARYLOU:

I don't think we have an alternative.

JACINTA:

I expect an increase in what I get from you.

MARYLOU:

No problem. The guys who use it can easily meet
A rise in the street price because the street is Wall Street.

JACINTA:

So how's the weather?

MARYLOU:

I haven't looked.

During the above, ZAC *looks in just for this exchange with* JAKE.

ZAC:

Good work, Jake.

JAKE:

I'd be OK if my hands didn't shake.

JACINTA *comes off the phone.*

JACINTA:

Good work, Jake. The franchise I got from Corman—what a pig—
I sell of course to some American.
You will arrange it, no wonder I am so fond,
And I put the money in a delicious Eurobond,
Yumyum.
I think that is all.
One more phone call,
Then I go see Biddulph, the white knight—
But you don't mention this to Zac, all right?

JAKE:

This deal's not enough?

JACINTA:

            What is enough?
Don't worry, Jake, you're making it.
Just keep on, taking and taking and taking it.

JAKE:

I do.

JACINTA *phones a shop.*

JACINTA:

   I like to order a tree. Maybe twenty feet tall. Fig, walnut, banyan? Lemon,
     yes that's sweet.

   Send it please to Zac Zackerman, Klein Merrick, and a card saying 'to
   Zac with love from Jacinta until we meet.'

DUCKETT *and* BIDDULPH. BIDDULPH *has a newspaper.*

BIDDULPH:

   Now Duckett, your image gets better and better.
   Have you seen this letter?

DUCKETT:

       No, show me the letter.

BIDDULPH:

   MPs of all parties and union leaders,
   Teachers and lawyers and ordinary readers
   All hope you'll succeed

DUCKETT:

       Oh let's have a read.

BIDDULPH:

   In stopping the raider who just wants a profit.

DUCKETT:

   But we want a profit.

BIDDULPH:

       We will make a profit.
   But at the right time and in the right place,
   With a smile on our very acceptable face.
   You do so much good, you give so much enjoyment—

DUCKETT:

   Youth unemployment.

BIDDULPH:

       Yes, youth unemployment,
   Swimming pools, pensioners, toy libraries, art—

DUCKETT:

   What's this about art?

BIDDULPH:

       You don't give a fart,
   I know it, they know it, you just mustn't show it,
   We're doing so well, Duckett, don't you dare blow it.

You've commissioned a mural called Urban and Rural,
It's sixty feet high—

DUCKETT:

I've commissioned a mural?

BIDDULPH:

And tomorrow you're joining the scouts for a hike.

DUCKETT:

I'm not sure I like—

BIDDULPH:

You go for a hike.
Your picture will be on the front of the *Mail*.
And we really can't fail.

DUCKETT:

You're sure we can't fail?
Sometimes I dream that I'll end up in jail.

BIDDULPH:

But you've done nothing wrong, you're an innocent victim,
Corman's the villain, you'll see when we've licked him.
He's sure to be up to some terrible schemes.

DUCKETT:

I just have bad dreams.

BIDDULPH:

Well don't have bad dreams.

DUCKETT:

I've done nothing wrong, I'm an innocent victim.

BIDDULPH:

And Corman will lose because we have tricked him.

Now we're meeting Señora Condor.
What the hell's she want I wonder.

JACINTA CONDOR *arrives.*

JACINTA:

Mr. Duckett. Miss Biddulph. As a major shareholder I have been wondering whether I should accept Corman's offer.

BIDDULPH:

You don't want to do that Señora Condor.

JACINTA:

I was hoping you could help me to make up my mind. I don't know how
much you know about my country.

BIDDULPH:

It's really absurd, from what I have heard,
You bear an intolerable burden of debt.

JACINTA:

My country is poor, it can't stand much more,
I really can see no solution just yet.
When I wish to borrow, much to my sorrow,
The banks here in Britain are overextended.

BIDDULPH:

I think they might lend a small sum to a friend,
And we hope this sad period is very soon ended.

JACINTA:

You think your bank will lend me money?

BIDDULPH:

I think if I explain the special circumstances it could probably be arranged.

JACINTA:

Señora Biddulph
You are pleased with yourself
And certainly so you ought.
And ah Señor Duckett
You don't know your luck, it
Is now my decision you get my support.

DUCKETT:

We get her support?

BIDDULPH:

            Just as we ought.

DUCKETT:

I sometimes have dreams that I'll end up in court.

JACINTA:

And now do you think it is time for a drink?

BIDDULPH:

Time for a drink!

DUCKETT:

            What do you think, Biddulph?

BIDDULPH:

I'm telling you, Duckett.
I begin to think fuck it.
Pull yourself together.

MERRISON *and* MARYLOU BAINES *at Marylou's office in New York.*

MERRISON:

So I've had three years pretty much in the wilderness.
I've had a great time skiing with my kids.
I've bred Tennessee walking horses. But I guess
Banking's in my blood. I miss the bids,
I miss the late nights, I miss the gambles.
So now I've got my own operation.
I can't forgive Durkfeld for the shambles
He's made of Klein Merrick. A great nation
Needs great entrepreneurs, not black plastic
And gray lino and guys in polyester.
   (I just bought a Matisse for seven million dollars,
   could have hung in the boardroom.)

MARYLOU:

I guess the old wound's beginning to fester.
It's about time you did something drastic.
Go for it, Jack. Why don't you sabotage
Durkfeld's deals? I've got a lot of stocks
Coming and going here in arbitrage
Should enable you to give him a few knocks.

MERRISON:

He's got his fingers in a lot of pies.

MARYLOU:

In the UK there's Corman Enterprise.

MERRISON:

You think I should step in as a white knight?

MARYLOU:

No, that's already happening all right.
Wouldn't it be far wittier to make
Corman himself a target?

MERRISON:

                I'll buy a stake
In Corman straight away. I'll get some little

Nogood company run by a real punk
To take it over with a lot of junk.
I'd really like to see Durkfeld in hospital.
Do you happen to have any Corman stock available?

MARYLOU:
Yes, I kind of thought it might be saleable.
How much do you want?

MERRISON:
How much have you got?

MARYLOU:
Let's talk to TK.

MERRISON *goes*.

TK? Sell Mr Merrison all the Corman we've got.
And guy all you can get straight away.
He'll give us a good price and take the lot.

TK:
OK.

SCILLA *and* GRIMES *playing Pass the Pigs*.

SCILLA:
Grimes and I were having a glass of poo and playing Pass the Pig,
Where you throw little pigs like dice. It's a good way to unwind
Because when trading stops you don't know what to do with your mind.

GRIMES:
Trotter!

SCILLA:
Except my mind was also full of Jake and how he'd been up to something
big.

GRIMES:
Razorback, snouter. Fucking pig out.
I knew Jake was up to something but I'd never have guessed that was
what it was about.

SCILLA:
He might have made a million. Trotter. Razorback.

GRIMES:
Marylou Baines! And he's in on it somehow, Zac.
Did he leave a will?

SCILLA:

I don't know.

GRIMES:

Trotter, snouter.
Fucking nuisance if he's died without a
Will,/fucking lawyers

SCILLA:

Daddy and I are next of kin.

GRIMES:

Will you marry me?

SCILLA:

Leave it out Grimes.

GRIMES:

Double snouter. I think I'm going to win.
I once threw double snouter three times.

SCILLA:

Are we playing a pound a point?

GRIMES:

Snouter, trotter.
There's the money he's made already. There's a lot o'
money still owing him, bound to be,
And why can't that be collected by you and me?
It's just a matter of tracing his contacts, innit.
They'll want him replacing./Snouter!

SCILLA:

You'll pig out in a minute.
There's someone who killed him.

GRIMES:

Risks are there to be taken.
Trotter, jowler. Fuckit, makin' bacon.
Do I lose all my points for the whole game?

SCILLA:

Yes, Grimes, isn't it a shame.
And I've got forty-five. Trotter, fifty./Snouter, sixty. Double razorback,
eighty. Hell.
I've pigged out. Back to forty-five.

GRIMES:

I'd have some questions for Jake if he was alive.
What about your old man?

SCILLA:

Denies he got a single tip.

GRIMES:

I bet he knows more/than he lets on.

SCILLA:

He'll be so pissed by now he might let something slip.

GRIMES:

He may know where Jake stashed the loot.

SCILLA:

Let's go round there now and put in the boot.
Really, this morning he couldn't have been fouler.
Let's drive/there now.

GRIMES:

Double leaning jowler!
Double leaning jowler as I live and breathe!

SCILLA:

He's so two-faced you don't know what to believe.
We'll make him talk.

GRIMES:

I'm winning! Double fucking leaning jowler!

SCILLA:

Bring the pigs.

GREVILLE *and* FROSBY *at Greville's house. Drinking.*

GREVILLE:

It's times like this you need an old friend.
We haven't seen each other for a while,
I blame myself but know that in the end
It's only you that travels that last mile.
It helps so much to have someone I'm fond
Of here to sit and drink and share my grief.
There's no one else I'm sure his word's his bond.
Talking things over gives me such relief.

FROSBY:

Greville, there's something—

GREVILLE:

Poor Jake. You knew him as a little lad.
Remember the wooden soldier you once made him?

FROSBY:

Greville, there's something—

GREVILLE:

He wasn't really bad.
Some bastard whizzkid probably betrayed him.
Poor Jakey, how could anybody sell you?

FROSBY:

Greville, there's something that I ought to tell you.

SCILLA *and* GRIMES *arrive.*

SCILLA:

Daddy!

GREVILLE:

Scilla!

SCILLA:

Grimes, a colleague. My dad. Mr. Frosby.

GRIMES:

Nice place you've got. High ceilings. Plenty of headroom.
Room for a chandelier. How many bedrooms?

GREVILLE:

Six, actually, now that you come to mention—

GRIMES:

That's all right. I could always build an extension.

GREVILLE:

It's not for sale.

GRIMES:

No, I was just thinking.
I'd give you half a million.

GREVILLE:

What are you drinking?

SCILLA:

Daddy. Tell me the truth if you're sober
enough to talk properly. About Jake.

GRIMES:

I'd get an alsatian and a doberman.

GREVILLE:

Darling, I think you're making a mistake.

SCILLA:

Do I know more than you? Marylou Baines.
Yes?

GREVILLE:

Now Scilla—

SCILLA:

Don't think you can smile a
Lot and not tell me. Ill gotten gains,
Right? Millions!

GRIMES:

I'll get a rotweiller.

SCILLA:

And nobody told me.

GREVILLE:

I know nothing about—

SCILLA:

Nothing?

GREVILLE:

Scilla, there's no need to shout.
Of course my son would make the odd suggestion.

SCILLA:

Where's his money?

GREVILLE:

But there's no question.
Marylou Baines?

GRIMES:

A rotweiller's a killer.

SCILLA:

What about me?

GREVILLE:

I protected you, Scilla.
It's bad enough to see a woman get work

Without her being part of an old boy network.

SCILLA:

Fuck off. I want my share.

GREVILLE:

       Your share of what?
Daddy's always given you all he's got.
My little girl! Jake seems to have been much bigger
Than poor old daddy knew. If it's as you say,
If we're really dealing with a six nought figure.
Where the hell's he hidden it away?

GRIMES:

Don't piss about. We haven't got all day.
Who's his solicitor?

GREVILLE:

       I'm afraid I don't—

GRIMES:

Who's his accountant?

GREVILLE:

       In any case I won't—

FROSBY:

Who is this? An awful lout.

GRIMES:

If he really don't know we should get back.

FROSBY:

Ordering everyone about.

GRIMES:

It might be more use talking to Zac.

SCILLA:

If you're holding out on me daddy you'll be sorry.

GRIMES:

We'll have your feet run over by a lorry.

FROSBY:

Who is this horrible young vandal?
I don't need to know his name.
Responsible for all the scandal.
He's the one you ought to blame.

GRIMES:

You've all been coining it for years.

FROSBY:

My lovely city's sadly changed.
Sic transit gloria! Glory passes!
And wonder I'm deranged,
Surrounded by the criminal classes.

GRIMES:

You've all been coining it for years.
All you fuckwits in the City.
It just don't look quite so pretty,
All the cunning little jobs,
When you see them done by yobs.

FROSBY:

He's the one you ought to blame.

GRIMES:

We're only doing just the same
All you bastards always done.
New faces in your old square mile,
Making money with a smile,
Just as clever, just as vile.

GREVILLE:

No, he's right, you killed my son.

GRIMES:

All your lives you've been in clover,
Fucking everybody over,
You just don't like to see us at it.

GREVILLE:

Scilla, I forbid you to associate with this oik.

SCILLA:

Daddy, you're trading like a cunt.
This is a waste of time. I'm going to see Corman again.

GREVILLE:

Scilla, wait, if you find out about Jake's money—

SCILLA:

Don't worry, I won't tell you, I'll protect you.

GREVILLE:

Scilla—

GRIMES:

If you want to sell the house I can pay cash.

SCILLA *and* GRIMES *leave.*

GREVILLE:

Because of yobs like him my Jake was led astray.
If it wasn't for that bastard he'd be alive today.
It's times like this you need an old friend—

FROSBY:

Greville.
It's me that told the DTI.
I can't quite remember why.
It didn't occur to me he'd die.

ZAC.

ZAC:

That afternoon things were going from bad to worse.
Jake was dead and I'd just as soon it was me they'd taken off in a hearse.
I'd just discovered Jacinta and Ajibala were no fucking help at all,
And I find Scilla hanging about in the hall.

ZAC *and* SCILLA *outside Corman's office.*

SCILLA:

Zac, I want to see Corman. Get me in.

ZAC:

Don't talk to me. We may not even win.
Jacinta Condor's supporting Biddulph which may wreck
The whole deal, and Nigel Ajibala's done god knows what with a two
million pound
check.

SCILLA:

Jacinta Condor? Nigel Ajibala?

ZAC:

I've got to get this sorted / before Corman finds out.

SCILLA:

But they were in Jake's diary.

ZAC:
>   Scilla, don't shout.

SCILLA:
>   Would either of them be likely to kill
>   Jake? Or more important still
>   Could they tell me about his bank account?
>   Which bank is it in? / And what's the total amount?

ZAC:
>   They've kicked this dog of a deal when I hoped they'd pat it. /
>   I've got to find them.

SCILLA:
>   And if it's in a numbered Swiss account, Zac, how do I get at it?

ZAC *goes.* MELISSA, *a model, enters.*

SCILLA:
>   Are you going to see Mr. Corman?—

MELISSA:
>   I don't know his name.
>   I'm having a picture taken. The PR
>   Consultant is in there with him, she's called Dolcie Starr.
>   Last time I did a job like this the bastard put his hand on my crutch.
>   I was ready to walk out, I said, 'What's your game?'
>   I hope nothing like that—

SCILLA:
>   Can I go instead of you?

MELISSA:
>   How much?

CORMAN *and* DOLCIE STARR, *a PR consultant.*

CORMAN:
>   My image is atrocious. 'Profiteering.'
>   'Decline of British Industry.' 'Robber gangs.'
>   There's even a cartoon here where I'm leering
>   At an innocent girl called Albion and I've got fangs.
>   I want to be seen as Albion's Mr. Right.
>   I need to be transformed overnight.
>   Can you make me look as good as Duckett?

STARR:

No, I'm afraid he's completely cornered the market
In fatherly, blue-eyed, babies, workers' friend,
Someone on whom the CBI can depend—

CORMAN:

I'm all that.

STARR:

No, you're none of that.

CORMAN:

Shit.

STARR:

Cheer up, Corman, you're the opposite.

CORMAN:

Then what am I paying you good money for?

STARR:

Let Duckett be good. And a bore.
Then you can be bad. And glamorous.
You'll have top billing by tonight.
Everyone loves a villain if he's handled right. /
Bad has connotations of amorous.

CORMAN:

Bad and glamorous?

STARR:

Two dimensions, spiritual and physical. First, spiritual.

CORMAN:

That's Duckett's area. He's a lay preacher. /
You don't want me to be a Moslem?

STARR:

No, secular spiritual. Arts. For you to reach a
Wide audience it's absolutely essential /
You sponsor

CORMAN:

Duckett sponsors arts.

STARR:

He sponsors provincial

Orchestras. You need the National
Theatre for power, opera for decadence,
String quartets bearing your name for sensitivity and elegance,
And a fringe show with bad language for a thrill.
That should take care of the spiritual.
Now the physical. It's a pity you haven't a yacht.

CORMAN:
I'll buy one now.

STARR:
       No, we'll work with what we've got.
I do recommend a sex scandal.

CORMAN:
Sex scandal? / That's the last thing—

STARR:
Will you let me handle this?
You think because you're already scandalous /
In the financial—

CORMAN:
I don't want—

STARR:
But that's the point. Fight scandal with scandal.
We provide a young girl who'll say you did it eight times a night.
Your wife is standing by you, so that's all right. /

CORMAN:
(I'm not married.)

STARR:
There could be a suggestion the girl might take her life—
If necessary we provide the wife.

CORMAN:
I'm not sure—

STARR:
There's ugly greedy and sexy greedy, you dope.
At the moment you're ugly which is no hope.
If you stay ugly, god knows what your fate is.
But sexy greedy *is* the late eighties.

CORMAN:

What about AIDS? I thought sexy was out.

STARR:

The more you don't do it, the more it's fun to read about.
We might have you make a statement about taking care.
Wicked and responsible, the perfect chair/man.

CORMAN:

I don't think I—

STARR:

We can take the pictures straightaway. / Melissa!

CORMAN:

Pictures?

STARR:

You don't have to do a thing, not even kiss her.

SCILLA *comes in.*

SCILLA:

Melissa's ill. I'm Scilla, the replacement.

STARR:

You need to stand more adjacent.

CORMAN:

I can't stop working while you take pictures. Zac!
Where the fuck's he gone and why isn't he back?

He recognises SCILLA.

You again?

SCILLA *and* CORMAN *talk while* STARR *takes photographs.*

SCILLA:

I've important news for you about Albion,
If you'll tell me more about Jake.

CORMAN:

What news?

SCILLA:

Jacinta Condor?

CORMAN:

What about her?

SCILLA:
How much did he make?

STARR:
Please look fonder.

SCILLA:
How much did you pay him?

CORMAN:
Two hundred grand.

SCILLA:
What did he do with it?

STARR:
If you took her hand.

CORMAN:
What about the señora?

SCILLA:
She's supporting Biddulph's bid.

STARR:
Could you be more a-
ffectionate—keep still please. Please smile. Smile, kid.

CORMAN:
I'll kill the bitch. /
I knew there was something funny.

SCILLA:
He was so fucking rich.
Who else gave him money?

CORMAN:
What else? Is that the lot?

SCILLA:
Ajibala.

CORMAN:
    What? what?

SCILLA:
More about Jake, or I won't say a word.

CORMAN:

I could name six companies he's dealt with, four merchant banks and two MPs and

that's only what I've heard.

Your brother was widely respected in the City.

Now what about Ajibala? have some pity.

SCILLA:

I'll tell you about him for a small fee.

Three companies, two banks and one MP.

CORMAN *whispers to* SCILLA. STARR *snaps enthusiastically.*

STARR:

That's the way. That's what we like to see.

Look as if you're having a lot of fun.

We'll have the front page story of the *Sun.*

SCILLA:

Ajibala's gone off with the two million you gave him.

CORMAN:

Not bought my stock? There's nothing going to save him. Zac!

He realizes about the pictures.

CORMAN:

Hang on a minute, you can't use these, this girl is the sister of the dead whizzkid in

today's papers.

STARR:

And that's a scandal with which you've got no connection?

CORMAN:

No, that's the scandal where there is a connection but I don't want it known, I just want

to be connected with the fictitious scandal where I've got a permanent erection.

(Eight times a night? Maybe four, let's be plausible.)

STARR:

But we can't let the whole story escape us.

This other scandal's a high-profile thriller.

Terrific pictures. / What's your name? Scilla?

CORMAN:

No, please—

SCILLA:

What's this about eight times a night?

STARR:

You make a statement to the press saying—

SCILLA:

Right. Keep paying or I'll agree.

Three companies.

CORMAN *whispers to* SCILLA.

Two banks.

CORMAN *whispers.*

One MP.

CORMAN *whispers.*

SCILLA:

I've never seen Mr. Corman before.

From what I do see he's an awful bore.

CORMAN:

Great. More! more! Don't skimp.

SCILLA:

He's physically repellant. What a wimp.

STARR:

OK OK, I get it. What duplicity.

Why don't you people appreciate publicity?

You've wasted a lot of film. Where's Melissa?

STARR *leaves.*

CORMAN:

Do you want a job? Most of the people who work for me are mentally defective.

SCILLA:

Maybe later when I've finished being a detective.

CORMAN:

Zac! Etherington!

I want blood. What the fuck's going on?

ZAC *comes in followed by* NIGEL AJIBALA.

ZAC:

Hold on, I've got Ajibala right here.

CORMAN:

Where's my money? You'd better start talking fast.
You can stick your cocoa beans up your arse.
Where's my two million pounds?

NIGEL:

I'm delighted to have this opportunity
Of explaining how by judicious speculation
I plan to increase the sum that you gave me so that I can buy even more
   shares in support
   of your acquisition.
I think I may certainly say with impunity /
That when you

ETHERINGTON *comes in with* GREVETT, *a DTI inspector.*

CORMAN:

Ajibala, I've been tricked.
I gave you two million pounds / on the strict
Understanding that you'd—

ETHERINGTON:

Mr. Corman. Mr. Corman. Mr. Corman.

GREVETT:

Do finish your sentence, Mr. Corman.

CORMAN:

What's going on? Who the hell's this?
Who let him in? Sack the receptionist.

GREVETT:

I identified myself to your receptionist
As Grevett from the Department of Trade and Industry. /
People don't usually refuse to see me.

CORMAN:

Very nice to meet you, Mr. Grevett.

ETHERINGTON:

I assured Mr. Grevett we'd be delighted to assist
With his inquiries in any way we could. /

We know the DTI is a force for good.

CORMAN:

Delighted.

GREVETT:

What was that about two million pounds?

ETHERINGTON:

I thought it might interest you, because it sounds /
Unusual, but in fact—

CORMAN:

What was it, Zac?

ZAC:

Mr. Corman is paying Klein Merrick, the bank I work for, two million
pounds for
advisory /
Services

ETHERINGTON:

The sum's derisory /
Considering the immense—

GREVETT:

I believed he was addressing this gentleman?

ETHERINGTON:

By no means.

CORMAN:

Mr. Ajibala, who supplies our cocoa beans.

GREVETT:

So the sum in question was to do with the cocoa trade?

ZAC *and* ETHERINGTON:

No.

CORMAN:

Yes. That is no, but we have made
Some arrangements to do with cocoa which were being discussed

ETHERINGTON:

But the two million pounds was a payment to Klein.

ZAC:

Yes, that side of the business is all mine.

GREVETT:

Mr. Ajibala, you can confirm I trust
That you never received the sum of two million?

NIGEL:

I only wish I had.

All laugh except GREVETT.

GREVETT:

The suggestion seems to cause you some amusement.
I have to establish you see that no inducement
Financial or otherwise was offered by Mr. Corman
To buy stock to help support his price.

NIGEL:

Two million pounds would be extremely nice.
But no, Mr. Grevett, I assure you.
An account of the cocoa trade would only bore you.

GREVETT:

And you Mr. Corman would confirm—?

CORMAN:

Absolutely.

GREVETT:

It sounded as if you were asking him to return
Two million pounds. I must have misunderstood.
You weren't asking—?

CORMAN:

No, no no, why should I?
I never gave him a two million pound check.

NIGEL:

So naturally he can't ask for it back.
I must be going. I've meetings to attend.
Good afternoon, Mr. Corman.

CORMAN:

Wait.

GREVETT:

What?

CORMAN:

Nothing.

SCILLA *waylays* NIGEL *on his way out.*

SCILLA:
I've got to talk to you. You were a friend
Of my brother Jake.

NIGEL:
Who? I never met him.

SCILLA:
It seems to be very easy to forget him.
Do you owe him money?

NIGEL:
This is crazier and crazier.
If you'll excuse me I have a very important meeting about cocoa stocks
in Malaysia.

NIGEL AJIBALA *leaves.*

GREVETT:
Does the name Jake Todd ring a bell?

CORMAN:
No. Oh yes, in the paper. Most unfortunate.
(I hope the stupid bastard rots in hell.)

GREVETT:
Not someone with whom you were personally acquainted?

CORMAN:
No, not at all. He seems to have been tainted /
By allegations of—

GREVETT:
I don't wish to be importunate,
But I was wondering if it would be possible for me to cast an eye
Over any papers relating to your interest in Albion, just a formality.

CORMAN:
This way.

GREVETT:
Your involvement, Mrs. Etherington, naturally goes a long way to reassure
us of the
transaction's total legality.

ETHERINGTON:

There could of course be aspects of which I wasn't aware because my participation
wasn't required.

CORMAN:

Etherington, you're fired.

GREVETT *and* ETHERINGTON *leave.*

CORMAN:

We'll give him a pile of papers ten feet high
And keep him busy till after the deal's completed.
Fuck the DTI, Zac, I refuse to be defeated.
I don't care if I go to jail, I'll win whatever the cost.
They may say I'm a bastard but they'll never say I lost.

ZAC:

Corman, there's one thing.
Gleason called and said he's seeing Lear at the National
Could you meet him and have a word at the interval
I don't know why you're being asked to meet a cabinet minister,
I hope it's nothing sinister.
But when the government asks you for a date, you don't stand them up.

CORMAN:

Fuck.

CORMAN *leaves.* ZAC *and* SCILLA *alone.*

ZAC:

Whether we'll get away with this is anybody's guess.
   (My guess is no.)
And to think Jacinta Condor—/ god, what an awful mess.

SCILLA:

She knew Jake, didn't she? Ajibala denied it.

ZAC:

He's the key to all the deals, of course they're going to hide it.

SCILLA:

I want to meet them.

ZAC:

            Scilla, we all have to lie low.

SCILLA:

I want to meet all his contacts because someone's going to know where /
his money is.

ZAC:

It'll be in a nominee company, and god knows where, no one except
maybe Marylou
Baines might know.

SCILLA:

Then I'll go and see Marylou Baines. / She's the one who made him.

ZAC:

No Scilla, I didn't mean—

SCILLA:

Yes, she'll know where his money is because she'll know how she paid him.
Do you think she owes him money? / Maybe I could collect.

ZAC:

Scilla—

SCILLA:

I'll go to New York / tonight.

ZAC:

Scilla, we must keep out of the news.
If you're going to be stupid I'll call Marylou and warn her and she'll
refuse—

SCILLA:

How much does Mr Grevett of the DTI suspect?
I could go and have a word / with him

ZAC:

Scilla, don't be absurd.

SCILLA:

I could have my picture in the papers
With Corman alleging all kinds of capers /
And linking him publicly with bad Jake Todd

ZAC:

Scilla, you wouldn't. God.

SCILLA:

So call Marylou Baines and tell her I'm on my way to Heathrow and she's
to see me. Do it.

ZAC:

At least you'll be out of England.

SCILLA:

I'll send you a postcard.

ZAC:

Scilla, I thought you were some kind of English rose.

SCILLA:

Go stick the thorns up your nose, bozo.

SCILLA *goes*.

ZAC:

Somewhere along the line I really blew it.

MERRISON *and* SOAT, *President of Missouri Gumballs, at a drugstore in Missouri.*

MERRISON:

So how would you like to acquire a multinational?

SOAT:

Mr. Merrison, this hardly seems rational.
My company is really extremely small.
You realize our only product is those little balls
Of gum you buy in the street out of machines?
If Corman took me over, I'd understand it.
But I'm really not cut out for a corporate bandit.
I've hardly got out from under my last creditor
And now you're trying to turn me into a predator.

MERRISON:

The smaller you are, the bigger the triumph for me.
I can raise four billion dollars of junk.

SOAT:

Mr. Merrison. I'm afraid I'm in a funk.
I don't know what to say. What're you doin'?

MERRISON:

I'm using you, Mr. Soat, to humiliate
Somebody I have good reason to hate.

SOAT:

I'm not sure—

MERRISON:

    I wouldn't like to ruin
Missouri Gumballs, it seems kind of dumb.

SOAT:

No no. No no no no. Don't take my gum.
I'll think about it. I've thought about it. Great.

CORMAN, GLEASON, *a Cabinet Minister, in the interval at the National Theatre.*

GLEASON:

Enjoying the show?

CORMAN:

    I'm not watching it.

GLEASON:

It's excellent of course, they're not botching it.
But after a hard day's work my eyes keep closing.
I keep jerking awake when they shout.

CORMAN:

It's hard to follow the plot if you keep dozing. /
What exactly is this meeting all about?

GLEASON:

Yes, Goneril and Reagan and Ophelia—
Good of you to come.
We have here two conflicting interests.
On the one hand it's natural the investor
Wants to make all the profit that he can,
And institutions' duty to the pensioners
Does put the onus on the short-term plan.
On the other hand one can't but help mention
The problems this creates for industry,
Who need longterm research and development
In order to create more employment.
It's hard to reconcile but we must try.

CORMAN:

I totally agree with the CBI.
Long term issues mustn't be neglected.
The responsibility of management—

GLEASON:

We—by which I mean of course the government—
Recognize that alas nothing's perfect.
That's something you learn in politics.
We want to cut the top rate of tax,
And profit related pay's a good incentive.
But we do think things have gone too far
In the quickprofit shortterm direction.
We wouldn't interfere in a free market.
But we are of course approaching an election.

CORMAN:

Absolutely and I hope to give
More than moral support to the party.
I've always been a staunch Conservative.

GLEASON:

My dear fellow, nobody doubts your loyalty.
That's why I have so little hesitation
In asking this small service to the nation.
Drop your bid. Give up. Leave it alone.

CORMAN:

Out of the question. Sorry. Out of the question.

GLEASON:

I absolutely appreciate the problem—

CORMAN:

Leave me alone will you to do my job.

GLEASON:

I'm sorry, Corman, but I must forbid it.
A takeover like this in the present climate
Makes you, and the City, and us look greedy.
Help us be seen to care about the needy.
Help us to counteract the effect of Tebbit.

CORMAN:

What if I say no?

GLEASON:

I wouldn't like to dwell on the unsavory
Story of that young man's suicide—

CORMAN:

Are you threatening me?

GLEASON:

        I do admire your bravery.
No, but my colleagues in the DTI
Did, I believe, call on you today.

CORMAN:

Leave it out, Gleason, I've had enough.
DTI? I'm going to call your bluff.
If my takeover's going to hurt your image
Another scandal would do far more damage

GLEASON:

Mr. Corman, I'll be brutally frank.
A scandal would not be welcomed by the Bank
Nor will it be tolerated by the Tories.
Whenever you businessmen do something shitty
Some of it gets wiped off on the City,
And the government's smelly from the nasty stories.

Meanwhile, 'Ladies and gentlemen take your seats' etc.

CORMAN:

Us businessmen? / The banks are full of crap.

GLEASON:

So if you persist and make a nasty mess
Not a single bank will handle your business.

CORMAN:

You can't do that, Gleason, don't make me laugh.

GLEASON:

Corman, please, don't make my patience snap.
I wouldn't want to miss the second half.
You drop the bid. We stop the DTI.

CORMAN:

You'd stop the scandal breaking anyway.
Are you telling me you can't control the press?

GLEASON:

Yes, but we'd break you. Do you want to try?
You drop the bid. We stop the DTI.

CORMAN:

Why pick on me? Everyone's the same.

I'm just good at playing a rough game.

GLEASON:

Exactly, and the game must be protected.
You can go on playing after we're elected.
Five more glorious years free enterprise,
And your services to industry will be recognized.

GLEASON *goes.*

CORMAN:

Cunt. Right. Good.
At least a knighthood.

ZAC *and* JACINTA, *exhausted, in the foyer of the Savoy.*

ZAC:

So he canceled the deal.

JACINTA:

And how do you feel?

ZAC:

Exhausted.

JACINTA:

　　　I get you a drink.
At least we can meet,
You're not rushed off your feet,
It's better like this I think.

ZAC:

Jacinta, I still can't forgive you for going to Biddulph, the whole deal
could have been wrecked.

JACINTA:

But I get more money that way, Zac, really what do you expect?
I can't do bad business just because I feel romantic.

ZAC:

The way you do business, Jacinta, drives me completely frantic.

JACINTA:

I love the way you are so obsessed when you're thinking about your bids.

ZAC:

I love that terrible hospital scam / and the drug addicted kids.

JACINTA:

(That's true, Zac!)

I love the way you never stop work, I hate a man who's lazy.

ZAC:

The way you unloaded your copper mines drove me completely crazy.

JACINTA:

Zac, you're so charming. I'm almost as fond

Of you as I am of a eurobond.

ZAC:

I thought we'd never manage to make a date.

You're more of a thrill than a changing interest rate.

JACINTA:

This is a very public place to meet.

ZAC:

Maybe we ought to go up to your suite.

They get up to go.

ZAC:

Did you ever play with a hoop when you were a child and when it stops
    turning it falls
    down flat?

I feel kind of like that.

JACINTA:

I am very happy. My feeling for you is deep.

But will you mind very much if we go to sleep?

GREVILLE, *drunk.*

GREVILLE:

Maybe I should retire while my career is at its pinnacle.

Working in the City can make one rather cynical.

When a oil tanker sank with a hundred men the lads cheered because
    they'd make a
    million.

When Sadat was shot I was rather chuffed because I was long of gold
    bullion.

Life's been very good to me. I think I'll work for Oxfam.

FROSBY, *with a gun.*

FROSBY:

    I thought the sun would never set
    I thought I'd be extremely rich
    You can't be certain what you'll get.
    I've heard the young say Life's a bitch.

    I betrayed my oldest friend.
    It didn't give me too much fun.
    My way of life is at an end.
    At least I have a friendly gun.

    My word is my junk bond.

DAVE *and* MARTIN *have just come out of a Chinese restaurant. Late night.*

DAVE:

    I've eaten too many crab claws.

MARTIN:

    You'll be sick in the cab again.

DAVE:

    You'll get stick from your wife again.

MARTIN:

    She don't care if I'm late.

DAVE:

    What's she up to then?

MARTIN:

    Watch it.

DAVE:

    Late city, no pity.

BRIAN, TERRY *and* VINCE *follow.*

BRIAN:

    Guy meets a guy and he says what do you do for a living and he says I hurt people. /

TERRY:

    Sounds like my girlfriend.

BRIAN:

    He says you hurt people, he says yes I hurt people for money. / *I'm a hitman.

TERRY:
Sounds like a trader

MARTIN:
How much was it?

DAVE:
Bet it was two fifty.

MARTIN:
Bet it was three hundred.

DAVE:
How much?

MARTIN:
Ten.

VINCE:
Two eighty five.

MARTIN:
Told you. All that crab.

DAVE *gives* MARTIN *ten pounds.*

BRIAN:
*Break a leg, five hundred pounds, break a back, a thousand /

DAVE:
I know him, he works for Liffe.

BRIAN:
And he says I'm glad I met you because my neighbor's carrying on with
my wife.
So he takes him home and says see that lighted window, that's where they
    are, I want
    her dead,
How much would it cost to shoot her through the head? *

TERRY:
You can't get rid of your money in Crete.
Hire every speedboat, drink till you pass out, eat
Till you puke and you're still loaded with drachs.

MARTIN:

DAVE: Drach attack! drach attack!

MARTIN:

DAVE: Drach attack! drach attack!

VINCE:

Why's a clitoris like a filofax?

DAVE and OTHERS:

Every cunt's got one.

BRIAN:

*And he says five grand.

And he says, now my neighbor what would it cost if you shot off his prick and his balls.

And he says that's five grand and all.

So he says ten grand! Yes all right, it's worth it, go on, so the hitman's stood there by the garden gate

And he points his gun at the window, and he's stood there and stood there, and he says get on with it, and the hitman says Wait.

Time it right / and I'll save you five grand.

DAVE:

I'll save you five grand.

MARTIN:

Two eurobond dealers walking through Trafalgar Square, one of them said what would you do if a bird shat on your head?

And he said /

I don't think I'd ask her out again.

DAVE:

I don't think I'd ask her out again

SCILLA *at Marylou Baines's office in New York.*

SCILLA, TK.

TK:

Hi, I'm TK, Marylou Baines's personal assistant.

SCILLA:

Tell Marylou Baines

I've just flown in from London, I've come here straight off the plane.

I'm Jake Todd's sister and I've got some information

That I didn't want to trust to the telephone so I've brought it myself personally to its
destination.

TK:

Ms Baines won't see you I'm afraid but if you'd like to give me the information instead,
I'm setting up in business myself and can guarantee you'd receive service second to
   none because it's always those who are starting up who work hardest because they
   want to get ahead.
So can I help you?

SCILLA:

I didn't spend six hours crossing the Atlantic
To be fobbed off by a personal assistant.

TK:

I'm sorry about this but it is part of my job description to be resistant.

SCILLA:

I warn you, I'm very tired and I'm getting frantic,
And Marylou will get a terrible fright
Tomorrow morning if she doesn't see me tonight.

TK:

If you just give me some indication of what your problem's about—

SCILLA:

Get out of my way. OUT OUT OUT.

MARYLOU *comes in.*

MARYLOU:

So. Todd's sister. You've come flying
From London with information?

SCILLA:

          No, I was lying.
You don't get information this time, Marylou.
I want to know things from you.

MARYLOU:

You can ask.

SCILLA:

I had been wondering if you killed Jake, but now I hardly care.
It's not going to bring him alive again, and the main thing's to get my share.

They left me out because I'm a girl and it's terribly unfair.
You were Jake's main employer so tell me please
How did you pay him his enormous fees?
Did somebody pass a briefcase of notes at a station under a clock?
Or did you make over a whole lot of stock?
Did he have a company and what's its name?
And how can I get in on the game?
You'll need a replacement in London who knows their way round the businesses and
    banks.
Can I suggest somebody?

MARYLOU:

    No thanks.

SCILLA:

If you don't help me I'll go to the authorities and tell them—

MARYLOU:

    Is this blackmail?

SCILLA:

Yes, of course. I can put you in jail.

MARYLOU:

I'll take the risk. I'm a risk arbitrageur.
So run off home.

TK:

And nobody in America runs better risks than her.

SCILLA:

You can stick your arbitrage up your arse.
If you don't tell me about his company
You'll find me quite a dangerous enemy.
I'm greedy and completely amoral.
I've the cunning and connections of the middle class
And I'm tough as a yob.

MARYLOU:

Scilla, don't let's quarrel.
My personal assistant's leaving. Do you want a job?

TK:

Right now?

MARYLOU:

Sure, TK, you said you wanted out,
Scilla wants in. So don't let's hang about.

MARYLOU *and* SCILLA *go.*

TK:

One thing I've learned from working for Marylou:
Do others before they can do you.

ZAC.

ZAC:

So Scilla never came back.
She sent me a postcard of the Statue of Liberty saying Bye bye Zac.
She never did find out who killed her brother but I'm sure it wasn't Cor-
man or Jacinta
or Marylou or any of us.
Who didn't want Jake to talk to the DTI? Who wanted him out of the
way?
The British government, because another scandal just before the election
would have
been too much fuss.
So I reckon it was MI5 or the CIA.
(Or he could even have shot himself, the kid wasn't stable.)
There's bound to be endless scandals in the city but really it's incidental.
It can be a nuisance because it gives the wrong impression
And if people lose confidence in us there could be a big recession.
Sure this is a dangerous system and it could crash any minute and I
sometimes wake up
in bed
And think of Armageddon, AIDS, nuclear war or a crash, and how will I
end up dead?
(But that's just before breakfast.)
What really matters is the massive sums of money being passed round the
world, and
trying to appreciate their size can drive you mental.
There haven't been a million days since Christ died.
So think a billion, that's a thousand million, and have you ever tried
To think a trillion? Think a trillion dollars a day.
That's the gross national product of the USA.
There's people who say the American eagle is more like a vulture.
I say don't piss on your own culture.

Naturally there's a whole lot of greed and

That's no problem because money buys freedom.

So the Tories kept the scandal to the minimum. Greville Todd was arrested and put in

prison to show the government was serious about keeping the city clean and

nobody shed any tears.

And the Conservatives romped home with a landslide victory for five more glorious

years.

(Which was handy though not essential because it would take far more than

Labour to stop us.)

I've been having a great time raising sixteen billion dollars to build a satellite,

And I reckon I can wrap it up tonight.

EVERYBODY.

SCILLA:

Scilla's been named by *Business Week* as Wall Street's rising star.

GREVILLE:

Greville walked out of the open prison but didn't get very far.

GRIMES:

Grimes does insider dealing for Scilla and Marylou (and he bought Greville's house).

JAKE:

Jake's ghost appeared to Jacinta one midnight in Peru.

CHORUS:

Five more glorious years, five more glorious years *B/U:*

We're saved from the valley of tears for five more glorious years

pissed and promiscuous, the money's ridiculous

send her victorious for five fucking morious

five more glorious years

CHORUS:

Five more glorious years, five more glorious years *B/U:*

We're crossing forbidden frontiers for five more glorious years
pissed and promiscuous, the money's ridiculous
send her victorious for five fucking morious
five more glorious years

END

KEEPING TOM NICE

Lucy Gannon

For Gerard & Norah Gannon
and
In Memory of
Mary Gannon

Keeping Tom Nice was first presented by the Royal Shakespeare Company at the Almeida Theatre, London, on August 9, 1988.

After twenty years of nursing, during which I had never tried to, or even wanted to, write anything at all, a playwriting competition was announced. I was a sucker for competitions and would try anything once, so I borrowed a typewriter and had a go. The competition, the Richard Burton Drama Award, was a nationwide search for new playwrights. I found that writing *Keeping Tom Nice* (which went on to win that first award, and then The Susan Smith Blackburn Prize) was so stimulating and quickly became so important to me that I couldn't stop. I've been writing, full time, ever since.

LUCY GANNON
1990

Author's Note

People have grown used to thinking about and "caring about" people who have genius, apparently, but are trapped within a disabled, wayward or nonfunctioning body. Tom isn't one of these geniuses. He's you or me, the person who serves us in the market or the man who sweeps the street, he could be within the accepted norms of intelligence or he could perhaps struggle to understand the simplest of sums. He has the right to be mentally ordinary or even dull just as he has the right to be an intellectual giant, and his dilemma is no less whichever he is. I do not believe that a person with high intelligence is any more precious or deserving of our care and understanding and compassion than someone with learning difficulties or an impaired understanding of the world. We're all in the soup together bright and dull alike, none of us have earned the brains we've got, so why all the desire to see something "extraordinary" in people like Tom, as if it is only this which deserves our attention? Few of us would ever get a glance from the rest of the world if this was true.

Having said that, the play is not about Tom. It is about looking after Tom, what that does to him and his family.

Characters

DOUG—Tom's father. Aged about 60. A well-educated man, middle class, used to be a middle manager in an engineering business and took early retirement to help look after Tom.

TOM—A man of 24. Severely physically disabled, unable to communicate, to feed or tend to himself, to walk or pick anything up even. We don't know how intelligent Tom is, but we know he uses language internally.

WINNIE—Tom's mother. Aged about 55. A pleasant, capable woman who has not had a career other than looking after Tom and the rest of her family.

CHARLIE—Tom's sister. 23 years old. Living away from home at university. She went to university late after working in an office for a couple of years and caught up with her A level exams at evening school. Doug always believed that she would go to university and it was to please him, to "make up" for Tom that she persevered and finally got there. A bright, apparently loving but immature woman.

STEPHEN—Tom's social worker.

The play takes place in an acting area, rather than a set. Only what is required is present. The time is free flowing, telescopic.

In the first half of the play, until Stephen enters the house, we can see him around the action—not a part of it, but there.

The Discords

An infrared camera can take a night photograph of a car park after a hot day and show where cars have been parked, reproducing an impression of them. The discords are what remain in the house after 24 years of this family living in it, doing the same things at the same times of day, saying the same words, the same pattern of words, thinking the same things, dreaming private dreams, for all that time. They are not happening in Tom's head, or anyone else's, some of the words have actually been said, some of them have remained unspoken, some they have not dared to say, but they are all real. I call them discords because the characters appear to be talking, to be answering each other, but in fact each phrase just skids off the next, each person deflects the words of the others with heart-breaking, unthinking skill. The unreality of these discords become apparent in the words, and shouldn't be self-consciously presented, as if their meaning is portentous, or more important than the rest of the play. The discords are the flotsam of four lives, that's all—they're not consciously presented to the world, and they are therefore revealing.

SCENE ONE
First Discord (Tom's)

TOM, *alone, in his wheelchair. Dark, growing gradually lighter but still dim until* DOUG *draws the curtains.*

TOM: Tom's here. Tom's here. Here. Juddering Tom. Dancing Tom. Jerking, juddering Tom, here. Tom sore bones. Bones. Bones aching in secret places. Bones boning in boney places. Razor bones on paper skin. Tom. Tom's here. Here. Daybreak Tom. Moonlight Tom. Just Tom.

(We hear a noise in the distance. TOM *is quiet for a moment.)*

Daddy! Daddy! Dark. Dark as Daddy. Dark. Dark. Father. *(Exploring the word.)* Father. Father? Fa . . . the . . . er. Dad. Daddy. Daddy father. Daddy! How many thoughts to morning? Sore bones, sore skin, sore, sore. Juddering-jerking, splaying, twisting, sore. Cold, dry, empty sore. Dry. Tom dry, dying for a cold wet gasping grabbing gulp. Tom. Poor Tom. Tom's cup. My cup. Sing-a-song, Tom, my cup. See Stephen-here-to-help-you, Tom's cup.

CHARLIE: *(off, coming on, stepping out from the shadows)* Look, he's reaching for his cup.

*(*TOM *looks around, straining his neck, his eyes rolling backwards his head lolls back and he strains to reach the cup, his movements tiny but ladened with effort.)*

CHARLIE: He's stretching for his cup.

WINNIE: *(off, coming on, stepping out from the shadows)* No good telling me dear, I can't hear you. Can't hear you.

CHARLIE: Look! Look!

WINNIE: I can't hear you dear, no good telling me.

CHARLIE: Tom! Yay! Tom!

*(*TOM *laughs on the intake of a breath.)*

WINNIE: It's no good, dear, he can't hear you. Can't year you.

CHARLIE: Stretching, straining, looking.

WINNIE: Jerking.

CHARLIE: Trying.

WINNIE: I meant to change his jumper.

CHARLIE: He's trying to pick up his bloody cup!

TOM: Tom's cup Charlie! *(He jerks back in frustration, a wordless yell.)*

WINNIE: I like him to look nice.

DOUG: *(off, coming on)* He looks nice.

CHARLIE: Don't you see? Don't you see?

DOUG: He looks alright. He is alright!

CHARLIE: He's reaching for his cup, are you blind?

WINNIE: I can't hear you, dear. I can't see. I choose not to listen, dear. I like to keep him nice.

(TOM, exhausted, allows his fingers to droop. Suddenly, cruelly, full light floods in, as DOUG wrenches back the curtains. TOM screws up his eyes in protest, his fingers splay again.)

DOUG: We do keep him nice. *(He goes to TOM and smiles down at him. His fingers play with TOM's, tip to tip. He leans over and rubs TOM's stubble playfully.)* Pushing the razor firmly over . . . and up . . . under the chin . . . pull his nose to get that bit there. . . .

(TOM snorts with laughter.)

WINNIE: That bit there.

DOUG: I know. On the humps of his jaw bones, little circles.

WINNIE: Oh, yes, he does look nice.

DOUG: *(admiring TOM's jumper)* Good color that.

WINNIE: Royal blue.

DOUG: Uniform blue. Smart and clean. *(He briskly mimes putting a jumper on TOM, practised in the task, crisp and efficient.)* Take his hand and push the sleeve on. . . . so. Take the neck, hold it open, ease it over his head. Lolling, sad head. The other hand. . . . so. Pull it all down . . .

WINNIE: There! That's it! Smart as a pin.

DOUG: *(smiling into TOM's face)* Clean as a whistle.

WINNIE: Bright as a button.

CHARLIE: Mad as a hatter. Daft as a brush. Silent as the grave.

(She looks at TOM *and pulls a face. He shouts, a sudden happy shout.)*

WINNIE: We like to keep him nice. We'll always keep him nice.

DOUG: For ever and ever.

CHARLIE: Amen.

(They look at TOM *and he looks back, anxious. His fingers and his head move in concern. They move nearer, peering at him. He closes his eyes.)*

SCENE TWO

TOM'S *Room. While this scene is going on* WINNIE *bustles around the room tidying up, getting rid of the talcum, the brush, flannel etc.* DOUG *watches her, a bone china tea cup and saucer in his hand. He is absentmindedly dunking a biscuit.*

WINNIE: I wish you wouldn't wander around with that cup in your hands, Doug.

DOUG: What do you want me to do with it? I tried balancing it on my head, but I can't see where I'm dunking my biscuits.

WINNIE: And that's a disgusting habit, anyway.

DOUG: I know. It gives you crumbs down your parting. Shall I give Tom a drink before I go?

WINNIE: It's too hot.

DOUG: I'm in no hurry.

WINNIE: I'll do it.

DOUG: Don't forget.

WINNIE: I don't forget. I never forget. What do you mean? *(She goes to a low table and moves a vase of flowers so that they are exactly central.)*

DOUG: Nothing. Another of those bloody pamphlets this morning. Wasting rate payer's money.

WINNIE: What was it this time?

DOUG: Some damn thing. *(He sees that she isn't watching and moves the flowers a couple of inches so that* TOM *can see them from his chair.)* Holidays or days out or social evenings. I don't know. Didn't read it. They're all the same.

WINNIE: You'd think that they'd have realized by now. There must be people who need them, people who'd be glad of being remembered. People who *need* them.

DOUG: We're on the list, see. Once you're on the list . . . remember how *The Reader's Digest* was calling my dad a most valued customer when he'd been dead twelve years? They get your name and that's it.

WINNIE: Oh, yes, *them.* But you'd think that social services had more sense.

DOUG: Charities. Half the time it's charities. There's a charity for everything these days. And self-help groups.

WINNIE: *(going to* TOM, *as if to lift up the rug around his legs)* Did you do his bag?

DOUG: I'll do it. My job. Leave it alone.

WINNIE: *(she lifts the rug anyway and then drops it back down)* There's hardly anything in it.

DOUG: I know. Self-help groups and discussion groups, support groups, associations. You can't get a boil on your bum without half a dozen committees standing around you, looking at it, and giving out information sheets.

WINNIE: *(stopping and enjoying the joke)* And people knocking on the door, wanting to tell you how big their boils are!

DOUG: ''Giving mutual support'' they call it.

WINNIE: Crying on each other's shoulders, more like.

DOUG: That's how minorities are born, Winnie. ''Civil rights for bum boils!'' ''Positive discrimination for bum boils!''

WINNIE: ''Holidays by the sea for bum boils!''

(They are silent for a split second.)

DOUG: Ah, yes, holidays.

WINNIE: *(bustling on)* I wish they'd leave us alone, I do. We're alright aren't we? What does Tom want with a holiday?

DOUG: Nothing. I'd better be off. Meals on wheels don't wait, and you know what the oldies are like if the stuff isn't actually on the boil.

WINNIE: Go carefully then.

DOUG: Always. *(He goes to* TOM *and looks at him fondly.)*

WINNIE: And wear your jacket.

DOUG: Be a good boy for Mum, eh? *(He gives* TOM's *cheek a little pat. It's too sharp and* TOM *jerks.* DOUG *touches him, gentler.)*

WINNIE: *(watching this small exchange but then turning away)* I'll get his drink.

*(*DOUG *and* WINNIE *exit.* WINNIE *returns almost immediately with the drink in a baby cup. She sits to the side of him, shakes out a pink bib, puts it around his neck. Notices the flowers and moves them back so that they are central again but out of* TOM's *vision. She smiles into his face.)*

WINNIE: There! That's better, isn't it? Now. A nice cup of tea.

SCENE THREE

STEPHEN *is working a stencilling machine, watching the copies as they come off, the strenuous movement of turning the handle mirroring his thoughts. We can hear the buzz of conversation, typewriters, laughter and phones ringing in the distance.*

STEPHEN: I find myself thinking about him all the time. In a meeting about someone else, some other problem, thinking about him. I look at strangers in the street, and I think of Tom. I go to a case meeting for someone entirely different. Different person. Different needs. Different . . . . and my thoughts are all on Tom. Wondering what he's doing. What they're doing. They always put his chair in the same place. Facing the same way, seeing the same things, looking at the same patch of carpet. The same strip of wallpaper. Whenever I visit, there he is. I turned his chair around once, and showed him the open window, the curtains fluttering in the summer breeze, but she came back in, his mother, and with a deft flick of the wrist she had him back to where he always sits. A quick flick. Like that.

WINNIE: *(sitting by* TOM, *still, smiling over at* STEPHEN) The sun. The sun hurts his eyes.

STEPHEN: "The garden," I said, "so that he can see the garden."

WINNIE: "Goodness Stephen!"

STEPHEN: In that bright, cheerful, patent leather, Marks and Spencers voice, ''He can't see everything.'' *Picking up his foot, which had dared to slip sideways, and slamming it down on the metal rest. (Slam.)*

WINNIE: Goodness me, dear. There's bound to be something he can't see. *(She exits.)*

STEPHEN: Only the world. Only the whole damn world.

SCENE FOUR

Tom's *Room.* TOM *is dozing in his chair. Room pristine as before. We hear the front door open and* DOUG *enters the room, goes to stand over* TOM *who is awake now, grinning at him, mild spasm.*

DOUG: *(calling)* I'm back! *(He touches* TOM's *hand and then takes off his outdoor clothes.)*

WINNIE: *(off)* I'm just mincing Tom's dinner.

DOUG: *(hanging his clothes up in the hall)* Any visitors? *(He comes back into the room and calls again.)* Any visitors?

WINNIE: *(entering)* Of course not.

DOUG: I thought that Stephen bloke might call today.

WINNIE: *(putting a bib on* TOM*)* No.

DOUG: He was a nice enough young man. *(Takes the dinner, to* WINNIE's *mild annoyance, pulls a chair up and sits down to feed* TOM.*)* 'Course, they all are. Nice and young.

WINNIE: *(mischief making)* I had the feeling that he was criticizing.

DOUG: Criticizing?

WINNIE: Looking. And thinking. You know. And when he went he said he hoped he'd see a lot of us.

DOUG: They've all said that, love. I'll believe it when I see it. There was that bloke, oh, a couple of years back . . . . we were going to see him every day, remember?

WINNIE: Oh, yes, that psychologist. What was his name?

DOUG: He was going to work bloody miracles. Come here every day, assess this, assess that, measure every damn thing. How often did we see him?

WINNIE: I think he got disheartened: that great pile of forms to fill in, thousands of little ticks—

DOUG: In thousands of little boxes!

WINNIE: And Tom couldn't do anything. Tom couldn't do a single thing. *(To her this is a simple statement, to* DOUG *it is a cause of terrible sadness which, his back to her, she doesn't see.)* I think he lost heart.

DOUG: They all lose heart, love. Same as this one will, this Stephen.

WINNIE: *(indignant)* He said he couldn't see the garden.

DOUG: Stephen did?

WINNIE: I came in and he'd moved Tom's chair.

DOUG: *(pulling a small face at* TOM*)* Well, never mind.

WINNIE: And his eyes. They look him up and down. Stephen looks up and down Tom and seems to take everything in. You can see him thinking.

DOUG: *(more interested, less patronizing)* What do you mean?

WINNIE: I came in from the kitchen and that Stephen was holding Tom's hand, sort of rubbing it with his thumb, and then he pushed the sleeve up and looked at his wrist.

DOUG: *(stopping abruptly)* He's had enough. What did he say?

WINNIE: *(looking at the food remaining)* Who?

DOUG: Stephen! What did he say?

WINNIE: When?

DOUG: When he was stroking Tom's hand—what did he say?

WINNIE: *(turning to go, taking the food dish)* Nothing. He didn't say anything. I'll put our lunch in the sitting room.

DOUG: I'll be right there. Tom's just about ready for a little nap. Aren't you Tom?

(He's taking TOM's *bib off wiping* TOM's *mouth with a damp flannel, with restrained violence.)* Aren't you, Tom? Ready for a "little nap." *(Struggling to keep his temper.)* These bloody social workers. What do you make of them, Tom? Do you like them, Tom? These bloody social workers?

(Slamming about now, pushing TOM's *footrests up, putting* TOM's *feet on a stool, placing a cushion under them, all caring tasks performed angrily.)*

At the end of the day, though, where are they? At meal times where are they? These precious bloody experts, eh? Where's precious bloody Stephen now? Now, when you need feeding. Now, when you need changing? God! *(Face thrust into* TOM's.) You stink! I said where is he now? Now that you're stinking? Bloody stinking? Don't look at me! Don't you look at me! *(Takes* TOM's *head and pushes it to one side so that* TOM's *looking at the wall.)* Don't you fucking look at me!

(Aghast at his own behavior but unable to stop, DOUG *strides to the back of the chair, trying to leave* TOM *alone. Unable to, he shoves his face up against* TOM's *again.)* Useless! Useless! Senseless, fucking useless!

(During the last three words WINNIE *has come to the doorway.)*

WINNIE: *(brightly, smoothly)* Come on, you boys. Our sandwiches are curling up and dying. And I thought Tom was going to have a nap? *(Drawing the curtains.)* I don't know, I really don't.

DOUG: *(going)* I'll wash my hands.

WINNIE: Well, don't be long. *(She takes a long look at* TOM *on the way out.)*

*(*TOM *sits alone, crying.)*

SCENE FIVE

STEPHEN *is standing, looking at* TOM *in the distance.*

STEPHEN: The first time I saw him, with his hair about his face, like sea weed on a drowned man, and his John The Baptist eyes, he caught me. Caught me with the eyes and the face of a prophet. They were getting him out of the bath, his long thin body, Christ's body, taken down from the cross and washed for burial. His Mother, like Mary Magdalen, no idea who the hell he was, saint or sinner, Messiah or man. And his father, shirt sleeves rolled up, red faced and sweating in the steam. Nightmare. Just another client. Nightmare.

S C E N E   S I X

First Discord ending. All are standing at a distance from TOM.

CHARLIE: Mad as a hatter. Daft as a brush. Silent as the grave.

WINNIE: We like to keep him nice. We'll always keep him nice.

DOUG: For ever and ever.

CHARLIE: Amen.

WINNIE: He's not in bed! *(She goes up to* TOM.) He's not in bed and the news half done. The weather soon.

DOUG: After the news.

WINNIE: But he's not in bed!

DOUG: Just for tonight. He's alright. Just for tonight. (WINNIE *takes hold of* TOM's *legs, waits for* DOUG *to take his body. Unwillingly, he does. They lift him onto the bed.)*

CHARLIE: Oh, listen to me. He's trying to reach.

WINNIE: Not a good idea, Doug.

CHARLIE: He's doing.

WINNIE: Bed sores.

DOUG: Just for tonight, no soap and flannel and one two three . . .

TOM: Sore bones.

(They stop for an instant, then carry on.)

DOUG: Just for tonight?

WINNIE: First time ever. Thin end of the wedge. Thin end of the slippery slope, I say.

DOUG: After twenty four years—a breather.

STEPHEN: I thought they'd jump at the chance. A week away from it all. Not much, but still, a breather. I thought they'd grab at it, but she said.

WINNIE: We'd worry about him so much.

STEPHEN: And he gave his tight little smile—

DOUG: Thanks all the same.

STEPHEN: And my words hang in the air between us all, "Well, if you change your minds . . . have second thoughts," and she smooths an imagined crease in the curtains.

STEPHEN, WINNIE: *(together)* "Oh, no, we'd miss Tom."

(Pause.)

STEPHEN: *(small shrug)* Helpless.

SCENE SEVEN

TOM'S *Room. Daytime. We hear the front door open, slam back on its hinges.*

CHARLIE: *(Off)* Yoo hoo! It's me! (TOM *crows with delight, slight spasm. We hear a bag being dumped.)*

DOUG: Charlotte? Winnie it's Charlotte!

CHARLIE: Hang on . . . (CHARLIE *enters like a whirlwind. Runs straight to the bed.)*

Tom! Tom! Oh Tommy Tom. Here I am!

(TOM *is screaming with laughter now. She takes his hands and kisses his face, gives him a little shake, laughing back.)*

Hello, you bugger. Here I am. Sort you out! Sort you out once and for all. Shake you up. *(He screams again. She hugs him.)* Oh, it's good to see you. *(Singing and playing with* TOM.) It is good to see you. Missed me? Missed me? Shall I sing? Shall I? *(Sings.)* "Oh, soldier, soldier, will you marry me, With your musket fife and drum?" "Oh, no, sweet maid, I canna marry you, For I have no clothes to put on." So, off she went, to her Grandfather's chest, And she brought him some clothes of the very very best And the soldier put them on. OOOOOh, soldier, soldier . . . will you marry me? *(She turns it into a mix-type song, repeating it, jumping up and "moon walking.")* Will you. Will you. Will you. Oh, soldier. Soldier. Marry me? Marry me? Marry me? *(He is laughing and now she joins in, falling down to rock him in time to her song.)* With your musket fife and drum? Oh, no, sweet maid, I cannot marry you, for I have a wife of my own. There. That was a lullaby. Darling Tom. As handsome as ever. Have you missed me? I bet you have. I bet, if you could manage it, you'd give me such a hug and you'd say, "Charlotte! God, I have missed you!" Wouldn't you?

STEPHEN: I want to get him away from there.

CHARLIE: Oh, I want to get you away.

STEPHEN: Out into the world.

CHARLIE: Wheel you along the road.

STEPHEN: Let him feel the rain on his cheeks.

CHARLIE: Take you to a disco.

STEPHEN: Lie him on the beach.

CHARLIE: So you can smell the sweat and the stale beer.

STEPHEN: So that he feels the wind in his hair and the salt on his lips. I do.

CHARLIE: I do. *(She hugs Tom again.)*

STEPHEN: But it's easier to lie awake at night worrying about that tight little home than it is to visit it. I sense something. And it stops me. It stops me in mid breath. I can't go in and snatch him out. And I can't stand by and mutely observe. And I can't get him out of my mind.

(DOUG *enters with* TOM's *meal on a tray.)*

DOUG: Off the bed, Charlotte. I wish you wouldn't do that.

CHARLIE: Me? Do what, Dad?

DOUG: You know full well what. We've told you often enough. Mauling him.

CHARLIE: Mauling him? Is that what I was doing? I was just saying hello, after being away for weeks and weeks.

DOUG: Sisters don't greet their brothers like that.

CHARLIE: Oh, God.

DOUG: It's not healthy.

CHARLIE: Bearing in mind that he's totally immobile, spastic, epileptic, and incontinent—oh, and aphasic—that's bloody funny, Dad. Really pertinent, that is.

DOUG: You know what I mean.

CHARLIE: Yes. I know what you mean. I'll go and unpack.

DOUG: How does he look, Tom?

CHARLIE: Frail. Frailer than I'd remembered.

DOUG: He's been poorly. He chokes a lot now, and he's losing weight. At night he shouts. Suddenly yells.

CHARLIE: Why?

DOUG: Who knows? With Tom, who knows? I think he's weary of it all.

CHARLIE: And you, Dad, are you weary of it all?

DOUG: What?

CHARLIE: What do you think of retirement?

DOUG: I don't think of it, love. I just live it. It's not so bad. I've got my greenhouse.

CHARLIE: And what about all your plans? The holidays in Scotland, the evenings out, the chess club? You were going to be so busy.

DOUG: We can't leave Tom. I thought that we could, but, when it comes down to it—we can't.

CHARLIE: Dad, the social services said that they'd take care of him, didn't they? Just an evening or two a week.

DOUG: I can't hand him over to a "they." I thought you were going to unpack? (CHARLIE *starts to go out but hesitates.*)

CHARLIE: Are you undressing him?

DOUG: We always undress him. You know that. Would you like to go to bed in all your clothes?

CHARLIE: I just thought. You always had him ready for bed so early.

DOUG: Yes, well, I always went to bed so early too, didn't I? So I could get up again at five o'clock to get Tom washed and dressed and in his chair before I left for work at seven o'clock. But I don't have to do that any more, do I? So now I sit with your Mother and watch TV for a while, OK? And after tea I lie him on his bed so that he gets a rest from that damn chair. And at supper time we heave him onto his bean bag so that he gets another little change. OK? Is that alright?

CHARLIE: Dad! Don't be so bloody touchy! I mean, I'm glad he stays up a bit longer . . . I only wondered, that's all—and I get a bloody lecture! (*She stomps off.*)

DOUG: When she was born, Tom, your sister, you were thirteen months old. We'd just been told about you, your Mother and me. Well, told as much as they knew, which wasn't much. Your Mother couldn't stop crying. She held Charlotte in her arms and cried for you. And I was angry. So blood angry.

We couldn't welcome her for grieving for you, and we couldn't grieve for
you for welcoming her. Guilty on all bloody counts. I took you in to see
her on the day that she was born. You weren't much bigger than her. It gave
us a shock to see that. We laid you side by side on the bed. Introduced you.
Same hair. Same features. Same perfect little hands. And I thought my heart
would break. I thought my heart would break, Tom. Like a sword had been
plunged through me. Agony. Agony so bad I wanted to scream and cry out
and clutch myself together, clutch myself together. Scream and cry and shit.
It clawed at my stomach and twisted my bowels, so that I wanted to shit.
Grabbed my bowels, wrenched the heart from me, wrung me out. There's
no pain like that, Tom, not in this world. To look at the two of you, lying
there, there's no grief like that. It's not to be endured. Even now, it's not
to be endured, even now. And it doesn't go away. Ever. Like a sword had
been plunged through me. ''And a sword will pierce your own heart, too.''
That's the bloody word you sent to your handmaiden. That's the message
you sent to Mary. A sword to pierce her heart. And mine! God! At least she
saw her son ''grow in stature.'' She saw him walk, she saw him run, she
heard him talk. Words from his lips. I'd let them crucify you for that, Tom.
Oh, God, I'd let them crucify you for that. I'd drive the nails in for that!
For one bloody word. Here! Give me the hammer, the nails, the cross! Give
them to me! I'll do it! I'll bloody do it! For just one word, I'll crucify my
Tom. I offer him to you. For just one word. I offer him. My son. My son.
My beloved son. My beloved son. *(He rests exhausted.* TOM *smiles uncertainly.)*

SCENE EIGHT

DOUG *slowly recovers and feeds* TOM *his meal, spooning in the food with
great patience, his back to* CHARLIE *who has entered and is slouched in*
TOM'S *wheelchair, rocking it. She puts her foot up on a piece of furniture,
watching* DOUG *critically. Now and then* DOUG *gives* TOM *a small smile, a
moue.*

CHARLIE: Why don't you ever talk to him?

DOUG: What sort of a question is that?

CHARLIE: A simple one. You never talk to him.

DOUG: If you say so.

CHARLIE: Oh, God!

DOUG: If you say so, it must be true mustn't it? Who could deny the truth of your words? Fresh from Olympus. *(Seeing her foot.)* Foot down.

CHARLIE: *(automatically obeying)* If he was a dog you'd talk to him.

DOUG: *(tidying the tray, the meal finished)* If he was a dog he'd feed himself. If he was a dog he'd go for walks. If he was a dog he'd bring me the bloody paper. As it is . . . it doesn't matter.

CHARLIE: It does matter. It matters that you think less of my brother than you would of a dog—

DOUG: I didn't say that.

CHARLIE: I heard that.

DOUG: I can't help what you heard. *(He starts to lift the rug on* TOM's *leg but then stops.)* If you could just pop out for a moment?

CHARLIE: Oh, God, here we go. The ritual of the bag. For God's sake, Dad, it's not incestuous for me to see my brother's piss.

DOUG: Charlotte!

CHARLIE: Sor-ry. Ur-ine. But we both know you're going to empty this bag. I've done it thousands of times. Me and Mum.

DOUG: Thank you. Thank you for that reminder, Charlotte. That "In case you've forgotten you senile old fool." Do you think that I don't know? Do you think that I don't know how often you and your Mother have tipped away his urine? I courted her once, to the sounds of Glenn Miller. I promised her the earth, to love and to cherish, to hold and to protect and to love, to the sounds of Glenn Miller. Do you really think that I don't know how many times she's tipped away my son's urine? Alright! here it is! *(He lifts the rug, and brandishes the catheter bag.)* A bag full of piss, as you bright, bloody young things would say. The total achievement of Tom's young life. The end result of every day and night, every day and night for the last twenty four years. Not much, some would say, but you can't fault his consistency. Can't do a lot, our Tom, but by God you should see him pee! We could get up coach parties! Fantastic peeing record holder! Pees all day long in the privacy of his own room! Steadily, stealthily, while you all think he's wasting his time, he's secretly peeing! Mind you, he's not the man he was. Time was, he didn't have a piss bag. Time was, you'd go into him at ten-to-six in the morning, and you'd find the bell all nice and warm and dry and you'd offer up a silent prayer, and creep over for the bottle, and creep back again, and try to carefully, ever so carefully, ease the bottle in, ease him into the bottle, and then . . . just as it was nearly . . . ever so nearly . . . there, he'd open his eyes, look straight at you, and let out a bloody bucketful. All over the place. Bloody gallons. But now, of course, he has a bag. And on dull days, when you're away at university, learning how bloody stupid the rest of us are, we sit around in here watching him pee.

(Pause.)

CHARLIE: I'm sorry.

DOUG: I talk to him. Sometimes. After twenty four years there's not a hell of a lot I haven't already told him. There's not a hell of a lot I can do for him, either, but at least I can give him some degree of dignity, privacy. At least I can do that much. Oh, I can't give him the sort of love you give him. I can't discount the years, the deadly routine, the tons of mush I've spooned into him, the tons of muck I've coaxed out, the rivers of urine I've tipped away. I can't discount it. All the weight and warmth and stink of it for all his life.

So be a good girl and humor your old Dad, would you? Bugger off while I empty this bloody bag. (CHARLIE *goes slowly, thoughtfully, while* DOUG *empties the bag into a plastic jug.* TOM *gurgles at him.*)

DOUG:*(smiling at* TOM*)* *"Pissssssssssss."*

(At the end of the hiss he pulls a face at TOM. TOM *laughs but almost immediately his eyelids droop.* DOUG *looks at him for a moment, stoney faced.)*

SCENE NINE
Second Discord (Charlie's)

Everything DOUG *and* WINNIE *say here is a cliche, a phrase* TOM'S *heard perhaps a hundred times. Everything* CHARLIE *says has been whispered to him alone. And so* DOUG *and* WINNIE *speak out while* CHARLIE *tends to speak quietly, just to* TOM *until* DOUG *and* WINNIE *are drawn into it.*

CHARLIE: At night I dream of him. In the day I think of him. Little things remind me.

WINNIE: That's nice.

CHARLIE: Little things. The smell of a soap. The curve of a man's chin. Hairs on an arm.

WINNIE: It's nice to think of him.

CHARLIE: The man smell of a young man.

DOUG: I choose not to hear that.

CHARLIE: The man smell of a young man. I choose to say it.

WINNIE: Goodness.

CHARLIE: Harmless things. The smell of soap.

TOM: Charlie. *(They don't hear.)*

CHARLIE: And I can't stop the thoughts.

DOUG: Charlotte!

WINNIE: Least said soonest mended.

DOUG: Best left unsaid.

WINNIE: Such a pretty name, Charlotte.

TOM: Charlie. Charlie chatterbox. *(They don't hear.)*

CHARLIE: The curve of a man's chin, hairs on an arm, the smell of a man, the smell of his soap, the tang of his sweat.

DOUG: Charlie.

CHARLIE: Reminders. The feel of him. The flesh of him.

WINNIE: We chose that name because it was so sweet. Charlotte.

CHARLIE: And the man who fills me, prods me, sweats on me, the man who holds me, breathes beer on me, pierces me, lies on me too long and whose skin melts onto mine in cold and sweaty union, becomes Tom.

DOUG: You know I don't like you doing that.

CHARLIE: When he's lain on me too long, and the pleasures has been shot, and our bodies are replete with the sameness of it all, I feel as if I have no strength, no breath, and as if the body crushing mine is Tom. (DOUG *has been combing* TOM's *hair and lets* TOM's *head fall back.)*

DOUG: You know I don't like you doing that.

CHARLIE: *(close)* As if it is Tom who saps all my strength.

WINNIE: A nasty dream.

TOM: My dream.

CHARLIE: A harmless dream.

DOUG: Off the bed, Charlotte.

TOM: Into bed, Charlotte.

WINNIE: I thought we'd have such fun.

CHARLIE: I only want to comfort him.

DOUG: Or yourself.

CHARLIE: Him.

WINNIE: He's alright.

CHARLIE: I love him.

DOUG: Or yourself.

CHARLIE: Him. I bring the world to him.

WINNIE: Your world.

DOUG: Not our world.

CHARLIE: A peck of dirt—

DOUG: Before he dies?

WINNIE: He's alright.

CHARLIE: But me . . .

WINNIE: She was always fond of him.

CHARLIE: I'm not alright.

DOUG: Bright.

WINNIE: We always said so.

CHARLIE: I'm not alright.

TOM: Poor Charlie. Poor Tom. Poor. Piteous.

CHARLIE: Listen. You have to listen.

DOUG: I choose not to hear that.

WINNIE: I choose not to.

CHARLIE: *(a cry)* Tom.

TOM: *(a shout)* Charlie.

(WINNIE *and* DOUG *exit.*)

SCENE TEN

CHARLIE *is looking down on* TOM *who is on his bean bag.*

CHARLIE: Right, Tom. Time for an update. Update time. Star date . . .
Where did we get to? I told you about the river . . . and the bridges . . .
now, let's see. People. Where will I start? Well, there's Sheila. She's, oh,
I dunno, about thirty-five, forty . . . old anyway. She wears black overalls
from Millets and she drinks real ale and cries into it because none of the
men fancy her! Then she gets pissed and she sits in the corner glaring at the
men and muttering "castrate the bastards!" and "Ireland for the Irish" and
all that sort of stuff. Anyway, she's sex mad. Permanently randy. Bernadette
says she had a transplant and they made a terrible mistake and gave her fully
functioning monkey glands. You'd like Bernadette. She's only there at
weekends. She's a Catholic. She works in a steakhouse and she's in love
with this horrible old married man. Manager of a cut price supermarket.
Really gross. To add insult to injury she turned vegan last week. Can you
believe it, Tom? A sinning Catholic vegan serving up bloody steaks all day
long. My God, it's pure Edna O'Brien! And the town! Oh, God, I wish I
could show you the town, Tommy. I walk around it, saying to myself,
"You're here, Charlie. Here. Look. Look and remember." I don't want to
forget any of it, not one bit of it! And the gigs! Oh, no, I was telling you
about the town. Remind me about the bands, eh? This is me, going out to
a lecture. Slam the door, scramble past the bikes in the passage, bloody
things. Down the steps, one, two, three. There! And the street's so narrow—
a back street in any other town, and God! There's loads of us, some in a
rush, some strolling, great gangs all talking together, no one looking where
they're going, like some big noisy crab, sideways. Some riding bikes. Millions riding bikes! Here comes one now—looking back over his shoulder
calling to someone—he hasn't seen me, damn man! *(She flattens herself
against an imaginary wall and flops down with relief at his passing.)* Phew!
He's gone! *(She laughs and caresses* TOM's *face, then grows suddenly quiet,
reflective.)* And it's all so lonely. I sit in my room and I think of you, Tom.
I think of you and wonder about you. It's nothing like I'd imagined. And I
can't tell Dad, can I? You're doing it for all of us, Charlotte, consolation
for how things are. Consolation prize. Oh, Tom. Twenty four years old and
stuck here with Mum and Dad. You're looking at me, Tom and I haven't a
bloody clue what you're making of all this. If you're making anything of it
at all. Are you with me, Tom? Are you? Talcumed and combed and laid to
rest on a clean and comfy bean bag . . . *(He laughs apparently involuntarily
as a baby laughs with wind, and this suddenly angers her.)* Do you give a
damn what happens to me? Do you? Wasting my time. Wasting my time,

because you don't care, do you? You don't give a damn if I'm here or there or dead or bloody gone, do you? I'm sorry, Tom. I'm sorry. You do care, don't you? You do listen. It's our bargain, isn't it? If I talk, you'll listen. It's them that make me like this. Them with all their "Off the bed, Charlotte!" and "You know we don't like you doing that," so prissy and shut-off and we-can-cope-ish. And they want to shut you off, too. As if you're some timid little baby needing total protection in a sealed bloody unit. Well, you're not. You're a man. A fully grown, fully blown man. Look at your beard, Tom. Feel it! *(She puts his hand to his chin.)* If it wasn't for some senseless accident of, God knows what, a long labor, sloppy nurses at a slow delivery—God knows, you'd be down at the pub right now, out there with the rest of them—fornicating with the best of them. And you're in working order, Tom, I know that, too. See, there are no secrets between us. Remember how I helped Mum to get you up, sometimes? *(She nuzzles into* TOM'S *neck and puts her arm around him. After a short time* CHARLIE *draws back from* TOM, *looking down at him, loving him. She slowly takes off her shirt, watching him all the time. His head jerks away and she slowly, gently, moves into his eye line again.)*

STEPHEN: When you walk up the path you're struck by the order of it all. Regimental. I can just see her now, slaughtering each weed as it pokes its little head above the ground. Him, relentlessly advancing on the ranks of grass with his grinding ravenous mower. "We like to keep busy." A small and shining house. A credit to them all. Enough to make you weep.

STEPHEN *draws nearer to the area where* TOM *and* CHARLIE *lie.* CHARLIE *is astride* TOM *now, bare breasted, trying to make him look at her. Wherever she moves he twists away, In the start of a fit. She doesn't recognize the fit, so involved with her own emotions. She takes his stiff, splayed hand and places it on her breast.* TOM *convulses, she scrambles off him, automatically moves something out of his way, and then she sits, watching.* TOM *is groaning now as he thrashes around. She starts to cry and pulls her shirt on, all the time watching* TOM. *Soon she is openly weeping. After a moment she goes to* TOM *and wipes his mouth.* STEPHEN *appears behind her.)*

STEPHEN: Erm.

(Charlie spins around and almost slips.)

STEPHEN: I'm sorry.

CHARLIE: *(afraid)* What do you want?

STEPHEN: Stephen. Tom's social worker. I'm sorry, I rang twice. Then, when I saw the back door standing open like that, I wondered if anything was wrong.

CHARLIE: Wrong? Why should anything be wrong?

STEPHEN: Look. Can we start again? I'm Steve. Tom's social worker. Well, the family's. And you must be Charlotte.

CHARLIE: I must be, mustn't I?

STEPHEN: Are you alright?

CHARLIE: I've been having a bit of a weep, actually. Put it down to hormones.

STEPHEN: We all need a weep from time to time.

CHARLIE: Do we? *(Relenting.)* You've missed Mum and Dad. They've gone out shopping. As soon as I walk in one door they grab their bags and run out of the other. Only chance they get to go together. Have a walk around and a cup of coffee like any other couple.

STEPHEN: Yes. *(He goes to crouch down by* TOM.*)* Hello, Tom. It's Stephen.

*(*TOM *snores gently.)*

STEPHEN: *(louder)* It's Stephen, here to help you. *(To* CHARLIE.*)* How is he?

CHARLIE: I don't know.

STEPHEN: Hello, Tom. Hello.

CHARLIE: They shouldn't be long.

STEPHEN: *(still looking at* TOM*)* Right.

CHARLIE: Sit down.

STEPHEN: *(not doing so)* Do you see any changes in him?

CHARLIE: Changes?

STEPHEN: Going away as you do. You know.

CHARLIE: Should I? He's a bit thinner. More frail. *(Pause.* STEPHEN *is still gazing at* TOM.*)* I wish you'd sit down.

STEPHEN: I'm very glad to have this chance to talk to you, actually. Do you mind if we talk? About the family?

CHARLIE: If we must.

STEPHEN: It's just that I don't seem to be getting anywhere with your parents.

CHARLIE: No?

STEPHEN: And they seem edgy.

CHARLIE: Do they?

STEPHEN: More worried, tense . . . even than they usually are. From what I've seen of them, that is.

CHARLIE: *(bored)* Yes.

STEPHEN: Please. Charlotte.

CHARLIE: Charlie. I'm more than Tom's sister, you know. I like to be called Charlie.

STEPHEN: I'm sorry. I didn't know.

CHARLIE: Not in your files, that bit? I do have a personality all of my own.

STEPHEN: Of course.

CHARLIE: There's no "of course" about it.

STEPHEN: God, this is so hard.

CHARLIE: Yes. Isn't it?

STEPHEN: *(plunging in)* I'm worried about Tom.

CHARLIE: *(her animosity begins to ease)* Worried?

STEPHEN: Concerned.

CHARLIE: Go on.

STEPHEN: I don't quite know how to put it into words. Tom. He's got something special. Some power. There's something powerful about him. Compelling. As if there's a real, hard intelligence there. I really feel as if there's a real intelligence there.

CHARLIE: And? It doesn't do him much good saying that. Or anyone else.

STEPHEN: It's a start.

CHARLIE: Don't fool yourself. A start to nothing. Others have seen what you've seen. Me, for a start. Then there was the district nurse, and some sort of education official, and when he got pneumonia one year there was the whole bloody staff of the medical ward. All charmed by Tom Davies.

There's been all sorts. *(She takes* TOM'S *leg and waves a foot at* STEPHEN.) Wave a leg at him, Tom. Yoo hoo! Here we are! Go to the back of the queue. You've actually joined rather a large body of opinion.

STEPHEN: But they treat him as if . . .

CHARLIE: And how should they treat him?

STEPHEN: I don't know.

CHARLIE: What exactly do you want them to do?

STEPHEN: I just don't know but . . . Widen his experience, change their attitudes—

CHARLIE: Sounds good. Be specific. *(Looks at* TOM, *still snoring.)* Tell him to be specific, Tom.

STEPHEN: That would need discussion.

CHARLIE: "Discussion"—What, as in "options" and "alternatives"?

STEPHEN: They won't discuss anything.

CHARLIE: They pride themselves on managing. Standing on their own two feet. Four feet.

STEPHEN: Is it so terrible, accepting a helping hand?

CHARLIE: You don't have to convert me. I'm just the piggy in the middle, I am. Look, twenty four years ago there was no help to be had. They've got into the habit.

STEPHEN: There's help now, if they'll take it.

CHARLIE: *(over him)* Just a cup of tea in the ward sister's office and the advice to put the baby into a home.

STEPHEN: *(desperately trying to get through to her)* I'm afraid that they'll leave it too late. I saw marks on his wrist.

CHARLIE: What?

STEPHEN: Marks. On his wrist. Eight days ago. (CHARLIE *goes to look.)* Oh, they'll have faded by now.

CHARLIE: What sort of marks?

STEPHEN: I don't know! Marks where they lifted him or held him in the bath or—I don't know. Perhaps he marks easily.

CHARLIE: I should have locked the back door. You could have been anyone. Gave me a start.

STEPHEN: Does he mark easily? *(She turns away and begins to fiddle with* TOM.) Charlie? Please?

CHARLIE: No. No. He doesn't mark easily.

STEPHEN: Thank you.

CHARLIE: Don't thank me!

STEPHEN: It's just another piece in the jigsaw. I only want to help them. *(Standing up.)* I'll try to get back tonight.

CHARLIE: They think the world of him.

STEPHEN: I know that. I only want to make things better.

CHARLIE: No one ever does.

STEPHEN: *(bending down to* TOM*)* I'll be back, Tom. I will. Look at me, Tom. *(He takes* TOM's *head gently in his hands).* Look at me.

CHARLIE: Leave him alone!

STEPHEN: I only—

CHARLIE: Don't move his head like that. Your will ruling his. Don't do it.

STEPHEN: I'm sorry.

CHARLIE: Everyone making him look at things. Manhandling him.

STEPHEN: Charlie . . .

CHARLIE: Mauling him. Just because you have the power.

STEPHEN: Mauling? I was only saying goodbye.

CHARLIE: You don't say "goodbye" like that. You don't grab my head and make me look at you. Perhaps he doesn't want to look at you! To be your flawed mirror! An image of what you could have been, an image of what he should have been! Perhaps that hurts him.

STEPHEN: *(exiting)* I'm sorry.

CHARLIE: *(fighting tears)* It hurts me.

SCENE ELEVEN

Later. DOUG *enters and he and* CHARLIE *tend to* TOM.

CHARLIE: Dad . . . Dad, Mum said something on the phone last week, about you moving.

DOUG: Moving?

CHARLIE: Said you'd looked at some of the new houses over at Lawton.

DOUG: She looked. I went along with her.

CHARLIE: They any good?

DOUG: Lovely, For gerbils.

CHARLIE: You're not going, then?

DOUG: Your Mum gets a bit fed up from time to time. She sees these lovely new show houses, and they've all got shining kitchens and brand new carpets, and there are no wheelchairs and cramped back rooms, and no commodes, and she just gets a bit . . . unsettled.

CHARLIE: Poor Mum.

DOUG: We're alright, Charlie. We don't want you worrying about us. Or about Tom. He's our responsibility.

CHARLIE: And my brother. But I wasn't worried about him.

DOUG: Your Mother mentioned the vague possibility to moving at some vague time in the distant future and you panicked. Panicked that Tom might get taken into care.

CHARLIE: No. No, I didn't. Not really.

DOUG: Not really. I don't want you worrying about your brother. I don't want you limiting your horizons because of him.

CHARLIE: But I don't Dad.

DOUG: When you have a handicapped child the whole family is handicapped . . . and I don't want you carrying your handicap through your whole life. Listen to me, Charlie. Tom's here. Please God, he'll always be here, well, as long as we are and as long as he lives. Leave him here. Leave him here and get on with your own life.

CHARLIE: You don't.

DOUG: I can't.

CHARLIE: Perhaps I can't either—(*As the words leave her mouth* DOUG *grabs her arm.*)

DOUG: Look at this place! Look at it! Look at it!

CHARLIE: Dad, you're hurting.

DOUG: This is where your fine feelings will get you! Right here! Do you think that I could bear to see you going down a road that ended up here? Turning into someone like me? Is this what you want for your fresh young life, is it?

CHARLIE: Dad, calm down.

DOUG: Nowhere. Nothing, Going nowhere doing nothing. I don't want that for you. A lifetime of keeping Tom nice. But this is where you'll end up, and the more interest you take in him now, the stronger a hold he'll have on you. He has the grip of a drowning man. *(Pause.)* No. Don't worry about them taking Tom away. We'll never let them do that. Don't worry about anything changing. Nothing's going to change. If they were to take him away, what would be left for us? There's only Tom for us. The Tom that is, the Tom that was, the Tom that ever will be.

CHARLIE: Oh, Daddy, what will you do?

DOUG: Do? Oh, we'll carry on for a bit. For a bit longer.

(CHARLIE *exits.* DOUG *fills a medicine funnel with bright pink medicine.)*

DOUG: Here we are, Tom. Before all that lovely tea leaves your tummy.

(He puts the funnel to TOM's *lips.* TOM *is in a small spasm.* DOUG *waits patiently for it to pass and then tries again. It is so thick that it wells up on* TOM's *lips.)* Bloody stuff. Come on, get it in, old man. Come on, for sweet Jesus sake . . . You stupid bloody . . . (He twists the funnel so that it is forced between* TOM's *lips.* TOM *appears to take it all and, just as* DOUG *is straightening up, satisfied, he spits it all back out again in a convulsive, choking cough.)*

Shit!

(Pink medicine everywhere. DOUG *mops it up, disgusted. Watches* TOM *warily.* TOM *calms down.* DOUG *starts to go but then* TOM *starts to choke.)*

Oh, God.

(He pulls TOM *off the bean bag and rolls him into his side. Panicking, he thumps between* TOM's *shoulder blades.* TOM *flails wildly, the choking turning into a whoop, his face congesting.)*

Oh, God! (WINNIE *runs in and makes as if to help.)*

DOUG: I'll do it! I'll do it!

WINNIE: Just rub between his shoulders, don't thump him.

DOUG: I know! I know! Just leave me alone . . . leave me.

(Gradually, as he thumps and rubs the choking dies down. TOM *takes a big shuddering gulp of fresh air.)*

DOUG: There. See. I could manage.

WINNIE: It's all over your sleeve. I'll get a damp cloth. (DOUG *looks at his cuff with distaste.)*

DOUG: I'll see to it. You sort him out.

(WINNIE *goes to* TOM *and with infinite patience wipes his face. She makes little soothing noises to him.)*

SCENE TWELVE
Third Discord (Winnie's)

DOUG *enters,* WINNIE *gets up and busies herself.*

DOUG: *(sitting down)* Come and sit down Winnie.

WINNIE: I cannot sit. You know that. I can't just sit.

DOUG: Then come and talk.

WINNIE: Talk?

CHARLIE: *(entering)* Come and talk, Mother.

WINNIE: What could I talk about?

CHARLIE: Your thoughts, Mum. Your thoughts at the kitchen sink.

WINNIE: It's a small house, dear. No room for thoughts. Just wheelchairs and lifting aids and beds.

DOUG: Come and sit.

WINNIE: I must be doing.

CHARLIE: Come and listen, then.

WINNIE: I cannot hear.

DOUG: Ah, come.

WINNIE: When I was a child I could not bear to share the Penny Arrow bar my mother used to buy for me.

DOUG: Come.

WINNIE: My thoughts are without words. They have no form.

CHARLIE: Blind fetus, curled up away from the light.

WINNIE: Yes. Yes . . . Suckling puppies, blind and groping.

CHARLIE: Suckling?

WINNIE: I have no will to move away.

DOUG: Then come here.

WINNIE: At my mother's house there was always a dog, and she was always called Meg.

DOUG: Come and sit beside me and let me hide my eyes against your body.

WINNIE: Always a Meg at the fireside. Two litters a year. Always the same.

DOUG: Let me nuzzle into your flattened breasts and the deep dark parts of you.

WINNIE: And I felt sorry for all those Megs when the pups were grown, but still greedy for her milk. Sharp teeth.

CHARLIE: She has no more milk to give.

WINNIE: All those Megs and all those teeth. Her back would arch as she tried to step away from their strong and angry little jaws, her tail tucked between her legs, and I thought, "How cruel. How cruel they all are."

DOUG: Only needing comfort.

CHARLIE: Bed warm bodies.

DOUG: Finding the tit.

CHARLIE: She has no more milk to give.

DOUG: I'll find her tit. Coax from it a blessing, a warm sweet blessing, take it in my mouth, her blessing.

WINNIE: She had a wooden box in the dark corner, by the range, Warm and quiet. "Shush now. Meg has her pups."

DOUG: A drop. A trickle.

WINNIE: All those generations of Megs. In her dark corner. And I thought, "How cruel they all are."

CHARLIE: How cruel you all are.

DOUG: How cruel you are.

WINNIE: How cruel.

(They exit.)

TOM: Steeephen. Steeeee phen. Stephen-here-to-help-you. At the end of the day Stephen. When I smell of fear and shit and love, Stephen. What, then? What then? Nothing. Dark nothing. And Father man. Daddy man. Father. Daddy. Man. Daddy. Daddy. Father! Bloody fucking Father! Father fucker! Fuck! *(The words strangle into a yell.)*

SCENE THIRTEEN

Night. DOUG *enters.*

DOUG: *(calling to* WINNIE, *off)* It's all right. He's just having a shout. I'll settle him down. Won't be long.

*(*TOM *is moaning, showing discomfort.* DOUG *lifts his head, settles him down again on his pillows.)*

Better? *(*TOM *moans again, screws his face up, ready for a shout.)*

Alright, alright, hang on. *(He adjusts* TOM'S *head again.)* TOM *is silent. After a moment* DOUG *turns to go but as soon as his back is turned* TOM *moans again.* DOUG *turns back, impatient now.)*

Shut up! Shut up! *(*TOM *shouts at him, battle declared.)* Shut up, you bloody bastard! Shut . . . I know what you shout. I know. After twenty four years, I bloody know. *(Glaring at each other.* TOM *gives a bark of a shout, defiant.* DOUG *lifts his head from the pillow and bangs it back down again.)*

Bloody . . . bloody . . . *(*DOUG *looks around and sees a bib, grabs it and rams it into* TOM'S *mouth.* TOM *roars all the more, his face congested, limbs flailing. The sight incenses* DOUG *even further and he digs his fingers into* TOM'S *belly. Stands back, crying now.* TOM *still moans and thrashes.* DOUG *grabs his head and pushes his face right into* TOM'S *and makes a vicious face, and an angry choking noise. He grabs a towel and beats the bed and* TOM *with it, but mostly the bed, until he is exhausted and* TOM *is crying. He drops the towel and slumps onto the bed.)* See. See what you've done to me. Christ. Oh, Christ. *(Takes the bib from* TOM'S *mouth.)* Alright, Son. All done. All done. There now. It's all done. *(After a few moments* TOM *is* *quiet, just an occasional sob.)* Round and round the garden . . . like a teddy bear . . . One step . . . Two step . . .

(Anticipating the line, TOM *takes a sharp breath in, delighted to be part of the game.* DOUG *sees the laughter welling in* TOM *and suddenly hugs him, rocking backwards and forwards, weeping. After a moment* DOUG *is calm.* TOM *is dozing.* DOUG *sits at his side, watching.)*

SCENE FOURTEEN

Day. WINNIE *enters in with a tray with a coffee for* DOUG *and a feeder cup for* TOM.

WINNIE: Look at you, you're nearly asleep.

DOUG: No I'm not. I was just telling Tom about the EEC.

WINNIE: Fat lot he wants to know about that. Or me. That Stephen phoned. He's coming over.

DOUG: Fair enough.

WINNIE: Very particular that we'd both be here.

DOUG: Well, we will be. When's he coming?

WINNIE: Before lunch. Sounded very mysterious. Will you give him his milk or will I?

DOUG: You can if you like.

WINNIE: Something about—oh, I don't know, Tom's rights to something or other.

DOUG: To what?

WINNIE: County council something or other. I had the washing machine spinning in my ear.

DOUG: Bloody hell, that's all we need isn't it? Someone telling us about Tom's rights. Where's Charlotte?

WINNIE: Out. Meeting some of her old school pals, I think.

DOUG: It would be today. Tom and me shattered. Well, I'm not taking any old nonsense from him.

WINNIE: He means no harm.

DOUG: Oh, God, I wonder what it's all about.

WINNIE: Well, it can't be anything to worry about, can it?

DOUG: No.

(WINNIE *exits.*)

SCENE FIFTEEN

STEPHEN *enters.* DOUG *greets him with a strained, polite nod.*

DOUG: All very mysterious. All this.

STEPHEN: Not really, not really mysterious. Erm . . .

DOUG: She's just coming.

STEPHEN: And Charlotte?

DOUG: Oh, no. We try to keep her uninvolved. Free.

STEPHEN: Are you alright, Mr. Davies?

DOUG: Tired. I get a bit tired.

STEPHEN: Of course.

DOUG: Not overtired, you understand. Just tired. (WINNIE *enters and sits down, expectantly.*)

WINNIE: There we are then, all present and correct.

STEPHEN: I hope I'm not holding up your lunch?

WINNIE: Not to worry.

STEPHEN: I'll try to be quick, then. The thing is, I know what sort of pressure you're both under. Well, you must be under a certain amount of strain.

DOUG: We haven't said so, have we?

STEPHEN: No. But I can see. Looking after Tom for so long. Looking after him so well.

DOUG: He's our boy.

STEPHEN: A man now. I mean, he doesn't get any easier, does he? Lighter? And you don't get any younger either.

(They don't give him any help, only regard him steadily.)

Anyway, first thing this morning I went to the County Offices on his behalf—

DOUG: His behalf?

STEPHEN: Looking at the possibilities. What's available. To help you. How we could ease the problem of—

DOUG: Problem? Who's talking about problems?

STEPHEN: Your life—Tom's life—

DOUG: Tom's life? What do you know about Tom's life?

STEPHEN: It's my job to know about Tom's life. To know something about it. And yours. To assist you—

DOUG: We don't want any "assistance."

WINNIE: Oh, Stephen, we've never asked for help. Never.

STEPHEN: I felt that I had gone as far as I could go. Here. I mean, there's only so much help you can get in this environment and—

WINNIE: We don't want strangers traipsing in and out.

STEPHEN: No. That's what I mean. I thought that if Tom had a new environment. Freeing you—*(He holds out a form which* DOUG *disregards but* WINNIE *looks at.)*

DOUG: Freeing? Freeing?

STEPHEN: I filled in this form, took it to the office. Got agreement in principle.

DOUG: Agreement? What form? What's he talking about Winnie?

STEPHEN: We can take Tom. We can—

DOUG: You young bastard!

STEPHEN: Mr. Davies!

WINNIE: Oh, Stephen, I don't think so, dear.

DOUG: Filling in forms! At County Offices! Forms with our names on, Winnie! You had no right!

STEPHEN: Tom! Tom has rights, Mr. Davies.

(DOUG *moves towards him and* WINNIE *restrains him.*) It's Tom's welfare and his rights that are my prime concern.

DOUG: You young bastard. So, you're going to tell me about Tom's rights, are you? You with your big red diary? You're going to be his advocate, are you?

STEPHEN: Couldn't we just sit back down and talk about this?

DOUG: Are you really arrogant enough to believe that anything you say could be more eloquent than the pleading that I see in my son's eyes?

STEPHEN: Pleading?

DOUG: Eyes that I've looked into for twenty four years? Do you?

STEPHEN: *(very still)* Why is he pleading, Mr. Davies?

DOUG: My god! The arrogance of the young! Eh, Winnie?

WINNIE: *(warning him, realising that* STEPHEN *is aware)* Doug . . .

DOUG: Go on, then. Make your accusations.

STEPHEN: Mr. Davies?

DOUG: Just make bloody sure that you can substantiate them . . . just be bloody sure!

WINNIE: Doug! Stop it!

DOUG: Because, if you can't find one mark on his body, if you can't come up with the marks, the proof, I'll have you! By God, I'll have you.

WINNIE: Doug! A holiday! *(She grabs the form and shakes it at him.)* That's what he's on about. A holiday! *(There is a silence.* DOUG *begins to laugh. The others look at him. They exit.)*

SCENE SIXTEEN

CHARLIE *enters and sits on the bed, plays with* TOM's *hands.*

CHARLIE: *(patting one of his hands against the other)* My mother said—I never should—Play with the gypsies—In the wood—

(WINNIE *comes to the doorway.*)

And if I did—

My mother would say—

WINNIE: There you are, Charlotte. I thought I heard the front door. Wondered where you'd got to.

CHARLIE: I'm here.

WINNIE: Well, I can see that now, can't I? I hope you're not overtiring him?

CHARLIE: Overtiring him? What exactly is he saving his strength for, then? A marathon? The entrance exam to The Royal School Of Music? Or perhaps a one man trip around the world on a bloody ripple bed?

WINNIE: That's enough.

CHARLIE: Where's Dad?

WINNIE: Lying down. That social worker came.

CHARLIE: Dad, lying down?

WINNIE: That young man upset your Father.

CHARLIE: Why? What did he say?

WINNIE: He wants us to go on holiday.

CHARLIE: My God. No wonder Dad had the vapors.

WINNIE: It wasn't very nice. It wasn't a very nice conversation. Your Father stormed off.

CHARLIE: Well, I don't know why you don't grab at the chance. You need a holiday, Mum.

WINNIE: We need nothing.

CHARLIE: I could look after Tom.

WINNIE: Ho, yes, I'm sure.

CHARLIE: They'll send someone to help with the lifting. Mum . . . I wish you'd give it a go.

WINNIE: Anyway, it's not up to me.

CHARLIE: Of course it is. He'd listen to you.

WINNIE: What, be another voice nagging in his ear? No, thank you.

CHARLIE: What is it you're so afraid of, you two? (WINNIE *reacts to this.*) You are, aren't you? You're afraid of something.

WINNIE: Don't be so silly. I wonder if your Father did his bag?

CHARLIE: Are you afraid that someone will be able to look after Tom as well as you do? Or better? Is that it? It is, isn't it? You want to be the only ones. The holy ones. Dedicated angels. Don't you? You make me sick.

WINNIE: *(stung by this)* Why are you so angry? What have we done to deserve such anger from you?

CHARLIE: You smooth the bed. *(She grabs it from under* WINNIE'S *hands and yanks the covers so that they rumple.)*

WINNIE: Charlotte!

CHARLIE: You hang flowered wallpaper in his room. You feed him mush when the doctor told you years ago to let him *chew.*

WINNIE: We don't want him to choke. We care about him—

CHARLIE: I'm angry because you leave him in here while you watch the TV in there—

WINNIE: His epilepsy!

CHARLIE: Because all he ever gets at Christmas is a pair of socks. One year a towel. A towel! All wrapped up in Santa Claus paper. But most of all I'm angry because you never, ever kiss him! I have never seen you kiss him. Hold him. In all the years—never! Oh, not now so much, not now when he's a grown man, but then. I remember kissing him. How I used to sneak into his room and slide into bed with him, and whisper to him, silly jokes and childish stories—We grew up together but I got all the kisses and he got, what? Soapy flannels? Passive exercises?

WINNIE: He needed those things!

CHARLIE: Not only! Not only! *(Softer.)* Oh, how could you *not* kiss him? His soft, sleeping body. His long, thin limbs. The curve of his eyelashes against his bed-warmed cheeks. For Christ's sake, Mum, whatever happened to him it happened inside you. That should draw you together, shouldn't it? He looks at you as if you were a God. A shining, breathtaking God. You know he does, don't you?

WINNIE: You're so good with words, madam! (CHARLIE *flounces out.* WINNIE *smooths the bedclothes, sits down with* TOM.)

WINNIE: A litany of despair, that's what she wants. Carefully fitted into the daily timetable. She doesn't look for tears and kisses and carryings on when there are sheets to be sluiced out and the smell to be expelled in great clouds of lemon aerosol. No. She's nowhere to be seen, then, when the tears are there. Each night brings with it the dull stale promise of what is waiting, and the cruel bright echoes of what could have been. You don't miss much, do you, love? You and I eat and sleep and keep our silence and they believe themselves to be the only ones to suffer. Only them. *(Slowly kisses him.)* Time enough for that when the years are over, Tom. Time enough for that when the suffering's done. Handsome boy. Lovely child. Precious darling heart.

SCENE SEVENTEEN
Last Discord (Doug's)

DOUG: Everyone gets tired, don't they?

CHARLIE: No room for me here any more.

DOUG: Don't they?

WINNIE: A perfectly natural thing.

CHARLIE: So crowded.

WINNIE: Phenomena. A perfectly natural phenomena.

DOUG: I just get so bloody tired.

WINNIE: He looks him up and down, and you can see him thinking!

DOUG: He's twenty-five next week.

WINNIE: Twenty-five!

DOUG: Quarter of a century!

CHARLIE: All dressed up and nowhere to go.

WINNIE: A round cake this year.

CHARLIE: A slice for Tom.

WINNIE: A small slice.

DOUG: A long time.

CHARLIE: On your back.

WINNIE: Ten candles, I'd thought. Round figure.

DOUG: Twenty-five to go. Piece of cake.

WINNIE: And butter icing. Pink and blue mixed. No writing, I'd thought.

DOUG: Like a nursery rhyme. Over and over.

CHARLIE: Happy birthday Tom.

DOUG: To the power of twenty-five. *(Anguish.)* Twenty-five years old!

CHARLIE: Like a red brick university.

DOUG: Pushing the razor up—

WINNIE: That bit there—

DOUG: I know.

TOM: Tom!

CHARLIE: My world.

WINNIE: Goodness, he can't see everything.

DOUG: My father died at seventy-five.

CHARLIE: A peck of dirt.

WINNIE: We like to keep him nice.

CHARLIE: Neat and tidy.

WINNIE: Safe and sound.

DOUG: Snug as a bug.

CHARLIE: Mutt and Jeff.

DOUG: My father died at seventy-five.

CHARLIE: And his father died at seventy-five.

WINNIE: Down hill all the way!

DOUG: Brakes off, then!

WINNIE: He always made me laugh.

DOUG: To the sounds of Glenn Miller.

WINNIE: Oh, what times we had.

DOUG: I just get so bloody tired at the end of the day.

WINNIE: Slippery slope I say. Thin end of the very thin wedge.

TOM: Tom!

WINNIE: Hardly a good idea, Dear.

DOUG: I'll do his drink, shall I?

CHARLIE: Empty his bag.

DOUG: My job, that.

WINNIE: Comb his hair.

CHARLIE: Flannel and soap and one . . .

DOUG: Two . . .

WINNIE: Three . . .

DOUG: Get it in, old man.

WINNIE: His blue today, or his green, what do you think, Daddy?

CHARLIE: Out there with the rest of them. Fornicating with the best of them.

WINNIE: Off the bed, Charlie.

TOM: Into bed Charlie.

WINNIE: Pass me that bib, Doug.

DOUG: Another fit.

WINNIE: A damp wipe, I think.

CHARLIE: Cotton bud.

TOM: Tom!

(Their actions mirror their words from now on, more and more frantic, nightmarish.)

CHARLIE: Like a teddy bear.

DOUG: His poor head.

CHARLIE: One step. Two step.

DOUG: Tickle under there!

CHARLIE: The curve of his chin.

WINNIE: The hollow of his neck.

CHARLIE: White talcum in a pink tub.

DOUG: *(angrily moving away from her)* How cruel you are.

WINNIE: Three times a day.

CHARLIE: After meals.

TOM: Tom!

DOUG: A sister's love—

CHARLIE: Never enough.

TOM: Tom!

CHARLIE: Tom!

TOM: Charlie!

DOUG: Wipe.

WINNIE: And wash.

DOUG: Dry.

TOM: Tom!

WINNIE: Powder. Spoon. Wipe.

DOUG: And wash.

CHARLIE: And powder.

DOUG: And spoon. Spoon the years one at a time. Twenty-five.

WINNIE: Fancy that. Twenty-five years!

CHARLIE: Doesn't time fly when you're—

WINNIE: Enjoying yourself! (DOUG *screams. The women look at him, mildly surprised, and then walk off. As the scream dies away he grabs the wheelchair and wheels* TOM *to one side of the area.*)

SCENE EIGHTEEN

The garden. DOUG *enters with a deckchair which he sets up and sits in next to* TOM.

DOUG: She'll complain. She'll tell me why she left you there and ask me why I put you here. And I'll say "Because he's light sensitive, dear." And she'll huff and puff for a bit and say something about the vitamins in sunshine, and "You could have told me, dear" and I'll say that I just have and she'll tell me not to snap. And I'll say I wasn't. And we'll have another frozen bloody pizza in frozen bloody silence. (*Quieter.*) I can't bear her petty thoughtless cruelties. Her bright and breezey tortures. Her blitheness. Her blindness. I will protect you from her. (*To himself.*) I can't bear her petty cruelties, but, by God, I will jealously guard my own.

WINNIE: *(entering)* Oh! I put him there!

DOUG: He asked me to take him in to the shade, dear.

WINNIE: I put him there to soak up some sun.

DOUG: He did, dear. Enough to take away what little sight he has.

WINNIE: The doctor said that he must have—

DOUG: His eyes burned out?

WINNIE: If you're going to be nasty then I think you'd better go for a walk.

DOUG: Not much point in going for a walk if I'm going to be nasty. If I'm going to be really nasty I might as well stay here, where I can put my soul and heart into it.

WINNIE: I'll do the lunch, then.

DOUG: I think I'll have my pizza unfrozen for a change.

WINNIE: You're in a very funny mood. *(She starts to go.)*

DOUG: I punish him! *(She stops but doesn't look at him.)* I pull his hair and twist his skin. Chinese burns, I think they call them. I pull his head back and shout in his face. right in his face. I pinch him. I take an ear in each hand and I squeeze, and I squeeze, hard. And his eyes stare and his legs thrash and I loathe him. Loathe him. (WINNIE *breaks the stem of a daffodil.*) But I never leave a mark. I don't think that I have ever left a mark. But I can't be sure. Never absolutely sure. I'm afraid that one day I'll kill him. I dig my nails into his sweet white flesh when I lift him. (WINNIE *crushes the flower.*) He'll be back, that young man, that Stephen. He said that he'll be back. He looked at me, Winnie, this morning he looked at me, and he knew. Winnie. He knew.

WINNIE: Actually I thought I'd give the pizza a rest today. Scrambled eggs. I'd thought. *(She drops the flower and makes as if to go but then stops.)* I'm not a Jesuit, Doug. A father confessor. And I'm not a fool, either. And I won't let you treat me like one. Not you, not Charlotte. No one's going to do that to me. I've learned to cope with what we've got. I get on with it and cope. I don't whine and I don't moan, I just cope. And I don't want to know, Doug. Do you understand me? I don't want to know.

DOUG: I can't stop myself.

WINNIE: It's a small house, Doug. And a stale confession.

DOUG: And there's no one else to stop me. Oh, God. Sometimes I think I'll leave him. Not to go in to him. But then, the thought of him, sitting awake, waiting. Waiting in the harsh electric light, waiting in the dark, sitting there all night long with his poor back aching and his poor head lolling, waiting for a father who will not come. And so, because I love him, I go in to him and—

WINNIE: I like to watch the ballet on TV, Doug. I like the precision. Every step planned, every glance weighed, considered. That's how I think of this family. Finely choreographed, around Tom. There are some steps that I must take and some that I must not take. Some things I may see and some that I must never see. In order that the ballet may go on. *(Pause.)* I can cope with that. I'm numbed to that. My guilty knowledge. My guilt. I don't want yours around my neck. It's not fair, Doug, it's not fair to tie that around my neck. *(She goes.)*

DOUG: All the weight and warmth and stink of it. (DOUG *remains sitting, gazing at the garden, toying with the crushed flower.* STEPHEN *enters and walks up to* DOUG *and looks out at the garden with him.)*

STEPHEN: Your garden is lovely.

DOUG: Isn't it? Everything in the garden is lovely, except this. *(Holds up the flower.)* Not quite lovely, not quite perfect. Easily crushed, so she crushed it, and went to clear up shit with cheerful precision. And now the question is, did she crush it because it was imperfect? Or is it imperfect because she crushed it? What do you think?

STEPHEN: I think we need to talk.

DOUG: "Why should the aged eagle spread its wings?" Do you know poetry?

STEPHEN: A bit.

DOUG: "A bit"! Poetry is the assurance we need that we are not the fools or the monsters we think ourselves to be. That we are a part of the human condition. "Because I do not hope to turn Desiring this man's gift and that man's scope I no longer strive towards such things. Why should the aged eagle spread its wings? Why should I mourn the vanished power of the usual reign?"

Not that I ever flew very high.

"For what is done, not to be done again, May the judgement not be too heavy upon us."

T.S. Eliot.

STEPHEN: It's beautiful.

DOUG: It is, isn't it? The melody of it is a comfort. An aesthetically pleasing way of saying "Do your worst. I'm past caring."

(Pause.)

STEPHEN: There is nothing I can do. Like you said, there is no proof. And I haven't come to pass judgement.

DOUG: No. You wouldn't. We've seen them come and go, Tom and me. Twenty odd years of professional carers. That's what you're called now, isn't it? "Carers." You care and you care and then you care some more.

STEPHEN: Somehow we've ended up on different sides, how did that happen?

DOUG: And then you care a bit more. Relentlessly caring. Unremittingly caring. Caring and caring until we're ready to cry out for mercy and lay down our arms and shamble along behind you, defeated.

STEPHEN: No!

DOUG: Dragging us to our knees.

STEPHEN: Christ!

DOUG: And still you care! Leave us alone! For Christ's sake, leave us alone. Twenty-five years ago there were no social workers. Welfare officers we had then. And district nurses and almoners. Look at your records. See all the names. You've worn out our carpets with your Hush Puppies, trekking back and forth over all the years. And now you! There has to be some sort of victory in life, there has to be. And they told us, your lot did, when we were sick of the screaming and the fits and the wet bed and the bloody awfulness of it all, that we were doing so well. So well! My God, they'd have done better putting a gun in our hands—

STEPHEN: Mr. Davies, this isn't doing you any good—

DOUG: But if you're tired enough, and desperate enough, and Tom doesn't respond in any way, in any bloody way at all, day after sodding day, you don't just need the praise. You don't just need it, you get to bloody believe it. You start to believe all that shit. And if people stop saying it, if ever they stop saying it, for any reason, if they stop saying it, then all those years become . . . futile. And the stupid thing, the funny thing, the bloody tragedy of it all, is that it's all lies.

STEPHEN: We can help you.

DOUG: Your holiday scheme, I suppose.

STEPHEN: Among other things.

DOUG: Why stop at a holiday?

STEPHEN: Start with a holiday—

DOUG: Why not a frontal lobotomy? Why not the total removal of all memory? Here, inject my veins with morphine . . . cut his bloody throat . . . why stop at a holiday?

STEPHEN: We could start with a holiday.

DOUG: Why are you so terrified at the prospect of a bit of heartbreak? Life is heartbreaking. Has always been. You can't change that. You and your lot. So bloody petrified at the very idea of a bit of unhappiness that anything is preferable . . . treachery, cowardice, abandonment.

STEPHEN: It's not abandonment. It's not any of those things!

DOUG: To me. Me and Tom. (DOUG *gets up and strides away to stand by* TOM *looking down at him.*)

DOUG: How could you explain to him that he hadn't been abandoned?

STEPHEN: For one week.

DOUG: For five minutes. He cries at night. I sit with him. How could I leave him for a week?

STEPHEN: That isn't why.

DOUG: What?

STEPHEN: I know why you won't leave him. The marks you spoke of.

DOUG: There are no marks!

STEPHEN: Not now, no. But tomorrow? If we agreed to take him tomorrow? Would there be no marks then? You're afraid that there would be, aren't you?

(DOUG *is staring at him, horrified.*)

STEPHEN: You don't know what you'll do to him between now and tomorrow, now and next week. You just don't know, do you?

DOUG: (*recovering*) What game is this? Cat and mouse? Hobson's choice? Well, whatever game it is, you can stuff it!

STEPHEN: Are you hurting your son, Mr. Davies? Doug, are you ill treating Tom?

DOUG: We have looked after him for so long.

STEPHEN: If we can be honest now we can make some good come of all this—

DOUG: And if not?

STEPHEN: It would be a police matter.

DOUG: Police?

STEPHEN: But without proof . . . I don't know.

DOUG: *(very calm now)* Who else have you told?

STEPHEN: Told? Well, everyone.

DOUG: Everyone?

STEPHEN: It's not a game, Mr. Davies. I've told everyone of my suspicions. All they are at the moment, isn't it? Legally.

DOUG: Who? Who have you told? The Doctor? (STEPHEN *nods.)* The physio? *(Nod.)* The hospital? My God! You bastard!

STEPHEN: Will you let us help you?

DOUG: Help? How? Watching me and watching Tom, examining Tom, talking to Charlotte, to Winnie, earnest young men with understanding eyes? Help? With everyone knowing? Everyone ''understanding''? Everyone?

STEPHEN: I had no choice. What else could I do?

DOUG: Christ knows. So. Now the praise has—finally—stopped. The victory is . . . gone. The lies are seen. The bag has no cat in it. Please. Please. Go.

STEPHEN: May I just have a word with Tom?

DOUG: My house.

STEPHEN: Doug.

DOUG: Goodbye, Stephen.

SCENE NINETEEN

The garden, evening. DOUG *goes off and returns wheeling* TOM. *He puts the chair next to the wheelchair.* DOUG *goes off and comes back again with a bottle of whisky, a bottle of* TOM's *pink medicine and a glass.* DOUG *sips his whisky, enjoying the evening sunshine.* TOM *is peaceful. [N.B. This scene is not continuous, we slip in and out of it. As the scene goes on* DOUG *becomes steadily drunker and more drugged,* TOM *becomes restless, anxious.]*

DOUG: So. Here we are, Tom. At the end of the day. Charlotte is on the train, rushing thankfully back to her friends, and your Mother is upstairs, with one of her heads, and we are here. So. Here we are. Father and son. But we're not alone, Tom. Never to be alone again if they have their way. From now on we'll know that they're there. That they know. Pushing back your sleeve and examining the flesh. Ghouls! Buggers! But the night's just as long as it ever was, and I'm still weary, and you still need to be changed, to be turned, to be fed, comforted. And I can't trust myself any more. Or her. And they can't stop me, and she won't stop me. Your nails need cutting. And, seeing the tension between us all, shimmering like heat on a long hard road, they treble it. Seeking to diminish it, they magnify it. *(Sings.)* "My soul doth magnify the Lord." Mine doesn't. Mine bloody doesn't. Does yours? No? It's a bugger, isn't it? We should have sat like this more often. Father and son. God it's years since I had a skinful. Medicine to make everything better. Every little thing.

(Pours some into his whisky tumbler, a little fuddled now.)

Raw, bleeding, foul, noxious things; cured. Sins of omission and commission; mended. Dank hidden deeds; obliterated. Frantic, obscene thoughts—all made well again!

(Toasts TOM *with the tumbler and takes a gulp.)*

Christ! No wonder you shouted.

(He quickly sloshes some whisky into the tumbler and swigs it back but the taste is still foul. He gets up and finds TOM'S *feeder cup, unscrews the top, pours whiskey into it and takes a drink.)*

That's better.

(He places the whisky and medicine bottles together.)

Quite a nice way to go, don't you think? Pink and amber. Boudoir colors. Oh, God. Regard this, Tom, as a confessional. Will you? Good lad. "She has been forgiven much, therefore she loves much." Well, I'm the other side of the coin. I have loved much and therefore I need to be forgiven much. The other side of the coin. Tails I lose. I did love you, Tom. Christ, how I loved you. That's not right, I do love you. Christ how I do love you. See?

(He takes a gulp of medicine from the bottle and washes it down with whisky straight from the bottle.)

No. Do it properly. *(Pours the whisky into the cup.)* You are my life and my mind. You are in my waking and in my sleeping. You are in my gut and in my blood and I love you. Love you. *(Another big gulp of whisky. He retches.* TOM *is growing more and more agitated.)* It doesn't do you any good if it tastes nice. You're a good lad, Tom, you are. (DOUG *shivers.)* You cold? You cold, son? You shouldn't be out here in the cold. Here . . . *(Struggles out of the cardigan.)* Have this. *(Drapes it over* TOM *clumsily.* TOM *is crying now.)* There you are, son. Tell you a secret? Your mother's pills . . . I took them all. One and all. Clever, eh? Not just a pretty face, your old Dad. If the booze doesn't get me the happy pills will. Pills will . . . pills will . . . pig's swill. Can't bear them knowing, see. Looking and seeing. All the years come to nothing. All the things they said, over all the years, come to nothing. I wanted to be such a good father, Tom. Such a good . . . Oh, Tom, don't cry. Don't cry. There's a good lad. Nothing to cry for, Tom. Lots and lots of people, Tom. All going to look after you . . . You'll be alright, you'll see. There now, there . . . shhh. Shush. Don't cry, son, don't cry. It's all over, Tom, all over. (DOUG *appears to fall asleep.* TOM *is thrashing wildly now, he cries out.* DOUG *stirs.)* All the weight and warmth and stink of it . . . (DOUG *sleeps on to death.* TOM *shouts in anguish. He manages to knock* DOUG's *knee.* DOUG's *head slumps. Gradually* TOM *quietens, wide eyed with grief.)*

(Slow fade.)

Appendix A

Chronological Listing of The Susan Smith Blackburn Prize Finalists, Plays, Judges, and Presenters (1978–1990)

I
1978–1979

HAPPY YELLOW
Tina Brown

THE LUNCH GIRLS
Leigh Curran

QUEEN CHRISTINA
Pam Gems

ARTICHOKE
Joanna Glass

NIGHTS ALONE
Valerie Harris

IN THE BLOOD
Lenka Janiurek

†GETTING OUT
Marsha Norman

*ONCE A CATHOLIC
Mary O'Malley

RENASCENCE
Terri Wagener

UNCOMMON WOMEN
AND OTHERS
Wendy Wasserstein

LOVED
Olwen Wymark

Note: Winners are indicated by an asterisk (*); runners-up are indicated by a dagger (†).

JUDGES

Walter Clemons
Harold Clurman
Michael Codran

Joan Plowright
Michael Rudman
Tom Stoppard

Presented by Joan Plowright, February 6, 1979, at the English Speaking Union, London

II
1979–1980

CLOUD NINE
Caryl Churchill

THE BEACH HOUSE
Nancy Donohue

FATHER DREAMS
Mary Gallagher

†CRIMES OF THE HEART
Beth Henley

THE ART OF DINING
Tina Howe

NASTY RUMORS AND FINAL REMARKS
Susan Miller

WE'RE ON THE ONE ROAD
Philomena Muinzer

VIRGINIA
Edna O'Brien

*DETAILS WITHOUT A MAP
Barbara Schneider

YSABELLE
Karen Duke Sturges

TALENT
Victoria Wood

FIND ME
Olwen Wymark

JUDGES

Peggy Ashcroft   André Gregory
Michael Billington   Jack Kroll
Howard Davies   Nina Vance

Presented by Irene Worth, February 13, 1980, at The Players, New York City

III
1980–1981

ANGELO'S WEDDING Part 1 of THE LORENZO TRILOGY
Julie Bovasso

DELI'S FABLE
Susan Dworkin

†TO GRANDMOTHER'S HOUSE WE GO
Joanna Glass

THE TIDE
Ann Jellicoe

WEDNESDAY
Julia Kearsley

*MY SISTER IN THIS HOUSE
Wendy Kesselman

MARGARET AND KIT
Shirley Lauro

THE FAMILY ALBUM
Byrony Lavery

KILLINGS ON THE LAST LINE
Lavonne Mueller

SALLY AND MARSHA
Sybille Pearson

TURTLES
Barbara Schneider

MOVING IN
Alison Watson

JUDGES

Anne Barton	Brendan Gill
Robert Cushman	Joyce Carol Oates
Geraldine Fitzgerald	Michael Rudman

Presented by Geraldine Fitzgerald, February 10, 1981, at The Players, New York City

IV
1981–1982

†DEATH OF A MINER
Paula Cizmar

CLOSE TIES
Elizabeth Diggs

*STEAMING
Nell Dunn

UNDER HEAVEN'S EYE . . , 'TIL COCK CROW
J. e. Franklin

SKIRMISHES
Catherine Hayes

A CONNECTICUT COWBOY
Shirley Kaplan

WONDERLAND
Margaret Keilstrup

STILL LIFE
Emily Mann

LAST LOOKS
Grace McKeaney

STUCK
Adele Edling Shank

KISS AND KILL
Susan Todd and Ann Mitchell

ISN'T IT ROMANTIC
Wendy Wasserstein

JUDGES

Elizabeth Hardwick	Arnold Wesker
Nancy Meckler	Edwin Wilson
Marina Warner	Joanne Woodward

Presented by Ronald Harwood February 22, 1982, at The Garrick Club, London

V
1982–1983

†TOP GIRLS
Caryl Churchill

MADONNA OF THE POWDER ROOM
Paula Cizmar

THE BROTHERS
Kathleen Collins

TAKE MY HUSBAND
Carol Ann Duffy

NEUTRAL COUNTRIES
Barbara Field

PLAYING IN LOCAL BANDS
Nancy Fales Garrett

WAITING
Julia Kearsley

TERRITORIAL RITES
Carol Mack

THE FLIP SIDE
Donna de Matteo

*'NIGHT, MOTHER
Marsha Norman

SALONIKA
Louise Page

SAND CASTLES
Adele Edling Shank

JUDGES

Maria Aitkin   Francine du Plessix Gray
Zoe Caldwell   Mel Gussow
James Fenton   Jonathan Lynn

Presented by Zoe Caldwell, February 22, 1983, at The Players, New York City

VI
1983–1984

*FEN
Caryl Churchill

HOSPICE
Pearl Cleage

DEAR
Roslyn Drexler

TYPHOID MARY
Shirley Gee

PLAY MEMORY
Joanna Glass

PAINTING CHURCHES
Tina Howe

ON THE HOME FRONT
Gail Kriegel

TRAVELER IN THE DARK
Marsha Norman

†COYOTE UGLY
Lynn Siefert

LADIES IN WAITING
Terri Wagener

JUDGES

Edward Albee	Ann Holmes
Howard Davies	Hilary Spurling
Christopher Hampton	Meryl Streep

Presented by Meryl Streep, February 24, 1984, at The Players, New York City

VII
1984–1985

WOMEN IN ARMS
Mary Elizabeth Burke-Kennedy

PERMISSION FROM CHILDREN
Kathleen Cahill

MRS. GAUGUIN
Helen Cooper

*NEVER IN MY LIFETIME
Shirley Gee

TOUCH AND GO
Debbie Horsfield

MOONYA
Cindy Lou Johnson

†WHEN I WAS A GIRL, I USED TO SCREAM AND SHOUT
Sharman MacDonald

EXECUTION OF JUSTICE
Emily Mann

WRENS
Anne McGravie

GOLDEN GIRLS
Louise Page

TEA IN A CHINA CUP
Christina Reid

UNDERSTATEMENTS
Susan Rivers

JUDGES

Beryl Bainbridge   John Guare
Robert Brustein   Benedict Nightingale
Colleen Dewhurst   Jules Wright

Presented by Peggy Ashcroft, February 25, 1985, at The Garrick Club, London

VIII
1985–1986

NO MERCY
Constance Congdon

*OURSELVES ALONE
Anne Devlin

THE CONDUCT OF LIFE
Maria Irene Fornes

CAMILLE
Pam Gems

TEA
Velina Hasu Houston

A SHAYNA MAIDEL
Barbara Lebow

COMING APART
Melissa Murray

†TALK OF THE DEVIL
Mary O'Malley

WINDHAWK!
Aishah Rahman

NIEDECKER
Kristine Thatcher

AMID THE STANDING CORN
Jane Thornton

JUDGES

Gordon Davidson	John Peter
Jane Howell	Maureen Stapleton
Julian Mitchell	George White

Presented by Janet Suzman, February 24, 1986, at The Garrick Club, London, London.

IX
1986–1987

WHILE OLDER MEN SPEAK
Kathleen Collins

MRS. VERSHININ
Helen Cooper

*HOW TO SAY GOODBYE
Mary Gallagher

BLESSÉ
Cindy Lou Johnson

QUEER FOLK
Rosie Logan

*A NARROW BED
Ellen McLaughlin

ETTA JENKS
Marlane G. Meyer

FIVE IN THE KILLING ZONE
Lavonne Mueller

BODY CELL
Melissa Murray

ROOSTERS
Milcha Sanchez-Scott

†FUGUE
Leonora Thuna

JUDGES

Sarah Pia Anderson	Jane Lapotaire
Francis King	Maria Tucci
Kenneth Koch	Linda Winer

Presented by Marsha Norman, February 23, 1987, at The Players, New York City

X
1987–1988

THATCHER'S WOMEN
Kay Adshead

*SERIOUS MONEY
Caryl Churchill

SOUTHERN COMFORTS
Kathleen Clark

WHEREABOUTS UNKNOWN
Barbara Damashek

†SAINT FLORENCE
Elizabeth Diggs

ABINGDON SQUARE
Maria Irene Fornes

RECLAIMED
Judy GeBauer

THE LUCKY SPOT
Beth Henley

DREAMS OF SAN FRANCISCO
Jacqueline Holborough

THREE WAYS HOME
Casey Kurtti

LOVE ON THE PLASTIC
Julia Schofield

JUDGES

Arvin Brown	Stanley Kauffmann
David Hare	Anna Massey
Julie Harris	Claire Tomalin

Presented by Anna Massey, February 22, 1988, at The Garrick Club, London.

XI
1988–1989

STARTING MONDAY
Anne Commire

THE STONES CRY OUT
Trista Conger

PLAYING WITH FIRE
Barbara Field

RAPING THE GOLD
Lucy Gannon

A KIND OF MADNESS
Nikki Harmon

MA ROSE
Cassandra Medley

KINGFISH
Marlane Meyer

FOR DEAR LIFE
Susan Miller

*THE HEIDI CHRONICLES
Wendy Wasserstein

†OUR COUNTRY'S GOOD
Timberlake Wertenbaker

ANGELA
Elizabeth Wyatt

SELF-PORTRAIT
Sheila Yeger

JUDGES

Michael Attenborough
Michael Coveney
Jon Jory

Fidelis Morgan
Edith Oliver
Jessica Tandy

Presented by Jessica Tandy, February 27, 1989, at The Century Association, New York City.

XII
1989–1990

DAYTRIPS
Jo Carson

THE COW JUMPED OVER THE MOON
Donna Franceschild

CHRISTCHILD
J. e. Franklin

¿DE DONDE?
Mary Gallagher

*KEEPING TOM NICE
Lucy Gannon

THE LADIES OF THE CAMELLIAS
Lillian Garrett

WARRIOR
Shirley Gee

OLYMPE AND THE EXECUTIONER
Wendy Kesselman

INFINITY'S HOUSE
Ellen McLaughlin

THE GEOGRAPHY OF LUCK
Marlane Meyer

†A HERO'S WELCOME
Winsome Pinnock

SHAKIN' THE MESS OUTTA MISERY
Shay Youngblood

JUDGES

Claire Bloom   Elliot Norton
Zelda Fichandler   Juliet Stevenson
John Gross   Nicholas Wright

Presented by Juliet Stevenson, February, 19, 1990, at The Reform Club, London

Alphabetical Listing of The Susan Smith Blackburn Prize Finalists (1978–1990)

Kay Adshead
Julie Bovasso
Tina Brown
Mary Elizabeth Burke-
  Kennedy
Kathleen Cahill
Jo Carson
Caryl Churchill
Paula Cizmer
Kathleen Clark
Pearl Cleage
Kathleen Collins
Anne Commire
Constance Congdon
Trista Conger
Helen Cooper
Leigh Curran
Barbara Damashek
Anne Devlin
Elizabeth Diggs
Nancy Donohue
Roslyn Drexler
Carol Ann Duffy
Nell Dunn
Susan Dworkin
Barbara Field
Maria Irene Fornes
Donna Franceschild
J. e. Franklin
Mary Gallagher
Lucy Gannon
Lillian Garrett
Nancy Fales Garrett
Judy GeBauer

Shirley Gee
Pam Gems
Joanna Glass
Nikki Harmon
Valerie Harris
Catherine Hays
Beth Henley
Jacqueline Holborough
Debbie Horsfield
Velina Hasu Houston
Tina Howe
Lenka Janiurek
Ann Jellicoe
Cindy Lou Johnson
Shirley Kaplan
Julia Kearsley
Margaret Keilstrup
Wendy Kesselman
Gail Kriegel
Casey Kurtti
Shirley Lauro
Bryony Lavery
Barbara Lebow
Rosie Logan
Sharman MacDonald
Carol Mack
Emily Mann
Donna de Matteo
Anne McGravie
Grace McKeaney
Ellen McLaughlin
Cassandra Medler
Marlane G. Meyer

Susan Miller
Ann Mitchell
Lavonne Mueller
Philomena Muinzer
Melissa Murray
Marsha Norman
Edna O'Brien
Mary O'Malley
Louise Page
Sybille Pearson
Winsome Pinnock
Aishah Rahman
Christina Reid
Susan Rivers
Milcha Sanchez-Scott
Barbara Schneider
Julia Schofield
Adele Edling Shank
Lynn Siefert
Karen Duke Sturges
Kristine Thatcher
Jane Thornton
Leonora Thuna
Susan Todd
Terri Wagener
Wendy Wasserstein
Alison Watson
Timberlake Wertenbaker
Victoria Wood
Elizabeth Wyatt
Olwen Wymark
Sheila Yeger
Shay Youngblood

Appendix B

Members of the Board of Directors of The Susan Smith Blackburn Prize

The late Lillian Hellman (Founding Director)

Michael Attenborough

Lady Ayer

William Blackburn

Betsy Dworkin

Ronald Dworkin

Cabanne Gilbreath

Lady Hale

Emilie S. Kilgore

Julia O'Faolain

Charles Perlitz

Meg Poole

Cabanné Smith

Edwin Wilson

EMILIE S. KILGORE graduated Magna Cum Laude from Smith College with a degree in art history. She studied in Paris and received an M.A. in art history from Goddard College. She worked at the Frick Collection in New York, and after moving to Houston, she developed and taught a course on awareness of visual arts. Later, she became a fine arts advisor, formed the Texas Commerce Bank Art Collection, and is at present the curator of the Fayez Sarofim Collection in Houston. She founded and directs The Susan Smith Blackburn Prize with her brother-in-law, William V. Blackburn, of London. She serves on the Houston Municipal Art Commission, is currently chairman of the board of Stages Repertory Theatre in Houston, and is active on the boards of other arts organizations in Houston and elsewhere. She has two sons and lives in Houston.